ENHANCING
JOB OPPORTUNITIES

William T. Grant Foundation
Book Fund

Bates College • Lewiston, Maine

ENHANCING JOB OPPORTUNITIES

Eastern Europe and the Former Soviet Union

Jan J. Rutkowski and Stefano Scarpetta
with Arup Banerji, Philip O'Keefe,
Gaëlle Pierre, and Milan Vodopivec

Europe and Central Asia Region

©2005 The International Bank for Reconstruction and Development / The World Bank
1818 H Street NW
Washington DC 20433
Telephone: 202-473-1000
Internet: www.worldbank.org
E-mail: feedback@worldbank.org

All rights reserved

1 2 3 4 08 07 06 05

This volume is a product of the staff of the International Bank for Reconstruction and Development / The World Bank. The findings, interpretations, and conclusions expressed in this volume do not necessarily reflect the views of the Executive Directors of The World Bank or the governments they represent.

The World Bank does not guarantee the accuracy of the data included in this work. The boundaries, colors, denominations, and other information shown on any map in this work do not imply any judgement on the part of The World Bank concerning the legal status of any territory or the endorsement or acceptance of such boundaries.

Rights and Permissions
The material in this publication is copyrighted. Copying and/or transmitting portions or all of this work without permission may be a violation of applicable law. The International Bank for Reconstruction and Development / The World Bank encourages dissemination of its work and will normally grant permission to reproduce portions of the work promptly.

For permission to photocopy or reprint any part of this work, please send a request with complete information to the Copyright Clearance Center Inc., 222 Rosewood Drive, Danvers, MA 01923, USA; telephone: 978-750-8400; fax: 978-750-4470; Internet: www.copyright.com.

All other queries on rights and licenses, including subsidiary rights, should be addressed to the Office of the Publisher, The World Bank, 1818 H Street NW, Washington, DC 20433, USA; fax: 202-522-2422; e-mail: pubrights@worldbank.org.

ISBN-10: 0-8213-6195-3
ISBN-13: 978-0-8213-6195-5
e-ISBN: 0-8213-6196-1
DOI: 10.1596/978-0-8213-6195-5

Cover photo by: Y. Hadar.
Cover design by: Naylor Design, Inc.

Library of Congress Cataloging-in-Publication Data

Rutkowski, Jan J., 1954–
    Enhancing job opportunities : Eastern Europe and the former Soviet Union / Jan J. Rutkowski, Stefano Scarpetta.
      p. cm.
    Includes bibliographical references and index.
    ISBN-13: 978-0-8213-6195-5
    ISBN-10: 0-8213-6195-3
    1. Job creation—Europe, Eastern. 2. Job creation—Former Soviet republics. 3. Labor market—Europe, Eastern. 4. Labor market—Former Soviet republics. I. Scarpetta, Stefano. II. Title.
HD5764.7.A6R88 2005
331.12'0420947—dc22

2005044730

Contents

Foreword	*xiii*
Acknowledgments	*xvii*
Acronyms and Abbreviations	*xix*

1. Overview   **1**

Changing Labor Markets in the Region	5
The Drivers of Labor Demand during the Transition	19
The Role of the Region's Policy and Institutions	24
The Policy Challenge: Promoting Job Creation in the Region	39

2. Main Labor Market Developments during the Transition   **61**

An Economically Diverse Region with Differing Labor Markets	61
Unemployment and Underemployment: Major Economic and Social Problems	63
Rebounding Real Wages, but Widening Wage Differentials	88
The Changing Nature of Jobs during the Transition	93
Labor Market Outcomes: Disappointing during the Transition?	97
Summary: Key Stylized Facts on Labor Market Transition in the Region	99

3. **Macroeconomic Policy, Output, and Employment: Is There Evidence of Jobless Growth?** — 107

   The Employment-Output Link during the Different Phases of the Transition — 108
   Any Role for Macropolicy to Influence the Employment-Output Link? — 114
   Summing Up: Employment Prospects in CEE and CIS Countries — 118

4. **Restructuring, Productivity, and Job Creation** — 125

   The Required Transformation of the Transition Economies and Progress So Far — 126
   What Is the Role of Firm Restructuring and the Entry and Exit of Firms for Job Creation? — 131
   What Is the Role of Firm Restructuring and the Entry and Exit of Firms for Productivity and Output Growth? — 137
   What Drives Restructuring of Existing Firms? — 147
   How Many Firms Enter and Exit the Market in Transition Countries? — 149
   Summing Up: Entry Conditions and Incentives to Create Jobs Are Essential for Improving Job Creation in the Region — 151

5. **The Investment Climate and Job Creation** — 155

   Importance of Investment Climate for Job Creation — 157
   Employers' Views on the Major Obstacles to Firms' Operation and Growth in the Region — 158
   The Impact of Investment Climate on Job Creation in the Region — 167
   Investment Climate: International Comparisons and Variations within the Region — 173
   Summing Up: Promoting a Better Investment Climate to Foster Job Creation — 183

6. **Labor Market Policy and Institutions: Combining Protection with Incentives for Job Creation** — 193

   The Role of Labor Market Policies and Institutions — 194
   The Divergent Paths of Wage Determination during the Transition — 194
   Employment Protection Legislation Remains Strict despite Reforms, Although Enforcement Is Variable — 209

	Taxes on Labor	217
	The Role of Passive and Active Labor Market Programs	221
	Summing Up: The Challenge of Labor Policy Reforms in Transition Economies	233

Bibliography — *243*
Index — *259*

Boxes

1.1	Geopolitical Country Groups Reflect Economic and Institutional Differences among the Region's Countries	6
1.2	In Most of the Region's Countries, Higher Investment Rates Are Necessary to Accelerate Economic Growth and Job Creation	40
2.1	Do Geopolitical Groupings Help in Assessing the Economic Performance of the Transition Countries?	64
2.2	The Challenge of Job Creation in Turkey	68
2.3	Employment in Moldova	69
2.4	International Migration Patterns in the Region	72
2.5	Growth and Job Creation in Low Income CIS Countries	78
2.6	Relative Position of Women in the Labor Market Has Not Deteriorated during the Transition, and New Employment Opportunities for Women Emerged in the Expanding Services Sector	80
2.7	Internal Migration in the Region in Search of Jobs	86
2.8	An Increase in Educational Wage Premiums Has Been an Important Factor behind the Rise in Wage Inequality	90
2.9	The Surge in Informality during the Transition: Key Features and Policy Challenges	94
3.1	An Empirical Investigation of the Possible Links between Employment, Output, and Macroeconomic Policy	119
4.1	Economic Development and the Employment Structure	128
4.2	A Consistent International Firm-Level Database	132

4.3	Assessing the Impact of Labor Reallocation on Productivity Growth	138
4.4	The Decomposition of Productivity Growth Using Firm-Level Data	143
5.1	Small Entrepreneurs Complain about the Business Environment in Bulgaria	158
5.2	Service Sector Employment Rate as an Indicator of Job Creation Potential	168
5.3	Stringent Employment Protection Regulations May Forestall Job Destruction, but at the Same Time They Discourage Job Creation	172
5.4	What the Official Data on Entry Barriers Do Not Show: Romania	176
6.1	The Role of Labor Market Policies and Institutions: Some International Evidence	195
6.2	Wage Bargaining in Estonia: A Radical Reformer	200
6.3	Innovative Ways of Targeting the Poor	226
6.4	Public Works and Workfare: An Alternative to the Unemployment Benefit?	228

Figures

1.1	The Payoff to Reforms in Transition Economies: Higher Output, but Still Insufficient Jobs, 1992–2003	2
1.2	Unsynchronized Job Creation and Job Destruction Can Give Rise to Unemployment	9
1.3	Unemployment Continues to Be High in Most Transition Economies	10
1.4	Employment Rates Have Declined and Are below the Lisbon Target of 70 Percent	11
1.5	Different Patterns of Labor Reallocation: The Czech Republic (CEE) vs. the Kyrgyz Republic (CIS)	15
1.6	Wage Inequality in the CIS Is Higher than in the CEE	18
1.7	Labor Reallocation Has Played an Increasing Role in Promoting Labor Productivity Growth in Russia	21
1.8	The Rate of Job Creation Is Higher for More Productive Firms in Moldova	22
1.9	Firm Entry and Exit Are Critical for Productivity Growth	25

1.10	Major Obstacles to Firm Activity, 2002	28
1.11	The Tax Wedge on Labor in the Region Is High, Often Higher than in Most OECD Countries	29
1.12	Obstacles to Business Operation and Growth Vary by Subgroup	31
1.13	The Region's Countries Have More Stringent Regulations on Hiring and Firing than OECD Countries Do	37
1.14	Labor Regulations Seem to Be a Binding Constraint Only in the New EU Member Countries and Not in the Other Parts of the Region	38
1.15	Access to Finance Is More Difficult in Transition Economies than in Market Economies at Similar Income Levels	43
1.16	Constraints Reported by Firms Vary across the Region's Countries	46
2.1	Unemployment Is High in Most CEE and SEE Countries, 2003	67
2.2	Employment-to-Population Ratio Is Low in Most of the Region's Countries	76
2.3	More Workers Are Hired in Regions with a Developed Services Sector, Educated Workforce, and Infrastructure (Poland's Regions, 1997)	84
2.4	Real Wages Have Rebounded in the Mid-1990s	89
2.5	Wage Inequality in the CIS Is Higher than in the CEE	91
2.6	Informal Sector Accounts for a Substantial Share of Total Employment, Especially in CIS	94
3.1	Output per Capita Growth Is Largely Driven by Productivity Growth	109
3.2	Inflationary Pressures Have Declined over Time in Most Countries	112
3.3	Employment Adjustment Has Been More Marked in CEE than in CIS Countries	113
3.4	Real-Wage Adjustments Have Been More Marked in CIS than in CEE Countries	114
3.5	Real Interest Rates Have Increased in Recent Years in CEE Countries	115
3.6	Share of Gross Fixed Capital Formation as a Percentage of GDP	116
3.7	Share of GFCF and Productive GFCF as a Percentage of GDP	117

3.8	Loosening of the Fiscal Stance in CEE Countries in Recent Years	118
3.9	Real Wages in the Public Sector Have Increased More Rapidly than in the Private Sector in CEE Countries	122
4.1	Different Patterns of Labor Reallocation across Transition Economies	129
4.2	Large Job Flows in Transition Economies	134
4.3	Unsynchronized Job Creation and Destruction Can Give Rise to Unemployment or Underemployment	135
4.4	Job Flow Rates, Selected Transition Countries, 1990–2001	136
4.5	Decomposition of Labor Productivity Growth, CEE Countries	140
4.6	Contribution of Reallocation to Russian Labor-Productivity Growth, 1986–2001	144
4.7	Sources of Productivity Growth in Transition and Emerging Economies	145
4.8	Relationship between Net Entry Contribution and Productivity Growth of Incumbents	146
4.9	Effects of Foreign and Domestic Privatization on Multifactor Productivity Growth (MFP)	148
4.10	Effects of Foreign and Domestic Privatization on Productivity, Employment, and Wages	149
4.11	How Many Firms Enter and Exit the Market?	150
5.1	Most Frequently Reported Major Obstacles to Firm Operation in the Region	159
5.2	Obstacles to Business Operation and Growth Vary by Subgroup	163
5.3	Smaller Firms Are More Constrained by the Investment Climate	166
5.4	Market Service Employment Is Higher in Countries with Easier Access to, and Lower Cost of, Credit	171
5.5	Excessive Market Regulation Hurts Job Creation	171
5.6	In Some of the Region's Subgroups, Time Spent Dealing with Government Regulations Is Still Substantial	174
5.7	Protection of Property against Crime Can Be Costly	174

5.8	Firms in the Region Rely to a Lesser Degree on Capital Coming from Formal Institutions than Do Firms in Other Regions	175
5.9	Starting a Business Is Not Easy in Many of the Region's Countries	178
5.10	Job Creation in the Region Is Likely to Be Hampered by Difficult Access to Credit	180
5.11	Markets in the Region Tend to Be Overregulated	181
5.12	Corruption Is High in the Region	182
6.1	Density and Bargaining Coverage, Early 2000s	198
6.2	Minimum-Wage-to-Average-Wage Ratio, 2002	206
6.3	Minimum Wage in Ukraine Accounts for a High Percentage of the Market Wage of Low-Skilled Workers, but It Is Not Enforced	207
6.4	Employment Protection Legislation in EU-8 and Other Selected Countries during the Transition	212
6.5	Transition Countries Have More-Stringent Regulations on Hiring and Firing than Do OECD Countries	213
6.6	There Are Significant Differences within the Region's Countries on EPL	214
6.7	Informality Tends to Be Higher in Countries with Strict EPL	216
6.8	The Region's Tax Wedge on Labor, 2003	218
6.9	Tax Wedge on Labor, the Region, and OECD, Early 2000s	219
6.10	Surge in the Tax Wedge in EU Transition Countries during the 1990s	220
6.11	Unemployment Benefit Replacement Rates Have Declined in EU Transition Countries during the 1990s	223

Tables

1.1	A Typology of Employment Protection Legislation and Enforcement	37
1.2	A Summary of Key Policy Measures to Improve Labor Market Outcomes in Transition Economies of the Region	45
2.1	Differences between Middle-Income European and Low-Income CIS Labor Markets	66

2.2	Flows into and out of Unemployment	74
2.3	Large Regional Disparities in Unemployment Rates, 2003	82
3.1	Significant Changes in the Correlation between Macroeconomic Variables and Labor Market Indicators	111
4.1	The Employment Structure in CEE and CIS Countries	127
4.2	The Evolution of Productivity, Wages, and Unit Labor Costs	142
5.1	Contribution of Investment Climate Components to Change in Service Sector Employment in the CEE EU Countries over the Past Decade	169
5.2	The Importance of Determinants of Job Creation Varies by Subgroup in the Region	172
6.1	EPL and Enforcement Typology	215

Foreword

In the last 15 years, the countries of Eastern Europe and the Former Soviet Union have made impressive progress in their historical transition from centrally planned to market economies. Building the institutional foundations of a market economy, they have developed a vibrant private sector and opened themselves to international trade. After an initial economic recession, this has ignited economic growth, which in turn has brought about higher incomes and reduced poverty. Currently, many of the countries in the Region are well-functioning market economies; eight of them have joined the European Union and an additional three transition countries, together with Turkey, are on the road to EU accession. Such a successful transition, achieved over a short period of time, exceeded many observers' expectations.

But the transition and recent growth have been disappointing in one key area—jobs. In countries across the region, job opportunities remain scarce. In many cases, job creation in the expanding new private sector still falls short of job destruction in the declining old sector. As a result, employment has decreased substantially in virtually all countries in the Region, and high unemployment has emerged in some of them. While some transitional unemployment was expected, the surprise lay in its persistence. Many workers displaced by structural shifts failed to find new jobs, and a significant number have either been unemployed for over a year or are in low-productivity occupations. In some of the new member states of the European Union, as well as in some acceding countries, the unemployment rate tends to be in double digits—as it is in some of the cohesion countries that joined the EU in previous rounds of enlargement. This carries significant social and political costs—long-term unemployment threatens to erode skills, aggravates poverty and inequality, and eventually leads to social marginalization. In the CIS countries, the jobs problem lies more in the quality of jobs—which are less productive and pay correspondingly little. Going forward, poor job prospects, if not improved, will act as a brake on the substantial poverty reduction that has occurred in the Region since 1998 and will undermine political support for reforms. Obviously, these problems are more pronounced in some countries—where reforms have been slow or delayed—than in others. But the lack of productive job opportunities is a common thread in virtually all transition economies.

This study, *Enhancing Job Opportunities: Eastern Europe and the Former Soviet Union*, focuses attention on the causes of these disappointing labor outcomes and points to the solutions. Why has the job creation record of transition economies been disappointing? One reason is that the size of the new private sector that generates jobs is still relatively small in many of the Region's countries. And there is still enough room for firms to increase output through downsizing and retrenchment—what is sometimes termed "defensive restructuring." For employment to grow, more firms need to engage in "strategic restructuring," which requires investing productively, hiring more workers, and finding new production niches. And why do firms not engage in more strategic restructuring? Often, they are discouraged by the poor investment climate—substantial risks, barriers, and costs associated with doing business.

Two other factors also play a role. In countries in the Region with strong institutions and enforcement capacity, strict employment protection legislation can actually inhibit hiring. Again, for many firms in the Region, the lack of adequate skills among available workers also proves to be a significant constraint to growth.

The pace of job creation and the reduction in unemployment in the Region can and should be accelerated. This study recommends a two-pronged strategy to create more and better jobs. First, in every country across the Region, the investment climate needs to be further improved to encourage new firms to enter the market, and for existing firms to grow. The specific needs differ across countries. In the low-income countries of the Former Soviet Union, the needs are basic: continued development of the institutions of a market economy and reducing risks. In the middle-income countries, such as the

Russian Federation and Ukraine, and in Southeastern Europe, the challenge is removing administrative barriers. In the new and prospective European Union members of Central and Eastern Europe, the necessity is improving the quality of regulations. Across the region, better governance, investments in human capital and in infrastructure, and ultimately building competitive economies integrated in a world economy are other key challenges.

Second, countries in the Region need to have institutional and regulatory reform to develop an adaptable labor market, where core worker rights are effectively protected but employers are not unduly constrained in adjusting the size and skill composition of their workforce to the changing product demand. Workers need to have incentives and skills necessary to take up available jobs, and be capable of moving to where the jobs are.

This book, part of a new series of regional studies, is intended as a contribution to the World Bank's goal to work more effectively with clients and partners in the Region to reduce poverty and foster economic growth through better utilization of labor resources. It complements the companion study on growth, poverty, and inequality, which examines in greater detail the critical link between labor market outcomes and poverty. Forthcoming studies on trade, infrastructure, migration, and demographics look at the key economic and social opportunities and challenges. I hope that these studies stimulate debate, promote better understanding, and spur action to bring about prosperity for all.

Shigeo Katsu
Vice President
Europe and Central Asia Region

Acknowledgments

This study was prepared by a team led by Jan Rutkowski and Stefano Scarpetta, who were also the main authors, and comprising Arup Banerji, Philip O'Keefe, Gaëlle Pierre, and Milan Vodopivec. Additional inputs were provided by John Haltiwanger and Paolo Saavedra. It draws on commissioned background papers by a number of researchers, including Tito Boeri, David Brown, Pietro Garibaldi, John Earle, Peter Huber, Paloma Lopez-Garcia, and Paolo Verme.

This work was supported by the Chief Economist of the Europe and Central Asia (ECA) Region, Pradeep Mitra, who has provided essential guidance throughout its implementation. The study benefited from useful comments and suggestions provided at various stages by Michal Boni, Daniela Gressani, Vladimir Gimpelson, Rostislav Kapelyushnikov, János Köllő, William Maloney, Mamta Murthi, Michelle Riboud, Michal Rutkowski, and Jan Svejnar.

Earlier versions of this study were presented at a World Bank Conference on Labor Market Stock-Taking: "What is the Role of Labor Market Policy in Promoting More and Better Jobs?" held in Washington, DC, on November 18–19, 2004, and at the Centre for Analysis of Social Exclusion (CASE) Conference titled "Europe after the Enlargement," held in Warsaw on April 8–9, 2005. The study benefited from the discussion following its presentation, and in particular from comments provided by Mikhail Dmitriev, János Köllő, and Jan Svejnar.

The study also benefited substantially from comments received from participants in a series of consultation meetings held in April 2005 at the International Labour Organization (ILO) in Geneva, the European Commission in Brussels, the Organisation for Economic Co-operation and Development (OECD) in Paris, and the U.K. Department for International Development (DFID) and the European Bank for Reconstruction and Development (EBRD) in London.

The World Bank Office of the Publisher coordinated the book design, editing, and production. Dina Towbin was the production editor. Francis Speltz and Timothy Whitehead edited the manuscript.

Acronyms and Abbreviations

AFR	Africa
ALMP	active labor market program
AW	average wage
BEEPS	Business Environment and Enterprise Performance Survey
BiH	Bosnia and Herzegovina
CEE	Central and Eastern Europe
CIS	Commonwealth of Independent States
CIS-7	low income CIS countries: Armenia, Azerbaijan, Georgia, the Kyrgyz Republic, Moldova, Tajikistan, and Uzbekistan
EAP	East Asia and Pacific
EBRD	European Bank for Reconstruction and Development
EC	European Commission
ECA	Europe and Central Asia
EIRO	European Industrial Relations Observatory
EMU	Economic and Monetary Union
EPL	employment protection legislation
EU	European Union
EU-15	European Union before the 2004 enlargement
EU-8	New EU-member countries (the Czech Republic, Estonia, Hungary, Latvia, Lithuania, Poland, the Slovak Republic, and Slovenia)

EUA-3	EU-accession countries (Bulgaria, Croatia, and Romania)
FBiH	Federation of Bosnia and Herzegovina
FDI	foreign direct investment
FYR	former Yugoslav Republic
GDP	gross domestic product
GFCF	gross fixed capital formation
GNI	gross national income
ICS	investment climate survey
ILO	International Labour Organization (plenary body) or International Labour Office (the secretariat and publisher)
IMF	International Monetary Fund
IQR	interquartile range
IZA	Institute for the Study of Labor
LAC	Latin America and the Caribbean
LFS	labor force survey
MENA	Middle East and North Africa
MFP	multifactor productivity growth
MNA	Middle East and North Africa
MW	minimum wage
NUTS	nomenclature of territorial units for statistics
OECD	Organisation for Economic Co-operation and Development
PPP	purchasing power parity
SAM	Serbia and Montenegro
SAR	South Asia
SEE	Southeastern Europe
SOE	state-owned enterprise
SSA	Sub-Saharan Africa
U.S.	United States
UB	unemployment benefit
UI	unemployment insurance
U.K.	United Kingdom
UN	United Nations
UNDP	United Nations Development Programme

Note: All dollar amounts are U.S. dollars ($) unless otherwise indicated.

CHAPTER 1

Overview

This study examines labor market developments and strategies for enhancing job opportunities in Eastern Europe and the Former Soviet Union during their historic transition from centrally planned to market economies. (This group of countries is called "the Region" in this study.)[1] It addresses three key questions: How has the process of economic transformation associated with the transition affected the labor market, and who are those who have been hardest hit? How far have the different countries progressed in the transformation process, and what are the key constraints against creating more and better jobs? How can public policy help promote job creation?

The transition from centrally planned to market economies has entailed profound institutional reforms and far-reaching structural changes. The countries of Eastern Europe and the Former Soviet Union have achieved impressive results in economic liberalization, privatizing state-owned enterprises (SOEs), and opening up their economies to international trade and capital flows. After a major plunge in the early phases of the transition, gross domestic product (GDP) per capita has recovered in many countries, being at or above the pretransition levels in many. Overall, there is a clear association between the reform effort (proxied by the European Bank for Reconstruction and Development [EBRD] transition index) and the recovery of GDP since the early 1990s (figure 1.1).

Despite some progress in recent years, labor market conditions remain difficult in most countries. For example, the employment-to-working-age-population ratio—a summary measure of the utilization of labor resources—is currently lower than at the beginning of the transition and often below the average of industrial countries (figure 1.1). Slack labor markets assume different dimensions in the Region's countries: high open unemployment, falling labor force participation, or a low-productivity employment trap.

In faster-restructuring countries such as Poland and the Slovak Republic, unemployment was 19 and 18.2 percent of the labor force in 2004, respectively, despite high rates of economic growth. In Hungary, the unemployment rate is relatively low (around 6 percent), but this rate is partly the result of falling labor participation: many workers have given up their job search and left the labor force.

FIGURE 1.1
The Payoff to Reforms in Transition Economies: Higher Output, but Still Insufficient Jobs, 1992–2003

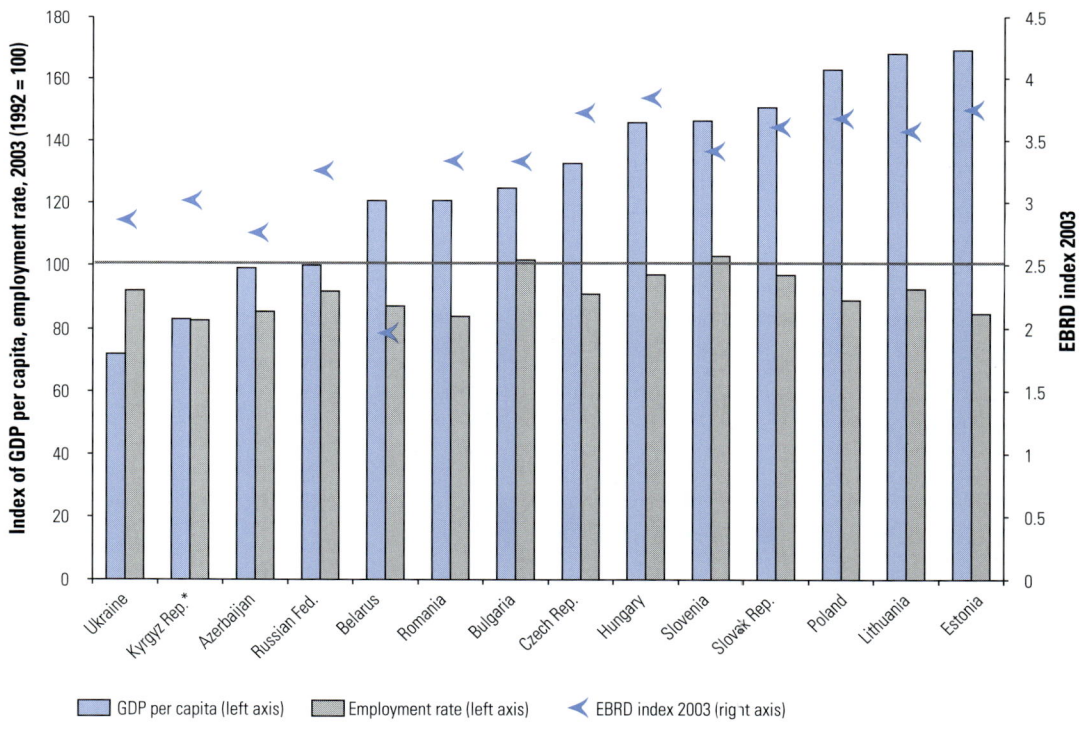

Sources: World Bank 2004c; ILO LABORSTA database; and EBRD Transition Report 2004.

Note: Data for the Kyrgyz Republic are for 2002. Data for Bulgaria, the Czech Republic, Poland, Slovenia, and the Slovak Republic refer to 1993; for Romania, data refer to 1994. The EBRD transition index is the simple average of the published indicators on Price Liberalization, Forex and Trade Liberalization, Small-Scale Privatization, Large-Scale Privatization, Enterprise Reform, Competition Policy, Banking Sector Reform, and Non-Banking Financial Institutions.

Open unemployment is less of a problem in the slower-reforming countries of the Former Soviet Union, such as Azerbaijan, Moldova, and Ukraine. However, much of their workforce is stuck in low-productivity employment in unrestructured and probably nonviable enterprises or has had to move back to subsistence agriculture. The employment levels of the central-plan period, when employment was not only a right but also a duty for most of those of working age, cannot be sustained in a market-based system. However, actual labor market conditions in most countries in the Region clearly indicate significant slack.

This has led to persistent disparities in the labor market. In the Region's economies, especially in Central European (CEE) and Southeastern European (SEE) countries, unemployment is typically of long duration, and many unemployed have difficulties in finding new jobs. The surge in unemployment was largely expected during the transition, given the need for major reallocation of labor across sectors, firms, and locations. But the persistence of unemployment—the share of those without a job for more than a year—is 40 to 50 percent in the EU-8 transition countries (annex 1.1), compared to below 40 percent in advanced market economies. A common assumption at the beginning of the transition was that high unemployment would be transient, declining once the emerging private sector started creating jobs. In reality, workers displaced in the "old" sectors have had limited chances to find jobs in the "new" sectors. In the Commonwealth of Independent States (CIS),[2] underemployment (low-productivity employment and hidden unemployment) is more prevalent.

Promoting the creation of more and better jobs remains a priority in the Region. Politically, creating viable and lasting employment will strengthen support for further market-oriented reforms. More broad-based employment growth—job opportunities for many workers and not only for the highly skilled and those in large cities—will also reduce social costs. For example, in Poland, a household whose head is unemployed is five times more likely to be poor than a household whose head is employed. In most other countries, such as Georgia, the Kyrgyz Republic, or the Russian Federation, unemployment raises the risk of poverty by at least a factor of two (World Bank 2005b).

The new market economy environment has contributed to the widening of wage disparities.[3] Although the increase in wage disparities is consistent with growing productivity differentials, market distortions have also played a role (particularly pronounced in CIS countries). The worst affected have typically been those who are the most vulnerable to shocks and least able to adjust to the new market paradigms: mostly less skilled and older workers. Thus, low employment and significant earnings inequality have translated into higher poverty and lower social welfare. These outcomes have improved in recent years, but serious problems persist for some of the weakest strata of the population.

What, then, is the way to more and better jobs in the Region? The specific mix of policies that each country needs to adopt varies, depending upon its particular economic and labor market situation. However, for all transition economies, addressing the issue of underutilization of labor requires a two-track strategy: ***increasing the pace of job creation*** by encouraging firm entry and expansion and ***facilitating the reallocation of jobs and workers*** away from old, less productive firms toward new, more productive firms.

The first part of this strategy requires further improvements in the investment climate and lowering the costs of doing business. Most countries in the Region have made substantial progress in their investment climate. However, there are remaining constraints. Operating a business in low income CIS countries carries high risks (for example, policy unpredictability, insecure property rights, weak contract enforcement, and unreliable infrastructure). In the middle income CIS countries (Belarus, Kazakhstan, Russia, and Ukraine), businesses face considerable administrative barriers (for example, numerous permits, inefficient regulations, and red tape). Doing business in CEE countries is hampered by high direct costs (for example, high taxation). Although there is substantial subgroup commonality, key constraints to firm entry and growth—and thus priorities for investment climate reform—are country-specific. They have been identified in this report in two ways: by comparing the regulatory and institutional settings in the Region's countries with those of other economies with a vibrant private sector and by exploiting enterprise surveys that directly ask entrepreneurs about the constraints they face in their operation and in their potential for expansion.

The second part of the strategy requires promoting adaptable labor markets and effective social safety nets to protect incomes of workers displaced in the wake of enterprise restructuring. In some countries (mainly in CIS and SEE), employment protection legislation (EPL) is stringent, but enforcement capacity is weak. These countries need to simultaneously liberalize EPL and promote compliance so that core worker rights are protected. In other countries (mainly CEE EU members), enforcement capacity is strong, and EPL is relatively flexible. They need to focus on addressing specific constraints to labor market flexibility. For example, where few regulations on temporary employment exist but regular employment is highly protected, these countries need to reduce protections granted to permanent workers to avoid creating labor market duality.

The rest of this overview develops these arguments in four parts:

- A summary of the key labor market developments during the transition, highlighting clear country differences in labor market conditions in the Region (see box 1.1 for a discussion on country grouping)

- A review of the process of job creation and destruction that examines enterprise restructuring, privatization, and entry of new ventures

- Highlights of the key constraints in the business environment that curb investment and job creation

- The set of policies still needed to create more and better jobs in the Region

Changing Labor Markets in the Region

The relatively poor record of job creation across the Region, despite the resumption of economic growth, remains the key area of concern for most policy makers. In the early phases of the economic transformation of the Region's countries, employment declined because of the major contraction in output. However, in the subsequent recovery periods, employment has not resumed as much as output has.

This is the case especially in CEE countries, where GDP growth has been sustained but employment has been fairly stagnant. Therefore, as in some EU-15 countries (annex 1.1), certain transition economies have recently experienced "jobless growth," with the number of jobs in the formal sector hardly responding to the growth in output. Poland is a good example: since the late 1990s, employment has been falling and unemployment persisting, despite relatively high rates of economic growth. In Hungary, the relatively weak labor demand has led to a fall in labor force participation. In other countries, such as those in the CIS, the link between output and employment has been stronger. In the early years of transition, this was associated with negative or very small output growth. Even when economic growth resumed in recent years, the strong link with employment has been associated with a generally poor quality of employment, with a rapid increase in the informal sector (including agriculture) as an employer of last resort.

Four main features characterize the labor markets of the Region during the transition:

> **BOX 1.1**
>
> **Geopolitical Country Groups Reflect Economic and Institutional Differences among the Region's Countries**
>
> The Region is large and economically diversified. Its subgroups of countries differ in their levels of economic development, institutions, industrial structure, and progress in market-oriented reforms. These differences, in turn, influence the characteristics and evolution of their labor markets.
>
> One way to group countries in the Region is to apply a traditional geopolitical grouping (annex 1.1). This approach clearly shows these countries' differences in their levels of economic development, institutional settings, and economic structure:
>
> - The following table shows a close correspondence between geopolitical location and differences in the level of *economic development*, as measured by the GDP per capita. All CEE EU-member countries belong to the group of the richest countries in the Region. All low income CIS countries belong to the group of the Region's poorest countries. Thus, geopolitical location is a good predictor of the level of economic development.
>
> **Geopolitical Location and Level of Economic Development Are Closely Related**
>
> | Geopolitical groups | Income groups: GDP per capita,[a] 2002 | | | Mean value US$ |
> | --- | --- | --- | --- | --- |
> | | Top tercile | Middle | Bottom tercile | |
> | CEE EU members | 8 | | | 12,984 |
> | CEE EU accession | 1 | 2 | | 8,032 |
> | SEE | | 3 | 1 | 5,685 |
> | Middle income CIS | | 3 | 1 | 6,122 |
> | Low income CIS | | | 7 | 2,428 |
>
> *Sources:* World Development Indicators; World Bank database; Bank staff calculations.
>
> *Note:* Numbers stand for the number of countries within the cell.
> a. GDP at PPP (current international dollars).

1. In many countries, job creation still lags behind job destruction, leading to employment decline. Overall, job reallocation (the sum of job creation and destruction) in the Region increased dramatically in response to transition—from less than 10 percent of the workforce in the late 1980s to more than 25 percent in the 1990s. The main differences across countries, however, are in job creation. Although countries lagging behind on reforms, such as those in the CIS, were able to contain job destruction in the early phases of transition, job destruction later rose to high levels but was not accompanied by new private initiatives to create new jobs.

- Similarly, a strong overlap exists between geopolitical location and quality of *institutions and governance*. Government effectiveness varies significantly between geopolitical groups, but variation within groups is relatively small.

- Geopolitical location also reliably corresponds to the progress of *economic transition* (as measured by the International Bank for Reconstruction and Development index). Countries that have either become members of the European Union or are candidates for membership have advanced the most in implementing market reforms. Economic transition is less advanced in the middle income and—especially—the low income CIS countries, while SEE countries occupy the middle position.

Naturally, use of the geopolitical taxonomy occasionally results in a misclassification of some countries from the economic perspective. Bulgaria and Romania, EU accession countries that thus fall into the CEE group, are closer to the SEE group in economic development. The borderline between middle and low income CIS countries is in some cases blurred. For example, in government effectiveness and regulatory quality, Armenia performs better than other low income CIS countries. Georgia, the Kyrgyz Republic, and Moldova, in turn, are more advanced in market-oriented reforms than other CIS countries.

Source: Bank staff analysis.

2. The nature of jobs has changed. The incidence of regular formal sector jobs has fallen, while the incidence of temporary and casual informal sector jobs has increased. This has led to increases in the segmentation of the labor market. There has also been a shift from less skilled, blue-collar manufacturing jobs toward more skilled, white-collar service sector jobs.

3. Wage growth has accelerated in recent years, but wage differentials have also widened substantially. Enterprise restructuring has led to significant improvements in productivity growth, which in turn has led to marked real-wage increases. At the same time,

returns to education and to market-related skills have risen, leading to a greater dispersion in the distribution of wages and a growing share of workers in low-paid jobs.

4. There is strong regional concentration of job creation within countries, which has brought about large regional disparities in labor market conditions.

These features of labor market adjustment to the transition shock have been common, to a varying degree, across the Region's subgroups of countries. At the same time, however, there have been considerable cross-regional differences in the nature of labor market adjustment, depending on region-specific features of the labor market. These four labor market factors are now discussed in turn.

Persistent Unemployment and Lack of Productive Jobs in the Region

The observed labor market outcomes in the Region's countries reflect different stages of the transition process and differences in underlying job dynamics (figure 1.2). All countries have experienced a surge in job destruction by downsizing and closing businesses. They have also seen job creation by new and expanding firms. However, the size of job creation and destruction, as well as their timing, has varied markedly across countries.

For example, Estonia and Slovenia experienced a short period of large job destruction in the early phase of the transition. This was followed by a period in which job creation and destruction went hand in hand (synchronized flows). More recently, incipient signs in these countries are emerging of job creation exceeding job destruction.

In contrast, many other countries are still struggling with job creation falling short of job destruction (for example, see Romania in figure 1.2). In Russia, job flows have been remarkably low, with job creation lagging behind job destruction for most of the past decade. In those countries where job destruction has been contained by slowing down the restructuring process, larger flows can be expected once the required transformation process has unfolded.

During the initial stage of the transition, high job destruction and low job creation resulted in growing unemployment and falling employment. Today, unemployment rates are in double digits in several CEE economies, in some cases above the Organisation for Economic Cooperation and Development (OECD) or EU-15 averages (figure 1.3). Unemployment rates reach highs of more than 30 percent in the former Yugoslav Republic of (FYR) Macedonia and 19 percent in Poland. In

FIGURE 1.2
Unsynchronized Job Creation and Job Destruction Can Give Rise to Unemployment

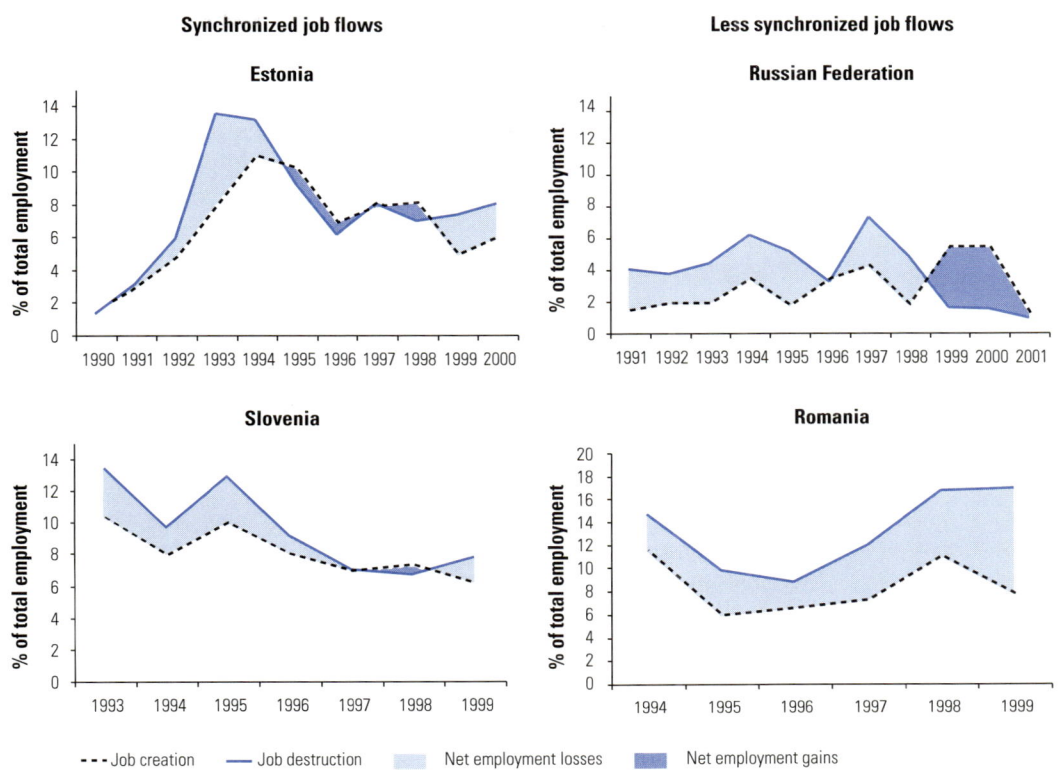

Source: Scarpetta and Vodopivec 2005.

most CIS countries, open unemployment tends to be lower (with Georgia, at more than 12 percent, being an outlier), but many workers are engaged in low-productivity activities or have moved back to subsistence agriculture (see the following discussion).

In CEE countries, high and persistent unemployment has been accompanied by a major fall in labor force participation rates, as workers became discouraged by lack of job opportunities and gave up their job search. In these countries, both open unemployment and low labor force participation have led to a low ratio of employment to working-age population (figure 1.4).[4] Employment-to-population ratios are below the EU's average and, for most countries, clearly below the Lisbon target of 70 percent of the working-age population.[5] However, in recent years there are signs that this negative trend in employment has been reversed in some countries, most notably the Baltic States—raising hopes that employment prospects are finally improving.

In CEE and SEE countries, the salient feature of unemployment is its long duration and prevalence among the young and the less edu-

FIGURE 1.3
Unemployment Continues to Be High in Most Transition Economies
Unemployment Rate in 2003, Percentage

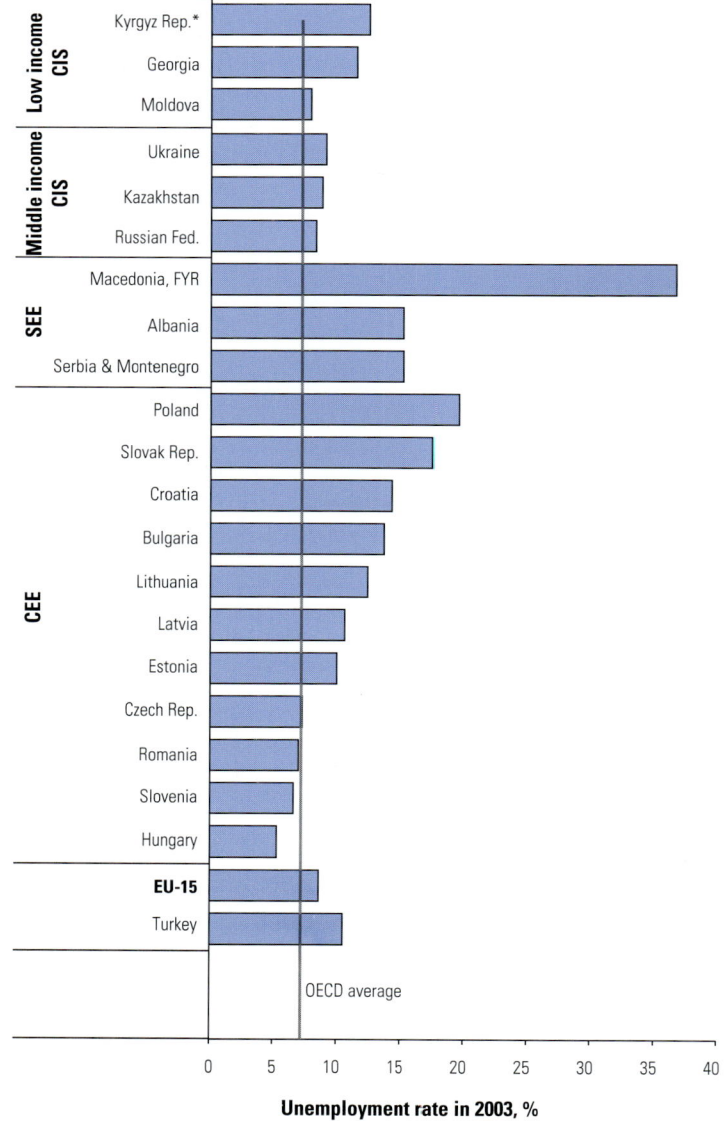

Sources: Labor Force Surveys (ILO [LABORSTA database], OECD); * 2002; and Labour Market in the CIS countries, Statistical Abstract, Interstate Statistical Committee of the CIS, Moscow 2004.

cated. These are problems observed in many EU countries, but assume particular severity in some of the Region's countries. More than 50 percent of the unemployed in many CEE countries have been without a job for more than one year (long-term unemployed), and

FIGURE 1.4
Employment Rates Have Declined and Are below the Lisbon Target of 70 Percent
Employment-to-Working-Age-Population Ratio in 2003

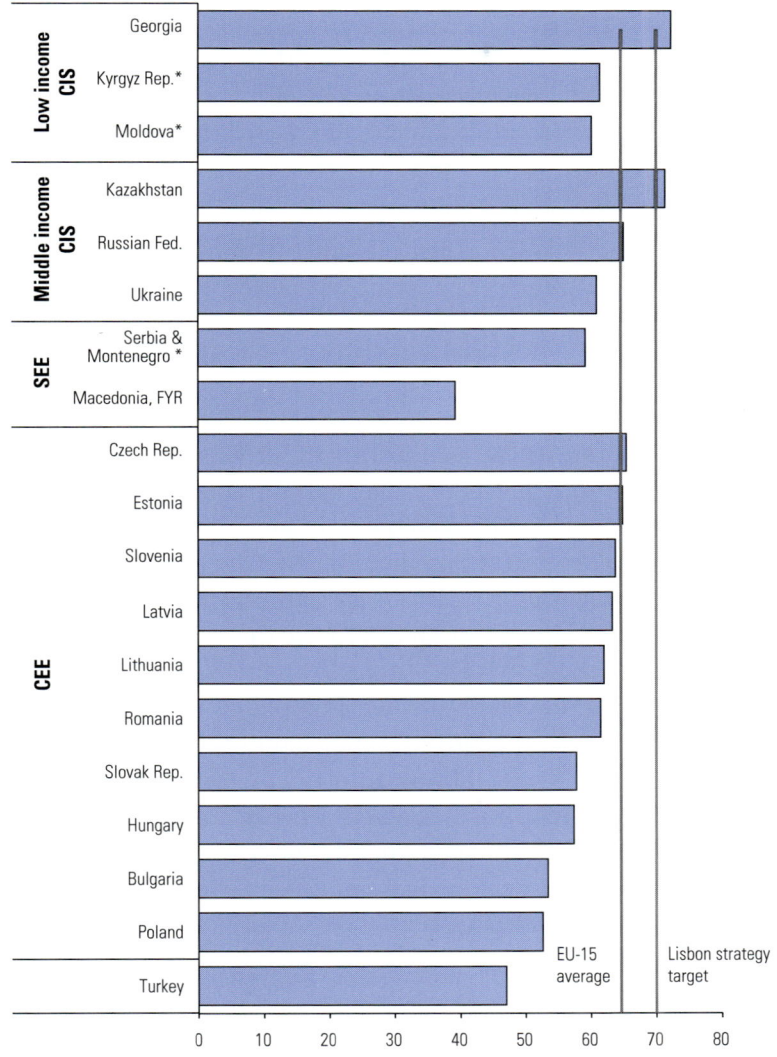

Sources: ILO (LABORSTA database); OECD; Eurostat; and Bank staff calculations.

Note: * = 2002

the proportion is still higher in SEE countries. The chances to escape unemployment are low by the standards of flexible labor markets and are similar to those seen in some EU countries with a stagnant pool of jobless people. Turkey, a nontransition economy, provides a telling contrast of a more dynamic labor market. Long-term unemployment there accounts for some 30 percent of total unemployment, which is similar to the proportion observed among more flexible EU labor markets.

Unemployment rates in transition economies are particularly high among less educated workers. For example, in Poland, a worker with primary education (eight years) is more than four times more likely to become unemployed than a worker with tertiary education. The employment rate for workers with primary education is less than 20 percent, compared with close to 80 percent for workers with tertiary education (United Nations Development Programme [UNDP] 2004). Youth is another group that suffers from high unemployment: on average, youth unemployment rates are twice as high as overall unemployment rates. In Bulgaria and the Slovak Republic, more than one-third of the youth labor force is unemployed, which also makes them poorer.

In many CIS countries, low open unemployment and high employment rates hide significant problems: delayed enterprise restructuring with persistent overstaffing and, especially in low income CIS countries, the dominance of low-productivity jobs in the informal sector to earn subsistence income. The latter feature is typical of developing countries, where social protection is ineffective and thus unemployment is not an affordable option for most workers. The natural implication is that unemployment in the CIS may worsen as restructuring progresses further. Enterprises will downsize more aggressively to be competitive, as they did in CEE, and unprofitable firms will close. Thus, inflows into unemployment are likely to increase as restructuring progresses. The extent to which this will cause an increase in unemployment will depend on the ease with which the displaced workers will find jobs in the new private sector (or in the informal sector).

The Changing Nature of Jobs

The greatest change since transition has been the shift from secure, though not highly rewarding, employment, to less stable jobs with greater earning potential. But in the low income CIS, casual and less formal jobs have also increased dramatically to levels observed in developing countries. For example, self-employment accounts for about 20 percent of total employment in EU transition economies and for about 50 percent of employment in low income CIS countries. Similarly, informal sector employment as a share of total employment is estimated at around 40–50 percent in the CIS.

Another feature of the changing nature of jobs in transition countries is the rapid increase in fixed-term employment contracts.

The characteristics of the jobs offered under temporary or informal arrangements and those of self-employment vary across individuals and countries. Temporary employment has been largely used by firms to circumvent the often rigid firing regulations for those on open-ended contracts. For example, in Croatia, most workers are hired using fixed-term contracts (World Bank 2003b). Informal jobs loom large among young, poorly educated blue-collar workers. They also seem to be a more frequent destination after a period of unemployment than formal sector jobs are. Informal workers also tend (on average) to have lower wages than formal sector workers do. The observed wage differentials between formal and informal sector jobs are largely the result of selection of workers in the two sectors: low-skilled and less experienced workers tend to be sorted into informal jobs, often in small firms with low-productivity potentials.

The nature of self-employment also varies greatly. For some low-skilled workers, especially in the poorer CIS countries, own-account jobs in retail and agriculture are subsistence activities. But for other, more skilled workers, self-employment is sometimes a preferred alternative to formal sector employment because self-employment offers better earning opportunities and more scope for entrepreneurship, especially in the more dynamic CEE countries.

The nature of jobs has also changed because of sectoral shifts and deindustrialization. Most CEE countries have witnessed a fall in the number of blue-collar manufacturing jobs and an increase in white-collar service sector jobs. In contrast, in most CIS countries, deindustrialization was associated with an increase in agricultural employment. Figure 1.5 illustrates these divergent patterns of job reallocation. In the Czech Republic, market services as a share of total employment increased by about 5 percentage points during the transition, while manufacturing's share fell by about 3 percentage points. In contrast, in the Kyrgyz Republic, market services gained little as a share of total employment. However, there was a dramatic fall in the share of manufacturing (about 17 percentage points) and a huge shift toward agriculture, which increased its share by some 20 percentage points. It is not clear whether the significant increase in the share of agricultural employment in the CIS countries is only temporary or represents a more profound and long-lasting reversion toward employment patterns more typical of countries with relatively low income per capita.

The skill content of jobs has shifted upward, especially in the new sector. The profiles of job creation and destruction during the transition differed in skills, occupations, and experience. Many jobs have been destroyed in low-skilled activities or in highly specialized manufacturing activities. Many jobs have been created not only in relatively more skilled activities but also in certain service activities that require low- and medium-level skills that are nonetheless different from those of the lost manufacturing jobs. In Estonia, for example, the share of nonmanual workers in total employment increased by 8 percentage points during 1990–2000; at present, nonmanual workers account for 55 percent of total employment. In Russia, the share of workers with tertiary education increased by 6 percentage points during 1992–2000 and currently exceeds 20 percent. A similar increase occurred in Poland and other CEE economies (Peter 2003). This skills mismatch between jobs destroyed in the old sector and those created in the new sector is one of the factors behind unemployment in transition economies. It requires reforms in the education system and efforts of requalification (Commander and Köllő 2004).[6]

Changes in the nature of jobs have affected men more than women. Many jobs have been lost in sectors dominated by male employment—heavy industry and the extraction industry—while new activities have been created in services where women tend to have easier access. As a result, men have suffered relatively more job losses than women have during the transition. For example, the female-employment-to-population ratio in CEE, at 54 percent, is close to the EU-15 average (56 percent), while the male ratio, at 65 percent, is significantly below the EU-15 average (73 percent).[7,8]

Wage Growth, Inequality, and Low-Paid Jobs

Wage increases in recent years have been associated with firm restructuring and productivity improvements. Enterprise restructuring benefited the insiders (that is, those workers who kept their jobs and those who managed to find new ones).[9] Wage growth has been the fastest in the low income CIS countries, where it averaged 2.8 percent annually. It was slightly slower in the CEE and SEE and in middle income CIS economies, where it averaged 2.5–2.6 percent annually during 1996–2002.

The change in the wage-setting mechanism, from administrative to market-based, has led to an increase in wage dispersion. The wage distribution was compressed under central planning because of the egalitarian ideology and the centralized wage-setting mechanism. For example, the wage premium for university workers over those with vocational education was just 20 percent.[10] Changes in the structure of the economy, and thus changes in relative demand for different types of labor, have given rise to various wage premiums to worker

FIGURE 1.5
Different Patterns of Labor Reallocation: The Czech Republic (CEE) vs. the Kyrgyz Republic (CIS)

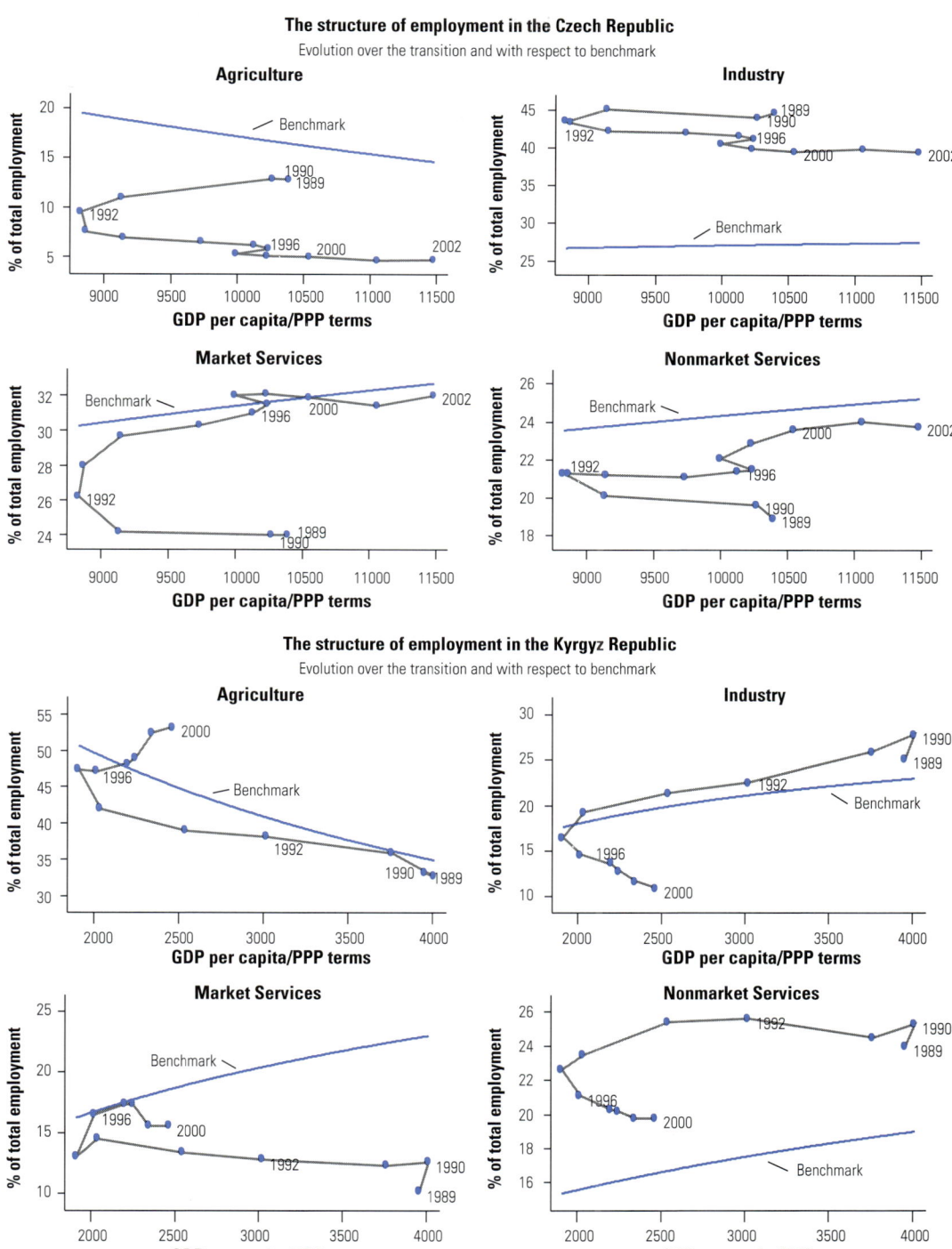

Source: Bank staff calculations based on the "Industrial Database for Eastern Europe" of the Vienna Institute for International Economic Studies.

Note: The market benchmarks are obtained through regressions of sectoral employment shares on GDP per capita and its square on a sample of 50 countries.

and firm characteristics (such as education and skills, occupation, or industry) that were not widespread in socialist times. A university-educated worker in Poland currently earns (on average) 70 percent more than a worker with basic vocational training. In the private sector, this premium to university education is even higher (160 percent).[11] These natural changes not only have contributed to the increase in wage inequality over most of the transition period but also have led to better market efficiency as wages become better aligned with productivity differentials. One should note that, although they remain high by the standards of industrial countries, wage inequalities have shown some decline in recent years (World Bank 2005b).

The gender pay differential has declined in many countries in the Region and is relatively small. On average, women earn some 20 percent less than men in comparable jobs, which is modest by international standards (Paci 2002). Thus, the gender wage differential has not been a factor behind the rise in wage inequality. After all, women in the Region benefited from the increase in returns to schooling more than men because (on average) they are better educated than men.

Though wage inequality is presently high in virtually all transition economies, there are substantial differences among the Region's subgroups of countries (figure 1.6). In European transition economies, wage inequality is high by EU standards, but still within the OECD range (although at its upper end). In contrast, in most of the CIS countries, wage disparities have reached very high levels characteristic of many developing countries. As an illustration, in CEE countries, the top-decile worker usually earns 4 to 5 times as much as the bottom-decile worker. In the Kyrgyz Republic, this ratio rises to 9, in Russia to 11, and in Azerbaijan to 13. In contrast, in the EU, the decile ratio varies between 3 and 4.

In countries where there is high earnings inequality, the labor market is divided into an increasingly large high-wage segment and a correspondingly large low-wage segment. For example, in the Czech Republic and Slovenia (where earnings inequality is relatively low), less than 5 percent of all wage and salary workers earn less than 50 percent of median earnings. In Serbia and Montenegro, this fraction exceeds 20 percent; in Russia, it goes up to 25 percent; and it reaches 30 percent in Azerbaijan.[12] The high incidence of low pay is of particular importance because it may translate into poverty. However, in the Region, consumption inequality tends to be lower than wage inequality because of multiple-earner households and extensive transfer systems in many countries. In the low income CIS countries and some SEE countries, remittances and other private transfers may also boost consumption levels (World Bank 2005b).

The minimum wage serves as a floor in European transition economies, reducing wage dispersion. In CEE and SEE, minimum wages are set at around 40 percent of the average wage. In contrast, in the CIS, minimum wages are much lower in relative terms. As a rule, they account for less than 20 percent of the average wage—often around 10 percent—which means that they are unlikely to be binding. This allows firms to maintain low-paid jobs, and as such it contributes to wage dispersion.

Geographical Labor Market Disparities

Labor market conditions vary substantially across geographical areas of most of the Region's countries, and in many cases such geographical disparities have persisted or even increased over time. For example, in 2003, differences between the regions with the highest unemployment rate and those with the lowest unemployment rate (usually the capital) exceeded a factor of 3 in all countries of the Region except Romania and Slovenia. These disparities in unemployment are also associated with large disparities in wages, with wages being lower in higher-unemployment regions. In Russia, the disparity in regional labor market conditions is much more pronounced, reflecting the immense economic heterogeneity of Russian regions.

Regional disparities tend to be persistent—regions showing better performance at the outset of the transition also tended to perform better in later phases—suggesting that they may be of a long-term nature, rather than a transitory phenomenon. Job creation and employment opportunities are clustered mainly around large urban agglomerations with diversified industrial structures—particularly with large and expanding service sectors, developed infrastructure, and a skilled workforce. In contrast, employment prospects are dire and unemployment high in monoculture (highly specialized) industrial regions, which suffer from idiosyncratic demand shocks. For example, in Bulgaria and Moldova in the early 2000s, employment was expanding almost exclusively in the capital region. During the same period, employment in Croatia grew in only 4 of 21 regions and in Poland in only 3 of 16 regions. Unemployment in rural agricultural regions is usually lower than that in regions with an industrial monoculture because workers in such regions have recourse to subsistence agriculture and can take temporary and seasonal jobs. In these regions, the problem is underemployment, rather than open unemployment.

The labor market inequalities are sustained by relatively low interregional migration. The main factors accounting for low interregional labor migration rates in transition economies include the following:

FIGURE 1.6
Wage Inequality in the CIS Is Higher than in the CEE
Ratios of 9th decile to 1st decile, 2002

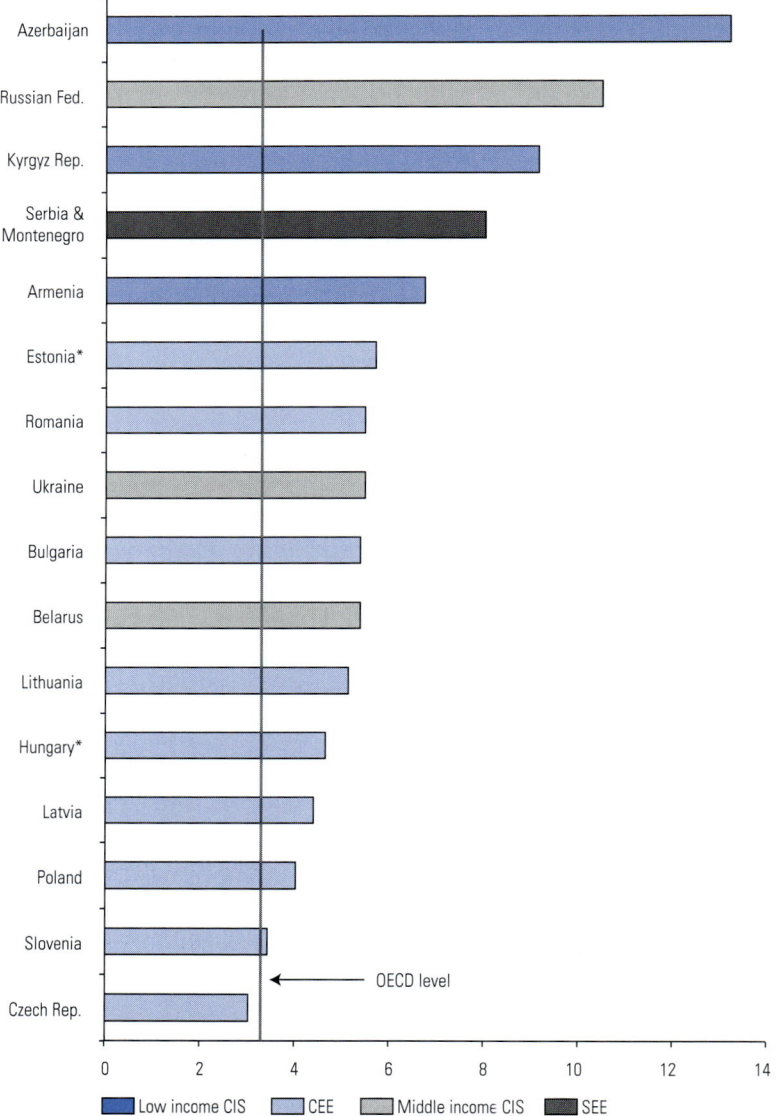

Sources: UNICEF TransMONEE database; and Bank staff calculations.
Note: * Signifies 2001.

- *High nationwide unemployment rates* may discourage internal migration because they indicate falling probability of finding employment. For example, in Bulgaria in the early 2000s, the unemployment rates were high in absolute terms, even in relatively low unemployment regions (for example, 14 percent in the capital city). A similar situation occurs in Poland.

- *Skills mismatch.* New jobs are created mainly in the service sector in urban regions, and these jobs may require skills not available to unemployed blue-collar workers in other regions. For example, it is estimated that in Bulgaria and Lithuania, more than 20 percent of the unemployed do not find a job because their skills fall short of employer requirements (World Bank 2002a and 2002c). Related to this is the inefficiency of the spatial matching (that is, the process by which unemployed workers find employment in other regions).

- *Social benefits* might have provided disincentives for migration, especially at an early stage of the transition (they were gradually reduced or abolished). In European transition economies, these were mainly cash benefits, while in CIS economies, they were usually in-kind benefits, such as firm-provided housing.

- *Informal safety nets* from informal sector employment or income from subsistence farming may induce job searchers to stay at home, rather than move elsewhere in the country.

- *Inefficiencies in the housing markets* greatly increase migration costs (for example, through high rents). The cost of renting a studio apartment in Warsaw accounts for around 70 percent of the average monthly net wage of a less skilled worker.

- *Liquidity constraints* may make migration an unaffordable option.

The Drivers of Labor Demand during the Transition

The observed changes in the Region's labor markets during the transition have been strongly influenced by the process of firm restructuring and massive reallocation of resources across firms, sectors, and locations. Faced with radical changes in the institution and market environment, firms in all countries have been forced to adapt their behavior. Some have been able to seize new opportunities, but many others have simply tried to survive in a market environment to which they were unaccustomed. The ensuing process of restructuring has involved major upgrading of technologies and production processes and hiring or (more often) laying off workers. As a result, some firms have managed to boost productivity, but some have been forced to exit the market. The process of economic transformation has been characterized by two interlinked processes:

1. *Within-enterprise reforms*, spurred by higher competitive pressure. These reforms comprise improvements in governance and management; better organization of producing and marketing; and introduction of new, more efficient technologies.

2. *A more efficient allocation of resources*, which also involved reallocation of jobs and workers away from declining, less productive firms, sectors, and regions toward expanding, more productive ones. Resource reallocation is important to promote output and productivity growth in any market economy, but it has assumed an even greater role in transition economies, given their highly distorted industrial structure inherited from the central-planning period. An important role in the process of reallocation of resources has been played by the entry of more productive firms and the exit of obsolete ones.

Restructuring of existing firms, reallocation of resources across them, and the entry and exit of firms have all contributed to shape the evolution of productivity and employment. The effects on productivity are massive. For example, figure 1.7 shows that the contribution to productivity growth of the entry and exit of firms and the reallocation of labor across incumbent firms in Russia has increased significantly during the transition period. In addition, there is evidence that more productive firms tend to create new jobs, while inefficient firms are destroying them in a number of countries, including Croatia, Lithuania, and Moldova (figure 1.8 illustrates this pattern for Moldova).

Firm Restructuring

Firm restructuring was a result of imposing market discipline on inherited enterprises and encouraging the creation and expansion of new enterprises. Discipline forced old enterprises to release assets and labor, which were then potentially available to restructured and new enterprises. It did this by hardening budget constraints, introducing competition in product markets, providing exit mechanisms, and monitoring managerial behavior to generate incentives for production and innovation. Encouragement entailed policies to create an attractive and competitive investment climate in which restructured and new enterprises had incentives to hire labor and to invest in expansion (World Bank 2002e, xvii).

Within-enterprise reforms engendered by the imposition of discipline resulted largely in labor shedding and what is called "defensive

FIGURE 1.7
Labor Reallocation Has Played an Increasing Role in Promoting Labor Productivity Growth in Russia

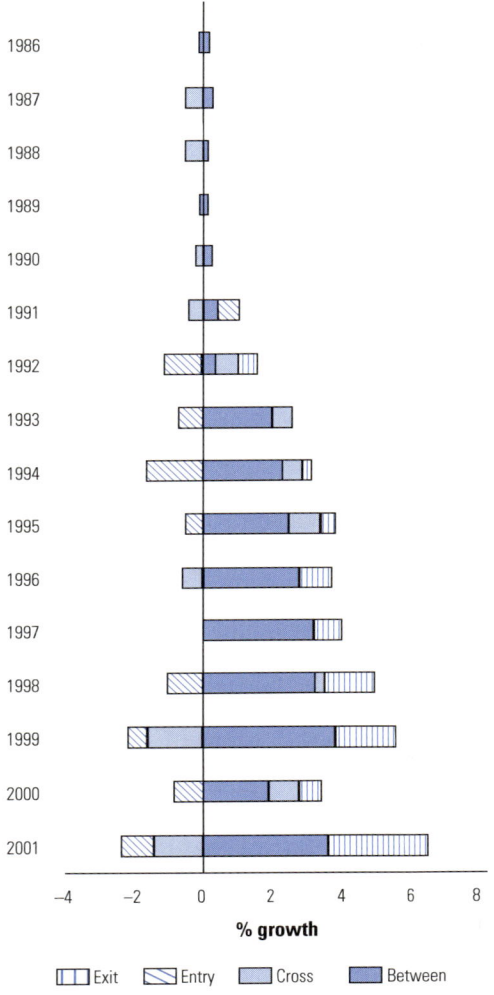

Source: Brown and Earle 2004.

Note: Entry: the contribution of new firms to overall labor-productivity growth; Exit: the contribution of exiting firms—as they tend to be less productive than the average, their exit contributes to raising productivity growth (on average); Cross: the product of changes in productivity and changes in market shares—it is negative if firms with rapidly growing productivity lose market shares; Between: captures the gains in aggregate productivity coming from a reallocation of resources from lower to higher productivity firms.

restructuring." Often, the impetus for defensive restructuring was privatization. In the "old" enterprises, productivity gains have been achieved largely through shedding redundant labor, which allowed the old firms to reduce costs and thus stay in the market. In addition, discipline led to the closure of other old, but inefficient firms, thus

FIGURE 1.8
The Rate of Job Creation Is Higher for More Productive Firms in Moldova
Employment Growth (percentage) by Productivity Level in 2001

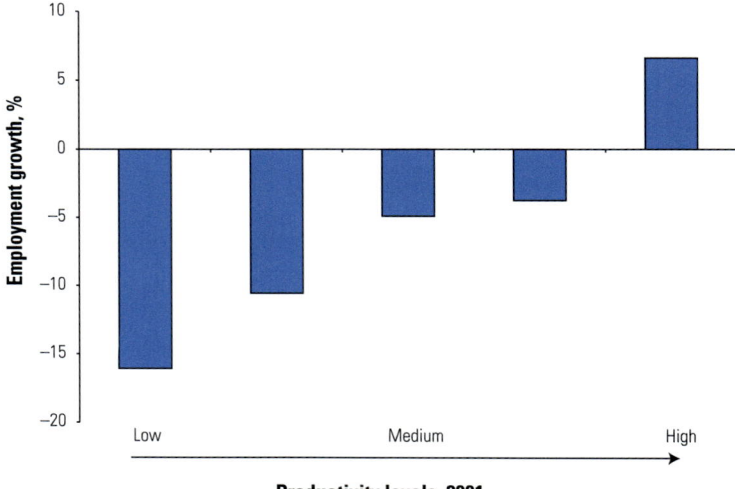

Source: Rutkowski 2004a.

raising average productivity. In addition, the entry of new firms further stimulated efficiency enhancements by incumbent firms. In background work to this report, which analyzed the effects of restructuring and reallocation of labor on productivity for a group of CEE countries, Russia, and Ukraine,[13] productivity growth was found to be clearly led by defensive restructuring and the associated labor shedding.[14] Indeed, those firms that achieved higher-than-average productivity growth during the transition period also experienced significant downsizing, with a fall in their share of total employment. At the same time, many low-productivity industries, sheltered from competitive pressure, have managed to contain job destruction, but may still have to go through a period of downsizing and restructuring, which will likely cause further increases in unemployment.

Strategic restructuring—with new investment and job creation—seems largely confined up until now to foreign-owned firms. For example, evidence for four countries (Hungary, Romania, Russia, and Ukraine) suggests that all privatized firms experienced significant improvements in their productivity performance. The acceleration in productivity was much stronger in foreign privatized firms, possibly because they had better characteristics even before the ownership change but also because of foreigners' advantages in accessing finance, new technologies, the latest managerial techniques, and world markets, which outweighed any disadvantages resulting from unfamiliarity with local conditions.

But where the differences between foreign and domestic privatization become even more evident is in employment. Foreign privatization is associated with increased employment and wages in all countries. Domestic privatization has been less kind to workers: wages suffered in all four countries, and employment rose in only a few instances. There are also significant differences across types of workers: employment composition and relative wage changes have been significantly biased toward white-collar employees. This is consistent with the idea that foreign privatization, by promoting the upgrading of production processes with new technologies, tends to be skill-biased. It also suggests that although foreign privatization has improved the welfare of workers overall, it has also increased inequality.

Reallocation of Labor and Firm Demographics

In all market economies, many firms enter and exit most markets every year. But in transition countries, the pace of firm creation and destruction during the transition has been phenomenal. In CEE countries, about 20–25 percent of firms were created or destroyed during the transition (compared with an average of 10 percent in OECD countries). Firm entry largely outpaced firm exit, which is obviously related to the process of transition and is not sustainable over the longer run. Yet it points to the fact that new firms not only displaced obsolete incumbents in the transition phase but also filled in new markets that were either nonexistent or poorly populated in the past.

The entry of new firms contributed markedly to job creation. As an example, in Russia, before the transition, firm turnover (entry and exit of firms) accounted for less than 20 percent of overall job turnover. During the transition, the contribution of firm turnover to job flows increased strongly. In the countries for which firm-level data are available, in the initial phases of the transition, the entry of firms contributed to about 40 percent of total job creation in Estonia, Hungary, and Latvia and to more than 70 percent in Romania and Slovenia.[15] Moreover, a stronger (positive) correlation exists in transition countries than in OECD countries between the number of entrant firms in a given country and industry and the overall job creation in that country and industry. By contrast, there is almost no correlation between exit of firms and job destruction, while in OECD countries this correlation is stronger. In other words, the entry of new firms plays a significant role in job creation. However, the exit of obsolete firms, while promoting productivity, does not strongly contribute to job destruction, which largely comes from downsizing of surviving firms.

Not surprisingly, the contribution of firm entry to overall job creation declined over the transition period. After having filled the pre-transition void in certain activities, the characteristics of job flows converged toward those observed in market economies: job creation and destruction come increasingly from within firm adjustment, rather than from the entry and exit of firms. In this context, Russia and Ukraine—two laggard reformers—saw the reverse patterns, with an increasing role of firm entry in total job creation in the second half of the 1990s.

Firm turnover is also important in promoting productivity. Contrary to the evidence in most OECD countries, where the lack of experience and small size often make new firms less productive than the average incumbents, in transition economies new firms have been more productive than existing firms. They have been able to fill in new market niches and adopt new and more efficient technologies. Thus, firm entry is critical not only for job creation but also for productivity growth. Figure 1.9 shows the contribution of the entry of more productive firms and the exit of less-productive ones to aggregate productivity in manufacturing. During the transition, in Estonia, Latvia, and Romania, 30 to 40 percent of overall productivity growth resulted from the creation and destruction of firms.

The Role of the Region's Policy and Institutions

All countries in the Region have made major progress in reforming their policy and institutional settings to accommodate the requirements of a market economy. But large differences remain in the investment climate across countries in the Region and, in different ways, all countries still have an ambitious agenda ahead to remove constraints to firms' entry, investment, and job creation. The initial deterioration of labor market conditions in most economies of the Region was the result of the transition shock, which caused a dramatic fall in output and a correspondingly large fall in labor demand. The resulting shedding of redundant labor and closing of loss-making enterprises caused large inflows into unemployment. Yet, the ability of the Region's economies to recover from the transition shock and to reduce unemployment has been largely determined by the rate of creation and expansion of new firms and consequently by the size of the new sector, as well as by the ability of existing firms to restructure to ensure profitability and improve competitiveness.

FIGURE 1.9
Firm Entry and Exit Are Critical for Productivity Growth
The Contribution of Entry and Exit of Firms to Total Labor Productivity Growth

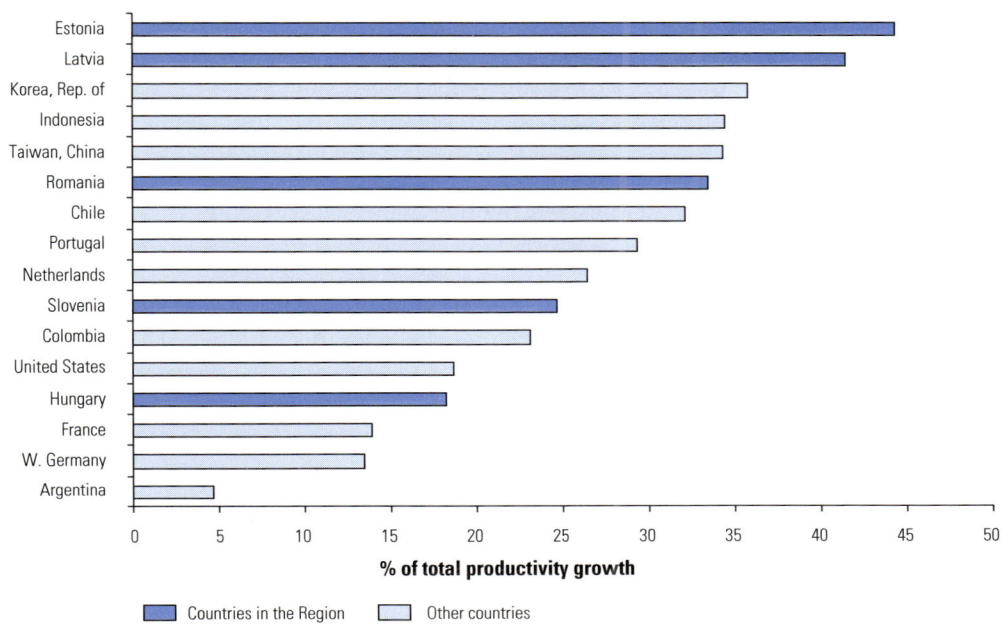

Source: Bartelsman, Haltiwanger, and Scarpetta 2004.

Note: Data show the sum of the contributions from new entrant firms and exiting firms to total labor-productivity growth in manufacturing. Data cover different periods for the countries. For all but three countries, the contributions are calculated on the basis of five-year rolling windows. For Hungary, Indonesia, and Romania, the data refer to three-year rolling windows and tend to underestimate the contribution of new firms to total labor-productivity growth.

The decision of firms to create more, and more productive, jobs and that of workers to stay in the labor market and seek more-rewarding jobs depend on a complex set of factors:

1. *Macroeconomic policy setting.* Macroeconomic instability and financial crises have both contributed to discouraging enterprises from undertaking new investment and creating new jobs. At the same time, the combination of relatively high interest rates and loose fiscal policy may have contributed in some CEE countries to reducing the employment content of growth.

2. *The cost of doing business.* Private investment is often discouraged in the Region's countries by a set of factors that increase the costs of new investment, the risk associated with it, and barriers to competition faced by firms.

3. *Wage flexibility* has increased during the transition in the Region; however, there are still instances in which wage floors or government intervention prevents wages from adjusting.

4. *Employment protection legislation.* Labor reallocation is also influenced by regulations on hiring and firing. Although several countries have reformed these regulations to better conform with market requirements, reforms have often focused on creating flexibility at the margin (for example, temporary contracts in CEE). And in the CIS countries, labor flexibility is often ensured by noncompliance with rigid regulations.

5. *Social benefits* played an important role in smoothing the costs of the transition, but overly generous benefits (as in the early phases of the transition in several CEE countries) weakened job search incentives.[16]

Each of these five factors—four on the demand side and one on the supply side—has played a different role across the countries of the Region. But, in general, the dominant role has been played by the demand-side factors, while the supply-side effects were relatively limited. Indeed, in transition economies, the rate of job destruction has been—and, in many cases, still is—higher than the rate of job creation, which has led to a fall in the number of jobs and an increase in unemployment. As a result, the number of unemployed per job vacancy is high in most transition economies. At the same time, the fraction of the jobless who receive unemployment benefits (20–30 percent) is relatively small. This suggests that the outflows from unemployment to jobs are mainly impeded by the lack of job openings, rather than by labor supply disincentives.[17]

Macroeconomic Policies

The transition to a market economy has been characterized in some countries by macroeconomic instabilities and financial crises that have had repercussions in the neighboring countries. Since the mid-1990s, there has been a tendency, especially in CEE countries, toward relatively tight monetary policy and loose fiscal policy. This combination is estimated to have contributed to jobless growth.[18] The tightening in monetary policy necessary to reduce inflationary pressures caused high real interest rates in the CEE since 1995. Empirical evidence suggests that high real interest rates tend to reduce capital investment and thus slow down the required adoption of new technologies and production processes, as well as the development of new activities. In turn, a slower pace of capital formation can easily translate into the postponement of defensive restructuring (see below), with less hiring of workers and thus a lower rate of employment growth.

There is also evidence of a loosening in fiscal policy in the aftermath of the 1998 recession, when employment was sharply declining.[19] Because fiscal loosening implied a likely future increase in interest rates, and possibly in the tax burden as well, forward-looking entrepreneurs reduced up-front hiring (Boeri and Garibaldi 2004). In addition, there was a crowding-out effect induced by an increase in labor costs. In the past five years, real wages in the public sector increased at a higher pace than those in the private sector in several CEE countries. In addition to worsening the fiscal balance, the associated high wage growth in the CEE public sector may have crowded out skilled workers from the private sector.

GDP growth also had a strong effect on employment in the second phase of transition, but again macroeconomic policies may have diluted its impact. There is evidence that the rise in real interest rates and the loosening of the fiscal stance contributed to weakening the potential effect of GDP growth on employment and unemployment (Boeri and Garibaldi 2004). In other words, employment and unemployment would have been more responsive to changes in GDP growth had the macroeconomic environment not changed at the same time.

Cost of Doing Business

Improving the investment climate requires further action not only in reducing the costs of investment and the risk associated with it but also in promoting competition in the market (World Bank 2004d). Priorities along these three dimensions differ from one country to another.[20]

High costs of doing business discouraged the creation of new firms and firm growth, leading to a lower pace of job creation. Objective indicators of the costs of doing business, as well as entrepreneurs' perceptions, indicate that there is substantial room for improving the investment climate in the Region and thus fostering job creation. In most of the subgroups of countries in the Region, economic and regulatory policy uncertainty and macroeconomic instability are seen as major obstacles (figure 1.10). High taxes, burdensome tax administration and associated corruption, and problems with financing access and cost also loom large.

Not surprisingly, most firms in the Region claim that taxes have a major impact on their costs. This is common to most firms around the world, and it is not by itself a source of major concern for policy makers. If properly used, tax revenues contribute to the provision of public goods and mitigate market failures. Two main aspects of the tax system have, however, a specific bearing on firms' costs in the Region.

FIGURE 1.10
Major Obstacles to Firm Activity, 2002
Proportion of Firms That Report the Following as Major or Severe Obstacles in the Region

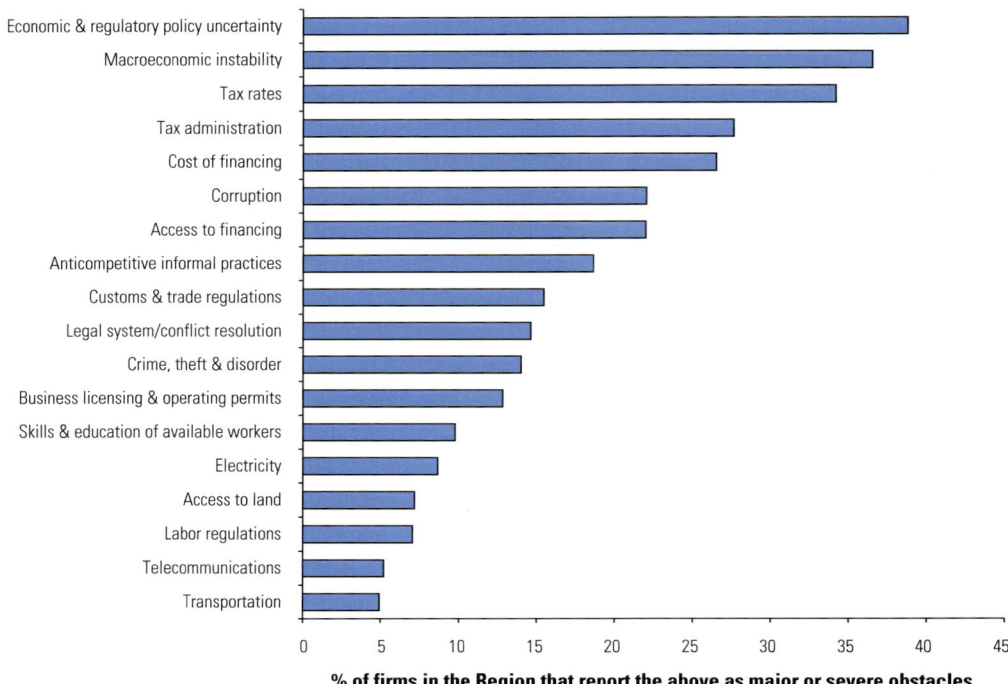

Source: EBRD–World Bank Business Environment and Enterprise Performance Surveys, 2002.

Note: Preliminary results from the new Business Environment and Enterprise Performance Survey (BEEPS) of 2005 are broadly consistent with those reported in this figure. However, some changes may have occurred for individual countries or subgroups of countries in the Region.

Tax rates—especially payroll taxes—are particularly high in European transition economies, reflecting, to a large extent, inefficiencies in the pension and health care systems. Taxes on labor use are among the highest in the world—in the Czech Republic, Hungary, and Romania, the tax wedge on labor use is around or even above 50 percent, while it is around 40 percent in the OECD countries (figure 1.11). Labor taxes lower labor demand by raising labor costs, but they also lower labor supply by reducing the real consumption wage.[21] In addition, they contribute to the growth of the informal sector. The result is lower formal sector employment. The employment effect of these taxes is especially strong in CEE economies, which combine high tax rates with effective enforcement.[22] Also, tax administration (for example, tax inspections) is particularly burdensome in the CIS countries, being associated with bureaucratic harassment and corruption.

Many firms in the Region also point to the difficulty of accessing finance and the costs of it as major constraints on their ability to invest and create new jobs. There are large differences in access to finance in the Region. For example, while domestic credit to the private sector accounts for more than 100 percent of GDP in the European Union, it is less than 30 percent in CEE, and it drops to 16 percent (on average) in the middle income CIS countries and to 10 percent in the low income CIS countries. The comparison between Croatia, with one of the most developed credit markets in the Region, and the Kyrgyz Republic, with one of the least developed credit markets in the Region, is stunning: in Croatia, domestic credit to the private sector represents more than 50 percent of GDP, while it represents only 4 percent in the Kyrgyz Republic. But even in Croatia, the credit market is less developed than in some developing countries, such as the Republic of Korea and Malaysia, where credit totals considerably more than 100 percent of GDP.[23]

Difficult access to credit is most common for small and newly established firms, which account for a large part of total job creation in most of the Region's countries. Improving financial markets and easing access to credit may therefore lead to significant improvements in the

FIGURE 1.11

The Tax Wedge on Labor in the Region Is High, Often Higher than in Most OECD Countries

The Difference between Labor Cost and Take-Home Pay as a Percentage of Labor Cost

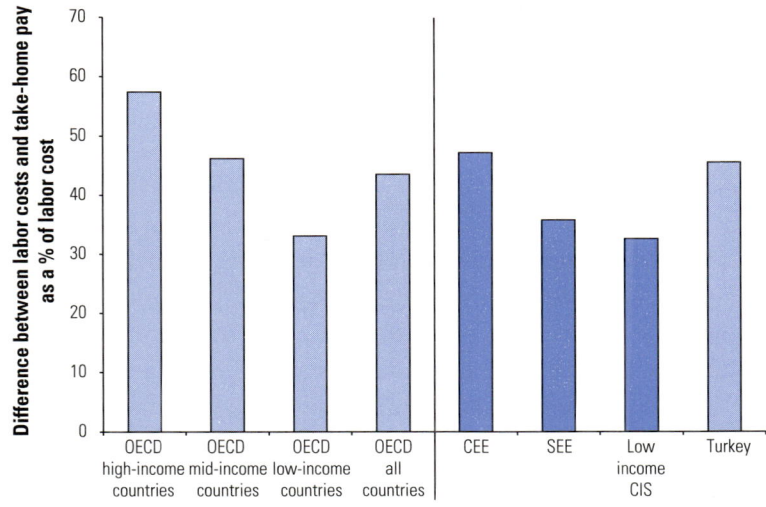

Sources: OECD 2004b for OECD and CEE OECD, except Slovenia (based on 2001); Bank staff estimates for others (using 2003). Tax wedge calculated with reference to the average worker without dependents. For countries in the Region, average workers do not include those involved in agriculture. OECD groupings exclude CEE OECD: (i) low (less than 40% wedge) includes Australia, Iceland, Ireland, Japan, Korea, Mexico, New Zealand, Portugal, Switzerland, UK, and USA; (ii) mid (40-50%) includes Canada, Denmark, Greece, Luxembourg, Norway, Spain and Sweden; (iii) high (51+ %) includes Austria, Belgium, Finland, France, Germany, Italy, and Netherlands.

labor market. In Latvia, where access to credit is considered one of the best in the Region and comparable to the EU-15 average, successful entrant firms almost double their employment in the first four years of life. By contrast, in Romania, where access to credit is considered one of the worst in the Region, successful new firms increase their employment by a mere 10–20 percent over the same time horizon.

Labor regulations do not rank among top business concerns in the Region, especially in the CIS. In the less-advanced economies of the CIS, they are dwarfed by more important and binding constraints. Although strict on the books, labor regulations are often only weakly or selectively enforced, and firms do not comply with them. Finally, in the slower-reforming transition economies (again, mainly in the CIS), where the restructuring effort still lies ahead, few firms have gone through major downsizing, constrained by high dismissal costs.

However, in European transition economies, where enforcement is stronger and enterprise restructuring more advanced, firms frequently view labor regulations as a significant obstacle to their operation and growth. In CEE, the proportion of firms complaining about labor regulations reaches as much as 30 percent, and it is only slightly lower in SEE (25 percent). For comparison, in low income CIS countries, this proportion is only 10 percent; it is somewhat more in middle income CIS countries, which reflects in part lax enforcement and in part lower pressures on adjustment.[24]

Although many investment climate concerns are common for most transition economies, there is also substantial variation in the relative importance of the obstacles. In the transition economies that recently joined the EU, labor-related issues, such as skills of the available workers, labor regulations, and taxation, figure prominently (figure 1.12, panel A). In other European transition economies, a combination of poorly functioning institutions (for example, ineffective legal systems and industrial conflict resolution) and bad governance (for example, anticompetitive and informal practices, as well as corruption) limit firm growth and job creation (figure 1.12, panels B and C). In the middle income CIS countries, the predominant part is played by administrative barriers, such as numerous licenses and operating permits, burdensome tax administration (with associated bureaucratic harassment and extortion), and inefficient regulations (figure 1.12, panel D). In the low income CIS countries, the constraints are more basic, ranging from unreliable infrastructure to underdeveloped institutions of a market economy (figure 1.12, panel E).[25]

One reason why labor-related issues are more pronounced in CEE, compared with those in other subgroups in the Region, is a faster pace of enterprise restructuring. First, a widespread job reallocation gives rise to a skills mismatch because the newly created jobs differ in

FIGURE 1.12
Obstacles to Business Operation and Growth Vary by Subgroup

Panel A—CEE, EU-Member Countries

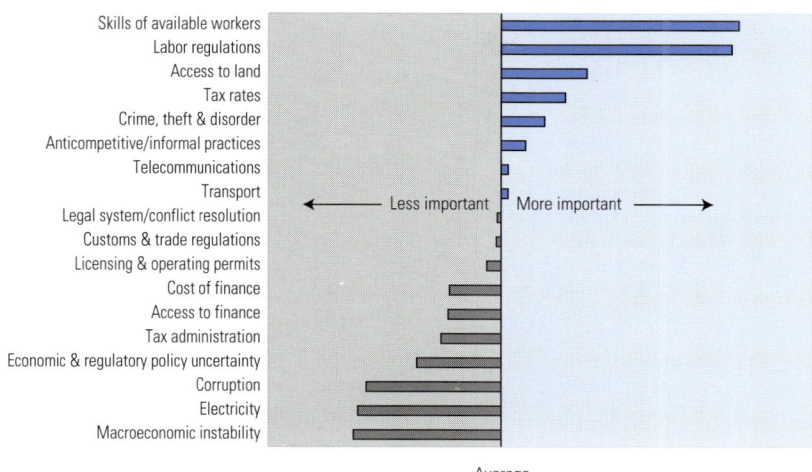

Panel B—CEE, EU-Accession Countries (Bulgaria, Croatia, and Romania)

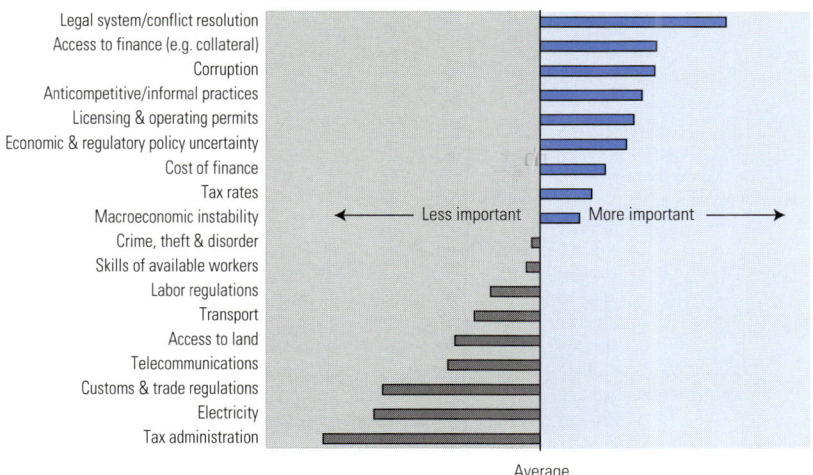

skill content from jobs that were destroyed. Thus, the relatively large job reallocation in CEE explains why employers there see the skills of available workers as a major constraint to firm growth. Second, labor regulations become an effective obstacle only if firms face competitive pressures to adjust the size and the composition of their workforce to stay profitable. This in turn explains why employers in faster-restructuring CEE countries complain more often about labor regulations, although on the books they are less strict than in other subgroups of countries in the Region.

FIGURE 1.12 (continued)

Panel C—Southeastern Europe

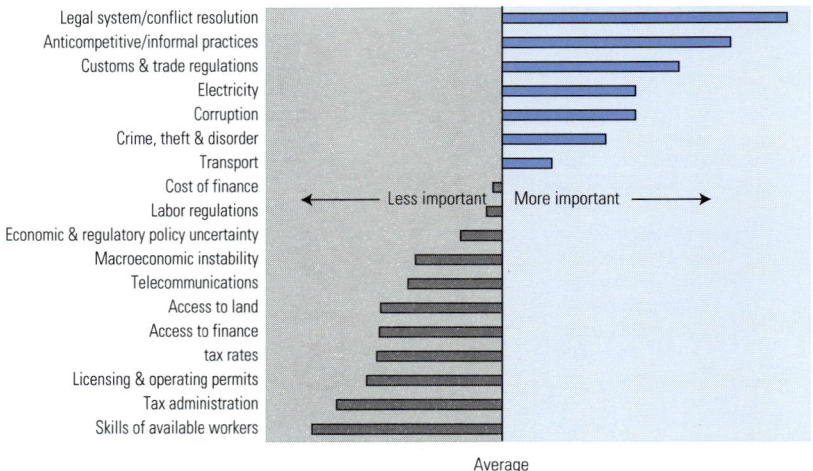

Panel D—Middle Income CIS Countries: Belarus, Kazakhstan, Russia, and Ukraine

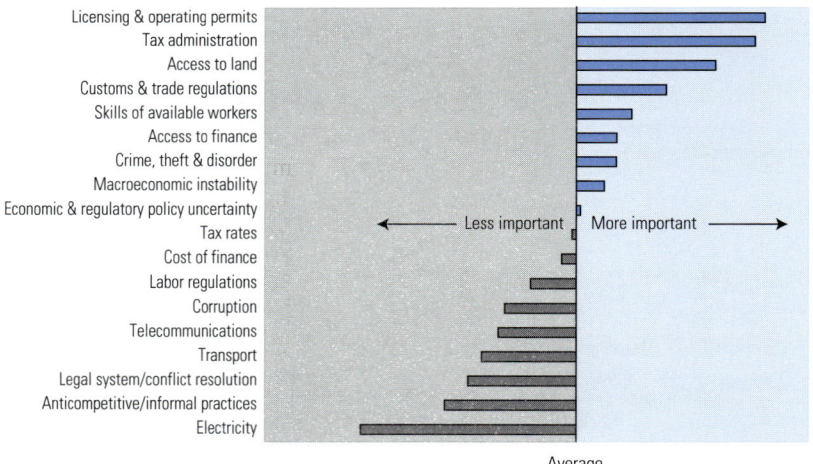

Administrative costs of setting up a new business affect the creation of new firms most in the CIS and SEE. Costs for setting up a new business tend to be higher in the Region than in many industrial and emerging Asian economies, being particularly constraining in many of the CIS countries and in the countries of Southeast Europe. By contrast, most Central and Eastern European countries of the Region—most notably the Baltic States—have made significant improvements in reducing start-up costs. For example, the number of

FIGURE 1.12 (continued)

Panel E—Low Income CIS Countries: Armenia, Azerbaijan, Georgia, the Kyrgyz Republic, Moldova, Tajikistan, and Uzbekistan

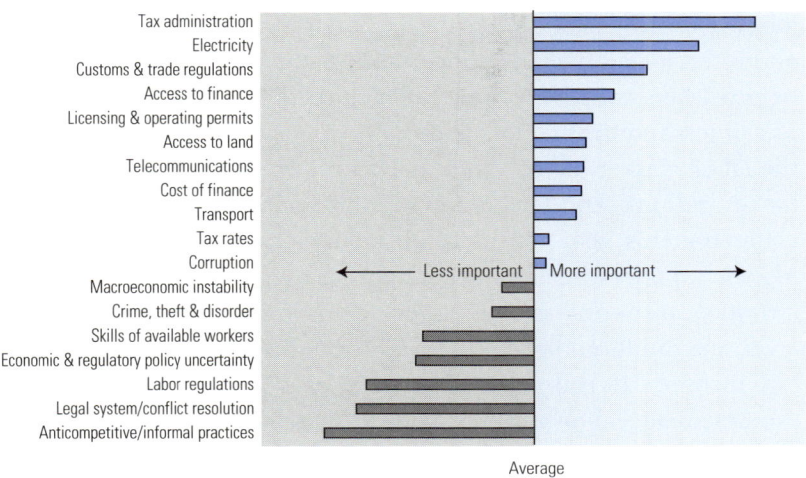

Source: EBRD–World Bank Business Environment and Enterprise Performance Surveys, 2002.

Note: Bars show the deviation from the regional and factor averages. Preliminary results from the new 2005 BEEPS are broadly consistent with those reported in this figure. However, some changes may have occurred for individual countries or subgroups of countries in the Region.

start-up procedures is just 3 in countries such as Ireland and Sweden and 7 or 8 in the Baltic States, but their number is 14 in Azerbaijan and Ukraine and 19 in Belarus. Thus, reducing business start-up costs in the Region may foster firm entry, facilitate formal sector growth, and as such bring about faster job creation.

Reducing the risks for firms and for workers is also a key challenge because they operate in a milieu of greater uncertainty. Firms in the transition economies have emerged during a period of profound economic and social transformation characterized by major macroeconomic shocks and profound structural changes. All these factors have certainly affected firms' perceptions about risk. Not surprisingly, most countries in the Region point to macroeconomic and political instability as one of the main sources of concern in their operations. But other factors also contribute to the perceived business insecurity: security of property rights and contract enforcement, frequent regulatory changes, arbitrary and selective application of the law, bureaucratic harassment and extortion, and crime are important issues in virtually all countries of the Region, although less so in the new EU members. Thus, strengthening the rule of law, developing effective market institutions, and improving governance are key elements of reducing risk and uncertainty and thereby fostering investment and job creation.

Workers also have to confront uncertainties in their career prospects and job stability. During rapid transition, in which many jobs are destroyed and others are created in different firms, sectors, and often locations, these uncertainties are high. Government can help workers cope with these rapid changes by insuring against the risk of job and income loss and improving the matching function of the labor market. Better labor market information, job search assistance, training, and facilitation of labor mobility can contribute to achieving this goal. Virtually all transition countries introduced income support schemes and a range of active labor market programs (ALMPs), although they are more generous (in coverage, benefit level, and duration) in CEE than in other subgroups, especially in the low income CIS countries. However, balancing income support to promote reallocation with possible job-search disincentive effects has been, and still is, a challenge in many CEE countries.

Introducing greater competition into markets has helped longer-term job creation in the Region. One of the most visible and pervasive changes during the transition was the introduction of competitive forces into markets for goods and services—by liberalizing prices and trade flows, by imposing harder budget constraints on state firms, and by shifting ownership to the private sector (World Bank 2002e). More-competitive product markets bring easier firm entry, less administrative barriers to firm growth, and greater firm efficiency, including wage adaptability. All these changes are conducive to faster job creation, although productivity gains can lead to job losses in the short term.

There are, however, large differences in the pervasiveness of competitive forces in the markets of the Region's countries, with product markets being most competitive in more-advanced CEE countries and least competitive in the CIS. For example, 90 percent of firms in Poland face significant competitive pressures and thus incentives to improve efficiency, while only 40 percent of firms face similar pressures in Georgia.[26] Some of these differences have been the result of different modes of privatization, which have often been the main trigger of firm restructuring and the promotion of efficiency.

The positive effect of privatization on productivity has been stronger in CEE countries than in the CIS countries because the former have placed fewer restrictions on—and sometimes actively encouraged—foreign participation in privatization and concentrated ownership. The defensive restructuring strategy adopted by many domestically privatized firms could go on for a while, given the large overmanning in previously state-owned firms, but further improvements in their performance will soon depend on their ability to invest, adopt new technologies, and hire new staff.[27] Promoting competition via easier entry of new firms and leveling the playing field can speed up the transition from defensive restructuring to strategic restructuring and job creation.

Wage Flexibility

The wage determination process in the Region has been decentralized and liberalized during transition and generally resembles that in mature market economies. But liberalization has gone much further in CEE than in SEE and the CIS.[28] In CEE countries, where the new private sector plays a bigger role than in other parts of the Region, wages are mostly determined at the enterprise level and linked to worker productivity. Union presence in the new private sector is weak and competition is high, so there is little space for workers to appropriate part of the firms' market rents[29] or for wages to be set above the competitive level. Evidence exists that regional wages are sensitive to regional unemployment rates (the so-called wage curve), as they are in mature market economies (Huber 2004). In contrast, wage setting in SEE and the CIS is less competitive, largely because of a still dominant role played by the "old" sector, including public and many privatized enterprises.

In some cases, wage rigidities in the form of binding minimum wages could have contributed to unemployment among disadvantaged groups. In many CEE countries, minimum wages are centrally set at a relatively high level (around 40 percent of the average wage). At this level, minimum wages may produce some disemployment effect among the less-skilled and younger workers, especially in economically depressed regions of the country where underlying market wages are well below the national average. For example, in economically depressed regions of Poland, the minimum wage is roughly 10 percent less than the average wage of low-skilled workers and 25 percent less than that of young workers (Rutkowski and Przybyla 2002). Similarly, the recent substantial minimum wage increase in Hungary was found to adversely affect job retention and job-finding probabilities of low-wage workers (Kertesi and Köllő 2003).

In SEE and especially the CIS, wage determination is more centralized and still influenced by the government. This is related to a higher share of the public sector in employment and the behavior of privatized enterprises, which often mimics that of state-owned firms. In addition, union bargaining power is significantly higher in the public sector than in the new private sector. As a result, the wage structure in the formal sector in SEE and the CIS is more rigid. Nonetheless, these countries have achieved a considerable degree of de facto wage flexibility through nonpayment or delayed payment of wages.

Employment Protection Legislation

Employment protection legislation (EPL) is (on average) stricter in the Region than in OECD economies (figure 1.13). Historically, employment protection has been particularly strict in CIS and SEE countries, and somewhat less strict in most CEE countries.[30] This means that employers in the CIS and SEE may face high—mainly procedural—costs of firing redundant labor. This is likely to discourage them from hiring in the period of economic upturn, to avoid future firing costs in some subsequent downturn. Apparently strict EPL in the Region might have contributed to a slow pace of job creation. However, the enforcement capacity in countries with strict EPL—largely in the CIS—is often weak, which means that the actual "bite" of the EPL tends to be less than implied by the law (table 1.1).[31]

In contrast, EPL is more binding in CEE because of stronger enforcement, despite more liberal regulations.[32] This assessment is consistent with the perceptions of employers, who deem labor regulations a significant obstacle in the new EU member countries (and also in Turkey), but not in the other parts of the Region (figure 1.14).

Available evidence suggests that the combination of stringent EPL with effective enforcement did indeed slow job creation in the Region. For example, in Croatia and the Slovak Republic, where EPL before the reforms was extremely strict and compliance was high, the rates of job destruction and job creation were much below those in CEE economies with more liberal EPL, such as the Baltic States, Hungary, or Poland (World Bank 2002a and 2003a). Thus, excessive protection of existing jobs comes at a price of slower job creation and also slower enterprise restructuring and productivity improvements. Moldova, where the rate of job turnover is relatively high, shows that strict EPL has little effect on enterprise restructuring if enforcement is weak (World Bank 2004a). All in all, EPL has likely slowed the pace of job creation in those countries of the Region that combined strict regulations with effective enforcement, such as the countries of the former Yugoslavia. In the rest of the Region, high firing costs might have adversely affected job creation in selected firms and had some effects on the composition of employment, but the overall effect on employment has likely been limited.

FIGURE 1.13
The Region's Countries Have More Stringent Regulations on Hiring and Firing than OECD Countries Do

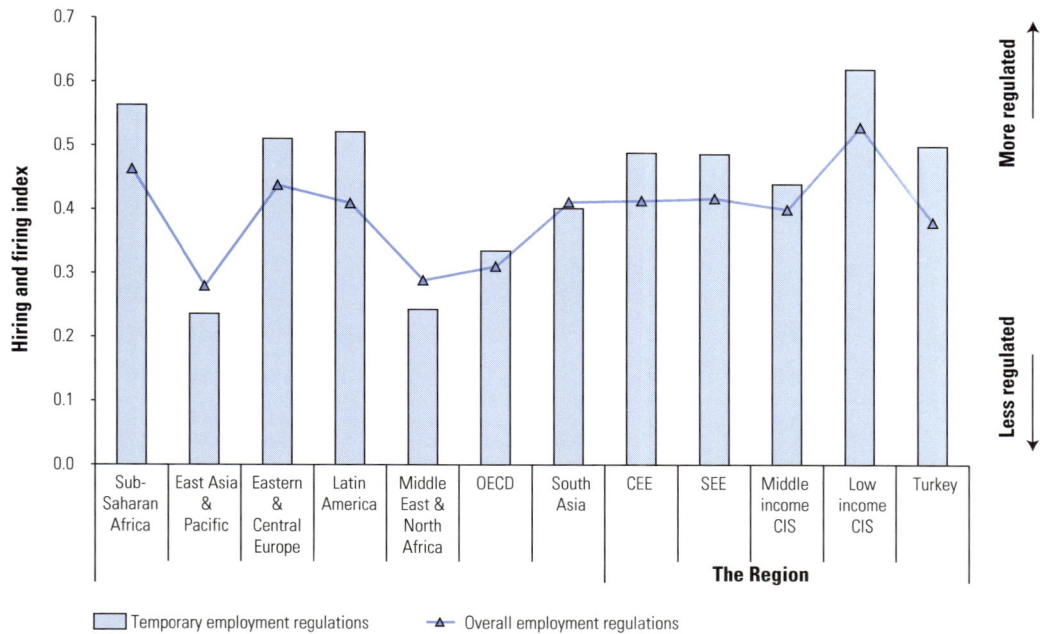

Source: World Bank, Doing Business Database (2005).

TABLE 1.1
A Typology of Employment Protection Legislation and Enforcement

	Flexible EPL	More restrictive EPL	Very rigid EPL
Weaker enforcement	Albania, Kazakhstan	Armenia, Georgia, Russian Federation, Serbia and Montenegro, Turkey	Azerbaijan; Belarus; Bosnia and Herzegovina; Kyrgyz Republic; Moldova; Ukraine; Uzbekistan
Intermediate enforcement		Bulgaria	Croatia; Macedonia, FYR; Romania
Stronger enforcement	Czech Republic, Estonia, Hungary, Poland, Slovak Republic	Latvia, Lithuania, Slovenia	

Source: Bank staff calculations.

Note: (a) Strictness is defined as whether country EPL index below world average EPL index in Doing Business 2005 (flexible), up to 20% higher (more restrictive) and more than 20% higher (very rigid). (b) The degree of enforcement is measured by the size of the informal economy—the higher the informal economy, the weaker the estimated degree of enforcement (Schneider and Klinglmair 2004 and country studies, where available). The typology is approximate because the indices are subject to margins of error.

FIGURE 1.14

Labor Regulations Seem to Be a Binding Constraint Only in the New EU Member Countries and Not in the Other Parts of the Region

Relative Importance of Labor Regulations, 2002

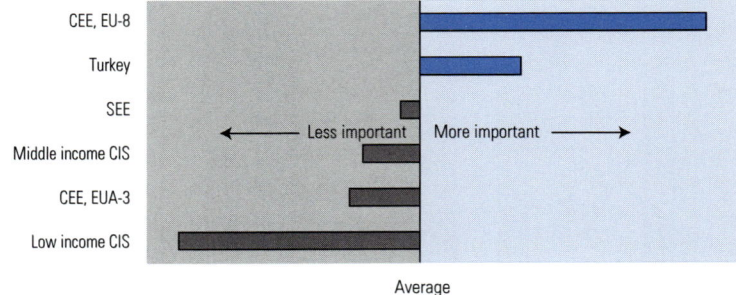

Source: EBRD–World Bank Business Environment and Enterprise Performance Surveys, 2002.

Note: Bars show the deviation from the regional and factor averages. Preliminary results from the new 2005 BEEPS are broadly consistent with those reported in this figure. However, some changes may have occurred for individual countries or subgroups of countries in the Region.

Social Benefits

One way to accommodate labor market slack in most of the Region's countries has been through the withdrawal of older workers through the promotion of early retirement schemes and disability pensions. This contributed to raising social expenditures and led to the surge in taxes on labor use. Moreover, social benefits were set at a fairly generous level at the beginning of the transition in many of the Region's countries, creating some disincentive effects on the supply side. The same happened with unemployment insurance benefits that provided income support for a long period of time (18–24 months in some countries) and a high replacement rate. But unemployment insurance benefits have been streamlined in all countries, and their generosity—and, in particular, their coverage—is fairly low nowadays: only 20–30 percent of the unemployed receive unemployment benefits in most of the Region's countries.[33] In CEE, unemployment benefits are more generous than in the CIS, but are still at the lower end of the OECD range. In the CIS, the generosity is so low that few unemployed have an incentive to register, which partly accounts for low registered unemployment in those countries.

Unemployment and other social benefits may have the largest effect in economically depressed regions. Despite their low overall generosity, unemployment benefits and other social benefits in CEE and SEE may create labor-supply disincentives in depressed regions, where they account for a higher proportion of the market wage. Family benefits and social assistance benefits are set at a national level and do not consider the large differences in the cost of living across areas of the Region's countries. Although very limited in the capitals and other dynamic regions, they represent a higher proportion of underlying market wages in more depressed areas.

In CEE, social benefits were a factor behind longer job-search duration and labor force withdrawal (especially initially, when their generosity was greater), but they facilitated restructuring and labor reallocation. For example, a study for the Slovak Republic found that workers who received unemployment benefits or social assistance spent more time (about two months longer) unemployed than workers who were not entitled to these benefits. At the same time, however, benefit recipients found new jobs more often, and these jobs turned out to be better matches than the ones obtained by nonrecipients (World Bank 2002d). In contrast, in the CIS, the lack of an effective social safety net made workers extremely reluctant to part with their jobs, contributing to the slower pace of enterprise restructuring. In addition, poor social safety nets in CIS countries caused widespread informal sector employment, including work in subsistence agriculture.

The Policy Challenge: Promoting Job Creation in the Region

The Region's countries face the daunting challenge of fostering the creation of more and better jobs. This challenge is not unique to these countries. Most Western European neighbors have faced high and persistent unemployment for a long time, and only some of them have succeeded in significantly improving labor market conditions. Creating more and better jobs requires improvements in the investment climate, a climate in which firms of all types find the incentives to invest productively, adopt new technologies, and ultimately hire more workers in more-productive, and thus more-rewarding, jobs. In the countries of the Region, this already complex task is part of an even broader process of economic transformation associated with profound institutional and structural changes. Ultimately, structural reforms and improvements in the investment climate are necessary to foster high investment rates and create foundations for sustainable economic growth (box 1.2).

In all of the Region's countries, there is substantial scope for investment climate improvements, although the conditions vary substantially across country groups. Obstacles to firm growth are generally more severe in SEE or low income CIS countries than in the new EU transition countries, where structural reforms have progressed the

BOX 1.2

In Most of the Region's Countries, Higher Investment Rates Are Necessary to Accelerate Economic Growth and Job Creation

Traditional growth theories emphasize the role of saving and investment in physical capital as important drivers of long-term economic growth. Investment is needed to expand and upgrade physical capital and thus promote output growth and productivity. And if technological progress is also embedded in physical capital, investment is needed to adopt new technologies and again to promote growth. Recent growth theories have also stressed the importance of complementary investment in human capital and the fact that there could be endogenous forces that counteract the traditional decreasing returns in investment in both physical and human capital.

The transition process from a central-plan to a market economy entails a massive investment in physical capital to replace obsolete equipment with new and to expand in new sectors and activities. The experience of some of the rapidly growing countries in East Asia clearly suggests that their extraordinary performance was also promoted by high investment rates, sustained for a prolonged period of time (World Bank 1993). For example, during the 1990s, the investment-to-GDP ratio in East Asian countries, such as Korea, Malaysia, or Thailand, averaged 36 percent. In most transition economies of the Region, the gross-investment-to-GDP ratio was around 20 percent over the past decade (figure A), largely resulting from low domestic savings. Higher investment rates may be necessary to accelerate or sustain economic growth and create new jobs. This in turn requires incentives for domestic savings and an environment in which firms find it profitable to invest and engage in strategic restructuring.

The impact of investment on economic growth and employment is also determined by the structure of investment. A part of gross investment is simply the replacement for depreciated capital and, as such, may not contribute to job creation.[a] Moreover, investment can either expand "productive" capital (such as machinery and equipment) and thus contribute to job creation or add to "nonproductive" capital (for example, housing), in which case its effect on employment is negligible. There is a substantial variation across countries of the Region in the proportion of total investment allocated to productive uses. Productive (nonhousing) investment as a share of gross fixed capital formation (GFCF) ranges from less than 60 percent in the Slovak Republic to about 80 percent in Poland and to some 90 percent in the Czech Republic. As a comparison, in Korea, productive investment accounts for 85 percent of GFCF.[b]

a. Gross investment minus capital depreciation is net investment, which would be a more relevant indicator of the potential for job creation; however, data on net investment are not available on a comparative basis.
b. National accounts of OECD countries (OECD 2003), average share for 1999–2003.

FIGURE A
In Many Transition Economies of the Region, Investment Rates Are below 20 Percent, Weakening Growth Prospects
Gross Fixed Capital Formation as Percentage of GDP (1999–2003 average)

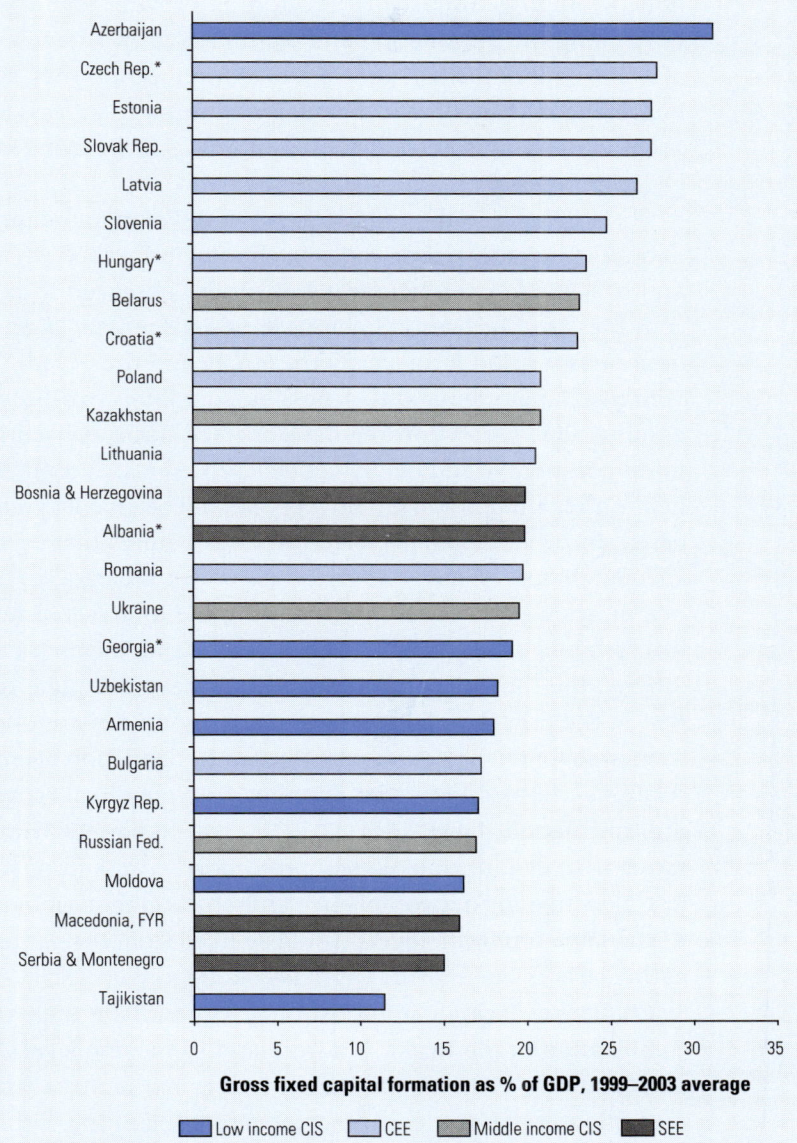

Source: World Development Indicators.

Note: * = 1998–2002.

most. But even in the most-advanced transition economies of CEE, the costs of doing business can be substantially lowered. Entrepreneurs in CEE still complain about high regulatory and economic policy uncertainty, difficult access to finance, poor governance, onerous regulations, and administrative barriers. There is also much to be done to improve infrastructure, from improving road conditions to developing the information and communication technology.[34] After all, the experience of developed market economies shows that improving the investment climate is a continuous process that should respond to changing economic conditions, globalization, and technological progress.[35]

The Region's countries also need to develop an adaptable labor market. Currently, labor codes in the Region, especially in the CIS and in SEE, go well beyond what can be observed in most OECD countries. But the overly generous provisions remain largely on paper because firms find it too costly to comply and thus evade or circumvent rigid labor regulations. A possible solution is two-pronged. First, employment protection regulations need to be revised to remove unduly restrictive and overly detailed provisions. Second, social partners—trade unions and employers—should be given a greater role in determining employment relations. This requires that both sides are adequately represented and that their power is balanced. Employers' organizations, adequately representing the interests of new private firms, should develop and have due voice, especially in the CIS and in SEE. At the same time, workers need to have adequate representation in the private sector—where currently unions are often nonexistent—so that their rights are protected. Deregulation of employment relations, coupled with strengthening the role of collective bargaining, can benefit both sides. Workers would benefit from de facto rather than de jure employment protection because firms would have less incentive for noncompliance and enforcement would be easier. At the same time, employers would be freed from regulations that are particularly costly to firms but of less value to workers.

Challenges facing countries of the Region have their source in a combination of the Region's history and its income level. Numerous administrative barriers (for example, permits) or strict employment protection are largely the legacy of central planning, although they are quite typical of developing countries across the world (Turkey is one example). Difficult access to finance or inefficient legal systems reflect institutions of a market economy that are underdeveloped because of both the history of central planning and the stage of economic development. Economic policy uncertainty, corruption, and crime have been engendered by the regime changes, although again they are typical of much of the developing world. Finally, poor infrastructure is closely associated with relatively low income levels.

How severe are the policy challenges? How far are the Region's subgroups from their natural comparators (that is, countries at a similar level of economic development that have been market economies)? This study focuses on one central dimension of the investment climate—access to finance—which is seen as a major obstacle to firm growth in virtually all countries of the Region. Figure 1.15 indicates that credit markets are underdeveloped in all of the Region's subgroups relative to their income level. For example, Armenia, Georgia, and Ukraine are at an income level similar to Bolivia's. But domestic credit to the private sector (as a share of GDP) is much higher in Bolivia: twice as high as in Ukraine and more than five times as high as in Armenia or Georgia. In the same vein, access to credit in Lithuania or the Slovak Republic is more limited than in Chile or Malaysia, in spite of a similar GDP level. This suggests that historical factors, such as the legacy of central planning, still have a bearing on the Region's economic performance. Evidence provided in this report indicates that access to finance has a significant impact on job creation. This, in turn, suggests that the Region's labor market problems at least partly stem from the uncompleted transition. Thus,

FIGURE 1.15

Access to Finance Is More Difficult in Transition Economies than in Market Economies at Similar Income Levels

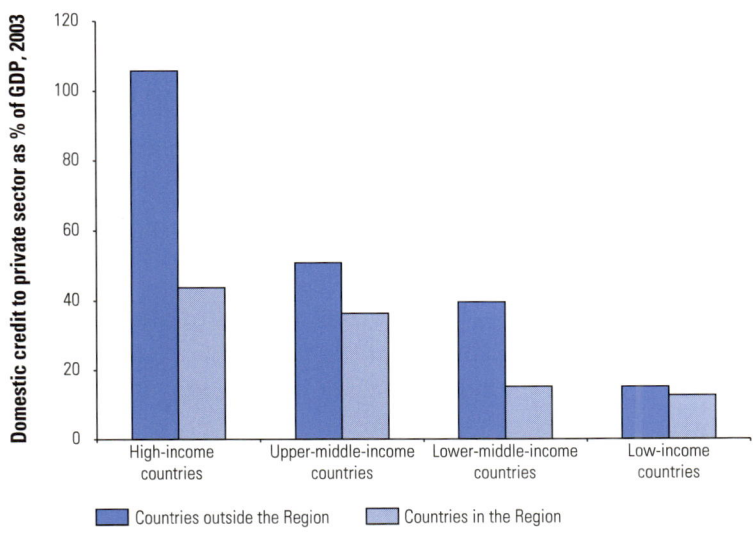

Source: World Development Indicators.

Note: * = Slovenia.

further structural reforms are necessary to develop the institutions of a market economy and foster labor demand.

There is no question that the Region's countries have been through major reforms already. The EBRD transition index attests to the many reforms that have been made in the past 15 years in privatization, enhancing competition, developing the financial market, and so forth. Reforms have to be seen, however, as a process through which constraints are identified and continuous improvement and fine-tuning of policies are made. International experience has shown that essential elements of reform processes include setting priorities, managing individual reforms, maintaining momentum, and strengthening government capabilities (World Bank 2004d). Setting priorities and sequencing reforms are of particular importance because too broad a reform agenda is difficult to implement and the impact is likely to be limited because of resource constraints, including "political capital," and opposition from the groups whose interests are likely to be hurt.

The policy priorities need to be set according to country circumstances. Although the transition countries of the Region have gone through similar economic changes over the past 15 years, they differ in their initial conditions, paths, speeds of reform, and consequently in their levels of economic development (figure 1.16). The next part of the overview highlights some of the main policy challenges the report has identified for each of the Region's subgroups: CEE, SEE, the middle income CIS countries (Belarus, Kazakhstan, Russia, and Ukraine), and the low income CIS countries. They focus on the labor market area of policy intervention, although in some subgroups, the improvements in the investment climate and the restoration of sustained growth are the key priorities for job creation, calling for a much broader policy agenda. Main policy priorities for each of the Region's subgroups are summarized in table 1.2.

Central and Eastern European Countries: Reducing the Cost of Labor and Mobilizing Labor Supply

These countries have generally started the macro and structural reform process earlier than other transition countries and have often adopted more aggressive reforms. They have achieved impressive results, with output exceeding its pretransition level. They have also successfully created institutions of a market economy, which has led to their EU accession. But these impressive results should not hide the turbulent phases of this massive transformation and its associated social costs. Moreover, impressive macro and structural reforms have not yet delivered major improvements in labor market conditions.

TABLE 1.2
A Summary of Key Policy Measures to Improve Labor Market Outcomes in Transition Economies of the Region

The Region's subgroups	Policy priorities
Central and Eastern Europe	• Reduce taxes on labor through reforming pension and health care systems • Enhance wage adaptability (for example, through reducing/differentiating minimum wages) • Liberalize employment protection regulations for permanent contracts • Improve labor supply incentives in backward, low-wage regions by adjusting benefit levels
Southeastern Europe	• Enhance product market competition and reduce administrative barriers • Reduce taxes on labor • Decentralize wage determination • Liberalize employment protection legislation
Middle income CIS	• Enhance product market competition and reduce administrative barriers • Decentralize wage determination • Deregulate labor relations and focus on enforcement of key labor standards • Improve the effectiveness of the social safety net to encourage labor reallocation
Low income CIS	• Develop key institutions of a market economy and invest in infrastructure • Reduce administrative barriers • Deregulate labor relations and focus on enforcement of key labor standards • Develop social safety net, particularly for those without access to formal insurance mechanisms

Source: Bank staff calculations.

Job opportunities in the formal sector are scarce, and unemployment is often high and persistent.

There is a substantial potential in CEE to foster job creation through addressing country-specific investment climate constraints. Although the investment climate in CEE is generally hospitable and notably better than in other subgroups of the Region, each CEE country can improve its investment climate along specific dimensions. For example, there is room for lowering start-up costs in Hungary and the Slovak Republic. Registering property is difficult in Croatia, and contract enforcement is extremely time-consuming in Poland. In Bulgaria and Romania, there is substantial room for improving access to finance and the efficiency of the legal system. In many CEE countries, corruption is still a serious problem. In general, the challenges are bigger for the EU accession countries (Bulgaria, Croatia, and Romania), where entrepreneurs identify more obstacles to business operation and more often perceive them as severe as in the new EU member countries.

Reducing taxes on labor is necessary to encourage hiring. To decrease such high rates in a fiscally viable way, reforms of health and pension systems must make the systems more efficient and sustainable. In particular, reviewing early retirement, disability, and sickness benefit policies should be part of the reform agenda, with the aim of tightening the eligibility criteria and eliminating the widespread abuse of the systems.

FIGURE 1.16
Constraints Reported by Firms Vary across the Region's Countries

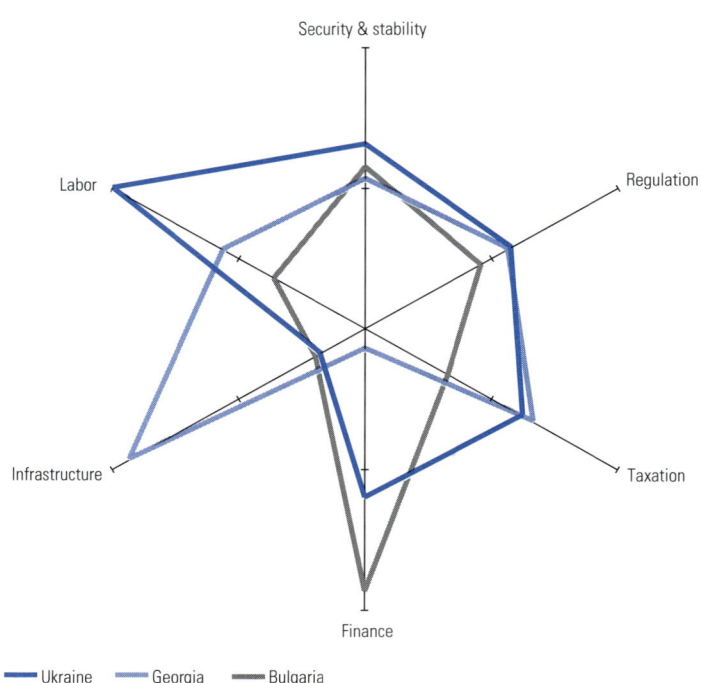

Source: From WDR 2005, with data from EBRD–World Bank Business Environment and Enterprise Performance Surveys, 2002.

Note: Preliminary results from the new 2005 BEEPS are broadly consistent with those reported in this figure. However, some changes may have occurred for individual countries or subgroups of countries in the Region.

Another way to facilitate job creation in CEE is to provide for greater adaptability of real wages to productivity and local labor market conditions. Decentralized (firm-level) wage setting has developed in most CEE countries, but some countries, such as Slovenia, have kept highly centralized bargaining. Some wage rigidities are also present in the state-owned and privatized firms, as well as in noncompetitive sectors of the economy. Most countries have kept a rigid coefficient system as a basis for wage setting in the public sector. Significantly, wage flexibility is limited by the mandated minimum wages, which tend to be relatively high in CEE.

Creating subminimum wages for young workers or in economically depressed regions, as in many EU countries, would promote job creation for less-productive workers who are hardest hit by unemployment. Poland set the example in CEE by introducing a youth subminimum wage (at 80 percent of the regular minimum wage) in an attempt to alleviate youth unemployment. Reform in this area is also important because social benefit programs are often tied to the minimum wage (that is, they are relatively high when the minimum wage is relatively high), creating additional disincentive effects on labor supply.

One common strategy to promote flexibility in the labor market in CEE countries has been the liberalization of fixed-term and temporary contracts. In this respect, CEE countries have followed the experience of many Western European countries that, faced with mounting pressure to promote flexibility, liberalized these atypical contracts while maintaining strict regulations for regular contracts. In Western Europe, this strategy has reinforced duality in the labor market, with some workers enjoying high and even increased protection in regular jobs, but others bearing the cost of greater flexibility by moving from one short-term job to another.

In CEE countries, creating jobs, even of short duration, can be beneficial, especially in a context of significant long-term unemployment. Still, it is important in the long term to foster regular employment creation. In this context, employment protection regulations for regular contracts should be liberalized in accordance with the recent relaxation of restrictions on the use of temporary contracts.

More generally, employment relations should be reformed to promote direct agreements between workers and employers.[36] For historical reasons, in many countries of the Region, the statutory labor standards are still very high, and detailed regulations cover virtually all aspects of employment conditions (for example, working time, employment protection, wage formation, and in-work benefits). This leaves little room for negotiations and thus impedes the development of genuine collective bargaining systems and stifles social dialogue. Instead, overregulation contributes to noncompliance and a steady drift toward informal arrangements. A greater role given to collective bargaining agreements in determining employment relations is thus a way to instill more flexibility into the labor market while balancing the interests of workers and employers.

Unemployment and related benefits have been reformed several times in most CEE countries, mainly to reduce the initial excessive generosity of the system. Therefore, the system does not currently create major labor supply disincentives. However, it may give rise to the "unemployment trap" in backward regions, where benefits account for a high proportion of the prevailing market wage of low-skilled labor. This is reinforced by the fact that some countries have extended benefit duration in backward areas or apply lax eligibility criteria. Although social assistance benefits are needed to cushion households from falling into persistent poverty, targeting and means testing should be reinforced to improve the effectiveness of these schemes.

Passive labor market programs are not sufficient to deal with the problems of long-term unemployment and discouragement. Stronger job creation by private firms is obviously the main avenue for addressing this serious social and economic issue. But active labor market programs, if properly designed and implemented, can also contribute by providing greater incentives for the unemployed to go back to work and for employers to employ disadvantaged individuals. Evidence suggests that ALMPs can improve the labor market prospects of some groups, although they do not increase aggregate employment and such programs may be costly. It is therefore crucial to pay special attention to their design and efficient targeting. They also need to be accompanied by monitoring and impact evaluation. The former enables the management of programs and fine-tuning, if necessary, while the latter provides feedback for future policies.

Investments in human capital are necessary to keep pace with the growing demand for high skills. Although the workforce in CEE is (on average) well educated, employers have difficulty finding workers with the right skills. The problem of the skills gap and mismatch hits the most advanced reformers in the subgroup. In countries like the Czech Republic, Hungary, Latvia, and Poland, 35–40 percent of employers see the skills of the available workforce as a significant obstacle. (The proportion is even higher in Estonia.) Evidence suggests that a substantial portion of the long-term unemployed in CEE lack the skills required by the employers. In some part, this reflects the failings of the educational system: workers need to be equipped with broad and transferable skills and provided with life-long learning opportunities to be able to meet the challenge of a dynamic labor market and to support firms' strategic restructuring.

Southeastern European Countries: Greater Stability, Law Enforcement, and More Competitive Markets

This subgroup of countries tends to be at an intermediary position between the most advanced CEE countries and the CIS countries. Unemployment is particularly high and persistent in SEE, and informality is pervasive. The reforms in the subgroup have been delayed and slowed by the regional conflict, which has also led to the disruption of regional infrastructure and economic ties. The subgroup of countries fares worse than CEE in product market competitiveness, administrative barriers, effectiveness of the legal system, corruption, crime, and disorder. Substantial investment climate improvements are thus necessary to foster firm growth and formal sector job creation.

Investment climate improvements in SEE require reforming institutions and changing government policies and behavior. One priority is to reduce corruption, which is widespread. Another is to enhance competition, because anticompetitive or informal practices are regarded as a major obstacle by almost 30 percent of firms in the subgroup. The same proportion of firms sees as a major obstacle to their operation the inefficient system of conflict resolution, which points to the need to reform the legal system. Finally, barriers to firm entry need to be removed, because starting a business in SEE can be difficult, time-consuming, and costly.[37]

The tax wedge on labor is slightly lower in SEE than in CEE countries, but it remains higher than the bottom end of OECD countries. Moreover, tax rates are identified as a major obstacle to operating a business by around 30 percent of firms. SEE countries should aim for a gradual reduction in payroll taxes, with a particular focus on health insurance taxes. This should be accompanied by efforts to improve compliance on tax payments by firms, including SOEs. Moreover, to make the reduction of payroll taxes fiscally viable, public-funded programs should be made more efficient. This entails tightening the eligibility criteria (for example, for early retirement and disability pensions) and reducing the abuse of the benefit system (for example, sickness benefits and disability pensions) by able-bodied individuals.

Wage setting in SEE may hamper achieving labor market equilibrium. Wage pressure arises because unions tend to be influential in these countries (partly because of the history of self-management before 1990). But the role of the government in wage setting also remains strong. Thus decentralized bargaining at the level of the firm should be encouraged to enhance wage flexibility. Sectoral wage negotiations appear to be a particular problem. For example, through the setting of specific minimum wages by sector, such bargaining leads to extremely high levels of wages. For example, in Bosnia and Herzegovina, the minimum wage in the 2004 telecommunications sector collective agreement was double the economywide minimum wage (itself a high 55 percent of the average wage), equivalent to 110 percent of the economywide average wage. The compression of the wage distribution that results leads to high unemployment for vulnerable groups such as youth and for some less developed regions.

Employment protection legislation remains fairly strict in SEE and clearly is not helping workers overall because a great number of "outsiders" are either employed in the informal sector or unemployed (figure 1.13). In fact, the share of formal employment decreases and an informal economy develops where enforcement of these strict regulations is difficult, especially because of the weak capacity of the administration. The way forward is to deregulate labor relations while protecting core worker rights and to leave the determination of employment conditions to bargaining between employers and workers. This should be coupled with improving the effectiveness of labor inspection in enforcing core labor standards.

Unemployment benefits tend to be at appropriate levels of generosity in SEE countries. However, work test requirements (that is, ensuring that the unemployed is available and willing to take a job, if offered) could be strengthened, especially in regions where labor demand is more robust. Also, employment offices should make a clear distinction between the unemployed who register to find work and those who register to gain eligibility for health care and other benefits. This will help to focus resources on those who need job search assistance and at the same time will provide a clearer picture of unemployment.[38]

ALMPs are currently insignificant in SEE countries. More fundamental investment climate improvements are needed to encourage job creation and improve labor market outcomes. However, the cost-effectiveness of ALMPs can be improved. ALMPs in SEE should be targeted at vulnerable groups (that is, those running a high risk of long-term unemployment). Given the limited capacity for designing costly programs, the most cost-effective way to improve the matching of unemployed to jobs in these countries is to improve the capacity of employment agencies to identify job vacancies and to provide job search assistance. Finally, to address the mounting issues of long-term unemployment, back-to-work benefits could be useful.

Social assistance performance is mixed across SEE countries. The evidence at the level of the subgroup suggests that the effectiveness of programs has been greater in countries where financing is more centralized, enabling targeting of the poorest areas. The current range of programs could be streamlined into core benefits to provide a decent but sustainable level of social assistance.

Middle Income CIS Countries (Belarus, Kazakhstan, Russia, and Ukraine): Removing Administrative Barriers, Promoting Restructuring, and Improving the Safety Net

These four countries have a high economic potential; however, the challenges are profound. Administrative barriers are still pervasive, and governance is often poor. Corruption is widespread. Competition is limited. Inefficient and burdensome regulations and numerous permits hamper business growth, as do underdeveloped financial markets.

Onerous tax administration and customs and trade regulations are seen as the key constraints to firm operation and growth in this subgroup. However, these are likely to capture a broader spectrum of investment climate issues, which include complex and often unintelligible regulations, their discretionary interpretation, bureaucratic harassment (for example, frequent, lengthy, and disruptive tax inspections), selective enforcement and associated uncertainty, and extortion. Therefore, improving the quality of regulations, reducing the red tape, and limiting the scope for bureaucratic discretion (along with other general improvements in governance) would create a more favorable investment climate and would support the development of the private sector and job growth.

Another important reform concerns wage determination. Even more than in SEE countries, the government has a strong role in wage setting in middle income and other CIS countries. In fact, the formal private sector tends to follow wage increases in the public sector. The role of the government in wage setting should be reduced and replaced with direct bargaining between employer and worker representatives. In most countries, this implies encouraging independent trade unions and employers' associations that are representative of the whole spectrum of firms (including small and newly established private firms).

Although labor codes were revised, labor relations tend to be over-regulated, and employment protection remains relatively strict (except in Kazakhstan), but often not enforced (figure 1.12 and table 1.2). This imposes rigidities, leaves little room for collective bargaining, and creates incentives for informal employment. As in other countries of the Region, deregulating labor relations and focusing on a set of core standards of worker protection, which can be effectively enforced, would be more efficient. This would more effectively protect basic worker rights while supporting labor market adaptability and reducing incentives for informality.

Given the low generosity of unemployment benefits in middle income CIS countries, mandatory severance pay for dismissed workers is one way to provide income support and facilitate job search, as well as make firms internalize the costs of dismissal. The mandatory severance pay should be related to job tenure with the terminating employer, with a ceiling so as not to impose excessive and unenforceable costs on firms.[39] At the same time, the procedural costs of dismissal (such as preventive measures, advance notice, required notifications, and negotiations) should be considerably reduced to facilitate enterprise restructuring and productivity growth.

The social safety net is underdeveloped in middle income CIS countries, inhibiting enterprise restructuring and locking workers into low-productivity jobs. To facilitate labor reallocation, middle income CIS countries need to move from the principle of protecting jobs to that of protecting workers. Income-support schemes need to be strengthened to reduce the social cost of worker displacement. Obviously, such schemes are costly and can create adverse labor-supply incentives. One option that addresses these concerns is workfare or public works. In essence, such schemes provide the unemployed with income, conditional on performing some socially useful work. The wage rate under such programs needs to be low to ensure self-selection of the neediest and to avoid competition with regular jobs. The participants should be encouraged to look for regular jobs, which may mean that work is less than full-time.

Countries that have not already done so should also consider using alternative approaches to targeting social transfers, such as proxy means testing or community identification of beneficiaries within national guidelines. In social insurance, middle income CIS countries should continue reforms of the pension system: this will adjust the system's dependency ratio to changing demographics and encourage other reforms that will stimulate formal sector labor supply to improve the contributions base for a given size of the working-age population.

Given the large share of informal employment, a significant proportion of people are not covered by social protection; therefore, a move to universalize social protection could be considered. Decoupling minimum pension schemes and health insurance from the labor market status of people (for example, through creating a universal minimum pension or expanding health insurance coverage to informal workers) are options currently considered for implementation in other countries outside the Region, such as Mexico. As with any of the measures proposed above, fiscal considerations would limit the menu of feasible options.

Low Income CIS Countries: Developing Institutions to Support the Formal Sector

This group of countries has drifted closer to the situation of low-income developing countries. They have great difficulties in creating jobs in the formal sector and have among the largest shares of informal economy (for example, in Azerbaijan and Georgia, the informal economy is estimated to account for more than 60 percent of GDP).[40] This situation means that large parts of the population are essentially unprotected against economic risk and receive no help from the state.

One key factor behind the low pace of job creation in the formal sector in the low income CIS countries is underdeveloped institutions of a market economy. This includes lack of enforcement of rules and regulations, economic and regulatory policy uncertainty, underdeveloped financial markets, inefficient regulations, bureaucratic harassment and corruption, and (last, but not least) poor and unreliable infrastructure. In particular, the unreliability of public infrastructure is a significant hurdle for firms in the low income CIS countries. It places them at a competitive disadvantage in relation to both their near neighbors in the middle income CIS group and their more-distant competitors in CEE (Steves, Fankhauser, and Rousso 2004). Thus, to meet the challenge of job creation, low income CIS countries need to strengthen the institutional underpinnings of a market economy to lessen the risks associated with doing business. They also need to reform their regulatory framework to increase its efficiency and remove administrative barriers (for example, customs and trade regulations rank high as a significant impediment to business operation in entrepreneurs' perceptions). An important component of the progrowth strategy is also the development and proper maintenance of the infrastructure.

Employment protection legislation tends to be strict in low income CIS countries, compared with the average for the entire Region (figure 1.12). At the same time, enforcement is lax or selective, meaning that the seemingly rigid regulations seldom are a binding constraint on firms. However, flexibility through nonenforcement is not an efficient combination because it undermines the rule of law, increases uncertainty, deprives workers of protection, and is not conducive to long-term productivity growth. Therefore, low income CIS countries, even more than other countries of the Region, need to focus employment legislation on core and enforceable labor standards. As in the middle income CIS countries, mandatory severance pay can be a way of providing workers with income protection (see above), but this option should be coupled with a substantial reduction in administrative procedures associated with layoffs.

In addition, low income CIS countries need to review the wage determination system and encourage direct bargaining between independent employers' associations and labor unions. This entails lessening the role of government and the development of genuine representation of labor and business, representing all segments of the economy (including the new private sector).

The restricted administrative capacity, large underreporting of earnings, and limited financial resources reduce the efficiency of current social protection programs, which end up protecting a few. Although these constraints limit the range of options available to these countries, a minimum level of protection for some basic risks could be provided to all, financed through general revenues. For example, a move to a flat-rate unemployment benefit system could be considered, financed through general revenues rather than payroll taxes. Moreover, given widespread informality, the need to reinforce social protection for those without access to formal insurance mechanisms should be considered. As in the middle income CIS countries, this could include greater use of public works (or workfare) schemes that are open to all those willing to work. However, the program wage rate should be set below the market level to ensure self-targeting of the most needy. In addition, social funds can serve to improve opportunities in poor areas.

Finally, given the large share of agriculture, policies should aim at improving employment opportunities in rural areas and raising the productivity of agricultural employment (World Bank 2005b). Investment in infrastructure and in human capital in agricultural regions can encourage the development of agribusiness and the creation of off-farm employment.

* * *

Productive job opportunities in the countries of Eastern Europe and the Former Soviet Union have to increase substantially to improve the growth prospect in the Region and reduce poverty. Workers who lost their jobs in the declining regions, industries, and firms often find it difficult to find a new, gainful job in the formal sector of the economy because, for most of the transition so far, fewer regions, industries, and firms expanded than declined. As a result, an accumulated pool of unemployment has developed especially in CEE and SEE. In the low-income CIS, by contrast, many laid off workers resorted to low-productivity jobs in the informal sector and in agriculture, because unemployment was not an affordable option. To meet the challenge of job creation, the Region needs to have more productive, competitive, and expanding firms. Lowering the costs of doing business and removing key constraints to firm operation and growth are the main routes to more and better jobs.

Many of the constraints differ across subgroups of countries in the Region, but there is also a common thread. The investment climate can be improved and job creation spurred by reducing economic and policy uncertainty, easing access to credit, lowering the burden of taxation, and removing administrative barriers to firm entry and growth. But the process of moving from the old jobs to the new ones also needs to be supported. This requires an adaptable labor market where employers have incentives to hire workers—incentives that are not weakened by unduly stringent employment regulations. At the same time, workers should have incentives to look for new jobs, even in other regions of the country or in other occupations. This requires lowering the cost of mobility (for example, by developing the housing and mortgage markets) and improving access to lifelong learning opportunities.

ANNEX 1.1
Geopolitical Taxonomy of the Region's Countries

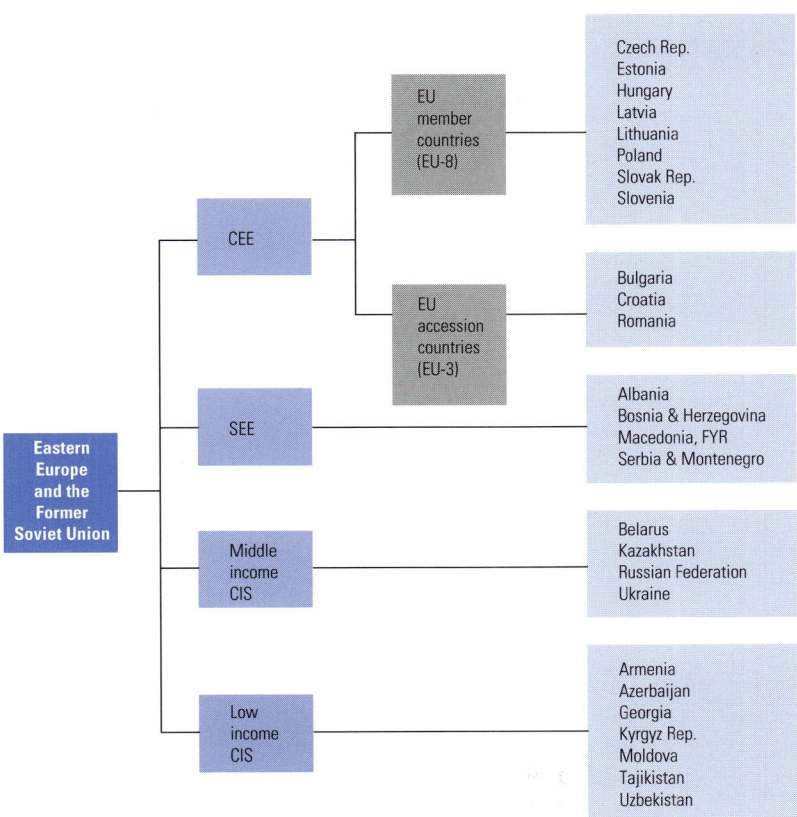

Note: The study focuses on the transition economies of Eastern Europe and the Former Soviet Union. Turkey is also included in some of the comparative analyses. The transition economies of Eastern Europe and the Former Soviet Union, plus Turkey, are all part of the World Bank's Europe and Central Asia (ECA) Region. Turkmenistan is not included in this Overview due to a lack of reliable country data.

ANNEX 1.2
Summary of Key Differences between Labor Markets in the Middle-Income European and the Low-Income CIS Economies

Labor market characteristics	Middle-income European transition economies	Low-income CIS transition economies
Main labor market issue	Unemployment	Underemployment
Adjustment to transition shock	Quantity (employment); labor moving to expanding services sector	Price (wages); labor shifting back to subsistence agriculture
Investment climate	Generally favorable	Less favorable
Market-oriented reforms and enterprise restructuring	Advanced	Less advanced
Employment protection legislation	Relatively liberal	Strict
Enforcement of labor market regulations	Relatively strong	Weak
Unemployment insurance system	Developed	Largely ineffective
Economic structure	Dominance of services and industry	Dominance of agriculture
Informal sector	Marginal, driven by tax evasion and avoidance of regulations	Large, driven by lack of job opportunities in the formal sector
Labor force location	Largely urban	Largely rural
Labor force skills	High	Mostly low
Productivity (wages)	High	Low
Earnings inequality	Modest	High

Source: Bank staff analysis.

Endnotes

1. See annex 1.1 for the taxonomy of the countries of this Region. The study focuses on the transition economies of Eastern Europe and the Former Soviet Union. Turkey is also included in some of the comparative analyses. The transition economies of Eastern Europe and the Former Soviet Union, plus Turkey, are all part of the World Bank's Europe and Central Asia (ECA) Region. Turkmenistan in not included in this Overview because of a lack of reliable country data.
2. The Former Soviet Union, except the Baltics.
3. These inequalities largely reflect differences in workers' productivity. However, in some cases wage differentials may be the result of the lack of more productive jobs for workers rather than their low-productivity potential.
4. Unless indicated otherwise, data on the Region's employment and unemployment presented in this report come from the ILO LABORSTA database, which contains national labor force survey (LFS) results. The data may differ from national sources and may not be strictly comparable across countries.
5. In March 2000, the EU heads of state and governments agreed on a strategy to promote competitiveness and a dynamic, knowledge-driven economy in Europe. The main issues for the realization of the Lisbon agenda for 2010 were the necessary investment in research and development, reduction of red tape to promote entrepreneurship, and achieving an employment rate of 70 per cent (60 percent for women). The actual employment-to-working-age-population ratio in the EU-15 was about 65 percent in 2004.

6. In principle, the skills mismatch problem can be addressed by training programs. However, in practice, the potential of training programs to successfully address large skills mismatches is limited for at least two reasons. First, if the skill profile of displaced workers is much different from the skill profile of new jobs, successful retraining can be extremely, if not prohibitively, costly. Second, for retraining to be successful, unfilled vacancies must exist for which the training participants can apply. If, however, job openings are few, as is often the case in transition economies, then training is of little help in finding a new job. Existing evaluation of training programs indeed confirms that training is often not very effective in addressing the mass unemployment resulting from large-scale industrial restructuring (Betcherman, Olivas, and Dar 2004).
7. 2002 data.
8. In virtually all modern societies, the female labor force participation rate is significantly less than the male one, which accounts for the higher male-employment-to-population ratio.
9. One reason why productivity gains have been translated into higher wages rather than employment is that they have been largely achieved through defensive restructuring by firms (that is, by eliminating overstaffing and shedding redundant labor). High hiring and firing costs may have contributed to discouraging firms from engaging in strategic restructuring and adopting new technologies and new workers (see the firm restructuring section in this chapter). The substantial real-wage growth, despite high unemployment, reflects a combination of market and institutional forces: employers maximizing profits by using efficiency wages (that is, wages set above the market-clearing level to motivate workers), union pressures, and government wage policies.
10. Rutkowski 1996.
11. Background calculations for World Bank (2001), using data from the firm-based 1998 Survey of Earnings.
12. Earnings dispersion—and thus the incidence of low pay—may be overestimated because of the practice of underreporting wages to avoid taxes on labor.
13. See Scarpetta and Vodopivec (2005) for the detailed analysis. See Grosfeld and Roland (1996) for a discussion of defensive versus strategic restructuring.
14. It should be stressed that, from a sectoral or macro perspective, defensive and strategic restructuring can be complementary—rather than opposing—strategies. Without a strategic reallocation of resources toward more productive use and the entry and expansion of a job-creating new private sector, it would not be politically feasible to engage in downsizing and defensive restructuring. Correspondingly, without hard budget constraints on state and unrestructured privatized firms, there is too much leakage of resources into the least efficient parts of the economy, crowding out the new private sector.
15. Scarpetta and Vodopivec 2005.
16. Generous social benefit schemes, including early retirement, were used (especially at the early phase of the transition) in CEE countries to facilitate enterprise restructuring and to move difficult-to-reemploy displaced workers (especially the older ones) out of the labor force.

Obviously, these schemes created adverse labor supply effects and contributed to low employment rates among older workers in CEE. However, they were deemed necessary to maintain political support for reforms. Moreover, the alternative to outflows to economic inactivity was either higher open unemployment or higher hidden unemployment, as in most of the CIS countries.

17. For example, in the early 2000s, there was only 1 vacancy in Poland for every 200 filled positions, which is four to five times less than in the United States, indicating the weakness of labor demand. At the same time, there were about 50 job seekers per vacancy. For comparison, in the United States, the unemployment-to-vacancies ratio is in the 2 to 3 range. The data on vacancies for Poland come from a special establishment-based survey of labor demand and in principle cover all available vacancies, not just those registered with employment offices (GUS 2003).

18. A caveat is necessary: conventional measures of the deficit may not fully capture changes in the fiscal policy stance. Many governments in the Region have reined in quasi-fiscal deficits, reduced arrears, and begun to get a grip on contingent liabilities since the financial crisis in Russia, which does not necessarily show in the fiscal deficit data.

19. It should be stressed that from an analytical standpoint, the association between fiscal loosening, output growth, and job creation is ambiguous.

20. This report uses primarily two sources of information to identify obstacles to business operation and growth: the EBRD–World Bank Business Environment and Enterprise Performance Surveys (also known as the investment climate surveys) and the World Bank Doing Business Database. For countries, the main route to identifying bottlenecks to firm growth and job creation is regular dialogue with the representatives of employers, including those representing newly established small firms. Additional insights can be gained through focus groups of employers and specialized surveys.

21. A growing body of evidence suggests that high levels of taxes on labor use can have detrimental effects on growth and on employment. This is particularly the case when taxes—in particular, social security contributions to pay for social benefits—are not transferred onto lower wages and thus raise labor costs for firms. If workers fully valued these benefits and were willing to trade them off for lower wages or greater effort, high taxes on labor use might not constrain firms' performance and job creation. The pass-through of taxes on wages, however, depends also on the existence of wage floors (for example, the minimum wage) and wage-bargaining systems. Evidence suggests that in countries with sectoral wage bargaining—as opposed to those with decentralized wage bargaining or fully centralized wage bargaining—the pass-through is more limited because workers have less incentive to internalize the effects of their bargaining on overall employment and unemployment. For evidence on the OECD countries, see Daveri and Tabellini (1997); also Elmeskov, Martin, and Scarpetta (1998). For evidence of the impact of the tax wedge on employment and unemployment in the Region during the transition, see Haltiwanger, Scarpetta, and Vodopivec (2004).

22. Employers in the Region often describe these taxes as substantially raising labor costs and having a strong negative impact on their hiring deci-

sions. For example, high taxes on labor were identified as the most important barrier to firm growth in a 2003 survey of small and medium-size enterprises in Poland (PKPP 2003).
23. The data come from the World Bank (2004c).
24. EBRD–World Bank Business Environment and Enterprise Performance Survey (BEEPS) data.
25. The conventional view is that low income CIS countries inherited well-developed infrastructure for their level of income. However, the public services infrastructure is unreliable, and the level of maintenance is low, which creates sizable obstacles to business. For example, power outages occur almost two-and-a-half times more frequently in low income CIS countries than in middle income CIS countries and almost 13 times more frequently than in CEE countries. The supply of water and the availability of mainline phone systems follow a similar pattern (Steves, Fankhauser, and Rousso 2004).
26. See World Bank (2004d), *World Development Report 2005,* based on data from BEEPS II.
27. Domestic privatization has usually been associated with management and employee buyouts and dispersed ownership. Foreign privatization, in contrast, has been associated with outsider control and more concentrated ownership.
28. This is not to deny that wages may be above the market-clearing level because of efficiency wages and other reasons, reflecting profit-maximizing behavior by firms. The point is that (except for minimum wages) there is no clear indication of institutionally induced wage rigidity in CEE.
29. "Rent" is extra profit that firms earn if there is little competition. Workers can share in part of this rent and raise their wages (appropriate it) if their bargaining power is high.
30. Most countries of the Region have reformed their EPL to reduce employment adjustment costs. Recently, substantial reforms were carried out in Bosnia and Herzegovina, Croatia, Poland, Serbia and Montenegro, and the Slovak Republic.
31. Enforcement is often selective and targeted at larger firms, where there is greater potential for extortion. So, even if compliance with EPL is low in general, some, mainly larger, firms may still be adversely affected by strict EPL.
32. Strong trade unions are an important part of the enforcement mechanism, so in countries where they are stronger (mainly in CEE and SEE), employment protection regulations tend to be more binding than in countries where unions are weaker (for example, in the CIS). Also, larger firms, where unions tend to be stronger, more often see EPL as a constraint than do small firms, where unions are weak.
33. For example, in Poland, unemployment benefit coverage was reduced from about 80 percent in the early 1990s to less than 20 percent in the early 2000s, largely by tightening the eligibility criteria (by introducing a requirement of 180 days of covered employment within the last 12 months). Benefit duration, initially indefinite, was reduced to 12 months in 1991. In addition, a flat-rate benefit (36 percent of the average wage) replaced an earnings-related benefit (up to 70 percent of one's previous

earnings). In Hungary, revisions to unemployment benefit regulations focused on reducing benefit duration: from two years in 1990 to three months to one year (depending on length of employment over the last four years) in 1993 (Dorenbos 1999).

34. For example, a recent investment climate assessment for Poland identified improving the quality of physical infrastructure as one of top priorities (World Bank 2004b).
35. OECD (2005) data suggest that foreign direct investment moves away from economies with more-regulated markets (for example, France and Germany) toward economies with less-regulated markets (for example, the United Kingdom and the United States).
36. Naturally, employment protection regulations need to be consistent with the ratified ILO conventions and, for the EU-member countries, relevant EU directives.
37. For example, in Serbia and Montenegro—the largest country in SEE—starting a business requires going through 11 procedures and takes 51 days. In Albania, the cost of starting a business represents one-third of the gross national income (GNI) per capita.
38. Croatia (which in this report is considered a CEE country, but has shared the problem of inflated unemployment registers with other former Yugoslav republics) provides an example of such an approach. It recently revised its unemployment statistics to distinguish between active job seekers and the passive unemployed.
39. In most OECD countries, the maximum mandatory severance pay does not exceed three months of salary (OECD 1999).
40. Schneider and Klinglmair 2004.

CHAPTER 2

Main Labor Market Developments during the Transition

Economic transition is associated with profound changes in the labor market. Labor resources are allocated by forces of demand and supply rather than by the decisions of the central planners. This fundamental institutional change, along with other transition shocks, spurs widespread employment and wage adjustments. Unemployment emerges and the wage structure changes. The nature of jobs changes, too. This chapter documents and discusses these changes. It shows that Eastern Europe and the Former Soviet Union (the Region) is an economically diverse region, and therefore its subgroup labor markets are also diverse.[1] The chapter looks at the labor market adjustment during the transition—the dynamics of employment and unemployment and the changes in the wage level and structure. Then it shows the changing nature of jobs in the wake of the transition. Next the chapter compares initial expectations with actual labor market outcomes. It concludes by summarizing key stylized facts on labor market transition in the Region.

An Economically Diverse Region with Differing Labor Markets

By its very nature, the transition—from a centrally planned to a market economy—that started in the Region in the early 1990s implied changes in the basic institutions of the economy. It decentralized economic decision-making processes, liberalized price and wage setting, and exposed enterprises to competition. Profitability and competitiveness increasingly became the major criteria of firm survival and growth. These major changes in the rules of the game, along with disintegration of traditional economic links, resulted in a substantial fall in output. This in turn led to a fall in labor demand, which forced firms to reduce employment or wages or, in practice, some combination of the two. Unprofitable firms went out of business or were transformed through restructuring and changes in governance and ownership. At the same time, new private firms began to enter the market. This process occurred in virtually all transition economies, although at varying speeds in different countries. Some countries, mainly in Central and Eastern Europe (CEE), implemented key market-oriented reforms early in the transition and were determined to continue economic restructuring, while others, mainly in Southeastern Europe (SEE) and the Commonwealth of Independent States (CIS), adopted a more gradual and less decisive approach.

Economies of the Region vary vastly in their levels of economic development, which influences the functioning of the labor market (see box 2.1). At one end of the spectrum are countries that are now members of the European Union; at the other end are the low-income countries of Central Asia. The first group is characterized by developed market institutions, more-advanced economic structures, and, correspondingly, relatively high levels of labor productivity. By contrast, the transition economies of Central Asia are much closer to those in low-income developing countries in their economic infrastructures. Their market-based institutions are relatively less developed or not effective on the ground, economic structures are dominated by agriculture, and their labor productivity tends to be low. Other economies of the Region, such as those of Southeast Europe, Russia, and Ukraine, fall somewhere between these two polar cases.

The differences in the levels of economic development across the Region are associated with significant differences in the key features of labor markets. The largely urban, services-oriented, and formal labor markets of EU transition economies perform differently from the mainly rural, agricultural, and informal labor markets of Central Asia. For example, the predominantly rural and informal labor markets in Tajikistan or Uzbekistan are very much different from the mostly urban and formal labor markets of the Czech Republic or Hungary. Similarly, the labor markets in Belarus or Ukraine, where market-oriented reforms are less advanced, differ from the labor markets in the Baltic States, which have a well-functioning market economy and are members of the European Union.

Labor market adjustments to the transition shock have been different in the transition economies of Europe and those of Central Asia. In Central and Eastern Europe, the high pace of enterprise restructuring and other structural reforms has led to an initial strong fall in employment and far-reaching reallocation of labor away from declining industries toward expanding ones, mainly in the services sector. In contrast, in Central Asia, the pace of enterprise restructuring has been slower. The drop in output associated with the transition was accommodated mainly by a fall in real wages. Many workers who were released from the oversized manufacturing sector moved back to subsistence agriculture. And the lack of job opportunities in the formal sector has led to the fast growth of the informal labor market and self-employment as a coping strategy.[2]

In European transition economies, the main problem is unemployment, which to a large extent results from the fast pace of enterprise restructuring. In CIS economies, the main problem is underemployment (hidden unemployment) and low productivity (for example, in subsistence agriculture). The low open unemployment in Central Asia reflects both the predominantly agricultural and informal nature of their economies—agriculture and informal sectors act as employers of last resort—and the slow pace of enterprise restructuring (for example, overstaffing is still prevalent in many enterprises).

The key differences between labor markets in the middle-income European transition economies and those in the low-income CIS economies are summarized in table 2.1. These differences must be borne in mind while reviewing labor market development in the rest of this report.

Unemployment and Underemployment: Major Economic and Social Problems

The transition shock caused a substantial fall in the number of formal sector jobs in all transition economies of the Region, although it was more marked in CEE and SEE than in the CIS economies. This in turn has led to considerable underutilization of labor. Underutilization of labor manifests itself in different forms, depending on policies toward the "old" enterprise sector and the prevailing mode of enterprise adjustment. Aggressive enterprise restructuring, encouraged by imposition of the market discipline that prevailed in

BOX 2.1

Do Geopolitical Groupings Help in Assessing the Economic Performance of the Transition Countries?

Eastern Europe and the Former Soviet Union is a large and economically diversified region. It encompasses subgroups of countries that differ in their level of economic development, institutions, industrial structure, and progress in market-oriented reforms. These differences, in turn, influence the characteristics and evolution of their labor markets.

The profound heterogeneity in the economic and structural characteristics of the countries of the Region makes it very difficult to analyze them as a group. One way to group the transition countries is to apply a traditional geopolitical grouping: Central and East European countries, which comprise two groups: CEE EU (EU members) and CEE EUA (EU-accession countries); Southeastern European countries (SEE); and CIS, which comprises middle income CIS countries (Belarus, Kazakhstan, Russia, and Ukraine) and low income CIS countries (Armenia, Azerbaijan, Georgia, the Kyrgyz Republic, Moldova, Tajikistan, and Uzbekistan).[3]

This geopolitical grouping also has a close bearing in the levels of economic development, institutional arrangements, and economic structure. For example, a close correspondence exists between the geopolitical location and differences in the level of economic development, as measured by GDP per capita (table A). All CEE EU-member countries belong to the group of the richest countries of the Region. And all low income CIS countries belong to the group of the poorest countries of the Region. Thus, the geopolitical location is a good indicator of the level of economic development.

Table A. Geopolitical Location and Level of Economic Development Closely Related

Geopolitical groups	Income groups: GDP per capita a), 2002			Mean value $
	top tercile	middle	bottom tercile	
CEE EU	8			12,984
CEE EUA	1	2		8,032
SEE		3	1	5,685
Middle income CIS		3	1	6,122
Low income CIS			7	2,428

Source: World Development Indicators World Bank database; Bank staff calculations.

Note: Numbers stand for the number of countries within the cell.
a) GDP at PPP (current international $)

Similarly, there is a strong overlap between the geopolitical location and the quality of institutions and governance. For example, government effectiveness varies significantly between geopolitical groups, but variation within groups is relatively small (table B).

Table B. Geopolitical Groups and Government Effectiveness

Geopolitical groups	Government Effectiveness Index, 2002			
	top tercile	middle	bottom tercile	mean value
CEE EU	8			0.67
CEE EUA	1	2		−0.07
SEE		3	1	−0.62
Middle income CIS		1	3	−0.74
Low income CIS		2	5	−0.85

Source: Kaufmann, Kraay, and Zoido-Lobaton 2004; Bank staff calculations.

Note: Numbers stand for the number of countries within the cell.

Finally, geopolitical location allows one to predict fairly well the progress of economic transition. Roughly speaking, the closer a country group is to Brussels, the more advanced it is in implementing market reforms (table C). Economic transition is most advanced in CEE countries and least advanced in middle and low income CIS countries, while SEE countries occupy the middle position.

Table C. Geopolitical Groups and Economic Transition

Geopolitical groups	EBRD index of the progress of the transition, 2001			
	top tercile	middle	bottom tercile	mean value
CEE EU	8			3.45
CEE EUA	1	2		3.03
SEE		2	2	2.61
Middle income CIS		2	2	2.36
Low income CIS		3	4	2.53

Source: EBRD Transition Report (2004); Bank staff calculations.

Note: Numbers denote the number of countries within the cell.

Naturally, there are cases when the use of the geopolitical taxonomy results in a misclassification of some countries from the economic perspective. For example, Bulgaria and Romania, which are EU-accession countries and thus fall into the CEE group, are closer to the SEE group in economic development. In turn, Croatia, which until 2004 was not officially an EU-accession country, in economic indicators is closer to EU transition economies than to EU-accession countries, let alone SEE countries. Finally, the borderline between middle and low income CIS countries is blurred in some cases.

In sum, the Region's economic diversity is well captured by the traditional geopolitical country grouping. This grouping fairly well reflects differences in the levels of economic development, institutional arrangements, and governance and in the progress of market-oriented reforms.

TABLE 2.1
Differences between Middle-Income European and Low-Income CIS Labor Markets

Labor market characteristics	Middle-income European transition economies	Low-income CIS transition economies
Main labor market issue	Unemployment	Underemployment
Adjustment to transition shock	Quantity (employment); labor moving to expanding services sector	Price (wages); labor shifting back to subsistence agriculture
Investment climate	Generally favorable	Less favorable
Market oriented reforms and enterprise restructuring	Advanced	Less advanced
Employment protection legislation	Relatively liberal	Strict
Enforcement of labor market regulations	Relatively strong	Weak
Unemployment insurance system	Developed	Largely ineffective
Economic structure	Dominance of services and industry	Dominance of agriculture
Informal sector	Marginal, driven by tax evasion and avoidance of regulations	Large, driven by lack of job opportunities in the formal sector
Labor force location	Largely urban	Largely rural
Labor force skills	High	Mostly low
Productivity (wages)	High	Low
Earnings inequality	Modest	High

Source: Bank staff analysis.

most CEE countries, led to high open unemployment. In contrast, the policy of protection through soft budget constraint, common in most CIS countries, led largely to underemployment (hidden unemployment) and associated low productivity (World Bank 2000).

Unemployment emerged at an early stage of the transition and rose sharply along with the restructuring process.[4] Currently it remains high in most transition economies of CEE and SEE, significantly above the level characteristic of mature market economies (figure 2.1). But unemployment is also high in Turkey, which is a nontransition economy at a level of economic development similar to that in many countries in the Region.[5] Albeit affected by major macro and structural changes over the past two decades and still afflicted by low participation, the country has not gone through the systemic changes of the transition economies (see box 2.2).

Unemployment rates in CEE countries are currently well above 10 percent, except in the Czech Republic, Hungary, Romania, and Slovenia. In SEE countries, unemployment rates are between 10 and 22 percent, except for FYR Macedonia (30 percent). Among the CIS group, Armenia, Georgia, Moldova, Russia, and Ukraine have unemployment rates above 6 percent. The other CIS countries are characterized by low *registered* unemployment rates, generally below 4 percent, and with little fluctuation over time. These latter rates, however, should be interpreted with caution because they refer to admin-

FIGURE 2.1
Unemployment Is High in Most CEE and SEE Countries, 2003

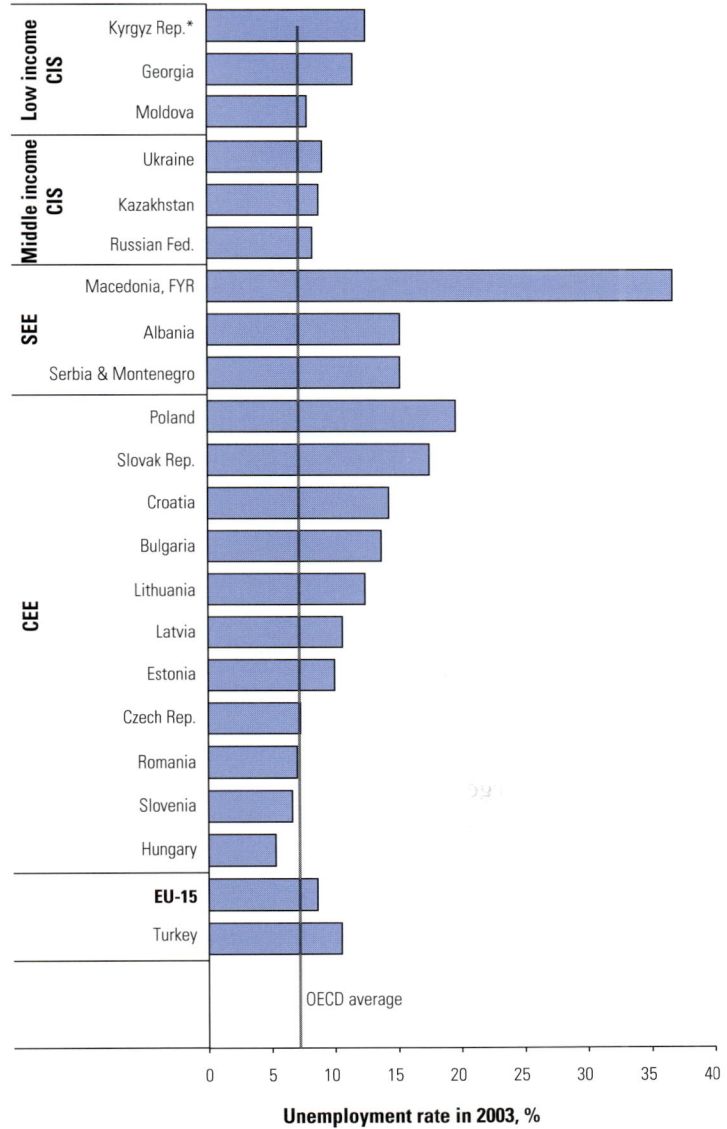

Sources: Labor Force Surveys (ILO, and OECD); * 2002 from Labour Market in the CIS countries, Statistical Abstract. Interstate Statistical Committee of the CIS, Moscow 2004.

istrative data that are highly influenced by the availability and generosity of social-benefit provisions.[6]

Low open unemployment in most CIS countries as a rule masks significant labor market problems. It is associated with artificially sustained, low-productivity employment in unprofitable firms, as well as

> **BOX 2.2**
>
> **The Challenge of Job Creation in Turkey**
>
> Turkey has suffered from poor labor market conditions since structural reforms were introduced in the 1980s. During 1980–2003, employment growth averaged just 0.8 percent, compared with 2.6 percent growth of the working-age population, and the labor force participation rate fell to 48 percent, the lowest in the OECD. Female labor force participation has been exceptionally weak, standing at less than 20 percent in urban areas. Currently, the working-age population is growing at more than 2 percent per year, and by 2020 more than 21 million new workers will have reached working age. Accommodating the needs of these new and existing workers represents a critical challenge for Turkey over the coming decades.
>
> Turkey's labor market outcomes reflect the interaction of demographic and economic factors. Like most other developing countries, Turkey is experiencing a rapid demographic transition that has generated a surge of new entrants to the labor market. Although these demographic forces have the potential to promote economic growth, absorbing them in the labor market requires sustained firm dynamism and job creation. Inadequate human and physical capital investment have so far prevented rapid expansion and job creation. Meanwhile, the demographic trends have been accompanied by a transformation of a fundamentally rural-agrarian society into an urban-industrial one. Cultural and institutional factors and an evolving occupational structure have led to changing roles, particularly for women, and have affected household preferences and labor force participation decisions.
>
> In the economic sphere in the early 1980s, Turkey abruptly abandoned a long-standing and inward-looking statist policy framework and began a transition toward a more outward-looking,

widespread informal sector and agricultural employment to earn subsistence income. Productive job opportunities are few, and underemployment is common. See box 2.3 on Moldova and World Bank (2003a) on Russia.

In recent years, unemployment has fallen in a few countries, most notably in the Baltic States. But in many other countries, such as Poland and the Slovak Republic, high unemployment rates persist despite resumed economic growth. And in other countries, mainly in those where reforms have been slow and delayed, such as Romania (until recently) and Serbia and Montenegro, unemployment continues to rise.

Long-Term Unemployment

The most worrisome and socially costly feature of unemployment in transition economies, particularly visible in CEE and SEE, is its long

free-market development model. The change quickly turned the economy around from a prolonged crisis in the late 1970s and produced spectacular results in trade performance. But subsequently long-standing policy failures were perpetuated in the new environment, contributing to inflation, macroeconomic instability, and weak investment. At the same time, integration into the global economy, though otherwise beneficial, increased vulnerability to external events, including two regional wars, economic disruptions in trading partners, and financial contagion.

The solution to the problem of generating employment is growth. In the medium term, the outlook is reasonably favorable. The external environment is promising, with growth and import demand picking up in European and the Region's trading partners. Turkey rebounded quickly from the 2001 crisis, and the confidence of international investors has been restored, at least for now. The government is implementing an IMF program, and early negotiations on EU admission seem likely, which should bolster reforms and raise Turkey's attractiveness as a destination for foreign direct investment (FDI). Nevertheless, medium-term growth will do little more than keep the labor market in a holding pattern. Making serious inroads into unemployment and low labor force participation will require a substantial improvement in macroeconomic performance.

In the longer term, Turkey is well situated in location and factor endowments. Some of the stress of absorbing large numbers of new labor market entrants will be alleviated as the working-age population gets older and its rate of growth slows. A recent overhaul of the educational system aimed at increasing human capital investment promises to increase competitiveness vis-à-vis international rivals. However, increasing the quantity and quality of investment is crucial to exploiting future opportunities and realizing Turkey's potential. Policies to improve the business climate and achieve macroeconomic stability must be top priorities.

Source: Keyfitz 2004.

BOX 2.3

Employment in Moldova

Moldova is an example of a country with relatively high employment and low unemployment rates, but where a large proportion of jobs is of low productivity and thus probably unsustainable. As much as 20 percent of privatized firms reported overstaffing in 2001. Moreover, 1 of every 10 workers was on a forced unpaid leave, and the average duration of such leave was three months. Many Moldovan firms close for a part of the year. Because of the low level of activity in poorly performing firms, the actual hours of work are very low. An average worker in Moldova works only 28 hours per week, while his or her Polish counterpart works 42 hours. Similar problems, although to a lesser degree, occur in Russia (World Bank, 2003f).

Source: World Bank 2004a.

duration. Once unemployed, workers find it difficult to find a new job. Consequently, a large fraction of the unemployed in the Region's transition economies are long-term unemployed (that is, jobless for more than a year). In CEE, 40 to 50 percent of the unemployed have been without a job for more than one year, and this proportion is higher than 60 percent in Bulgaria and the Slovak Republic. These figures are high by OECD standards and similar to those observed in Southern European countries with a stagnant unemployment pool. Available data also point to a high persistence of unemployment in SEE. For example, more than 80 percent of the unemployed in FYR Macedonia have been without a job for more than one year.

The crux of the unemployment problem in European transition economies is thus the low chances of finding new employment, rather than high inflow into unemployment. Russia and Turkey provide an interesting contrast of more dynamic unemployment pools. Russian and Turkish workers tend to leave unemployment sooner, and therefore the incidence of long-term unemployment is much lower (about 30 percent).

Labor Force Withdrawal

The increase in unemployment has been one symptom of the fall in labor demand during the transition. Another closely related symptom is the often large fall in labor force participation. Many workers become discouraged by the lack of job opportunities and give up the job search, ceasing to be part of the labor force. In 2002, the economically active population accounted for around 60 percent of the working-age population in Hungary and FYR Macedonia and for more than 70 percent in Belarus, the Czech Republic, Estonia, Lithuania, and the Slovak Republic. In this context, Bosnia and Herzegovina, Moldova, and Turkey are clear outliers, with official participation rates below 55 percent (in the first two cases, down from more than 60 percent in the mid-1990s).

From an economic viewpoint, the effects of labor force withdrawal are similar to those of unemployment: both reduce the amount of available labor and, as such, translate into lower output and diminish growth prospects. For instance, in the early 2000s, the unemployment rate in Poland was much higher than in Hungary. However, so was the labor force participation rate. As a result, both countries had similar employment rates, which is the most relevant measure of the utilization of labor resources.[7]

Some decline in labor force participation was probably to be expected during transition. Participation rates were particularly high during the central-planning period, when work was not only a right but also a duty for all people of working age. The withdrawal of older workers from the labor market—often taking advantage of early retirement schemes—imposed significant costs on fragile budgets, but was probably inevitable, given the difficulty of reemploying the workers. In contrast, the withdrawal of women and youth is reducing the growth potential of transition economies and contributing to widening income disparities.[8]

Greater International Migration Flows

Cross-border migration has increased in the Region during the transition. Although in some countries migration was linked to conflicts and ethnic reasons in the early years of the transition, migration has increasingly been driven by economic reasons in most recent years. Pressures from a growing working-age population and the lack of employment opportunities have led nationals from the low income CIS countries toward richer countries of the Region, especially Russia, which have themselves become both significant receiving and sending countries. Many nationals of these countries migrate to Western Europe because of increased economic payoffs to migration. In particular, temporary migration (that is, either seasonal or moving back and forth) is sizable (box 2.4).

Falling Employment Rates and Persistent Unemployment

The level of unemployment depends on the probability of becoming unemployed and on the expected duration of the unemployment period. The latter in turn depends on the probability of escaping unemployment by finding a job. Therefore, the level and duration structure of unemployment vary depending on the relationship between the inflow rate and the expected duration of unemployment.

In a *dynamic labor market*, the risk of losing a job may be high, but so are the chances of finding a new one. Therefore, the expected duration of unemployment will be short, which will result in a "moderate" unemployment rate (or a low unemployment rate if inflows into unemployment are low). An opposite example is that of a *stagnant labor market*. In such a market, the risk of losing a job may be low, but so are the prospects of finding a new one. The expected duration of unemployment periods will be long, and the level of unemployment will be elevated, despite low inflows into joblessness. If inflows into joblessness increase (for example, because of economic downturn, restructuring, or demographical pressures), unemployment will reach a high level.

> **BOX 2.4**
>
> **International Migration Patterns in the Region**
>
> **The Changing Nature of Migration**
>
> In the first half of the 1990s, international migration in the Region was a direct consequence of the breakup of the communist system in Eastern Europe and the Soviet Union. Because of the creation of new countries in the former Soviet Union, the former Yugoslavia, and the former Czechoslovakia, millions of people became de facto migrants (that is, foreign born): for example, within the Soviet Union, 43 million individuals were living outside their homeland. Moreover, the end of restrictions to movement led to the resumption of pre-Iron Curtain era migration (for example Jewish emigration to Israel or ethnic German migration to Germany). In addition, civil wars and conflicts in the area led to further ethnic migration.
>
> From the mid-1990s, international migration became increasingly economically driven as individuals weigh the expected costs and benefits of moving to another country to improve their quality of life. Overall, two main directions of flows have emerged: migration from Eastern Europe to Western Europe (especially to Germany and Austria) and migration from low income CIS countries to resource-rich CIS countries (especially to Russia, but also transiting through Azerbaijan and Kazakhstan).
>
> The movements from new EU members to old EU members are expected to be limited and temporary. The experience of Southern European countries joining the EU with much lower income levels than the then members is illustrative. After an initial increase in migration when joining, and as economic and social development occurs, through (for example) foreign direct investments spurred by membership, emigration starts declining to be progressively replaced by temporary or circular (seasonal) migration. All new EU members are currently both significant sending and receiving countries, and a few (the Czech Republic, Hungary, the Slovak Republic, and Slovenia) have already become net immigration countries.
>
> The movements from low income CIS countries and among CIS countries have to be viewed in the context of a history of movements within the Former Soviet Union (FSU), making northern FSU countries attractive destinations for those in southern FSU countries. Young and growing populations in the poorly developed Central Asian countries are likely to move north to FSU countries, which are seeing aging and decreasing working-age populations. Belarus and Russia have already become net immigration countries. Lack of progress of reforms, poor governance, and low quality of public services in some CIS countries are strong incentives for out migration.

A typical example of a flexible, dynamic labor market is that of the United States. There, 66 percent of the unemployed find a job within a year (Boeri and Terrell 2002). The median duration of unemployment fluctuates around 10 weeks, and correspondingly the incidence

Again, as the differentials in governance decrease across countries, migration flows are expected to become multidirectional rather than directed at a few receiving countries, and return migration will become more attractive.

Recent Evolution

Accurate data on migration are notoriously difficult to obtain, but some tentative observations can be made from available data. Consistent with the changing nature of migration just described, countries that had above-average migration flows in the early phase of transition saw these subsequently decrease. Net emigration in absolute terms was largest in Lithuania and Poland. Relative to population size, net emigration was largest in Estonia. Hungary reported, both in absolute and in relative terms, the largest net gain from migration, followed by the Czech Republic. Although the number of Central Asian nationals living permanently in Russia has increased moderately, there is evidence that temporary migration has increased significantly.

International Migration and Labor Markets

The receiving country may be affected in two main ways: flows of new migrants may have an impact on wages and employment of prior residents, and immigration may have fiscal implications. The current literature on immigration in the United States, Europe, and Australia suggests only small effects on labor market outcomes of native populations. The fiscal contribution of migrants is found to depend on the composition of immigration, highly skilled migrants contributing the most to the fiscal balance.

For the sending country, on the one hand, migration may relieve tensions on the labor market (for example, in resource-poor countries that have growing working-age populations, such as Central Asian countries). On the other hand, the emigration of disproportionately young and better-educated individuals may be an issue because growth may be further depressed by poor labor supply.

There is evidence that *circular or return migration* may be welcomed by both sending and receiving countries. Receiving countries may prefer temporary migration that responds to specific labor demand and may be reduced in economic downturns. Sending countries may benefit from greater remittances, as migrants keep stronger ties to their home country with a view to coming back, and from better-skilled returning migrants (although this is not always the case). For example, there is evidence that Albanians who have been abroad earn more than those who never went, while the stayers would have earned even more abroad than those who left.

Sources: World Bank forthcoming; Lucas 2005.

of long-term unemployment is very low: in 2002, the number of unemployed with a period longer than one year accounted for 8.5 percent of total unemployment in the United States, and usually the percentage is even lower (OECD 2003). Labor markets in CEE are in sharp contrast to the U.S. example. As can be expected, flows from employment to unemployment tended to be higher, as transition economies underwent rapid restructuring, which by its very nature is associated with a high rate of job destruction. However, the main difference lies not in the inflow rate, but in the outflow rate, which was much lower in CEE than in the United States. The chance that a worker finds a job within a year after entering unemployment is substantially higher in the United States than in virtually all transition economies. Roughly speaking, the probability that an unemployed person finds a job in transition economies is half that in the United States. Thus, all else being equal, if the outflow rate from unemployment to jobs in Poland, say, were the same as in the United States, then the Polish unemployment rate would be about one-fourth lower (15 percent instead of 20 percent).[9]

Some examples of the differences in flows into and out of unemployment are shown in table 2.2.

Data in table 2.2 suggest that high unemployment in transition economies was initially the product of relatively high inflows into unemployment and limited outflows to jobs. Most of the economies were thus in the high unemployment/depressed (stagnant) labor market state. As the restructuring process slowed with the progress of the transition, the initially high inflow rates gradually declined, although

TABLE 2.2
Flows into and out of Unemployment
As a proportion of the origin stock

Country	Year	Employment to Unemployment	Employment to Out of the Labor Force	Unemployment to Employment	Unemployment to Out of the Labor Force	Out of the Labor Force to Employment	Out of the Labor Force to Unemployment
Central and Eastern European Countries							
Bulgaria	1994–1995	0.059	0.092	0.323	0.244	0.092	0.044
Czech Republic	1994–1995	0.013	0.028	0.496	0.129	0.042	0.012
Czech Republic	1996–1997	0.08	0.025	0.457	0.101	0.04	0.008
Czech Republic	1998–1999	0.018	0.025	0.335	0.09	0.036	0.017
Poland	1992–1993	0.04	0.076	0.361	0.158	0.095	0.045
Poland	1993–1994	0.04	0.063	0.354	0.159	0.074	0.043
Slovak Republic	1994–1995	0.023	0.045	0.237	0.078	0.018	0.017
Former Soviet Union							
Estonia	1992	0.048	0.097	0.465	0.093	0.143	0.036
Estonia	1997	0.047	0.04	0.372	0.064	0.074	0.038
Russian Federation	1992–1993	0.032	0.058	0.52	0.157	0.087	0.014
Russian Federation	1995–1996	0.056	0.062	0.395	0.145	0.076	0.034
Memorandum							
United States	1992–1993	0.028	0.053	0.659	0.288	0.043	0.161

Source: Boeri and Terrell 2002.

they still remain higher than in the United States. This entailed a movement toward the moderate unemployment/stagnant labor market state because the job-finding chances hardly improved and thus the duration of unemployment remained high. Currently, unemployment is a rather stagnant pool: few workers enter unemployment, but also few are able to exit it. However, recent examples of a substantial fall in unemployment in some CEE countries (for example, Lithuania) suggest that these successful countries might have begun a movement toward a moderate unemployment/dynamic labor market. It is obviously an open question whether the movement will continue toward the low unemployment/dynamic labor market state.

Employment Rates below EU Average

Because of rising unemployment and falling participation, employment rates (employment as a percentage of working-age population) declined sharply in most transition economies. Roughly 15 percent of the population of working age who would have been employed under the old regime has become nonemployed (that is, unemployed or out of the labor force). In virtually all of the Region's countries, the employment rate is presently below the EU average of 65 percent and way below the Lisbon target of 70 percent for 2010 (figure 2.2). For CEE countries, meeting this target would require a major effort of job creation in the years to come.

Employment rates remain relatively high in some low income CIS countries. But rather than a sign of good labor market outcomes, these high employment rates are often a symptom of a slow pace of restructuring and the permanence of many low-productivity jobs. These include informal sector jobs, subsistence farming, and nonviable jobs in the formal sector characterized also by a high prevalence of wage arrears, forced unpaid leave, and short working hours. These jobs can exist only as long as enterprises are not subject to competition and receive direct or indirect subsidies (for example, tax arrears, nonpayment of utility bills) (see box 2.5).[10] The high employment rates in these countries therefore partly reflect low value added and poorly paid work.

In some transition economies of both CEE and the CIS, there are signs of incipient employment growth. Since the early 2000s, the employment rate has increased in the Baltic States, Hungary, and Slovenia in CEE, and in Armenia, Georgia, Russia, and Ukraine in the CIS.[11] However, whether this growth is sustainable and represents a turnaround point remains to be seen. In some of these countries, especially in the CIS, major restructuring effort still lies ahead, which may imply an acceleration of job destruction.

FIGURE 2.2
Employment-to-Population Ratio Is Low in Most of the Region's Countries

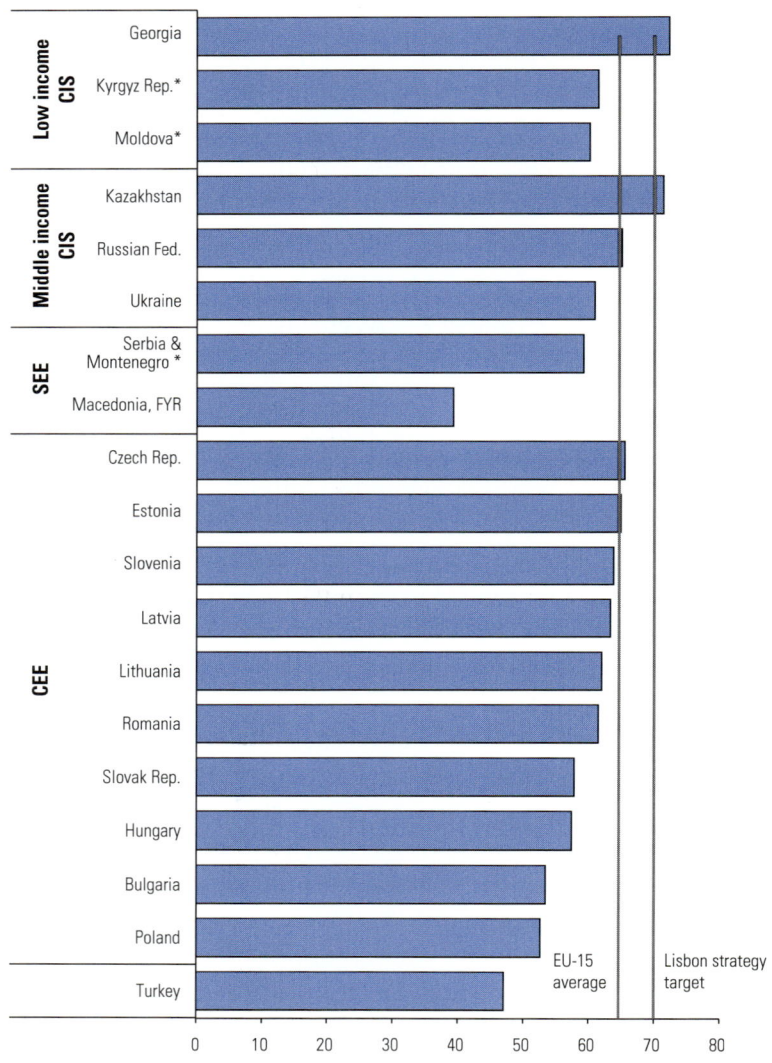

Source: Labor force surveys (ILO).

Note: * signifies 2002.

Male Employment Rates Affected More

As is common in most industrial economies, male employment rates are higher than female employment rates in all transition economies of the Region. This results from the difference in the labor force participation rates, which are lower for women, rather than from the difference in the unemployment rates, which tend to be similar for men and women in the Region. This is not surprising because the female labor force participation rates are lower than those of men in virtually all societies, and the transition countries are no exception to this regularity.

If anything, the gap between male and female labor force participation rates is smaller in the Region than in the OECD countries. In nearly two-thirds of the Region's transition economies, women's activity rates increased relative to men's. In effect, there has been a general increase in the share of women in the labor force over the past decade in the Region (Paci 2002). Thus, by international standards, male rather than female labor resources are underutilized in the Region's transition economies. To illustrate this point for the CEE countries, there is a 6-percentage-point gap in the male labor force participation rates between the EU-15 and CEE. This gap is even bigger in the male employment rate: 64 percent in the CEE compared with 73 percent in EU-15. In contrast, no such gap between CEE and EU-15 exists for the female employment rate.

How can these particularly low male employment rates be explained? One possible explanation is that the restructuring process has been biased against manual, less-skilled labor, which has put men at a disadvantage. The industries that have been declining, especially heavy industry, were employing predominantly male labor. In contrast, the expanding service sector relies to a much greater extent on female labor. Moreover, the restructuring is associated with the increase in the relative demand for higher, mainly nonmanual, skills, which benefits women more, because in many transition economies women tend to be better educated than men. In other words, there is indication that during the transition the demand for male labor, which tends to be manual and less skilled, has been hurt more than that for female labor, which tends to be nonmanual and more skilled.

In addition, the female labor force participation rates were very high by international standards in most socialist countries, and therefore the gender gap in labor force participation was relatively small. The transition shock lowered both male and female employment rates, but although it has brought female employment rates to the EU level, it brought the male rates well below the EU level (box 2.6).

Less-Skilled and Young Workers

Unemployment rates in transition economies are particularly high among less-educated workers and are disproportionately low among well-educated workers, especially those with university education. For example, a worker with primary education (eight years) in Poland

BOX 2.5

Growth and Job Creation in Low Income CIS Countries

The low income CIS countries historically suffered from a certain degree of underdevelopment vis-à-vis other Soviet republics, and this development gap was increasing during the 1980s. The output fall unleashed by the early transitional postindependence reforms exacerbated this gap as the low income CIS countries experienced a deeper recession between 1990 and 1994 relative to other transitional economies. In the subsequent stabilization period, the macroeconomic trends became progressively positive, and growth was reestablished in all the countries considered after the Russian financial crisis in 1997. A period of substantial and sustainable GDP growth followed.

Yet net job creation continued to be negative or slow (especially in the formal sector) during the expansion period, a trend that constrained the transmission of growth benefits to people. According to available evidence, the elasticity of poverty reduction to growth was modest and delayed by two to four years vis-à-vis the initial phase of GDP growth. Thus questions arise as to what factors may be constraining employment growth in the low income CIS countries and what policy mix might be needed to reverse this trend.

A number of coexisting factors have constrained job creation in these countries. They are related to both the structural heritage of the pretransition period and the nature of economic transition in the Region. The countries entered the transition period with significant excess labor in most enterprises. The recession of the early 1990s accentuated this phenomenon as employment declined markedly slower than did GDP. The resulting losses in productivity were fully reflected in real-wage losses. In other words, most people kept their job, but lost part of their income.

Growth recovery also took place only in a few sectors, mostly capital-intensive, and in a few export-oriented firms. Moreover, enterprises remained largely unrestructured and could still be characterized by significant labor hoarding. Economic growth was in fact supported by either capital investments or by labor-productivity growth (with a steep increase in real wages). Therefore, the later period of mostly jobless growth is largely explained by the productivity-margin gains that were available in existing enterprises.

How real-wage growth could have coexisted with excess labor in the market is partly explained by the dual labor market behavior of the low income CIS economies. Many workers who lost their jobs in manufacturing moved back to agriculture, which for many became the only possi-

is more than four times more likely to become unemployed than a worker with tertiary education. At the same time, most of the unemployed are workers with secondary education, especially those with narrow vocational skills, because in the centrally planned economies this was the most prevalent form of education. This unemployment

ble form of subsistence, as well as an escape from urban unemployment. Consequently, they did not compete with formal urban sector workers and did not exert downward pressure on wages.

Industry and agriculture followed two rather different paths during the transition. The agricultural sector initially experienced a fall in output—but a fall that was much more limited than what was visible in other sectors. This is explained by land privatization that allowed a large number of small farmers to increase production and productivity and progressively replace state farms in the market. But agriculture remained a rather isolated sector, with few backward and forward linkages to the industrial sector. In the industrial sector, the collapse of the state system was not offset by private initiatives. Moreover, the post-1997 growth in the industrial sector tended to be narrowly based and concentrated in a few—typically capital-intensive—industries, while manufacturing stagnated. As a result, the demand for agricultural production has hardly increased, constraining agricultural production to the subsistence level. Thus, agriculture and industry not only followed different paths, but paths that produced very little employment or benefits for the average household.

Summing up, the following features distinguish economic transition in low income CIS economies from that in middle income CIS and other more-advanced transition economies:

- Lower economic performance than middle income CIS countries before the transition
- A different economic structure, with a smaller urban sector and a larger agricultural sector
- Deeper and faster recession than elsewhere in transition during 1991–1996
- Larger output-employment gap during the recession and faster labor-hoarding growth during the 1990s
- Slower and narrower structural reforms during the recession
- Faster reforms and faster growth rates during the growth period (1997–2003)
- Slow or nil job creation during the growth period (explained by productivity gains in existing enterprises)
- An agricultural sector currently confined largely to subsistence
- A very small industrial manufacturing sector delinked from the agricultural sector

Source: Verme 2004.

pattern indicates a labor market premium to education and high skills, also visible in the structure of wages (see Widening Wage Differentials section later in this chapter).

Youth is another group that suffers from high unemployment. On average, youth unemployment rates are twice as high as overall

BOX 2.6

Relative Position of Women in the Labor Market Has Not Deteriorated during the Transition, and New Employment Opportunities for Women Emerged in the Expanding Services Sector

Despite an ideology of gender equality and high labor force participation, different forms of gender discrimination were evident under the central-plan period in many of the transition countries. In particular, there was evidence of a gender pay gap, mainly because women were prevalently working in low-paid, white-collar occupations. This wage gap was relatively small by international standards but, in practice, societies continued to reflect the model of a "male breadwinner," which considered women as secondary workers.

In the context of major economic changes associated with the transition to a market economy, there was a concern that women would be disproportionately affected by worsening labor market outcomes so that preexisting gender gaps in employment and wages would increase. The reduction in state-financed social services, such as kindergartens, forced many women to withdraw from the labor market to take on family responsibilities. At the same time, jobs with a clear female connotation remained or even expanded during the transition, while many male-oriented jobs were destroyed, contributing to the erosion of the male breadwinner model.

After 15 years of transition, female unemployment rates are generally similar to men's rates and are even lower in some cases. In a number of countries, however, female labor force participation declined more sharply than did men's. Two main concerns persist:

unemployment rates. This proportion is not different from that in mature market economies; however, given high overall unemployment rates, joblessness among youth often reaches dramatic levels. For instance, in Bulgaria and the Slovak Republic, more than one-third of the youth labor force is unemployed.

Youth unemployment matters because it prevents new entrants in the labor market from gaining experience and developing labor market skills. Youth unemployment is also closely associated with poverty in some of the transition countries. For example, in Bulgaria and FYR Macedonia, the incidence of poverty among the unemployed youth is significantly higher than the average. In this case, the likely reason is that young people in poor families cannot afford to be out of the labor force. Low family income forces people to enter the labor market at a relatively young age. As long as young people are searching for jobs, they are counted as unemployed, and in this sense poverty gives rise to youth unemployment. Obviously, prolonged and unsuccessful job search by young family members can also contribute to poverty.

- Although the gender wage gap remains small, there is evidence of some wage discrimination in the Region. This wage gap can largely be explained in gender differences in the returns to some key individual characteristics, primarily education. In fact, the relatively small size of the gender pay gap largely results from the fact that women in the Region tend to be better educated than men, which helps to contain the wage gap in many of the transition countries.

- New gender differentials may have been created because of the increase in the size of the informal economy. On the one hand, the informal economy may offer employment opportunities to women in a context of a small, formal private sector and shrinking public sector. On the other hand, the informal economy does not provide adequate social protection, and there is some evidence that women are more vulnerable as they concentrate in lower-end jobs.

All in all, there is little evidence that the transition has been harder on women than on men, although women's labor market status varies greatly across countries. There is, however, some concern that the gender dimension of some developing phenomena—such as the rise of the informal sector—may hurt women disproportionately, but this hypothesis has not yet been tested. More generally, there is a need to mainstream gender issues into the debate about reforms of the labor market and social policy. This is particularly so given that many employment-protection provisions granted to women during the socialist era (for example, generous maternity-leave provisions with extended rehiring guarantees) may actually hurt women's employment prospects in a competitive labor market by raising the cost of employing women relative to that of employing men.

Sources: Paci 2002; Paci and Reilly 2004.

Either way, youth unemployment is significantly correlated with poverty (see also Kolev and Saget 2003).

Those in Backward Areas

Labor market conditions vary substantially across geographical areas of most of the transition countries, and in many cases such geographical disparities have increased over time. Large differences in the unemployment rate within countries illustrate the severity of regional labor market disparities. Differences between the regions with the highest unemployment rate and those with the lowest unemployment rate (usually the capitals) exceeded a factor of 3 in all countries but Romania and Slovenia in 2003.[12] These disparities in unemployment are also associated with large disparities in living standards. Regional GDP per capita levels ranged from 60 percent to up to more than 200 percent of the national average in most transition economies (table 2.3). The disparity in regional labor market conditions is much more

TABLE 2.3
Large Regional Disparities in Unemployment Rates, 2003

	Average	Minimum	Maximum	Coefficient of variation	Capital city region
Czech Republic	7.5	4.2	14.8	40.1	4.2
Hungary	6.3	3.3	11.3	31.1	3.6
Poland	20.1	8.5	33.4	25.8	18.3
Romania	7.0	5.9	8.6	14.8	—
Estonia	10.6	0.4	17.4	32.2	9.0
Latvia	10.4	8.2	15.4	22.7	10.8
Lithuania	12.3	7.5	16.9	20.4	11.7
Slovenia	7.3	4.7	10.2	29.8	4.7
Slovak Republic	17.2	7.1	23.9	36.3	7.1
Russian Fed. (2002)	8.0	1.4	44.0	56.3	1.4

Source: Huber 2004.

Note: Registered unemployment rate, NUTS III level.

pronounced in Russia, which is not surprising, given the immense economic heterogeneity of the country's regions. In Moscow and St. Petersburg, open unemployment is negligible (less than 4 percent), while in Dagestan and (even more so) in Ingushetia, it is alarmingly high (24 and 44 percent, respectively). Even leaving these extreme cases aside, regional labor market conditions within Russia vary much more than those in European transition economies.[13]

High regional unemployment is usually coupled with lower labor force participation (resulting from discouragement), giving rise to the low employment/population ratio in high-unemployment regions. Differences between maximum and minimum employment rates range from more than 10 percentage points to more than 25 percentage points in transition economies; however, there are notable exceptions to this pattern. For example, the high-unemployment (nearly 20 percent) southwestern region in Romania has at the same time the highest employment rate (70 percent). In contrast, the low-unemployment (11 percent) capital region has by far the lowest employment rate (56 percent). This confirms that unemployment and nonparticipation are often different signals of poor labor market conditions and should be considered together. Nonetheless, the prevailing pattern is that of high unemployment being associated with low labor force participation, and thus low employment rates (Bornhorst and Commander 2004).

Job Creation Concentrated around Large Urban Agglomerations with Modern Economic Structure

Regional unemployment inequality reflects strong regional concentration of job creation and employment growth. Job creation and employment opportunities are clustered mainly around large urban agglomerations with diversified industrial structures, particularly with large and expanding service sectors, developed infrastructures, and skilled workforces (figure 2.3). In contrast, employment prospects are dire and unemployment high in monoculture (highly specialized) industrial regions, which suffer from idiosyncratic demand shocks. For example, in Bulgaria and Moldova, employment expanded almost exclusively in the capital region (Rutkowski 2003c and 2004). Employment grew in only 4 out of 21 regions in Croatia and in 3 out of 16 regions in Poland (Rutkowski 2003c; World Bank 2001). Unemployment in rural agricultural regions is usually lower than in regions with industrial monoculture because workers in such regions have recourse to subsistence agriculture and can take temporary and seasonal jobs. In these regions, the problem is underemployment rather than open unemployment, a pattern more characteristic of developing countries.

Regional labor market disparities are not specific to countries of the Region—they also occur in developed market economies. However, transition economies stand out in two respects. First, most transition countries display a degree of variation in unemployment rates that is generally higher than in most industrial (OECD) countries. For example, the coefficient of variation of unemployment for France and the United States is roughly one-half that for the Czech Republic and one-third that for Hungary (Boeri and Scarpetta 1996; Bornhorst and Commander 2004). These large differences in regional unemployment rates are associated with strong concentration of net job creation in a few relatively economically vibrant regions and the dominance of job destruction in most other, economically depressed, regions.

Second, labor market imbalances tend to be highly persistent in transition economies.[14] Regions showing better performance at the outset have also tended to perform better in later phases. Correlation coefficients of the rank position of regions over time suggest strong persistence in the relative position of regions along different labor market indicators (Huber 2004). In other words, regions at the bottom (or at the top) of the regional distribution at the beginning of the transition were still in the same position late in the transition. Again, there are some important exceptions. Particularly in Bulgaria, Romania, and Russia, which may be considered as countries that were slightly slower in their reform process, there were some important changes in the regional distribution of unemployment rates, particularly in the early transition, and a similar observation applies to Estonia for wage levels.

FIGURE 2.3
More Workers Are Hired in Regions with a Developed Services Sector, Educated Workforce, and Infrastructure (Poland's Regions, 1997)
Panel A

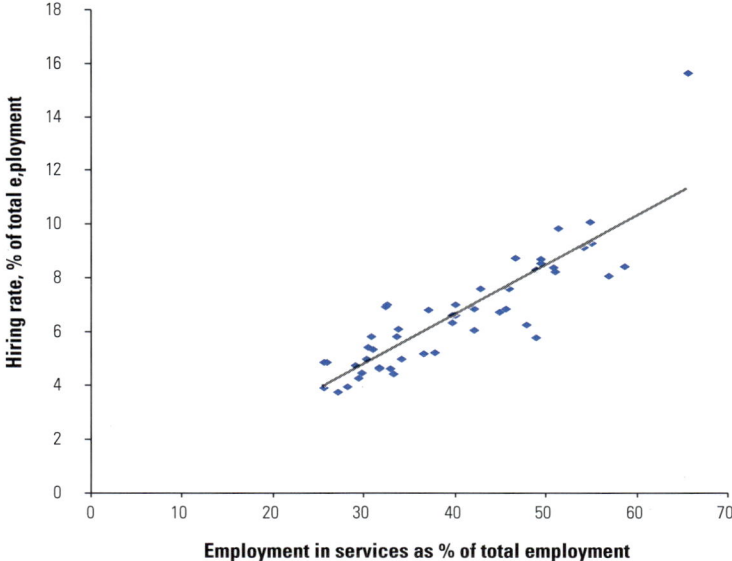

Panel B

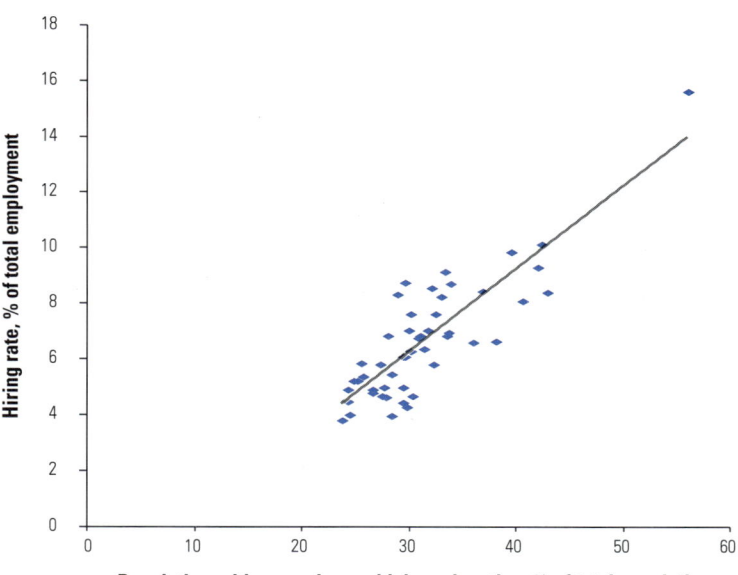

Panel C

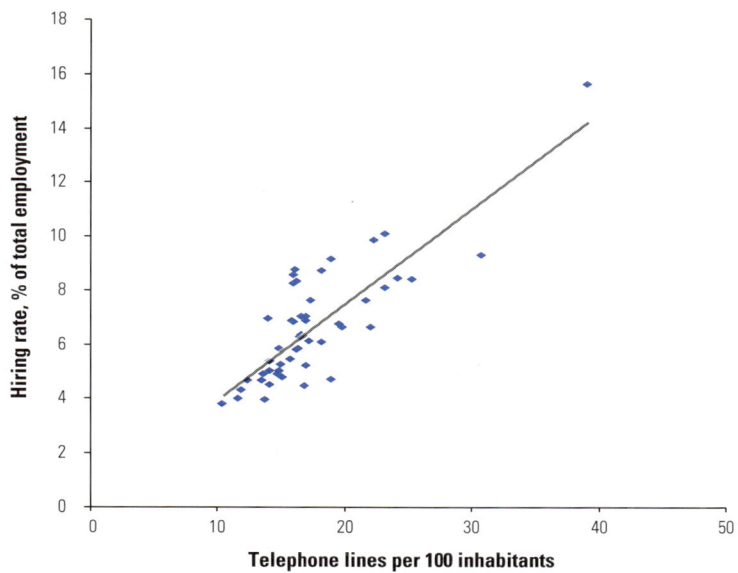

Source: Rutkowski and Przybyla 2002.

The strong persistence of regional labor market disparities suggests that they may be of a long-term rather than a transitory nature.[15] Even though some of the divergence may be transitory, regions in the long run may become clustered into two distinct groups of prosperity: one covering a relatively small number of well-off regions, the other comprising a large number of relatively poor regions. This points to the weakness of equilibrating mechanisms, such as wage adjustment or interregional labor mobility, to accommodate region-specific shocks (Boeri and Scarpetta 1996; Fidrmuc 2004; Huber 2003; Bornhorst and Commander, 2004).

Limited Labor Mobility

Interregional migration in most transition economies is low relative to that of the European Union.[16] Furthermore, results show that migration rates in transition countries have fallen during the transition, although regional disparities have widened.[17] Commuting may be a substitute for migration, but evidence is scarce that this is indeed the case. A study on Hungary points to the high cost of transport as a potential barrier to commuting (Boeri, Burda, and Köllő 1998). Still, the pattern of migration is clear: people move away from declining regions, which offer few job opportunities, to expanding regions, often the capital city and other large urban agglomerations, where employment prospects are better (box 2.7).

BOX 2.7

Internal Migration in the Region in Search of Jobs

Internal migration within transition economies generally appears quite low by international standards, and it is now declining from a peak in the early 1990s. Still, migration in the Region responds to differences in labor market conditions: people move away from regions where job opportunities are scarce toward regions offering better employment prospects—found largely in capital regions and other large urban agglomerations.

Internal flow levels increased sharply in a number of countries at the beginning of the transition. The largest of these streams were movements to national commercial and investment capitals from isolated, peripheral communities. For example, more than 1 million people relocated to more centralized areas of Russia from Siberia and the Russian North and Far East. This represents about 12 percent of the population of these areas. Russian census takers discovered nearly 13,000 "ghost towns" in peripheral regions where cities that had once existed have become fully depopulated and another 35,000 where the population had dwindled down to 10 or fewer people. This mass depopulation has been explained, apart from population aging, by large out-migration to urban areas—mainly to Moscow, where the population increased by 1.5 million from 1990 to 2002.

Similar patterns of considerable internal migration from peripheral regions to urban centers are evident in other parts of the Region. For example, although Albania and the Kyrgyz Republic have been net emigration countries since the early 1990s, the populations of Tirana and Bishkek have increased 41 and 23 percent, respectively, over the past decade as internal migration increased.[18] In Poland, a clear pattern exists of people moving to where jobs are: large net migration flows are associated with hiring rates (figure A).

Low and falling migration in the face of large regional disparities in income and unemployment rates in the transition countries presents a puzzle. A number of explanations have been put forward:

- High nationwide unemployment rates might have discouraged internal migration because they suggest a low probability of finding employment (Decressin 1994). For example, in Bulgaria in the early 2000s, the unemployment rates were high in absolute terms even in relatively low-unemployment regions (for example, 14 percent in the capital city). A similar situation occurred in Poland.

- Spatial skills mismatches occurred. Unemployed workers in declining regions (largely less-skilled blue-collar workers) might have been reluctant to migrate to expanding regions because they lacked the skills in demand in these regions (white-collar skills in

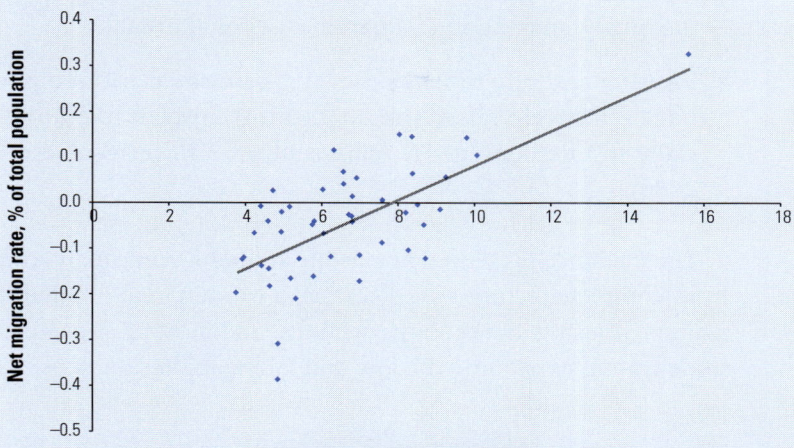

Figure A Job Opportunities Are a Driving Force behind Migration Flows
Hiring Rate and Migration Rate in Poland's Regions, 1998

Source: Rutkowski and Przybyla 2002.

Note: Each dot represents one region in Poland in 1997.

Yet, the overall trend in the Region points to declines in internal migration since the early 1990s. Much of the spike in migration, especially in CIS countries, appeared to be driven by "diaspora" migration—the return of people to their ethnic homelands—and the movement of workers away from peripheral areas that had been assigned to them or their families by the Soviet central planners. These two effects appear to have run their course, and consequently migration has slowed despite persistent income and quality-of-life differentials.

Source: World Bank staff.

the services sector). In addition, spatial matching (that is, the process by which unemployed workers find employment in other regions) might have been inefficient (Faini and others 1997).

- Social protection mechanisms, being set at national levels, provide relatively generous income support to the unemployed or the inactive in regions with low costs of living (see chapter 6 for more details), therefore discouraging migration.

- Informal sector income may induce job searchers to stay at home rather than move elsewhere in the country.

- Inefficiencies in the housing markets have likely constrained migration. This may be especially relevant in countries where rent controls are important and taxation of housing transactions is high. For example, the cost of renting a studio apartment in Warsaw represents around 70 percent of the average monthly net wage of a less-skilled worker.

- Liquidity constraints could have prevented potential migrants from moving by making the migration costs unaffordable.

- Housing and other in-kind benefits associated with employment have effectively raised the opportunity costs of migration, especially in monoenterprise regions in the CIS (Friebel and Guriev 2000).

The evidence presented in existing studies—while delivering a far-from-complete picture—suggests that a combination of liquidity constraints, housing market imperfections, and in-kind transfers may go some way in explaining the low and falling migration rates.[19]

Rebounding Real Wages, but Widening Wage Differentials

The early stage of the transition was associated with a deep drop in real wages, another manifestation of the fall in output and labor demand. During this initial stage, wages fell more in the CIS economies than in European transition economies, which was an unavoidable consequence of the limited employment adjustment to the output drop in the CIS. (In contrast, in European transition economies, the adjustment was more through employment reduction.)

Significant Wage Rebounds in the Mid-1990s

Unlike employment, wages have rebounded relatively quickly. Since the mid-1990s, real wages have grown in all transition economies at a relatively high pace.[20] However, despite the growth, in most countries the *measured* real wages are still below the pretransition level (figure 2.4), but in purchasing power, real wages have probably increased more than wage statistics suggest.[21] Notwithstanding problems with real-wage measurement, in some early reformers (that is, the Czech Republic, Hungary, and Poland), wages are already higher than before the transition.

The real-wage growth that has occurred during the second stage of the transition is a reflection of concomitant productivity improvements (see chapter 4). Productivity gains resulting from enterprise restructuring were translated into higher wages, but at the same time contributed to the low elasticity of employment in relation to output growth.[22] Therefore, the beneficiaries of productivity growth have

FIGURE 2.4
Real Wages Have Rebounded in the Mid-1990s

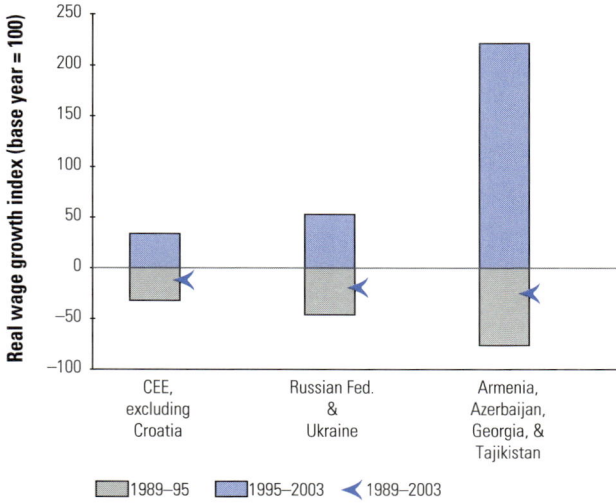

Sources: UNICEF, TransMONEE database, Bank staff calculations.

been the insiders (that is, workers with jobs) rather than the outsiders (that is, those without salaried employment).

Widening Wage Differentials

The wage distribution was compressed under central planning, resulting from the egalitarian ideology and the centralized wage-setting mechanism. Wages were not aligned with productivity, and the returns to human capital were relatively low, which dampened the incentives to invest in skills and education. The change in the wage-setting mechanism, from administrative to market-based (though this change has been less pronounced in the public sector, especially in CIS and SEE), has led to a sharp increase in wage dispersion. More-productive and expanding firms tend to pay higher wages in general, and especially to workers whose skills are in high demand.[23]

Moreover, technological progress and structural shifts, such as that from the manufacturing sector to the services sector, raised relative demand for, and thus wages of, white-collar, skilled workers. At the same time, the process implied deterioration in the relative wages of less-skilled, blue-collar workers employed in declining manufacturing industries. For example, a university-educated worker in Poland currently earns (on average) 70 percent more than a worker with basic vocational training does. In the private sector, this premium to university education is even higher (160 percent).[24] Under central planning, the differential was merely 20 percent.[25] The changes in the structure of the economy, and thus changes in relative demand for different types of labor, have given rise to various wage premiums to worker and firm characteristics (such as education, skills, occupation, industry, and location) and contributed to the increase in wage inequality. In particular, the increase in returns to education is the single most important observable factor accounting for the increase in wage inequality during the transition (box 2.8).

BOX 2.8

An Increase in Educational Wage Premiums Has Been an Important Factor behind the Rise in Wage Inequality

The rising wage inequality reflects an increase in wage premiums to various worker and firm characteristics. The increase in wage premiums to education is the most important observable factor that has caused the increase in wage dispersion in virtually all transition economies.[a] Under central planning, wage differentials between highly educated workers and less-educated workers tended to be relatively small. Evidence for CEE and Russia shows that the situation changed dramatically during the first few years of the transition (Fleisher, Peter, and Wang 2004). Wages and salaries of well-educated and highly skilled workers have gone up, while wages of less-educated workers have gone down, not only in relative terms but often also in absolute terms. These developments have led to a substantial increase in returns to education, especially to university education. At present, the annualized rate of return to education is similar or higher than that in Western European economies (Orazem and Vodopivec 1995; Vecernik 1995; Rutkowski 1996 and 2001; Kertesi and Köllő 2001; Newell and Reilly 1999; Munich, Svejnar, and Terrell 2005; Peter 2003).

The premiums to high skills and education (especially university education) are particularly high in the private sector. For example, in Poland, while less-educated workers earn the same or less in the private sector, university-educated workers (on average) earn twice as much in the private sector as they do in the public sector (Rutkowski 1998).

The pace of the increase in returns to schooling has been positively related to the speed of market reforms. Returns to education increased faster in countries where regulatory and institutional constraints on wage setting were removed earlier. For example, in Ukraine, where the pace of market reforms has been slow, the increase in returns to schooling has been modest, and they are still lower than in the faster-reforming economies of CEE and in Russia (Fleisher, Peter, and Wang 2004; Gorodnichenko and Peter 2004).

a. Evidence comes from CEE, Russia, and Ukraine. An earlier study (Newell and Reilly 1996) found that returns to university education in Uzbekistan in 1995 were significantly lower than in CEE, Russia, and Kazakhstan.

Wage inequality is presently high in virtually all transition economies; however, there are substantial differences among the Region's subgroups (figure 2.5). In European transition economies, wage inequality is high by EU standards, but still within the OECD range (although in its upper end). That is, wage disparities are large,

FIGURE 2.5

Wage Inequality in the CIS Is Higher than in the CEE

Ratios of 9th decile to 1st decile, 2002

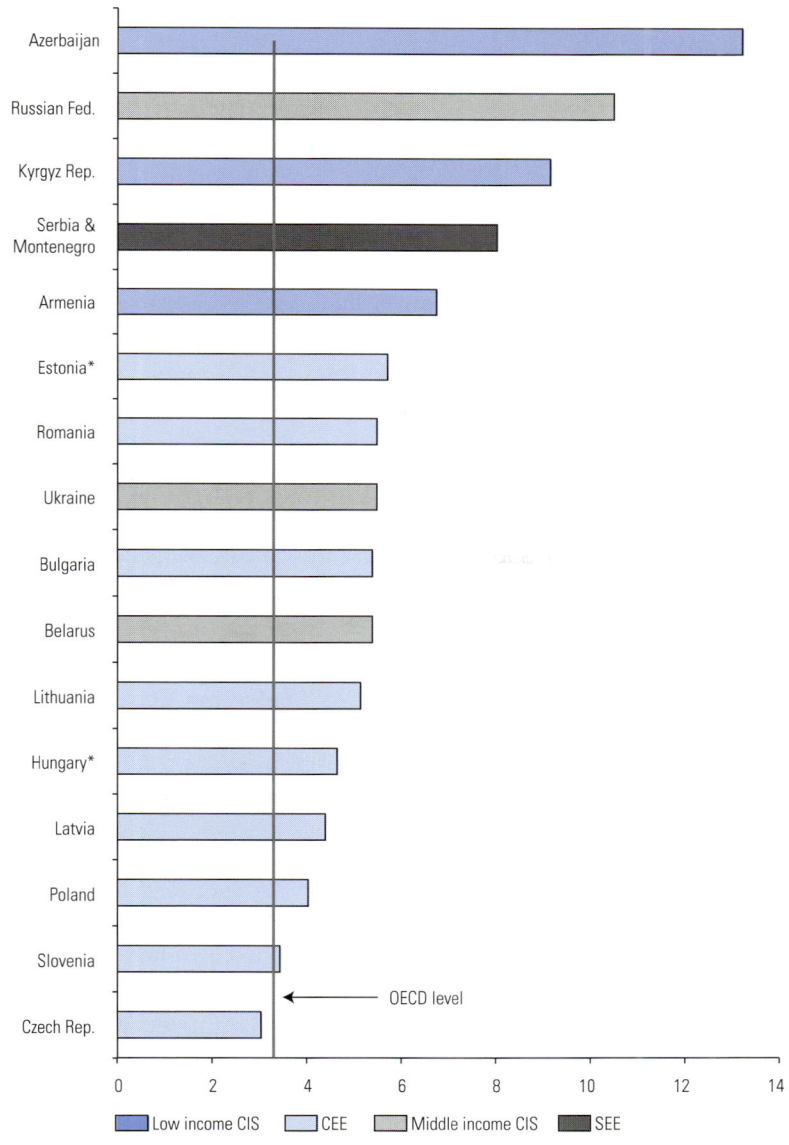

Sources: UNICEF TransMONEE database; Bank staff calculations.

Note: * Signifies 2001.

but not exorbitant. In contrast, in most of the CIS, wage disparities have reached the extremely high levels characteristic of developing countries. The gap between workers at the bottom of the wage distribution and those at the top has become dramatic. As an illustration, in EU transition economies, the top decile worker usually earns four to five times as much as the bottom decile worker. In the Kyrgyz Republic, this ratio amounts to 9, in Russia 11, and in Azerbaijan 13. In contrast, in the EU, the decile ratio varies between 3 and 4.

In CEE countries, wage distribution has widened mainly at the upper tail, which means that high wages have become more prevalent. In the CIS, the wage distribution has widened at both the lower and the upper tails, which implies the emergence of both very low and very high wages. As a result, the wage position of low-paid workers has deteriorated in the CIS much more than in CEE.

The widening earnings differentials contribute to the growing labor market segmentation in the Region.[26] In high earnings–inequality countries, the labor market is divided into the increasingly large high-wage segment and the swelling low-wage segment. The high incidence of low pay is of particular importance, as it often translates into poverty (World Bank 2000). For example, in the Czech Republic or Slovenia (where earnings inequality is relatively low), less than 5 percent of all wage and salary workers earn less than 50 percent of median earnings. In Serbia and Montenegro, this fraction exceeds 20 percent; in Russia, it goes up to 25 percent; and it reaches 30 percent in Azerbaijan.[27]

In European transition economies, minimum wages are set at a relatively high level, accounting for around 40–50 percent of the average wage. This acts as a floor on the wage distribution and is thus likely to lessen wage variation. In contrast, minimum wages in the CIS are much lower in relative terms. As a rule, they account for less than 20 percent of the average wage, often around 10 percent, which, together with weak enforcement, means that they are unlikely to be binding. This allows firms to maintain low-paid jobs and as such contributes to wage dispersion.

Wage dispersion also reflects the large disparities in regional labor market conditions discussed above. In theory, wage flexibility can act as an equilibrating mechanism and can be expected to lessen regional unemployment disparities. In practice, however, this mechanism is moderately effective, although in most CEE countries, wages were found to be responsive to regional unemployment (Huber 2004).[28] Wage flexibility is limited in many cases because of institutional factors, such as collective bargaining agreements or national minimum wages, which often do not allow for regional differences in labor market conditions. In addition, even lower wages in economically underdeveloped

The Changing Nature of Jobs during the Transition

Job security was one of the salient features of the socialist economic system that has been undermined during the transition. Under central planning, the bulk of workers had permanent, full-time jobs in state-owned companies. The transition has been associated with the emergence and expansion of self-employment and informal sector employment and—a related development—a growing incidence of irregular, casual, or temporary jobs.

Expanded Informal Sector

The size of the informal sector (measured by its share in total output or employment) varies significantly across subgroups within the Region, as well as across countries. Still, the informal sector is an important source of jobs in all subgroups and in most countries (figure 2.6). Its role in the Region is much greater than in OECD countries. The informal sector contributes to GDP nearly twice as much in CEE countries as it does in OECD countries (29 and 17 percent, respectively, in 2000).

Informality tends to be smaller—although not negligible—in the more-advanced CEE countries, while it is particularly large in economies of the CIS. In CEE, between one in five and one in four workers is engaged in the informal sector. In other European transition economies, the proportion goes up to one in three. In the CIS, every third to every second worker has an informal sector job. The cross-country variation is substantial. On one end of the spectrum are the Czech and Slovak Republics, where the informal sector accounts for around 15 percent of employment, which is close to the OECD average. The percentage is about twice as high in Bulgaria, Estonia, and Latvia and reaches 40 percent in Belarus, Russia, and Ukraine. In Azerbaijan and Kazakhstan, the informal sector accounts for half of the economy. The characteristics of jobs in the informal economy vary across countries, but also within each country across individuals (box 2.9).

Self-Employment Also Expanding

Another dimension of the change in the structure of employment during the transition is the increase in self-employment. Self-employ-

FIGURE 2.6
Informal Sector Accounts for a Substantial Share of Total Employment, Especially in CIS

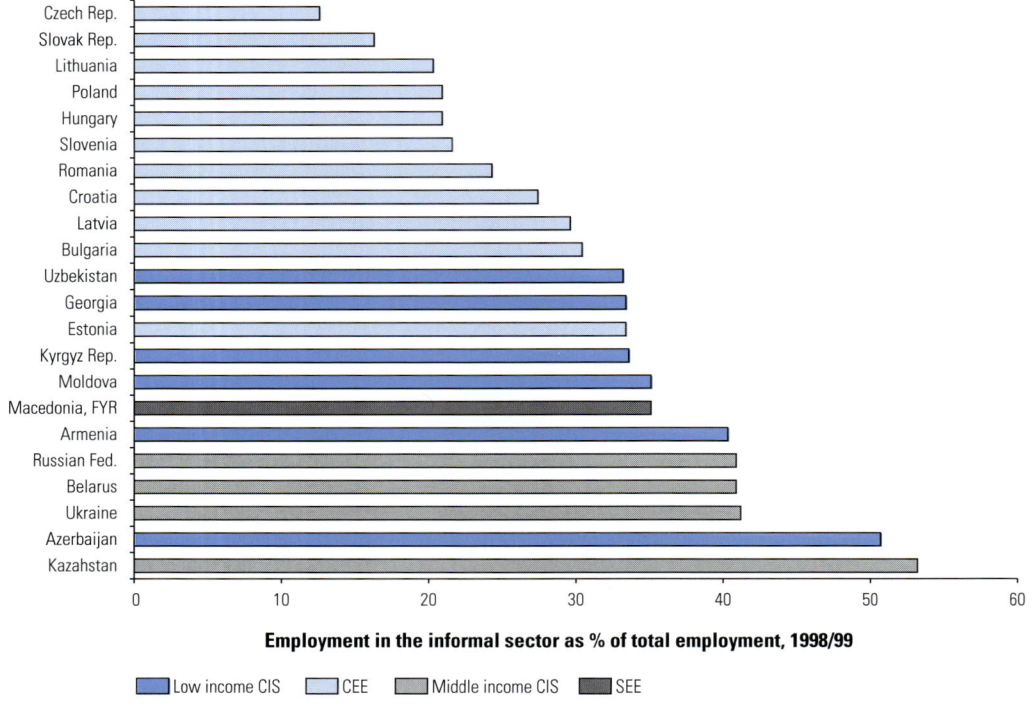

Sources: Schneider 2002; Schneider and Klingmair 2004.

BOX 2.9

The Surge in Informality during the Transition: Key Features and Policy Challenges

The characteristics of informal activities vary within each transition country and across them; nonetheless, there are some common patterns. In a number of countries in the Region, mainly in CEE, the rise in informal activities is associated with high taxes and strict regulations in product and labor markets. In other countries, including the low income CIS group, the informal economy has a clear rural connotation and has played the role of an employer of last resort to provide subsistence income.

Different motives drive firms and workers into informality. Many small firms choose to stay informal because fixed costs—such as licenses or permit fees (and even bribes)—tend to impose a disproportionate burden on them, and they prefer to remain invisible to public officials. Professional workers may prefer to develop their own activities as self-employment rather than working as employees when taxes on labor use are high and social benefits from affiliation to

(continues on the following page)

BOX 2.9 (continued)

the social security uncertain. At the same time, informal employment may be the only available alternative for less-skilled workers displaced in the wake of enterprise restructuring.

Microeconomic evidence from Household Panel Data in four transition economies (Albania, Georgia, Hungary, and Ukraine) sheds some light on the incidence of informality[29] and self-employment across different groups of workers and on the mobility in and out of informality and self-employment.

The incidence of informality varies substantially across different workers. The youth, poorly educated, and unskilled blue-collar workers are disproportionately represented among the informal workers. In Ukraine, for example, unskilled workers account for one-third of informal sector employment, compared with less than one-fifth of formal sector employment. In Hungary, the unskilled account for about 70 percent of informal workers, while they account for only 50 percent of formal sector workers. In pay, informal sector jobs are comparable to formal sector jobs, once due account is taken of individual and firm-specific characteristics. In other words, the observed wage differentials between formal and informal sector jobs are largely the result of selection of workers in the two sectors; low-skilled and less-experienced workers tend to be sorted into informal jobs, often in small firms with low-productivity potentials. At the same time, high-skilled workers in self-employment tend to earn more than similar workers in formal sector jobs, especially when taking account is made of the fact that they tend to work longer hours.

The analysis of the transition across the different types of jobs in the Region suggests a number of common patterns across countries:

- In all countries, informal workers have a higher chance of moving into unemployment than into formal jobs.

- At the same time, exit from unemployment is more likely to take place to an informal job than to a formal one.

- Mobility into and out of self-employment is more limited than mobility into and out of informality.

- Informality and self-employment are also more likely entry points into the labor market than formal employment is.

Individual characteristics not only affect the type of job that workers hold but also their chances of moving from one type of job to another. In all four countries, young workers are more mobile than adults and especially older workers. The unskilled are generally more mobile than skilled workers and are more likely to move into informality than skilled workers. Finally, women have less access to self-employment and more likely to be in formal employment than in informal jobs. However, they also have higher chances of moving out of the labor force if they lose their formal job.

Source: Duryea and others 2005.

ment plays the most important part in low income CIS countries, where (on average) it accounts for 50 percent of total employment. The share of self-employment is much lower in middle income CIS countries (17 percent) and in CEE (20 percent). By way of comparison, in EU-15 countries, self-employment accounts for about 15 percent of total employment.

What are the reasons behind the surge in self-employment? On one hand, people are *pushed* into self-employment by a lack of work opportunities. In this case, self-employment is the only available means of earning subsistence income. Sometimes employers also force workers into self-employment to lower hiring and firing costs. For example, in Bulgaria and Poland, some health care sector employees were turned into independent self-employed contractors. This obviously inflated the number of self-employed, although there was no corresponding change in the nature of jobs. On the other hand, people can be *pulled* into self-employment if the expected benefits, mainly earnings, exceed those of wage employment. Self-employment, then, is a voluntary welfare-maximizing choice among different alternatives. In such a case, self-employment often becomes a springboard for firm creation.

In reality, self-employed workers make up both categories—aspiring entrepreneurs and those for whom self-employment is a last-resort grasping for survival where regular jobs are scarce and poorly paid. However, there is some evidence that in the Region, the push factors tend to prevail and that most of the self-employed resort to self-employment to avoid unemployment and earn at least subsistence income (Earle and Sakova 2000; Verme 2004). The recourse to subsistence agriculture (as has happened in Poland, FYR Macedonia, and Romania and in the most of the CIS) supports this point.

Service Sector Jobs Replacing Manufacturing Jobs

The reallocation of jobs and labor, which has been an integral part of the transition, entailed an increase in service sector employment and a decline in manufacturing employment. The expansion of the service sector has been more pronounced in CEE than in the CIS. For example, the share of market services in total employment during the 1990s went up by about 14 percentage points in Estonia, but only by a mere 2 percentage points in Russia (see chapter 4 for more details).

Deindustrialization and the expansion of the service sector have been associated with the change in the skill profile of labor demand. The skill content of jobs has shifted upward, especially in the new sector. Jobs destroyed during the transition were disproportionately low-skilled, blue-collar jobs. In contrast, newly created jobs tend to require higher educational attainment and white-collar skills. Thus, job creation in the new sector has been biased against low-skilled workers, largely because of skill-biased technological change. For example, in Estonia, the share of nonmanual workers in total employment increased by 8 percentage points during 1990–2000, so that presently nonmanual workers account for 55 percent of total employment. In Russia, the share of workers with higher education increased by 6 percentage points during 1992–2000, and it currently exceeds 20 percent of the workforce. A similar increase occurred in Poland and other CEE economies (Peter 2003). Clearly, job destruction has fallen mostly on manual workers, who are mainly unskilled (Commander and Köllő 2004). This mismatch between the skill content of jobs that are being destroyed in the old sector and those that are being created in the new sector contributes to structural unemployment in transition economies.[30]

Labor Market Outcomes: Disappointing during the Transition?

In most cases, the labor market outcomes that have emerged during the transition were expected and have been an unavoidable consequence of the profound institutional changes and restructuring associated with the transition. Some unemployment, for instance, is a natural phenomenon in a market economy, in which workers continuously move across jobs and the process is not frictionless. In addition, the pace of industrial restructuring, which is a salient characteristic of the transition, is bound to contribute to unemployment by creating structural mismatches.

Persistent Unemployment and Growing Labor Market Disparities: Sources of Concern

There have been, however, a few unpredicted, negative outcomes. The first is persistently high unemployment and the long duration of unemployment periods. High unemployment was expected to be transient. It was assumed that a fast-growing private sector would soon absorb workers released from the shrinking public sector, so that workers would experience only relatively short periods of unemployment. This has proved not to be the case. Workers who lost their jobs found it extremely difficult to find new ones because the pace of job creation lagged behind the pace of job destruction for a long time (see Chapter 4). As a result, unemployment has become a stagnant pool. Only in those countries such as the Baltic States, where the rate of job creation has picked up and caught up with the rate of job destruction, have outflows from unemployment increased and unemployment started to decline.

The second outcome has been the sharp increase in, and high level of, wage inequalities. Again, some increase in wage inequality was expected and was a desirable phenomenon, improving labor market incentives. However, in many countries, wage inequalities have reached extremely high levels.[31] This may undermine the sense of fairness and negatively affect worker morale and motivation. Moreover, wage inequalities translate into income inequalities and thus can have a negative effect on poverty.

The third unanticipated, negative outcome has been the development of dual labor markets: the often shrinking formal sector offering considerable employment protection, and the growing informal sector promising little job security. This can be mainly traced to high labor taxes and to strict labor regulations. But while for some workers, mainly in the poorer CIS countries, the informal sector is the employer of last resort, for others, mainly in richer CEE countries, it is a preferred alternative to work in the formal sector, offering better earning opportunities and more scope for entrepreneurship.

The fourth unexpected outcome was the significant growth of regional labor market disparities. This largely reflects strong regional concentration of job creation and high unemployment coinciding with low wages. A few centers of job creation and good employment prospects have emerged, surrounded by depressed regions where few new jobs are being created and employment opportunities are scarce.

These negative labor market outcomes—in particular, the high and persistent unemployment along with high wage inequality—have a number of important welfare implications:[32]

- The underutilization of labor resources translates into lower output and therefore lower welfare.

- Unemployment and wage disparities translate into even larger income inequalities.

- Large income inequalities imply, all else being equal, higher poverty rates.

- Long-term unemployment and persistent poverty often lead to social exclusion.

- Unemployment, inequality, and eventually poverty carry high economic, social, and political costs.

For all these reasons, improving labor market performance is critical for poverty reduction and the political sustainability of market-oriented reforms.

A widespread assumption concerning labor market outcomes during the transition was that they would initially deteriorate because of intensive restructuring, but then improve as the reforms started to bear fruit. Put differently, one could hypothesize that changes in labor market outcomes are U-shaped. Is this hypothesis borne out by the evidence? Although the transition has been under way for more than 10 years, it is too early to tell. It has taken longer for labor markets to adjust to the transition shock than initially assumed, and the process of transformation is still far from complete, at least from a microperspective (see below). Therefore, one currently observes a dynamic process whereby key labor market variables, such as employment and unemployment, continue to adjust to various shocks associated with the transition. Present levels of employment and unemployment are thus unlikely to represent steady-state values. Some countries, where reforms have been slow, are still on the downward slope of the U curve. That is, employment is relatively high and open unemployment low, as for example in Moldova or Ukraine. Other countries are close to the bottom of the U (that is, unemployment is high and employment low, such as in Bulgaria or Poland). But it seems that some countries have already started to move up the right-hand side of the U curve (that is, employment has started to increase and unemployment to fall). Examples include the Baltic States of Estonia, Latvia, and Lithuania, as well as Bulgaria and Hungary. Particularly in the Baltic States, the employment rate, after being well below the EU average, is presently quite close to it. The gap is narrowing.

It is noteworthy that the EU average employment rate is significantly below the one that was prevailing under central planning. This suggests that there is probably no return to the extraordinarily high employment rates observed before the transition (at least in the short to medium term). But reaching the current EU average employment rate should not be seen as the ultimate objective. After all, this rate is considered too low by the EU, as illustrated by the Lisbon target of raising the employment rate to 70 percent of the working-age population from the current level of 65 percent. Therefore, even in the most successful transition economies, there is room for improving labor market performance.

Summary: Key Stylized Facts on Labor Market Transition in the Region

The main features of labor market transition in the Region can be summarized as follows:

- Transition has led to a substantial underutilization of labor, negatively affecting social welfare and growth prospects. However, the adjustment to the transition shock has taken different forms in various subgroups of the Region. In the European transition economies, the job fall has translated into open unemployment. Within this group, there are differences in labor market conditions associated with the pace of enterprise restructuring and the rate of job creation. In the CIS, the fall in labor demand has led largely to underemployment (hidden unemployment). Many workers hold low-productivity jobs in unrestructured and unprofitable enterprises, in the informal sector, and in subsistence agriculture, which is the employer of last resort.

- Limited job opportunities have also led to discouragement and massive labor force withdrawal, especially among younger and older cohorts, as well as women. The combined effect of unemployment and labor force withdrawal was a substantial fall in the employment-to-population ratio. This fall was stronger in European transition economies than in CIS countries.

- The low open unemployment and high employment rates that prevail in many CIS countries hide significant problems in their labor markets. They often indicate delayed enterprise restructuring with persistent overstaffing and—especially in low income CIS countries—to the dominance of low-productivity jobs in the informal sector to earn subsistence income. The latter feature is typical of developing countries, where social protection is lacking and so for most workers unemployment is not an affordable option.

- Coping strategies of displaced workers differed between European and CIS transition economies, too. In European transition economies, many displaced and discouraged workers took advantage of relatively generous nonwork benefits (early retirement and disability pensions, unemployment benefits, and social assistance). In most CIS countries, these benefits are less available and many laid-off workers have moved to subsistence agriculture, self-employment, and casual work in the informal sector.

- Although the emergence of unemployment in the wake of the transition was expected, its persistence is a source of major concern. In particular, outflows from unemployment to jobs have been low in many cases, leading to a buildup of a large pool of long-term unemployed, with a negative effect on their employment prospects.

- Real wages fell sharply during the early phase of the transition, but have rebounded since the mid-1990s, following the resumption of economic growth. The fall in wages was much more pronounced in the CIS economies (where enterprises restructured slowly and were reluctant to lay off workers) than in European economies (where enterprises restructured by shedding redundant labor). The uniform wage growth during the second stage of the transition (when economic growth resumed), coupled with limited, if any, employment growth, implies that output and associated productivity growth are translated into higher wages, rather than into higher employment.

- Wage inequalities have increased substantially across the Region; however, the increase has been more moderate in European than in CIS transition economies. As a result, the current level of earnings inequality is still relatively modest in CEE and SEE, while it is very high by international standards in most CIS countries. One important driving force behind the growth in wage inequalities has been the increase in returns to education and high (white-collar) skills. However, wage inequalities also reflect firm-specific characteristics, such as profitability, ownership, industry affiliation, location, and so forth.

- The segmentation of the labor markets has been an important feature of the transition in the Region's countries. Although the informal sector has become sizable in European transition economies (by European standards), it often accounts for the bulk of the private sector in some low income CIS countries, resembling developing countries in this respect. In European transition economies, the informal sector is mainly driven by tax evasion, as well as by the avoidance of strict regulations. In contrast, in CIS countries, the informal sector is largely the employer of last resort. The informal sector there is concentrated in agriculture, while in European transition economies, it is concentrated in the expanding services sector. The growth of the informal sector is associated with the increased incidence of casual jobs, as well as with self-employment.

- Regional disparities in labor market conditions across the Region are large and persistent. Job creation and employment prospects are heavily concentrated around large urban agglomerations with diversified economic structures and, in particular, an expanding service sector. These growth poles are surrounded by economically depressed regions, often one-company towns, where job opportunities are scarce and unemployment is high. Equilibrating forces are too weak to alleviate the imbalances. Labor mobility in the Region is relatively low, resulting from (among other things) an underdeveloped housing market. Although regional wages tend to respond to regional unemployment, this is not enough to entice the entry of new firms and investment, which are prerequisites for job creation.

- Labor market transition has created both losers and winners. The former include less-skilled blue-collar workers in declining industries and regions, among whom unemployment is high and wages are low and falling in relative terms. The latter constitute well-educated white-collar workers who find employment mainly in the expanding services sector and who command high wages. The dramatic shift of labor demand away from low-skilled labor—giving rise to high unemployment and the fall in relative wages—is one of the most notable features of labor market transition in the Region.

- There are signs of an emerging divide between labor markets in the transition economies of Europe and those of Central Asia. Labor markets in European transition economies in many respects resemble those in developed economies of Europe, in both positive (for example, productivity growth) and negative aspects (for example, high and stagnant unemployment). In contrast, labor markets in low-income CIS countries seem to become similar to those in other low-income countries, with typical characteristics such as the dominant informal sector, underemployment, and low-productivity employment.

Notes

1. The study focuses on the transition economies of Eastern Europe and the Former Soviet Union. The transition economies of Eastern Europe and the Former Soviet Union, plus Turkey, are all part of the World Bank's Europe and Central Asia (ECA) Region. Labor market developments in Turkey are discussed in a separate box (box 2.2). Turkmenistan is not covered in this chapter because of lack of reliable data.
2. Self-employment and informal sector employment have acted as shock absorbers in many transition economies, providing a source of earnings and helping the displaced workers to avoid poverty. At the same time, informal sector jobs in the CIS are often of low productivity and casual in nature.
3. See annex 1.1 for the country grouping within the Region.
4. The scope of this chapter is limited to the presentation of basic labor market trends and patterns in the Region. A comprehensive overview of labor markets during the transition is provided in Svejnar (1999). Useful analysis of labor market outcomes during the transition is also provided in Boeri and Terrell (2002), Riboud and others (2002), and Haltiwanger, Scarpetta, and Vodopivec (2003).

5. Turkey's GDP per capita at PPP is close to that of the average for SEE and middle income CIS.
6. This report uses internationally comparable indicators of unemployment based on the labor force surveys. For some countries, however, these data are not available, and the report refers to administrative data on unemployment as collected by labor offices. These latter data are not fully comparable with those of other countries and may also vary over time because of changes in unemployment benefit systems that change the incentives for the unemployed to register with the labor offices.
7. However, employment has started to grow in Hungary since the early 2000s, while it has continued to decline in Poland, so the employment rates in both countries have diverged.
8. Female labor force participation rates continue to be high in most transition economies. Before the transition, they were extraordinarily high by international standards, so their fall may represent a movement toward an equilibrium. The fall in the youth labor force participation, in turn, partly reflects the increased demand for higher education, which has led to a dramatic increase in college enrollments. For example, in Russia, the number of college students increased more than two times during the transition.
9. Outflows from unemployment to jobs account for about two-thirds of all outflows from unemployment (the other being to inactivity), so doubling the outflows-to-jobs rate (holding the outflows-to-inactivity rate constant) results in shortening the average duration of unemployment and thus lowering the unemployment rate by one-fourth.
10. Russia does not fully fit into this pattern because the labor market there is quite vibrant, providing jobs to migrants from other CIS countries. Still, many jobs are in the informal sector and of low productivity. For example, according to Goskomstat (Russian Federation State Statistics Committee) data, more than 40 percent of firms in Russia were reporting losses in 2002.
11. Measurement of employment and its changes is not straightforward, and various sources, using different definitions, show somewhat different trends. In particular, employment data coming from household-based surveys (for example, labor force surveys and household budget surveys) differ from those coming from establishment-based surveys. The former cover self-employment and informal employment in addition to regular employment and thus use a broader definition of employment than the latter, which cover only regular (registered) employment.
12. In the OECD countries, the ratio of the maximum to the minimum regional unemployment rate is around 3. The coefficient of variation in most cases is in the range of 25 to 30 percent (OECD 2000). These values should be regarded as illustrative only because they depend on the number and size of regions. In general, the greater the level of aggregation (that is, the larger the regions), the less is the variation in unemployment rates.
13. Regional variations in labor market conditions in Russia are less pronounced and similar to those in CEE if one weighs regional indicators by the labor force.
14. Regional disparities also tend to be persistent in many Western European economies (Italy being the best-known example), but much less so in the United States. A high degree of persistence in transition economies is

somewhat surprising, given the large-scale reallocation of resources associated with the transition.
15. Recent econometric evidence by Römisch (2001) for EU-accession candidate countries and new member states, by Profit (1999) for the Czech Republic, and by Solanko (2003) and Granberg and Zaitseva (2002) for Russia, supports this hypothesis. They find that divergence has been accompanied by an increased polarization of regions.
16. Fidrmuc (2004), comparing internal migration in the Czech Republic, Hungary, Poland, the Slovak Republic, and Slovenia with that in Germany, Italy, the Netherlands, and Spain, concludes that migration rates are largely ineffective in reducing regional disparities in the new EU countries. Ederveen and Bardsley (2003) find evidence that, after controlling for methodological and data construction differences between studies, migration in the new EU countries is less reactive in particular to differences in unemployment rates. In addition, Andrienko and Guriev (2003) state that overall migration in Russia is low, although Russia is the only country—aside from Hungary—where migration rates approach European levels, but clearly fall short of U.S. levels (EBRD 2003).
17. Fidrmuc (2004) for the big central European candidate countries, Hazans (2004) for the Baltic states, Kallai (2003) for Romania, and Andrienko and Guriev (2003) for Russia all find this decline in migration rates to be a stylized fact of the transition period in the countries they analyze.
18. Caution is required in interpreting these finding as these studies may differ in methodology and definitions. The cross-country comparability of migration rates is limited as these depend on the size and degree of homogeneity of regions and these vary across countries.
19. Kallai (2003) and Andrienko and Guriev (2003) provide some evidence on the importance of liquidity constraints in shaping migration in Russia and Romania. Bornhorst and Commander (2004) argue that housing market imperfections are an important aspect.
20. The substantial real-wage growth despite high unemployment reflects a combination of market and institutional forces: employers maximizing profits by using efficiency wages (that is, wages set above the market-clearing level so as to motivate workers), union pressures, and government wage policies.
21. The purchasing power of wages under central planning was overestimated because prices of many consumer goods were set below the equilibrium level, as attested by widespread shortages. Therefore, the fall in real wages during the initial stage of the transition, when prices were liberalized, was most probably overestimated.
22. One reason why productivity gains have been translated into higher wages rather than employment is that they have been largely achieved through defensive restructuring by firms—that is, by eliminating overstaffing and shedding redundant labor (see chapter 4). High hiring and firing costs may have contributed to this process (see chapter 6).
23. There is some econometric evidence that in Russia the relationship between a firm's wage rates and its performance (profitability or productivity) is particularly strong—stronger than in CEE countries. This points

to a less-competitive labor market in Russia because, under perfect competition, wages are independent of firm performance (Gimpelson and Kapelyushnikov 2005).
24. Background calculations for the World Bank (2001), using data from the firm-based 1998 Survey of Earnings.
25. Rutkowski 1996.
26. The contribution of wage inequality to overall income inequality is substantially larger in CEE, where wages account for a high share of total income, than in the CIS, where wages account for a much lower share (World Bank 2000).
27. Earnings dispersion and thus the incidence of low pay may be overestimated as a result of the practice of underreporting wages to avoid taxes on labor.
28. The estimation of the so-called wage curve, which is the relationship between individuals' wages and regional unemployment rates (controlling for human capital and other characteristics), shows that for a sample of CEE countries, wages are at least as responsive to regional unemployment rates as in most developed market economies (Huber 2004).
29. Informal employees are identified as those who do not have a written contract or who are not affiliated with the social security system.
30. In principle, the skill-mismatch problem can be addressed by training programs. However, in practice, the potential of training programs to successfully address large skills mismatches is limited. First, if the skill profile of displaced workers is much different from the skill profile of new jobs, then successful retraining can be extremely, perhaps prohibitively, expensive. Second, for retraining to be successful, there need to be unfilled vacancies for which the training participants can apply. If, however, job openings are few, as is often the case in transition economies, then training is of little help in finding a new job. Existing evaluation of training programs indeed confirms that training is not an efficient tool for addressing mass unemployment resulting from large-scale industrial restructuring (Betcherman, Olivas, and Dar 2004).
31. It is an open question whether existing wage differentials reflect a labor market equilibrium or are still of a disequilibrium nature.
32. The term "unemployment" is used in its broad meaning, which covers workers of working age who withdraw from the labor force, as well as different forms of underemployment.

CHAPTER 3

Macroeconomic Policy, Output, and Employment: Is There Evidence of Jobless Growth?

This chapter looks at the links between economic growth and employment trends in the countries of the Region during the transition to a market economy and assesses the possible roles of macroeconomic policies in shaping these links. Output and employment fell significantly in the early phases of the transition in all countries of the Region. In the subsequent phases of output recovery, employment has been somewhat slow to grow, giving rise to the concern that the transition countries were developing symptoms of a jobless growth, or at least of low-employment-content growth.

The macroeconomic performance of transition economies is marked by two major episodes of output loss, which have also affected the links between subsequent output and employment. The first was the widely documented transitional recession; the second was the recession following the 1998 Russian financial crisis. During the first episode, the output loss brought a decrease in employment and an increase in unemployment. Yet, such labor market adjustment was smaller in the CIS countries than in CEE countries, partly because the former group of countries experienced large wage flexibility.

This chapter argues that the labor market response to the second episode was different in CEE countries that had progressed the most in the transition. In those countries, the output recovery was not associated with job creation. This chapter assesses whether jobless growth in those CEE countries can be accounted for by a particular set of macroeconomic conditions. It suggests that the positive link between employment and output growth was potentially still present, but it was counterbalanced by a combination of high real interest rates and a loose underlying fiscal policy. In the years to come, low real interest rates, possibly linked to euro adoption, and strong emphasis on fiscal discipline may prove beneficial for the job-creation potential of CEE countries.

This chapter is organized as follows: Section 1 analyzes the relationship between output and labor market variables during the different transition periods. Section 2 discusses the possible channels through which macroeconomic policies might have lessened the responsiveness of employment to economic growth. Section 3 presents the employment outlook in CEE, in view of EU accession, and in the CIS, given the delayed restructuring.

The Employment-Output Link during the Different Phases of the Transition

The pace and depth of restructuring and the macro- and micropolicy stances largely influence labor market developments in transition economies. The noticeable feature of the transition in most of the countries of the Region is that output recoveries have not been associated with major rebounds in employment growth. A good starting point is to describe the various contributions of the labor market to per capita growth. To this end, figure 3.1 presents output per capita growth decomposed into labor-productivity growth, changes in the employment rate (employment divided by the working-age population), and changes in demography (working-age population divided by total population).

The Response of Employment to Output Has Changed.

Two main phases can be identified, each characterized by a different response of the labor market to output performance. The first phase refers to the transitional recession, while the second phase starts with the 1998–99 financial crisis in Russia and extends to the most recent years.[1] Not surprisingly, when output declined in the first phase, employment fell and was only partially compensated by increases in productivity. But even when output growth resumed in the second phase, it was largely driven by productivity growth, with further declines in employment in most countries.

FIGURE 3.1
Output per Capita Growth Is Largely Driven by Productivity Growth

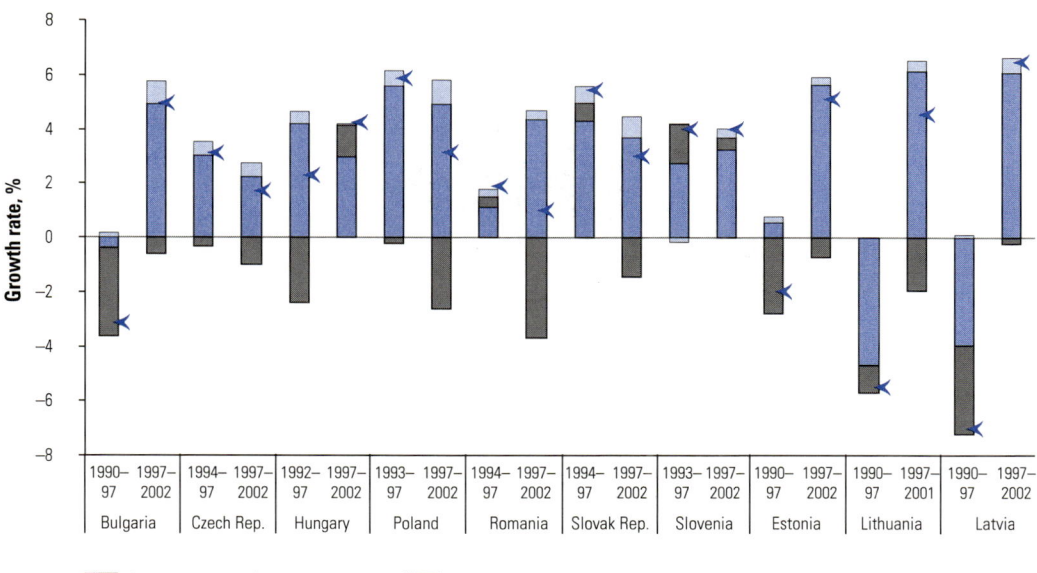

Source: Bank staff calculations.

The (quantity-based) labor market response to output losses in the first phase was larger in CEE than in the low income CIS countries, Russia, and Ukraine. This resulted from the more intense process of economic restructuring in the former countries, which inevitably involved quantity adjustments. But it also resulted from the greater downward rigidity in real wages in CEE countries, compared with that in Russia, Ukraine, and other CIS countries.

The labor market response to the second episode was different in the CEE countries. Although the output decline associated with the 1998–99 Russian financial crisis again led to job losses, the subsequent recovery did not generate marked net job creation in CEE countries. What has been the relative importance of macroshocks in shaping key labor market outcomes? How pervasive are jobless growth and high structural unemployment? And what is the relationship between the labor market outcomes and the macroeconomic policy stance?

Until 1997, Output and Employment Moved in Tandem in CEE Countries

Table 3.1 presents correlations between the key macroeconomic variables (GDP growth and inflation) and labor market outcomes (changes in unemployment, employment, and real-wage growth). In the transitional recession period, GDP and employment changes were strongly and positively correlated in CEE, suggesting that there were employment losses during the early recession while employment started to improve as growth gained momentum. A similar picture emerges when one looks at the correlation between changes in output and unemployment. In other words, during the initial phase of the transition, employment was responsive to changes in output.

In the CIS countries, the elasticity of employment in relation to output was insignificant in the first stage of the transition, while the wage output correlation was strong. This suggests that in the initial period of the transition, price (real-wage) adjustments were more important than quantity (employment) adjustments in the CIS.

In Recent Years, Employment Seems to Be Less Responsive to Output

The labor market response during the second phase of the transition was different. This phase began with a balance-of-payments crisis in the Czech Republic and the Russian financial crisis and covered the 1998 recession, with the subsequent strong output recovery in CEE and in Russia, Ukraine, and the low income CIS countries. However, consistent with a weaker employment output correlation (table 3.1) compared with the first stage of the transition, the subsequent output recovery was not associated with job creation in a subset of CEE countries.

Jobless growth was not uniform across CEE countries. There were some obvious exceptions, such as Hungary (which experienced only one year of jobless growth), the Czech Republic (which experienced two episodes of more than 3 percent growth with modest job destruction), and the Slovak Republic. Conversely, countries such as Bulgaria, Lithuania, Poland, and Romania had several years of jobless growth.

At the same time in the CIS group, the employment output correlation has become stronger in the more recent period, while the wage output correlation has weakened.

It is also noticeable that inflation and changes in unemployment were positively correlated during the first phase of the transition. This suggests that inflation was associated with the start of economic restructuring, the absorption of monetary overhang, and an overall collapse of the centrally planned economy inherited from the previous system and that such inflation was close to the hyperinflation limit. By the mid-1990s, inflation had declined everywhere below the 20 percent threshold (figure 3.2). Noticeably, the reduction in inflation was accompanied

TABLE 3.1
Significant Changes in the Correlation between Macroeconomic Variables and Labor Market Indicators
(Contemporaneous Correlations between GDP Growth and a Set of Macro Variables)

First Episode: 1990–97	Real GDP growth	Inflation	Real-wage growth	Employment growth
CEE countries				
Real GDP growth	1.00			
	—			
Inflation	−0.59	1.00		
	0.00	—		
Real-wage growth	0.60	−0.37	1.00	
	0.00	0.01	—	
Employment growth	0.46	−0.20	0.19	1.00
	0.00	0.16	0.25	—
Change in unemployment	−0.55	0.10	−0.29	−0.60
	0.00	0.43	0.03	0.00
CIS countries				
Real GDP growth	1.00			
	—			
Inflation	−0.28	1.00		
	0.01	—		
Real-wage growth	0.44	−0.37	1.00	
	0.00	0.02	—	
Employment growth	−0.01	−0.12	0.19	1.00
	0.94	0.41	0.32	—
Change in unemployment	0.05	0.13	−0.01	−0.02
	0.75	0.43	0.95	0.90
Second Episode: 1998–2003	**Real GDP growth**	**Inflation**	**Real-wage growth**	**Employment growth**
CEE countries				
Real GDP growth	1.00			
	—			
Inflation	−0.36	1.00		
	0.00	—		
Real-wage growth	0.30	−0.18	1.00	
	0.02	0.17	—	
Employment growth	0.29	0.03	−0.01	1.00
	0.03	0.80	0.96	—
Change in unemployment	−0.40	−0.11	−0.11	−0.39
	0.00	0.38	0.42	0.01
CIS countries				
Real GDP growth	1.00			
	—			
Inflation	−0.15	1.00		
	0.19	—		
Real-wage growth	0.30	−0.56	1.00	
	0.06	0.00	—	
Employment growth	0.17	0.08	0.22	1.00
	0.22	0.56	0.21	—
Change in unemployment	−0.19	0.01	0.09	−0.32
	0.21	0.98	0.64	0.04

Sources: Bank staff calculations; Boeri and Garibaldi 2004.

Note: p-value in italics; — = not available.

by a convergence in macroeconomic developments within each group of countries. Differences across groups were still large by the mid-1990s and reflected differences in the initial trajectories: early inflation was much more moderate in CEE than in the CIS countries.

Real Wages and the Pace of Restructuring Affected the Output-Job Links

Why was the quantity adjustment larger in CEE countries than in the other transition economies? There are different but interrelated explanations for this. When CEE countries started the transition, they had in place effective safety nets, notably relatively generous unemployment benefit systems and social assistance of the last resort schemes, which constrained wage adjustment from below.[2] This

FIGURE 3.2
Inflationary Pressures Have Declined over Time in Most Countries

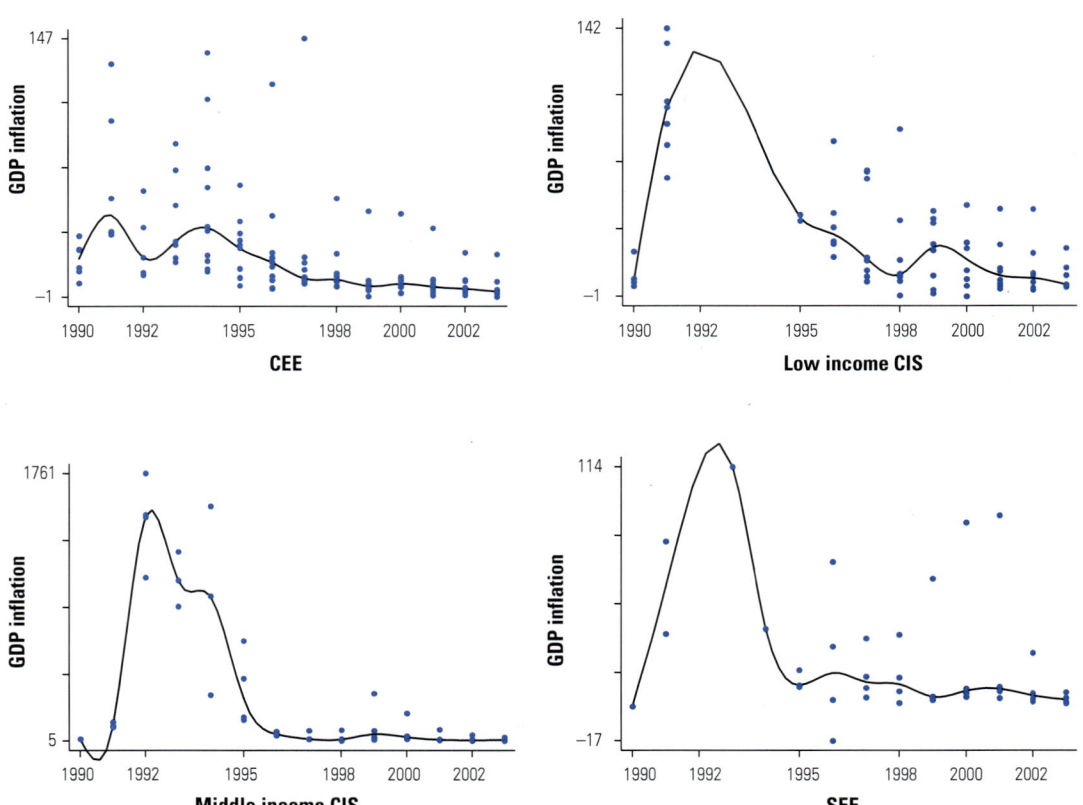

Sources: World Development Indicators; Boeri and Garibaldi 2004.

Note: Inflation (GDP deflator) 1990–2003.

induced more job destruction than in the CIS, where wages ended up bearing most of the costs of adjustment (figure 3.3). Within-group variation in the levels of unemployment in CEE can also be explained in institutions moving the labor force participation margins (see chapter 6). In some countries, the decline in employment rates was mainly accompanied by the growth of unemployment; in other countries, it was the rise of inactivity that mainly absorbed employment declines (see chapter 2). Finally, the pace of sectoral reallocation largely affected (and was influenced by) the possibility of using wage adjustments instead of labor mobility to accommodate the transition shocks. In countries (mainly CEE—see chapter 4) where sectoral transformation proceeded speedily, labor had to be relocated across firms, industries, and locations, and the price adjustment could not substitute for that. At the same time, the greater willingness of workers to move because of the presence of safety nets probably contributed to speeding up the sectoral transformation.

The behavior of real wages is also consistent with this interpretation. Indeed, as suggested by figure 3.4, real-wage adjustments in CEE countries were much less marked than in the CIS.[3] In the latter group of countries, the cumulative decline in real wages during the transitional recession was on the order of 60–70 percent, compared with 20–25 percent in CEE. Later on, the CIS also experienced a rapid recovery, interrupted only in 1999, while real-wage evolutions in CEE flattened out at one-digit rates.

FIGURE 3.3
Employment Adjustment Has Been More Marked in CEE than in CIS Countries

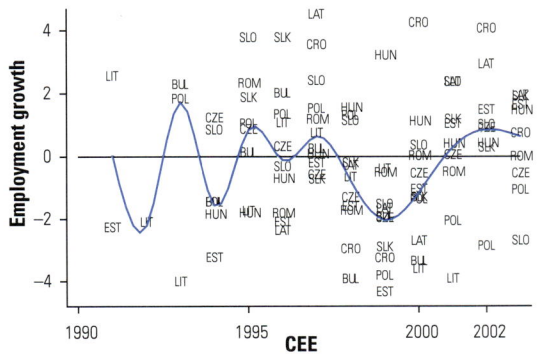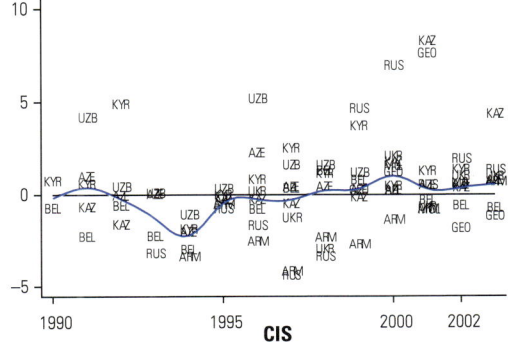

Sources: ILO (LABORSTA database); Boeri and Garibaldi 2004.

Note: Employment growth in CEE and low and middle income CIS countries, 1990–2003.

FIGURE 3.4
Real-Wage Adjustments Have Been More Marked in CIS than in CEE Countries

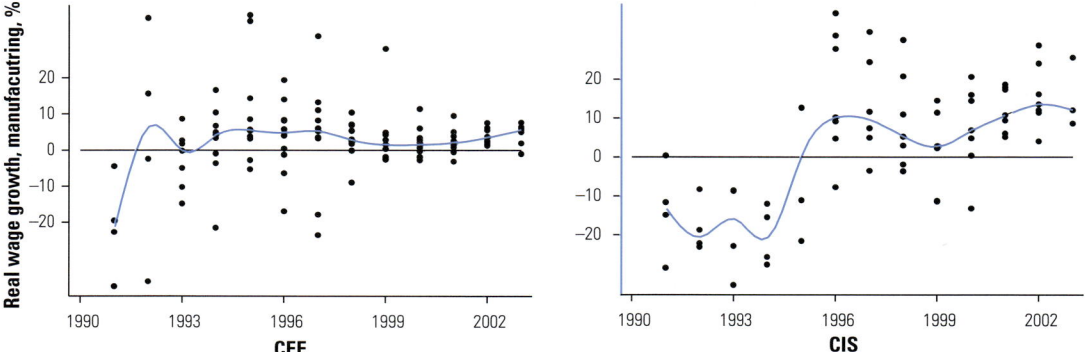

Sources: ILO (LABORSTA database); World Development Indicators; Boeri and Garibaldi 2004.

Note: Growth in real manufacturing wage 1990–2003 for CEE and low and middle income CIS countries.

Any Role for Macropolicy to Influence the Employment-Output Link?

The uncertainties associated with the transition, the major reforms it implied, and the associated economic volatility affected firms' ability to do business (see chapter 5). Such a climate was probably not conducive to carrying out further investment or employment creation. In recent years, such policy uncertainties have faded, and although further reforms are needed, employers are likely to face less economic and policy uncertainty in the coming years, especially in countries that have joined the European Union.

The significant weakening of the employment-output link in CEE countries in the second phase of the transition was primarily the result of the large overstaffing that existed in most firms in the central-planning period. This overstaffing largely enabled firms to promote growth without hiring many more workers. (This explanation is developed in more detail in chapter 4.) Changes in monetary and fiscal policy may also have contributed to the observed jobless growth. In particular, this section argues that higher real interest rates and changes in the fiscal stance are possible factors that contributed to jobless growth.

Real Interest Rates Have Increased in Recent Years

Real interest rates have been positive and sizable since 1995, mainly as a reflection of the tightening in monetary policy necessary to reduce inflationary pressures. Figure 3.5 also highlights a remarkable increase in real interest rates following the 1998–99 recession. Such behavior is linked to the financial turmoil that hit the Region in the aftermath of the 1998 Russian crisis.

There are various channels through which an increase in real interest rates could contribute to jobless growth.[4] One important channel is the complementarity between new capital investment and job creation. High real interest rates tend to reduce capital investment, and transition economies certainly need large quantities of capital for completing the restructuring process.[5] In particular, the adoption of new technologies and production processes, as well as the development of new activities in the service sectors, requires the hiring of workers. If real interest rates are high, this process of developing new activities can be slowed. Instead, firms are pushed toward defensive restructuring and tend to increase output through more-productive use of existing capital and labor. Especially in transition economies, output and productivity growth could also be achieved by further rationalizing current production techniques and eliminating the still large labor hoarding.

As an illustration, figures 3.6 and 3.7, respectively, show gross fixed capital formation for countries of the Region and of East Asia and a decomposition of gross fixed capital formation for the Czech Republic, Korea, Poland, and the Slovak Republic. Consistent with the idea developed above, figure 3.6 shows that investment has been (on average) lower in the transition countries than in East Asian countries over the 1990s. More important, some evidence exists that productive investment (measured as GFCF minus investment in housing) has been consistently lower in transition countries (figure 3.7).

FIGURE 3.5

Real Interest Rates Have Increased in Recent Years in CEE Countries

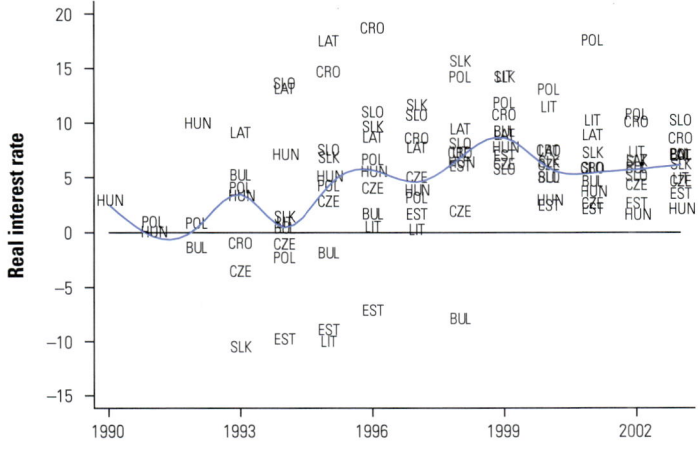

Sources: World Development Indicators; Boeri and Garibaldi 2004.

FIGURE 3.6
Share of Gross Fixed Capital Formation as a Percentage of GDP (1990–2003 Average)

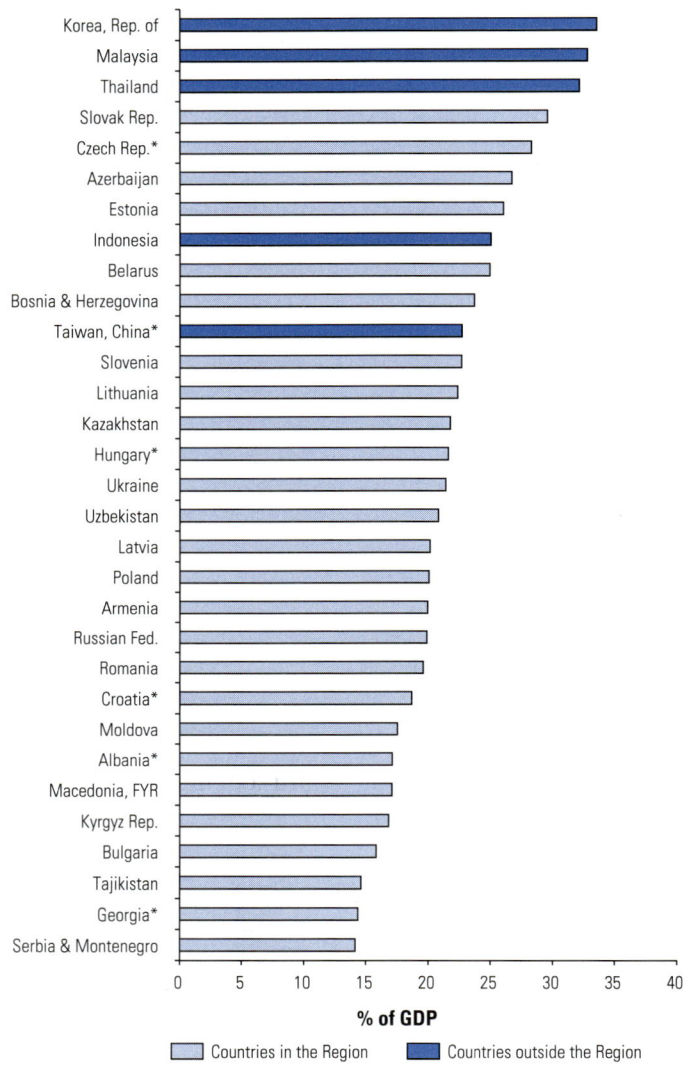

Source: World Development Indicators 2004.

* 1990–2002

Fiscal Policy Has Been Loosened

Expansionary fiscal policy is a usual response in times of economic downturns; fiscal expansion is expected to counteract the associated decrease in employment. The fiscal loosening that followed the 1998 recession can be interpreted as such a policy response (figure 3.8). However, in CEE countries, there could have been a connection between such fiscal loosening and jobless growth.

FIGURE 3.7
Share of GFCF and Productive GFCF as a Percentage of GDP (1990–2003 Average)

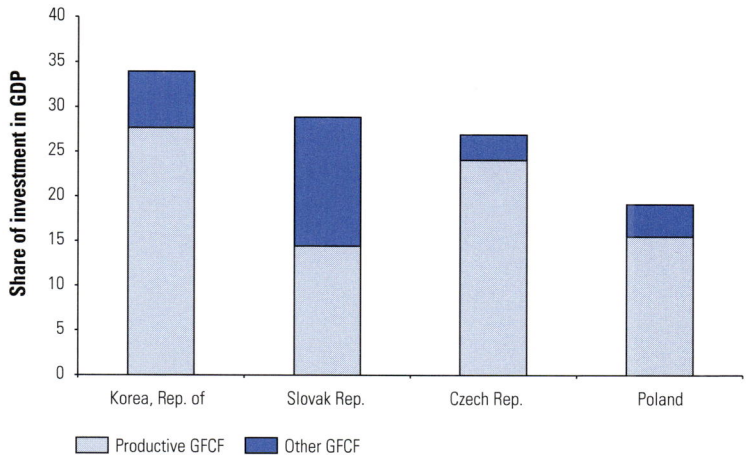

Source: National accounts of OECD countries (OECD 2003).

Note: GFCF = gross fixed capital formation.

Changes in the fiscal stance can affect employment if they alter the credibility and expectations of private employers about future changes. Fiscal loosening in CEE countries implies a likely future increase in interest rates and possibly in the tax burden. The anticipation of these adverse effects is akin to a negative capitalization effect in the private sector. In other words, forward-looking entrepreneurs identify fiscal loosening as presaging a future increase in interest rates (and possibly in taxes) and so reduce their hiring upfront. This is particularly likely in CEE countries, which, as mentioned above, have known many years of policy uncertainty, significantly affecting the way enterprises do business, and which have already seen real interest rates increase from those of the mid-1990s.

A second channel that links fiscal loosening to jobless growth is a crowding-out effect induced by an increase in labor costs. As shown in figure 3.9, real wages in the public sector increased in the past five years at a higher pace than those in the private sector in several CEE countries. In addition to worsening the fiscal balance, high wage growth in the public sector may have negative effects on private sector job creation, crowding out private sector employers from hiring skilled workers and possibly creating a wage-drift effect from the public to the private sector.

How important have these changes in macroeconomic policy settings been in driving the jobless growth observed in some CEE countries? To shed light on this question, a simple econometric analysis is

FIGURE 3.8
Loosening of the Fiscal Stance in CEE Countries in Recent Years

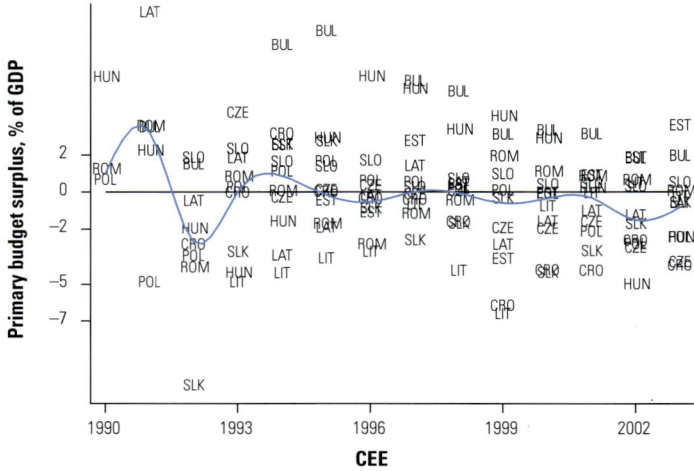

Sources: World Economic Outlook Database; Boeri and Garibaldi 2004.

performed.[6] Its results suggest that GDP growth had a strong effect on employment and unemployment in the second phase of transition. However, during the second phase, the impact of growth on the labor market was mediated by adverse macroeconomic policy changes. The rise in real interest rates and the loosening of the fiscal stance contributed to weakening the potential effect of GDP growth on employment and unemployment. In other words, employment and unemployment would have been more responsive to changes in GDP growth had the macroeconomic environment not changed at the same time (see box 3.1).

Summing Up: Employment Prospects in CEE and CIS Countries

The Employment Prospect Is Likely to Improve in EU Transition Countries and Accession Countries

For the CEE countries that have joined the EU, macroeconomic policy is likely to evolve in the years to come in a favorable way for the labor market. It is likely that interest rate premiums will decline following EU accession, reflecting a lower investment risk. Therefore, lower interest rates in the new EU transition economies may promote investment in new technologies and production processes and in job

BOX 3.1

An Empirical Investigation of the Possible Links between Employment, Output, and Macroeconomic Policy

This box provides an attempt to link employment growth to economic growth and a set of policy variables. It is illustrative of the possible linkages between these factors (see Boeri and Garibaldi [2004] for details). The analysis focuses on CEE economies, where there is clearer evidence of jobless growth.

If $\Delta ln e_{it}$ is employment growth in country i between time t-1 and time t and $\Delta ln y_{it}$ is GDP growth during the same period, the basic regression is as follows:

$$\Delta \ln e_{it} = \alpha_i + \beta \Delta \ln y_{it} + \delta post97_t + \beta_1 post97_t \Delta \ln y_{it} + \gamma_1 r_{it} + \gamma_2 ps_{it} + \varepsilon_{it} \qquad (3.1)$$

where r_{it} is the real interest rate and ps_{it} is the primary surplus. The employment equation 3.1 also features country-fixed effects (α_i where the indicator "i" denotes different countries) and a $post97_t$ dummy aimed at capturing the effects of employment growth of the second episode. Notice further that the regression includes an interaction term between GDP growth and the post-1997 dummy. That term should capture any change in the employment-output relationship that occurred during the same episode. Finally, ε_{it} is a white noise error term. The time period used was 1992–2002 for nine countries. Because of missing observations in some countries and time periods, the total number of observations is 75.

The results of the econometric exercise are reported in the table below. The poor employment performance since the 1998 recession seems also associated to the worsening of the fiscal stance, as indicated by the significant effect of the primary budget variable. An important result also concerns the size and statistical significance of the interaction term between GDP growth and the post-1997 dummy. The coefficient β_1 clearly indicates that in the employment growth regression, the employment-to-output elasticity did *not* change significantly over time, but the partial effect of output on employment was undone by the worsening of the fiscal stance.

The second column reports the results of the unemployment regression. The results suggest that high real interest rates had adverse effects on the increase in unemployment. Remarkably, the second column of the table suggests that unemployment became more sensitive to GDP growth in the aftermath of 1998, although the coefficient is estimated with a large standard error. According to those estimates, the pickup in growth since the year 2000 should have induced CEE countries to experience a sizable reduction in the unemployment rate. The fact that this reduction in unemployment did not take place is largely attributed to adverse effects of the interest rate hike.

(continues on the following page)

BOX 3.1 (continued)

Panel Regressions on Employment Growth and Change in Unemployment

	CEE	
	employment growth	change unemployment
gdp growth	**0.19**	**−0.13**
	0.03	0.01
post97	0.03	**0.93**
	0.97	0.087
gdp growth*post 97	0.04	−0.17
	0.78	0.11
primary surplus	**0.22**	−0.77
	0.07	0.31
real interest	−0.03	**0.03**
	0.22	0.05
Observations	79	89
R^2	0.19	0.22
FIXED Effect		
Years	92–02	92–02

Source: Boeri and Garibaldi 2004.

Note: P values are in italics.

Various robustness tests (not reported) suggest that other macrovariables, notably the current account deficit, the investment-to-GDP ratio, and the amount of foreign direct investment in dollars, do not appear to be significant in this multivariate analysis.

creation, finally pushing firms beyond the defensive restructuring strategy (see chapter 4). An early adoption of the euro may reinforce this effect. Indeed, real interest rates in the Euro Area are much lower than those experienced by most CEE economies, and adopting a common currency will provide a low interest rate environment.[7]

There could also be an additional beneficial effect on the labor market stemming from a change in the fiscal stance. For CEE countries that are now members of the EU, there is an obligation to avoid deficits in excess of 3 percent of GDP, whether or not they take part in the Economic and Monetary Union (EMU).[8] Although tightening fiscal policy may reduce resources for needed infrastructure development, it may also improve expectations of private firms about the ability to contain interest rates, thereby promoting investment and job creation. Similarly, if fiscal prudence leads to wage moderation in

As an illustration, the figure below shows the expected relationship between output growth and employment growth in CEE countries over the 1998–2002 period *had macropolicies remained unchanged* (see the corrected correlation line). The figure suggests that employment would have increased more had the macropolicy setting not changed.

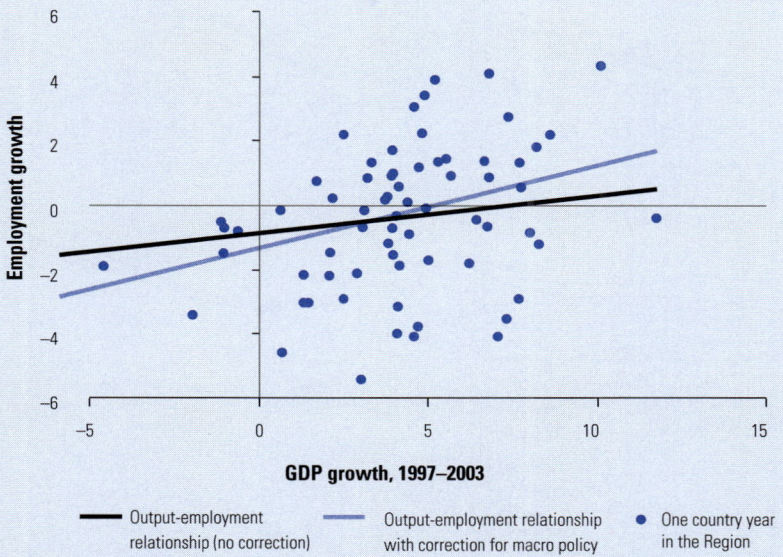

Source: Bank staff calculations, using ILO (LABORSTA database) and World Development Indicators.

The corrected output-employment relationship is obtained by assuming no change in macroeconomic policies over the observed period.

the public sector, then this may also have positive spillover effects on wage dynamics in the private sector, stimulating employment.

CIS Countries Are Still Lagging Behind in Restructuring, and More Employment Adjustment Is to Be Expected

The job prospects in CIS countries largely depend on their progress in structural reforms. Evidence suggests that there is a strong link between output and growth, but the latter has been modest for most of the transition period. Moreover, as discussed below, structural changes, including the reallocation of resources to more-productive activities, have been relatively lacking to date. And even if this modest progress has not resulted in very high levels of unemployment or low participation, it has negatively affected growth and the living

FIGURE 3.9
Real Wages in the Public Sector Have Increased More Rapidly than in the Private Sector in CEE Countries

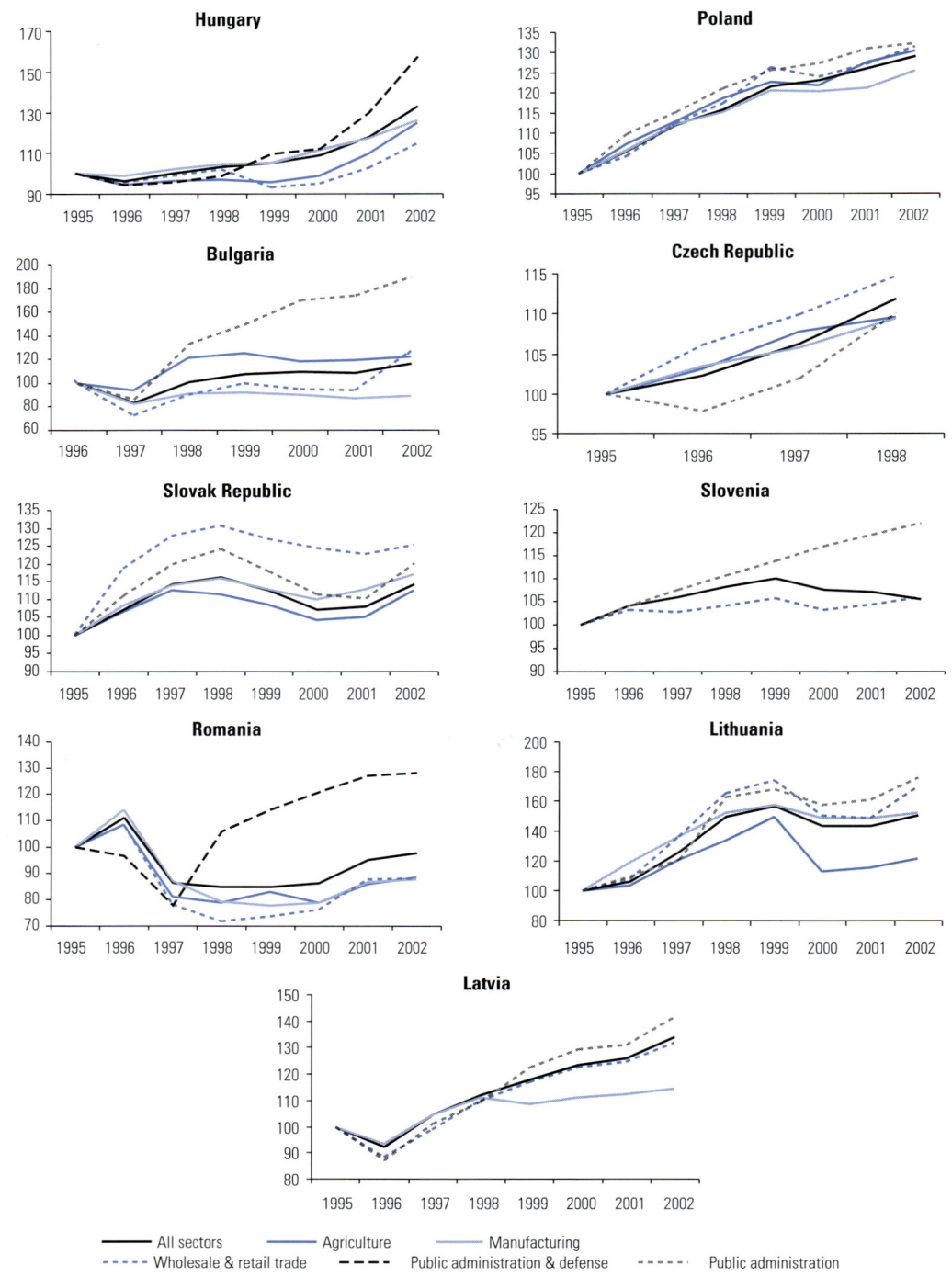

Source: LABORSTA database.

standards of the population. These issues will be addressed in the next chapter of this study.

Notes

1. The cutoff point between the first and second transition phases is somewhat arbitrary. In the aftermath of the Russian financial crisis, most of the transition countries experienced a significant slowdown in economic activities; but the size of the slowdown differed significantly, being stronger in the CIS countries than in most CEE countries.
2. This hypothesis is proposed by Boeri and Terrell (2002) and Garibaldi and Brixiova (1998).
3. The data refer to manufacturing because of measurement problems in other sectors.
4. Several theoretical and applied papers have also suggested a possible role for real interest rates in influencing unemployment. In particular, Phelps (1992 and 1994), in the "customer market" model of pricing, suggests that an increase in real interest rates lowers incentives to invest in expanding market shares. Thus, the increase in marginal production costs resulting from a rise in interest rates is likely to be followed by a rise in price markups that, in turn, should have negative effects on employment. Moreover, in an intertemporal model, if workers have nonwage income, an increase in the rates of interest may reduce the expected utility of being employed.
5. Microdata on labor demand of firms in transitional economies confirm a strong complementarity between capital and labor (Svejnar 1999; Boeri and others 1997).
6. The econometric analysis includes regressions of both employment growth and changes in unemployment rates against a set of variables: GDP growth, the primary surplus, the real interest rate, a post-1997 dummy, and a variable capturing the change in coefficient in the GDP growth variable post-1997.
7. Yet, real interest rates are not under full control of the monetary authority, and the real interest rate is partly a market-determined variable. Indeed, some increase in the real interest rate in the aftermath of the Russian financial crisis was probably inevitable, and such country risks would not be fully eliminated by early euro adoption.
8. This obligation is not obviated by the fact that members states not participating in EMU are not subject to the financial penalties for noncompliance.

CHAPTER 4

Restructuring, Productivity, and Job Creation

Faced with radical institutional and policy changes, enterprises in all transition countries have been forced to adapt their behavior. Some have been able to seize new opportunities, but many others have simply tried to survive in a market to which they were unaccustomed and ill-prepared. The ensuing process of restructuring has involved shifts in technology, suppliers, and customers; abandoning old production lines and introducing new ones; and hiring and (more often) laying off workers—and has resulted in improved productivity of some firms, but also in the death of many others.

The pace and depth of enterprise restructuring and the restructuring and reallocation of resources across firms are determined by the extent to which previously nonexistent control mechanisms of enterprise efficiency have emerged during the transition. A number of key factors are responsible for these efficiency increases, including improvements in corporate governance (for example, changing of managers), brought on by privatization, and stronger competition in product markets, not least because of the opening to foreign markets. The systemic environment of firms (that is, the investment climate) has also improved, with the liberalization of conditions for entry, the reduction of state paternalism via the hardening of the budget constraint, price liberalization, and macroeconomic stabilization. All these factors have taken different forms in CEE, CIS, and SEE, with very different implications for output, productivity, and employment growth.

How successful have countries been in reallocating resources to more productive uses? Is the process over, or are countries still struggling with restructuring their economies? Moreover, is there a role for policy to influence the pace and nature of the process of labor reallocation? And are different approaches to reallocation and restructuring associated with different labor market outcomes?

The Required Transformation of the Transition Economies and Progress So Far

Economic Structures Were Often Far from Those in Market Economies

One way to assess the size of the structural gap that transition economies inherited from the centrally planned period is to compare their employment distribution by sectors with those prevailing in market-oriented economies of similar income per capita.[1] This exercise offers only an illustration of the potential scope of structural changes expected in the transition economies in their process of convergence toward market-based economic systems, not least because the latter vary a great deal across market economies. Bearing in mind these caveats, table 4.1 shows the distribution of employment by sector for transition economies at the beginning of the transition and in 2002.[2] In the table, the sectoral deviations from the market benchmark are also aggregated into a synthetic distortion index, which measures the deviation from the market benchmark (see box 4.1).[3]

Taken at face value, the distortion index suggests that at the beginning of the transition period, CEE countries had an economic structure that was further from the market economy benchmark than that of the CIS countries. Given their level of income per capita, CEE countries already had a relatively small agricultural sector and a largely oversized industrial sector.

During the transition, all countries experienced a sideways-U shape change in the employment structure, driven by the evolution of output, with an initial large decline followed by a recovery. By 2002, CEE countries had managed to move closer to a market-based structure of the economy. The European CIS countries have also shown some sign of convergence toward the market benchmark in recent years, but are still very far away from it and would require major adjustments in the years to come. The other CIS countries have

TABLE 4.1
The Employment Structure in CEE and CIS Countries

Share in employment	CEE countries		CIS countries	
	1989–90	2002	1989–91	2000
Agriculture				
Actual	17.8	14.5	30.9	39.0
Benchmark	23.2	22.3	32.1	43.1
Industry				
Actual	42.0	32.4	30.3	18.3
Benchmark	26.0	26.2	23.8	20.4
Market-oriented services				
Actual	20.9	29.7	13.6	17.9
Benchmark	28.5	28.9	24.3	19.4
Nonmarket services				
Actual	18.8	23.3	23.3	23.0
Benchmark	22.4	22.7	19.8	17.0
GDP per capita (1995 US$)	7,268	7,627	4,603	2,706
Distortion index	17.0%	12.1%	13.7%	13.0%

Source: Bank staff calculations.

Note: The distortion index is defined as half the sum of the absolute value of (s − s*) where s is the actual share of employment in a sector and s* is the benchmark share. The benchmark shares are calculated as described in the text.

seen increases in agriculture and little progress in the development of a modern service sector. They have moved closer to the market benchmark by becoming poorer rather than by progressing toward modern economies (see figure 4.1 for the example of the Kyrgyz Republic; see Scarpetta and Vodopivec [2005] for the other countries). It could be argued that with the removal of subsidies from the Former Soviet Union, these countries have reverted to the income levels that are more consistent with their comparative advantages and underlying economic characteristics.

Shifts to Market Services in CEE

Looking at changes in the sectoral composition of employment suggests that all transition countries experienced a process of deindustrialization, but this was associated with significantly different patterns across them. In most CEE countries, except for Romania, deindustrialization was associated with a reduction in employment in agriculture. In 2002, the share of agriculture in total employment in most CEE countries was close to what is seen in many EU countries. By contrast, the CIS countries—and, within the group, the poorest countries in particular—saw a rise in relative and even absolute employment in agriculture (see figure 4.1 and Scarpetta and Vodopivec

BOX 4.1

Economic Development and the Employment Structure

Using large cross-country data sets, a number of stylized development patterns have been identified (Chenery and Taylor 1968; Rowthorn and Ramaswamy 1997). The share of agriculture in GDP and employment tends to fall as economies grow richer. The share of industry in GDP and employment tends to increase with income per capita, but the relation is nonlinear (that is, at higher levels of income per capita, employment in industry shifts toward services). Finally, the share of services and, in particular, market-oriented services rises monotonically with income per capita. Raiser, Schaffer, and Schuchhardt (2003) propose a market-economy benchmark based on regression analyses on a cross-section of 50 countries. For each sector, the share in employment is regressed on the log of GDP per capita and its square. (The results are shown in the table below.) Because all sectoral regressions fit the data quite well, this section uses the fitted curves as benchmarks in the analysis of the distortion in economic structures and the evolution of these structures over the transition. It should be stressed that similar conclusions concerning the distance from the market-based economic structures can be obtained using real benchmarks, such as the EU average or the North EU and the South EU benchmarks (see Aiginger and others 1999 and Landesmann 2000).

More important, benchmark comparisons are generally performed to compare underlying features of economies at their steady state. Transition economies are in fact evolving rapidly, and the observed employment structures—even in most recent years—should not be taken to represent their new steady state equilibrium.

Benchmarking Regressions (standard errors in parentheses)

Independent variables	Dependent variable: share of employment in			
	Agriculture	Industry	Market service	Nonmarket services
Log GDP per capita	−0.38390	0.32560	0.08198	−0.03740
	(0.036)	(0.019)	(0.576)	(0.808)
(Log GDP per capita)^2	0.01082	−0.01600	0.00058	0.00548
	(0.293)	(0.042)	(0.945)	(0.533)
Constant	2.78970	−1.37035	−0.49013	0.12316
	(0.001)	(0.023)	(0.441)	(0.853)
R^2	0.883	0.4544	0.7141	0.4784
F(2, 47)	176.4	19.57	58.71	21.55
Number of observations	50	50	50	50

Source: Raiser, Schaffer, and Schuchhardt 2003.

[2005]), often as the employer of last resort, given the lack of job openings in other sectors.

Further downsizing in industry could be expected in CEE countries if they are to move toward a market economy industrial structure. Moreover, despite some significant shifts in employment toward mar-

FIGURE 4.1
Different Patterns of Labor Reallocation across Transition Economies

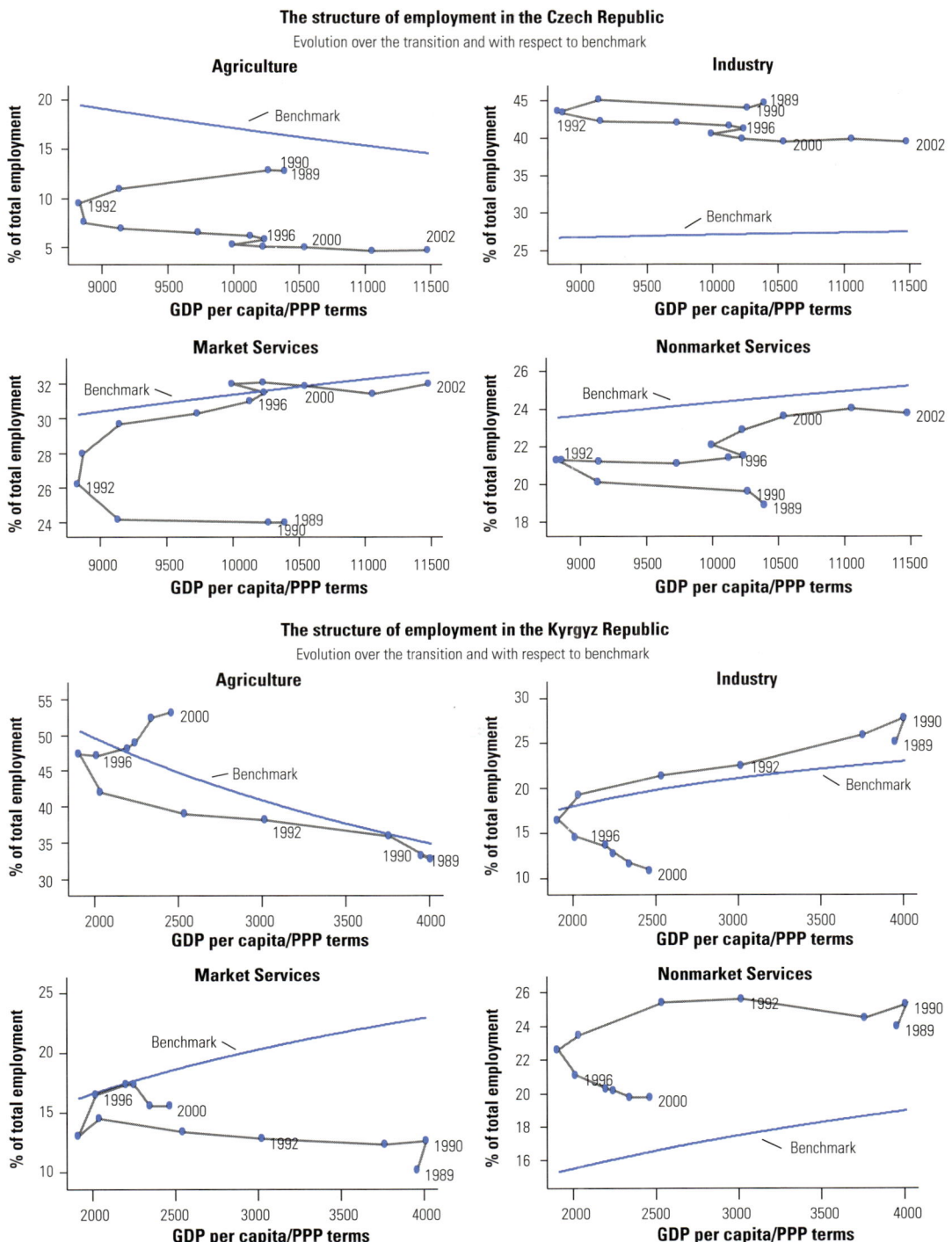

(continues on the following page)

FIGURE 4.1 (*continued*)

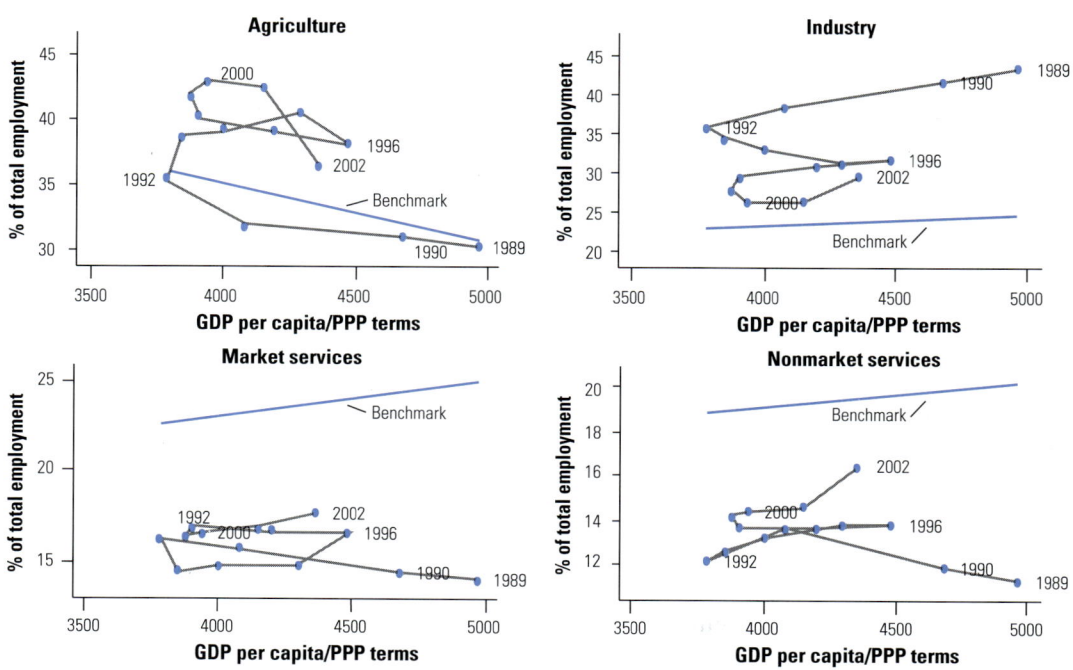

The structure of employment in Romania
Evolution over the transition and with respect to benchmark

Source: Authors' calculations.

ket services (trade, finance, transport, and communication), they still have only 30 percent of employment in these activities, and Romania has an even smaller market service sector. At the same time, most CEE countries have shares in employment in nonmarket services (public administration and social services) that are greater than what would be expected in market economies at a similar level of development, with significant implications for public finances.

Backward Shifts to Agriculture in Many CIS Countries

For the middle income CIS countries, there are signs of positive convergence (that is, associated with income growth) in the most recent years. The size of the required employment reallocation, however, remains daunting. Major shifts can be expected away from agriculture and possibly industry, especially toward market services. This will imply major changes in skill requirements and in work habits, as well as changes in the location of workers away from declining regions and toward expanding areas.

The poorer CIS countries, by restructuring the least, are paradoxically quite close to the market-based benchmark. The lack of reforms has been associated with major declines in income per capita, which has in turn brought them closer to low-income market economy benchmarks. Sustained economic growth in these countries is likely to trigger major pressures to reallocate labor along the lines of their European counterparts. But there are greater uncertainties as to whether the poorer CIS countries have the economic and institutional capabilities to pursue an aggressive transformation of their economies.

What Is the Role of Firm Restructuring and the Entry and Exit of Firms for Job Creation?

The analysis of shifts in employment across sectors hides a greater dynamism taking place within sectors, because of new firms entering the market and displacing obsolete units and because of within-firm restructuring in the struggle to survive and possibly expand market share. In this context, it is of importance to first assess the size and characteristics of job flows (job creation and destruction) and then link them to productivity and output growth.

Job Creation and Destruction Have Surged Rapidly

Not surprisingly, job reallocation (the sum of job creation and destruction) increased dramatically in response to transition: from less than 10 percent of the workforce in the late 1980s to more than 20–25 percent in the 1990s (see box 4.2). Job creation and job destruction rates in transition countries exceeded those in developed countries or were at about the same level, and they lagged slightly behind the average job flows in the sample of developing countries (figure 4.2). Once the initial years of transition are excluded, the average rates of job reallocation and excess job reallocation for the transition countries were 25 and 21 percent, respectively, thus exceeding the average of developed countries with 24 and 20 percent, respectively, but falling behind developing countries. It is quite remarkable that it took only a few years for the job flows in transition countries to increase from very low levels to the levels of flow present in mature market economies.

In Some Countries, Job Creation Has Lagged behind Job Destruction

The timing of job creation and destruction has played an essential role in shaping labor market outcomes. In all transition economies, job

BOX 4.2

A Consistent International Firm-Level Database

Available data at the firm level are usually compiled for fiscal and other purposes, and (unlike macroeconomic data) there are few internationally agreed-on definitions and sources, although harmonization has improved over the years. The data used in this chapter are based on a harmonized firm-level database for 24 OECD, transition, and emerging economies. The data set used in the study was collected in various stages. Most recently, the firm-level project organized by the World Bank collected indicators for 14 countries (Estonia, Hungary, Latvia, Romania, and Slovenia; Argentina, Brazil, Chile, Colombia, Mexico, and Venezuela; Indonesia, Republic of Korea, and Taiwan [China]). An earlier OECD study collected indicators based on information on firms from Canada, Denmark, Germany, Finland, France, Italy, the Netherlands, Portugal, the United Kingdom, and the United States (see Bartelsman, Haltiwanger, and Scarpetta [2004] for details). The main source of the data and the period covered for the five transition economies included in the sample are presented in the table below. The analysis of firm demographics is based on business registers, censuses, social security databases, or employment-based registers containing information on both establishments and firms. Data for the analysis of productivity growth come more frequently from business surveys. Using these data, time-series indicators on firm demographics were generated for disaggregated sectors for each country.

Basic Characteristics of the World Bank Firm-Level Database

Country	Firm demographics and survival			Labor productivity			
	Source	Period	Threshold	Source	Period	Threshold	Sectors
Estonia	Business Register	95–01	Emp ≥ 1	Business Register	95–00 to 96–01	Emp ≥ 1	All
Hungary	Fiscal register (APEH)	92–01	Emp ≥ 1	Fiscal register (APEH)	92–96 to 97–01	Emp > 1	All
Latvia	LURSOFT and State Social Insurance Agency	96–02	Emp ≥ 1	LURSOFT and State Social Insurance Agency	96–01 to 97–02	Emp ≥ 1	All
Romania	Business register	92–01	Emp ≥ 1	Business register	95–98 to 96–99	Emp ≥ 1	All
Slovenia	Statistical Office of Slovenia, Accounting data. Business registry data	92–01	Emp ≥ 1	Statistical Office of Slovenia, Accounting data. Business registry data	92–97 to 97–01	Emp > 1	All

Source: Bartelsman, Haltiwanger, and Scarpetta 2004.

destruction surged first in the early 1990s, but the response of job creation differed across countries. Many CEE countries, which advanced rapidly in the transformation of their economies, saw job creation rapidly catching up with job destruction (see, for example, Estonia and Slovenia in figure 4.3), giving rise to balanced (synchronized) job flows. In other countries lagging behind in economic transformation, job creation continued to be lower than job destruction for prolonged

Definition of Key Concepts

Entry rate is defined as the number of new firms divided by the total number of incumbent and entrant firms in a given year.

Exit rate is defined as the number of firms exiting the market in a given year divided by the population of origin (that is, the incumbents in the previous year).

Labor productivity growth is defined as the difference between the rate of growth of output and that of employment[a] and, whenever possible, controls for material inputs.

Job creation rate equals employment gains summed over all plants that expand in a given year, divided by the average employment in the period.

Job destruction rate equals employment losses summed over all plants that contract in a given year, divided by the average employment in the period.

Job reallocation rate is the sum of all plant-level employment gains and losses that occur in a given year.

Comparability Issues

Two prominent aspects of the data have to be borne in mind while comparing firm-level data across countries:

Unit of observation. The data used in this study refer to "firms" rather than "'establishments." Firm-based data are likely to more closely represent entities that are responsible for key aspects of decision making, compared with plant-level data. Nevertheless, business registers may define firms at different points in ownership structures; for example, some registers consider firms that are effectively controlled by a "parent" firm as separate units, while others record only the parent company.

Size threshold. Although some registers include even single-person businesses, others omit firms smaller than a certain size, usually in the number of employees, but sometimes in other measures (such as sales). Data used in this study exclude single-person businesses.

Source: Bartelsman, Haltiwanger, and Scarpetta 2004.

a. Available data do not allow the control for changes in hours worked, nor do they distinguish between part- and full-time employment.

---

periods (see, for example, Russia and Romania in figure 4.3), giving rise to either large increases in unemployment or falls in participation.

The main differences across countries are in job creation rather than job destruction. Although countries lagging behind on reforms were able to contain job destruction in the early phases of transition, job destruction later took off to high levels. At the same time, however, delaying macro- and microreforms prevented new private initia-

FIGURE 4.2
Large Job Flows in Transition Economies

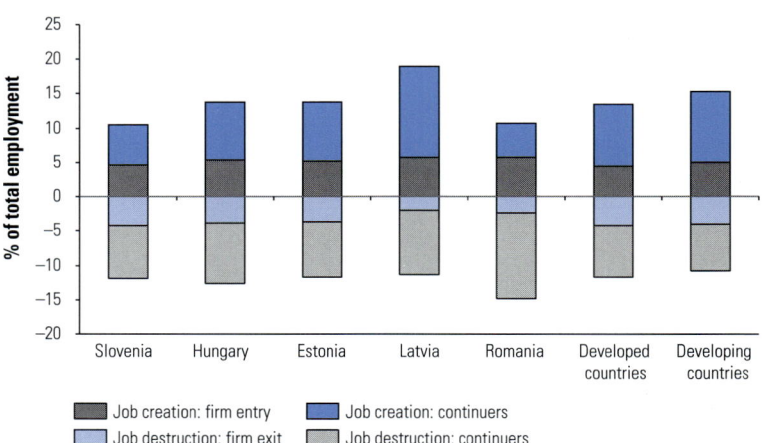

Source: Bartelsman, Haltiwanger, and Scarpetta 2004.

Note: Estonia: 1997–2000. Hungary:1994–2000. Latvia: 1994–99. Romania: 1994–2000. Slovenia: 1993–2000. Developed countries: West Germany 1978–99, USA 1989–97, Italy: 1988–93, U.K. 1987–98, Portugal 1984–94, Finland 1989–98, France 1991–96, Canada 1985–97, Denmark 1982–94, Netherlands 1994–97. Developing countries: Argentina 1997–2001, Mexico 1987–2000.

tives from emerging and creating new jobs. Thus, job creation did not catch up with job destruction, leading to net job losses. In other words, slowing down the required transformation of the economy cannot prevent job destruction, but risks reducing incentives for job creation, with a consequent buildup of unemployment or nonparticipation.

Job Creation Largely Depends on the Ability of New Firms to Enter the Market and Hire Workers

An essential channel for job creation in transition economies is the creation of new firms. As an example, in Russia, before the transition, firm turnover (entry and exit of firms) accounted for less than 20 percent of overall job turnover. During the transition, the contribution of firm turnover to job flows increased strongly. In the countries for which firm-level data are available, during the initial phases of the transition, the entry of firms contributed from about 40 percent of total job creation in Estonia, Latvia, and Hungary to more than 70 percent in Romania and Slovenia.

Moreover, there is a stronger (positive) correlation between the number of entrant firms in a given country and industry and the overall job creation in that country and industry in transition countries than in OECD countries. By contrast, there is almost no correlation between exit of firms and job destruction in transition countries, while

FIGURE 4.3

Unsynchronized Job Creation and Destruction Can Give Rise to Unemployment or Underemployment

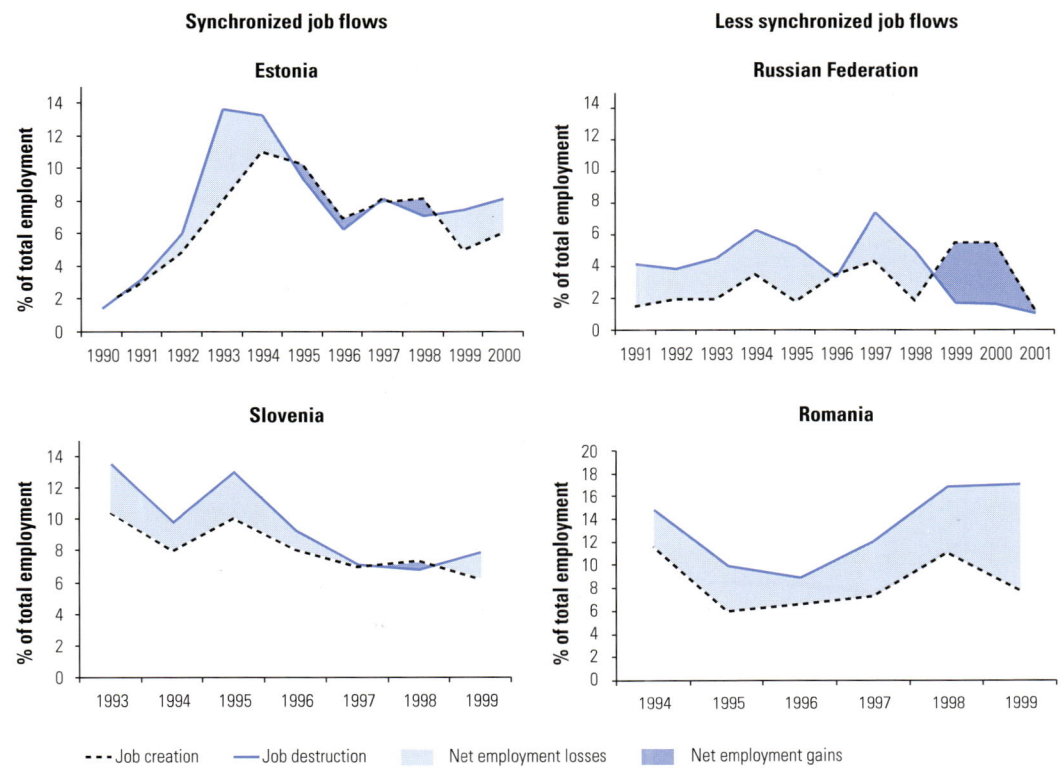

Source: Bartelsman, Haltiwanger, and Scarpetta 2004.

in OECD countries this correlation is stronger. In other words, entry plays a significant role for job creation, but the exit of obsolete firms, while promoting productivity, does not strongly contribute to job destruction, which largely comes from downsizing of surviving firms.

Not surprisingly, the contribution of firm entry to overall job creation declined over the transition period (see figure 4.4). After having filled the pretransition void in certain activities, the characteristics of job flows converged toward those observed in market economies: job creation and destruction come increasingly from within firm adjustment, rather than from the entry and exit of firms. In this context, Russia and Ukraine—two laggard reformers—saw the reverse patterns, with an increasing role of firm entry to total job creation in the second half of the 1990s.

Notably, the contribution of firm closure to job destruction followed the opposite trend than that of firm entry and job creation.

FIGURE 4.4
Job Flow Rates, Selected Transition Countries, 1990–2001 (percentage)

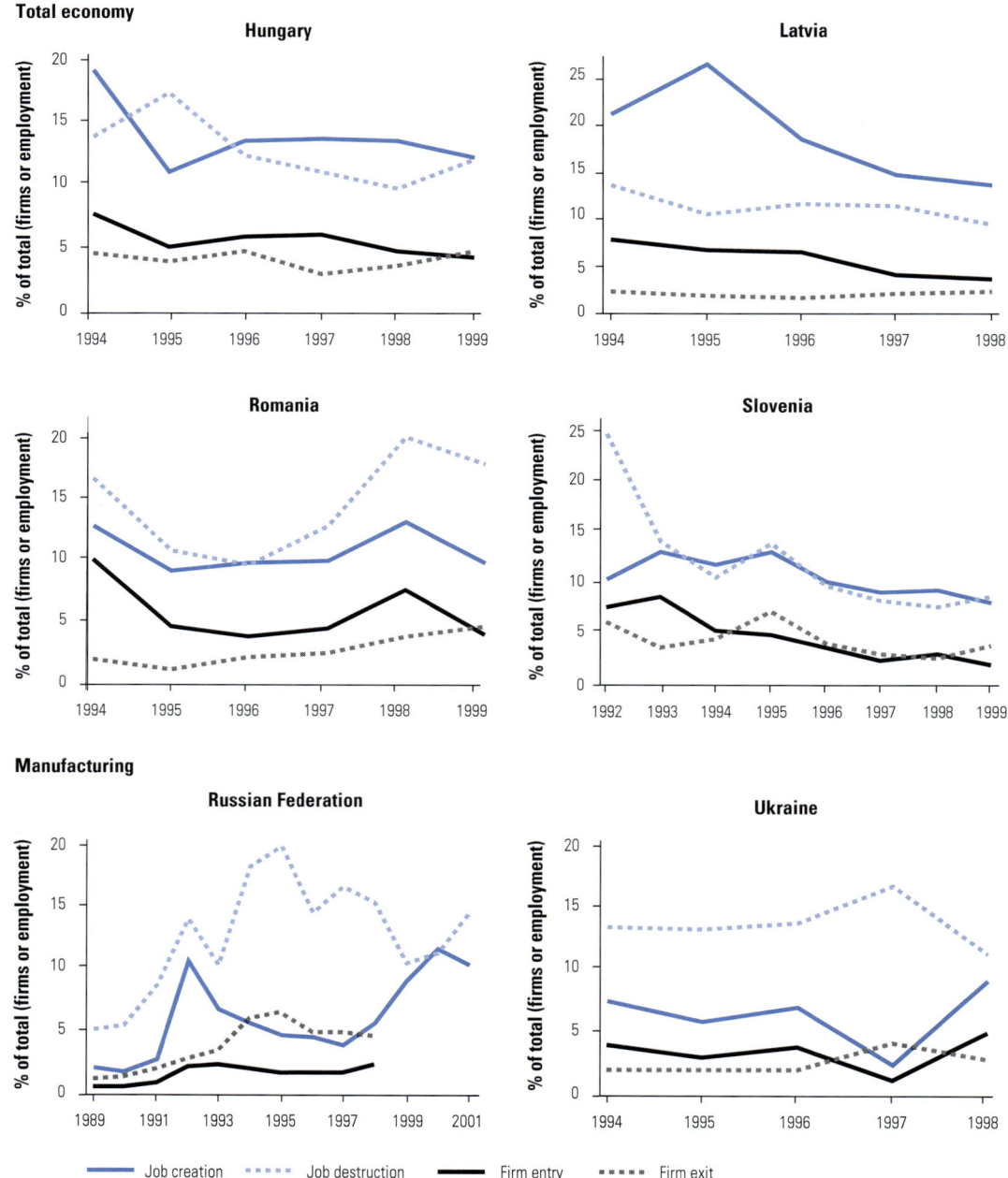

Sources: Bartelsman, Haltiwanger, and Scarpetta 2004; Brown and Earle 2004.

Competitive pressures have increased over the transition process, and in all the countries for which data are available, the share of job destruction resulting from firm exits increased later in transition.

How does the share of job flows attributable to firm turnover compare with that of nontransition countries? For the sample of countries included in the analysis, the entry of firms contributed (on average) 38 percent to the total job creation rate (ranging from 25 percent in Latvia to 50 percent in Romania), exceeding this share in OECD countries and developing countries, where it amounted to slightly more than 30 percent (on average). This suggests that the entry of firms indeed played an exceptionally important role in job creation in transition countries. In contrast, at 28 percent, the average share of firm exits in job destructions was below that in the group of OECD and developing countries, where it was around 35 percent.

What Is the Role of Firm Restructuring and the Entry and Exit of Firms for Productivity and Output Growth?

If restructuring and creative destruction are important for employment, they are also essential for promoting productivity and output growth. At least during the initial phases of the transition, these two objectives—employment growth and productivity—have been conflicting because firms have attempted to promote productivity by reducing overstaffing.

In Manufacturing, Productivity Growth Is Largely Resulting from Within-Industry Restructuring

The effects of restructuring and reallocation of labor on productivity are analyzed at different levels for a group of CEE countries, Russia, and Ukraine.[4] This is first done by exploring the reallocation across manufacturing industries (see box 4.3). Then it is done by looking at how productivity growth is accounted for by within-firm growth, shifts in employment across existing firms, and the entry and exit of firms.

In CEE economies, despite major changes in relative prices and revealed comparative advantages, most productivity growth over the past decade has come from changes within each manufacturing industry, rather than from shift of resources from less- to more-productive industries (figure 4.5). The effect of reallocation of labor from less- to more-productive industries is positive, albeit small. The results of the decomposition also suggest that those industries that contributed the most to aggregate labor-productivity growth in manufac-

BOX 4.3

Assessing the Impact of Labor Reallocation on Productivity Growth

The effects of shifts in sectoral shares on aggregate productivity growth can be calculated using different techniques. In all cases, it is crucial to consider the shift of employment not only from sectors with low-productivity growth to sectors with high-productivity growth but also from sectors with low-productivity levels to those with high-productivity levels. The reason is that the positive contribution to aggregate productivity of the high-growth sectors may be offset by their lower-than-average productivity levels. One approach (equation 4.1) is to express the productivity for the economy as a whole as the sum of the productivity level of each sector weighted by the sectoral employment shares:

$$P_m = \frac{Y_m}{L_m} = \sum_{j=1}^{n} \frac{Y_j}{L_j} * \frac{L_j}{L_m} = \sum_{j=1}^{n} P_j * S_j \qquad (4.1)$$

where Y is output, L is employment by sector ($j = 1.....n$) and the total economy (m), P is labor productivity (Y/L), and S is the sectoral employment share. In a discrete time perspective, the expression (equation 4.1) can be rewritten as follows:

$$\frac{P_m^t - P_m^0}{P_m^0} = \frac{\sum_{j=1}^{n}(P_j^t - P_j^0) * S_j^0}{\sum_{j=1}^{n} P_j^0 S_j^0} + \frac{\sum_{j=1}^{n} P_j^0 * (S_j^t - S_j^0)}{\sum_{j=1}^{n} P_j^0 S_j^0} + \frac{\sum_{j=1}^{n}(P_j^t - P_j^0) * (S_j^t - S_j^0)}{\sum_{j=1}^{n} P_j^0 S_j^0} \qquad (4.2)$$

for a current year t and a base year 0.

The first term on the right-hand side is the *within industry contribution* to overall productivity growth. The second term can be defined as the *net shift effect* (that is, the contribution coming from changes in the sectoral composition of employment). The third term is derived as a residual and represents the joint effect of changes in employment shares and sectoral productivity: it is positive if sectors with above-average productivity growth increase their share of total employment; it is negative if either expanding sectors have below-average productivity growth or sectors with high-productivity growth are also declining in their shares of total employment.

The data used for the productivity decomposition in this study refer to 14 manufacturing industries in the manufacturing sector of 11 CEE countries. They refer to 1989–2002, although for a number of countries data coverage is more limited.

turing were also shrinking in size, while those with below-average productivity growth gained—in relative terms—in employment shares.

Industries Have Boosted Productivity by Reducing Overstaffing

The dominance of within-industry changes in total productivity growth is a common result for OECD countries, especially in recent years. But in previous decades, when structural changes were more marked, even in OECD manufacturing, productivity was also largely driven by substantial shifts in employment from less- to more-productive industries. Why is this not occurring on a large scale in CEE economies, despite massive changes in the patterns of demand, trade, and the use of production factors?

Most industries have experienced job losses: first because of the decline in demand, and then to maintain or reinforce productivity by reducing the large overstaffing of the centrally planned era. The fact that the industries with above-average productivity growth are those that have shed relatively more labor confirms the hypothesis advanced above: productivity growth has been driven by a process of "defensive restructuring" rather than by reallocation of production factors to the most-productive uses (strategic restructuring).[5] Also, many low-productivity industries—being sheltered from competitive pressure—have managed to contain job destruction, but may still have to go through a period of downsizing and restructuring, with further effects on employment and unemployment rates.

Wage Growth Did Not Vary as Much as Productivity Growth across Industries

Have wages responded to different productivity performance of industries and firms during the transition? Table 4.2 presents the average growth rates of labor productivity, real wages, and unit labor costs in manufacturing during the early phases of the transition and the most recent period. It also shows the within-manufacturing dispersion of each of these variables (coefficients of variation), as well as the correlations between labor-productivity growth and real-wage growth.

The picture is rather heterogeneous across transition countries and time periods. Two of the countries (Romania and Slovenia) even had a negative interindustry correlation between real-wage growth and labor-productivity growth, and in most of the other countries the cor-

FIGURE 4.5
Decomposition of Labor Productivity Growth, CEE Countries

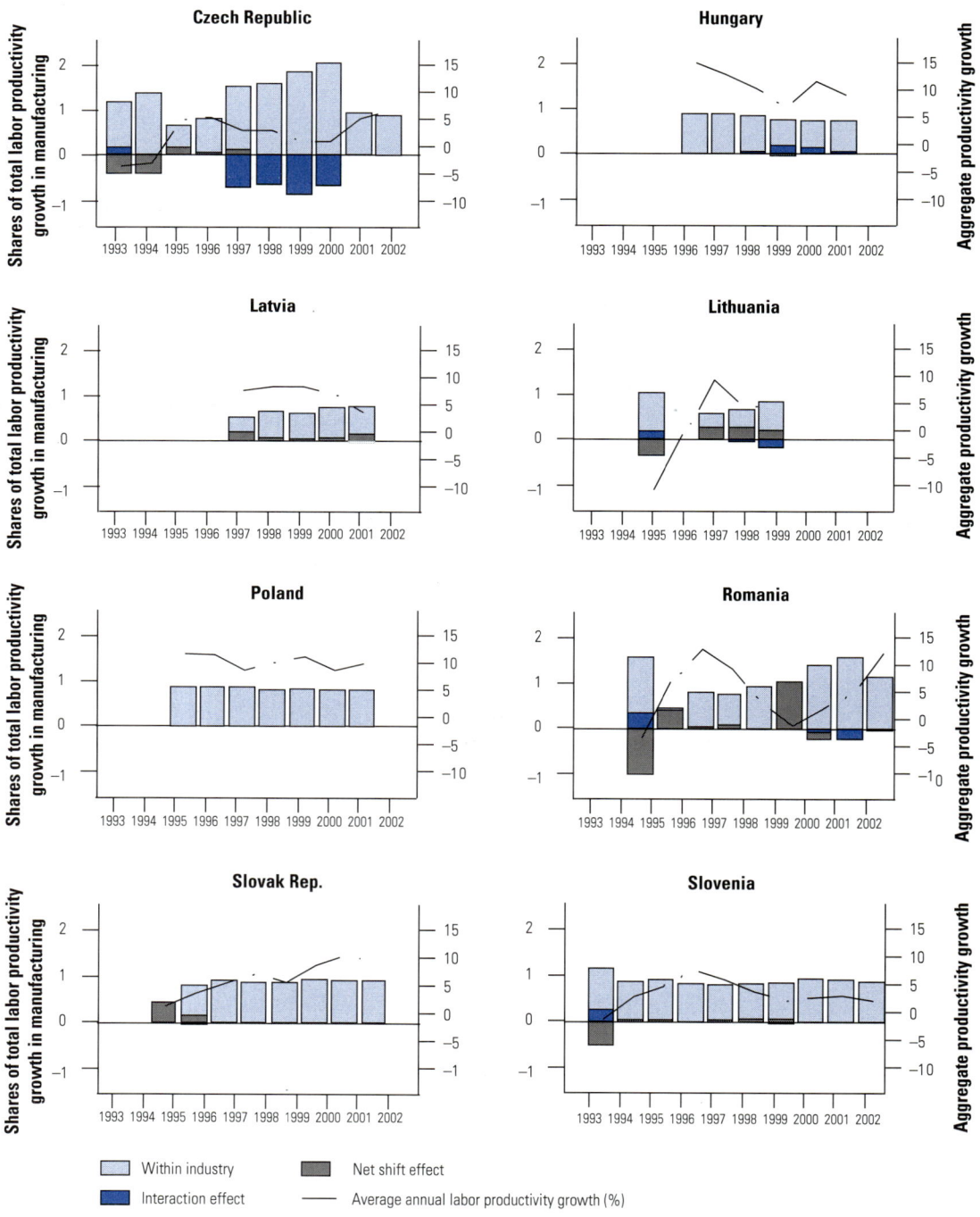

Source: Bank staff calculations.

relation was positive, but not very strong. Most likely, industries that were more exposed to competitive pressures and privatization combined downsizing with wage moderation to survive, while industries sheltered from competition were able to resist restructuring and maintained real-wage growth despite poor productivity performance. The second phase of the transition saw a significant increase in the interindustry correlation of real wages and productivity, indicating that market mechanisms played their role in a more effective way. The closer association between real-wage and productivity growth in the more recent years is also related to the fact that it is often difficult to reduce nominal or even real wages to compensate for negative or only modest productivity growth, as observed in the early phases of the transition.

Another interesting element emerging from the table is that across manufacturing industries, many countries had a lower dispersion in interindustry real-wage growth than in labor-productivity growth in the second phase of the transition. The result is that differences in labor-productivity growth also showed up in changes in relative unit labor costs (that is, industries with above-average productivity growth also improved their relative position in relative unit labor costs).

CEE Countries Are Gaining Comparative Advantages in High-Technology Industries

These changes in unit labor costs are modifying the comparative cost advantages of industries in most transition countries. At the beginning of the transition, most countries had comparative advantages with respect to Western European countries in low-technology industries (textiles, clothing, footwear, and leather products) and in resource-intensive industries (wood, chemicals, nonmetallic minerals, and so forth). Over time, however, one can observe a general pattern of catching up of productivity by medium- and high-technology industries such as machinery, electrical equipment, and transport, outpacing productivity increases of low-technology industries where relative productivity growth has been stagnant or very small (Landesmann 2000). By contrast, real-wage growth has been similar in these industries to that observed in medium- and high-technology industries that experienced major productivity improvements. This wage drift between industries implies that countries are gaining comparative (unit cost) advantages in the medium- and high-technology industries or alternatively that they are losing comparative advantages in those sectors that are labor-intensive and where transition countries were expected to gain significant shares of EU market shares.

TABLE 4.2
The Evolution of Productivity, Wages, and Unit Labor Costs

		Manufacturing					
		1992–95			1996–02		
		Average[1]	Corr. coef.[2]	Corr.	Average[1]	Corr. coef.[2]	Corr.
Bulgaria	Avg. labor productivity growth				0.69	0.60	
	Avg. real wage growth (3)				2.66	−0.16	
	Avg. unit labor cost (EURO) growth (4)				7.83	1.43	
	Correlation labor productivity and real wages (5)						0.61
Croatia	Avg. labor productivity growth				5.78	1.61	
	Avg. real wage growth (3)				2.66	1.23	
	Avg. unit labor cost (EURO) growth (4)				0.10	0.18	
	Correlation labor productivity and real wages (5)						0.48
Czech Rep.	Avg. labor productivity growth	0.33	−0.37		3.90	0.55	
	Avg. real wage growth (3)	−1.25	−0.80		3.81	3.17	
	Avg. unit labor cost (EURO) growth (4)	4.48	1.95		4.34	0.94	
	Correlation labor productivity and real wages (5)			0.51			0.84
Estonia	Avg. labor productivity growth	6.28			10.02	2.88	
	Avg. real wage growth (3)	5.20			4.52	0.58	
	Avg. unit labor cost (EURO) growth (4)				2.58	1.90	
	Correlation labor productivity and real wages (5)						0.58
Hungary	Avg. labor productivity growth	14.91	2.05		8.28	0.96	
	Avg. real wage growth (3)	0.23	−0.13		3.40	2.97	
	Avg. unit labor cost (EURO) growth (4)	−8.83	−1.56		−1.00	0.32	
	Correlation labor productivity and real wages (5)			0.40			0.35
Latvia	Avg. labor productivity growth	1.57	−0.08		7.22	1.49	
	Avg. real wage growth (3)	7.70	0.46		2.02	1.11	
	Avg. unit labor cost (EURO) growth (4)				4.03	0.72	
	Correlation labor productivity and real wages (5)			0.12			0.23
Lithuania	Avg. labor productivity growth				5.78	0.98	
	Avg. real wage growth (3)				5.06	1.97	
	Avg. unit labor cost (EURO) growth (4)				14.40	2.80	
	Correlation labor productivity and real wages (5)						0.71
Poland	Avg. labor productivity growth	10.67	2.39		8.92	3.28	
	Avg. real wage growth (3)	3.13	1.27		2.94	1.84	
	Avg. unit labor cost (EURO) growth (4)	1.03	0.37		0.83	0.35	
	Correlation labor productivity and real wages (5)			0.39			0.41
Romania	Avg. labor productivity growth	0.90	0.09		5.18	0.93	
	Avg. real wage growth (3)	−6.18	−2.64		−1.09	−0.16	
	Avg. unit labor cost (EURO) growth (4)	−4.66	−0.42		0.96	0.42	
	Correlation labor productivity and real wages (5)			−0.44			0.24
Slovak Rep.	Avg. labor productivity growth	1.82	0.24		7.68	1.46	
	Avg. real wage growth (3)	2.45	1.13		3.19	2.51	
	Avg. unit labor cost (EURO) growth (4)	13.48	3.04		0.87	0.50	
	Correlation labor productivity and real wages (5)			0.78			0.75
Slovenia	Avg. labor productivity growth	2.56	0.60		2.92	−0.07	
	Avg. real wage growth (3)	3.08	1.68		4.41	2.03	
	Avg. unit labor cost (EURO) growth (4)	3.68	0.49		3.80	0.56	
	Correlation labor productivity and real wages (5)			−0.31			0.73

Source: Authors' calculations.

Note:
1. Weighted average across 14 manufacturing industries (in percent)
2. Unweighted average divided by the standard deviation (in percent)
3. Average monthly wages, real (defl. CPI) annual changes in percent.
4. Unit labor cost (EURO) - annual in percent
5. Correlation between average growth rates in real wages and labor productivity growth.

Firm Creation and Destruction Is Also Vital for Promoting Productivity Growth

One interesting result emerging from the previous section is that productivity growth was largely driven by performance within each manufacturing industry, rather than by reallocation of resources across manufacturing industries. To shed more light on this result and proceeding to the level where the core action of restructuring is taking place, this section analyzes firm-level data to assess how restructuring of existing firms and the process of creative destruction (that is, the entry of new firms that displace old and obsolete units) contribute to productivity growth.

There are a number of ways in which aggregate productivity can be decomposed into a within-firm component and other components related to the reallocation of resources across firms. The approach used in this section distinguishes five different components of productivity growth: the *within component*, accounting for productivity growth taking place within firms; the *between component*, capturing the increases in aggregate productivity that come from high-productivity firms gaining market shares or from low-productivity firms losing market shares; the *covariance* or *cross component*, a term that combines changes in market shares and changes in productivity (it is positive if enterprises with growing productivity also experience an increase in market shares); and components attributable to *entry* and *exit* of firms (see box 4.4 for further details).

BOX 4.4

The Decomposition of Productivity Growth Using Firm-Level Data

One approach (equation 4.3) used to decompose productivity growth is from Foster, Haltiwanger, and Krizan (2001). It uses base-year market shares as weights for each term of the decomposition:

$$\Delta P_t = \sum_{Continuers} \theta_{it-k} \Delta p_{it} + \sum_{Continuers} \Delta \theta_{it}(p_{it-k} - P_{t-k}) + \sum_{Continuers} \Delta \theta_{it} \Delta p_{it} \\ + \sum_{Entries} \theta_{it}(p_{it} - P_{t-k}) - \sum_{Exits} \theta_{it-k}(p_{it-k} - P_{t-k}) \quad (4.3)$$

where Δ means changes over the *k*-years' interval between the first year ($t - k$) and the last year (t); θ_{it} is the share of firm *i* in the given industry at time *t* (it could be expressed in output or employment); p_i is the productivity of firm *i*, and *P* is the aggregate (that is, weighted average) productivity level of the industry. The first term is the *within component*; the second term is the *between component*; the third term is the so-called *covariance* or *cross component*; and the fourth and fifth terms are the *entry component* and *exit component*, respectively.

FIGURE 4.6
Contribution of Reallocation to Russian Labor-Productivity Growth, 1986–2001

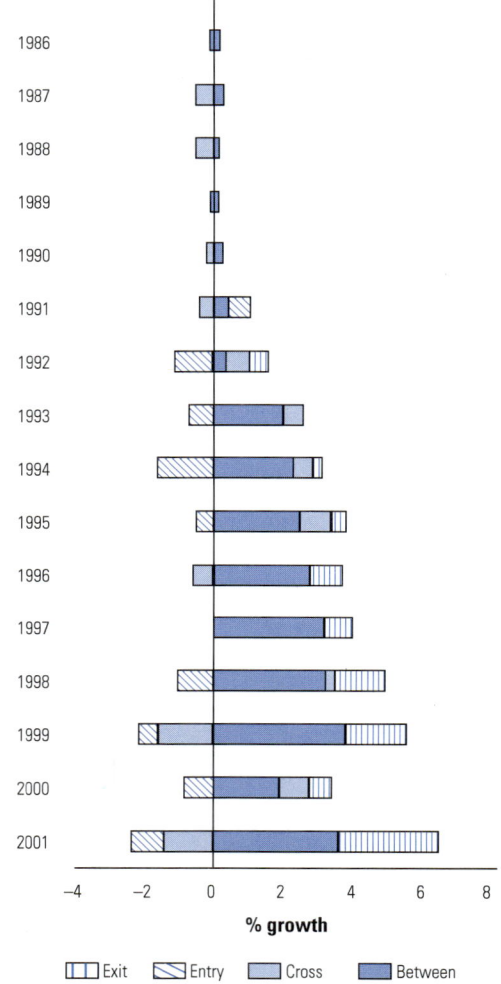

Source: Brown and Earle 2004.

Note:
between = productivity growth resulting from reallocation of labor across existing firms
entry = productivity growth resulting from entry of new firms
exit = productivity growth resulting from exit of firms
cross = changes in market share and changes in productivity

Firm-level data for a sample of CEE countries plus Russia and Ukraine suggest that since the beginning of the transition, reallocation of employment across firms and industries has gained a stronger role in promoting productivity growth (figures 4.6 and 4.7).[6] Nevertheless, efforts to promote greater efficiency within each firm also play an important role. Also, confirming the findings obtained with more aggregate data, there is little evidence of labor reallocation across existing firms from the least- to most-productive units. If anything, firms experiencing an increase in productivity were also losing employment shares (that is, their productivity growth was associated with restructuring and downsizing, rather than expansion) (figure 4.7).

The net entry effect (entry plus exit) is generally positive in most transition countries, accounting for between 20 percent and 50 percent of total productivity growth. In particular, there is clear evidence that the exit of obsolete firms released resources that could be used more effectively by new or existing firms. Although lack of experience and small size often make new firms less productive than the average incumbent in OECD countries, new firms in transition economies are (on average) more efficient than the incumbents. They have been able to fill in new market niches and adopt new and more efficient technologies, thereby contributing to productivity and output growth.

FIGURE 4.7
Sources of Productivity Growth in Transition and Emerging Economies
Labor productivity decomposition shares: manufacturing, three-year differencing, real gross output

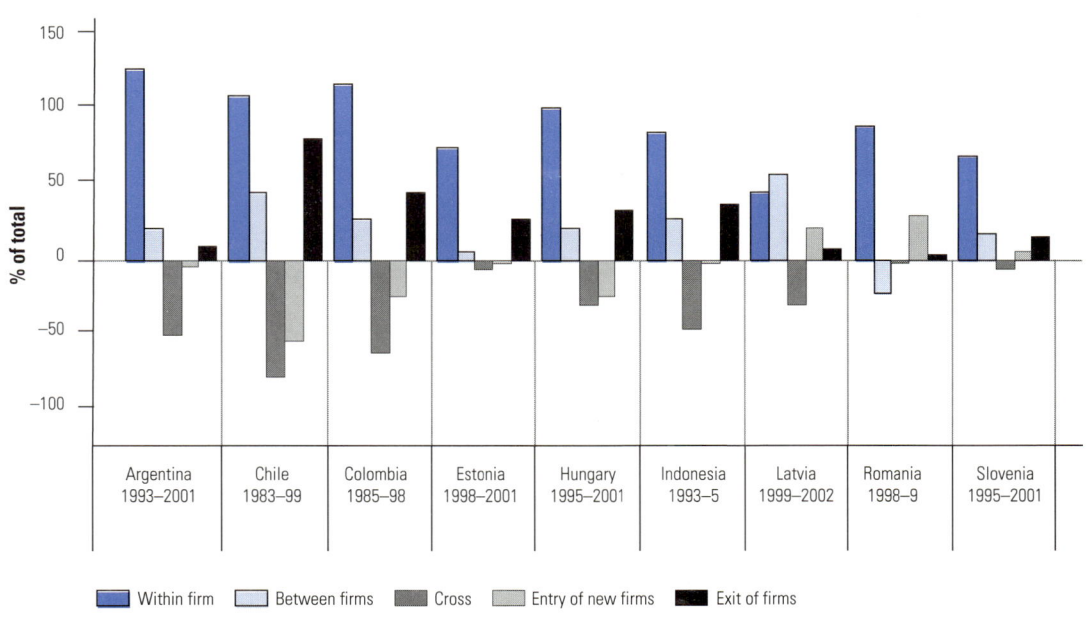

Source: Bartelsman, Haltiwanger, and Scarpetta 2004.

Note:
Within = within firm productivity growth
between = productivity growth resulting from reallocation of labor across existing firms
entry = productivity growth resulting from entry of new firms
exit = productivity growth resulting from exit of firms
cross = changes in market share and changes in productivity

In Medium- and High-Technology Industries, New Firms Are Better at Harnessing New Technologies

Dividing manufacturing industries into a low-technology group and a medium- and high-technology group suggests important differences in the sources of productivity growth. Defensive restructuring seems to be largely concentrated in low-technology industries, where the contribution of new firms to productivity growth is modest (Scarpetta and Vodopivec 2005). By contrast, the entry of new firms plays a strong role in boosting productivity in medium- and high-technology industries. This is consistent with the idea that in areas where there are greater opportunities for adopting newer and better technologies, new firms play an essential role.

New Firms Also Promote Productivity of Incumbents by Raising Market "Contestability"

The role of entry and exit of firms is also important in reinforcing competitive pressure on incumbents. The risk that new firms may steal market shares from incumbents and the risk of failure both act as strong disciplinary devices to promote better performance by incumbents. A first look at such contestability effects is provided in figure 4.8, which presents the correlation between the contribution of net entry in a country or sector (using time averages from the

FIGURE 4.8
Relationship between Net Entry Contribution and Productivity Growth of Incumbents

Firm entry and productivity growth of incumbents: five-year differencing, real gross output, country and industry time averages

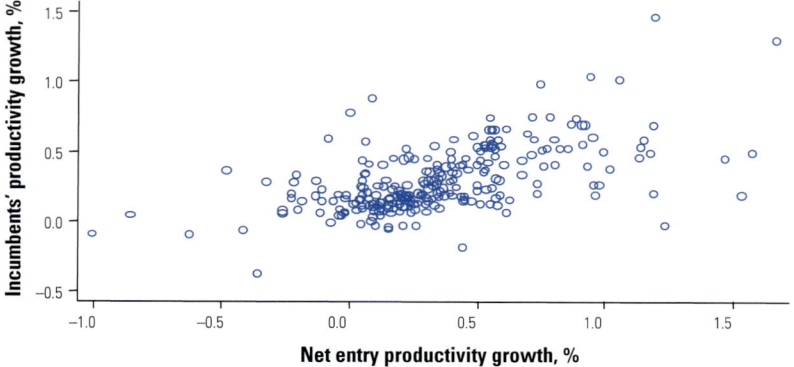

Source: Bartelsman, Haltiwanger, and Scarpetta 2004.

Note: Correlation coefficient: 0.58, statistically significant at 1 percent. Each dot is one country-industry observation. Excludes Brazil and República Bolivariana de Venezuela. Outliers excluded.

country-sector-year data) and the productivity growth from incumbents (the *within component* in the productivity decomposition). Interestingly, a strong positive and statistically significant correlation exists between the net entry contribution and the productivity growth of incumbents. This finding is suggestive that there is a relationship between the creative destruction and within-firm sources of productivity growth.[7]

In sum, while existing firms have largely responded to the need to improve performance by reducing overstaffing—especially in traditional sectors—the creative destruction process has boosted productivity growth, both directly by the entry of new, more-productive firms that have displaced less-productive units and indirectly by reinforcing market contestability.

What Drives Restructuring of Existing Firms?

Restructuring of Existing Firms Has Been Largely Influenced by Privatization

Privatization has often been the main trigger of firm restructuring, and transition countries have used different privatization methods, have transferred ownership at different paces, and have left different roles for the state as shareholder in privatized firms. All these factors have played a role in fostering the reduction in inefficiency and in promoting firm development.

Transition countries have generally privatized small firms quickly and completely, while the privatization of large firms has proceeded more gradually. Among transition economies, CEE countries privatized both small and large firms faster and more comprehensively than SEE or CIS countries. The dispersion of both small- and large-scale privatization progress has been by far the largest in the CIS, while it has been relatively uniform in CEE countries, particularly for small-scale privatization.

Privatization Has Promoted Firm Performance

Privatization strongly improved enterprise performance, but its effects vary substantially by type of privatization and by groups of countries. The recent "quantitative" survey of Djankov and Murrell (2002), based on meta-analysis of 93 empirical studies from various transition countries, finds that outside owners have been more effective in improving performance than insiders and that privatization methods generating concentrated ownership—particularly by foreigners—improved performance the most. Firms with diffused outsider ownership performed virtually the same as state firms, and worker-owned firms performed the worst. Productivity effects of privatization also vary strongly across countries. In Central and Eastern Europe, these effects have been more statistically significant and greater in size (often adding several percentage points to enterprise growth) than in the CIS (Djankov and Murrell 2002).[8]

A more in-depth assessment of the privatization process in four countries (Hungary, Romania, Russia, and Ukraine) sheds further light on these issues (figure 4.9). It suggests that the effect of foreign privatization on performance is strikingly similar across countries, in contrast to the effects of domestic privatization. This suggests that foreigners' advantages in accessing finance, new technologies, the latest managerial techniques, and world markets far outweigh any disadvantages resulting from unfamiliarity with local conditions and weak political connections.

The privatization methods used in Hungary and Romania also resulted in concentrated ownership from the time of privatization, whereas mass privatization in Russia and Ukraine led to dispersed ownership by employees and small outside investors.[9] Secondary trading has resulted in more-concentrated ownership in Russia and Ukraine, but this has taken time. This raises the possibility that if ownership concentration is a necessary condition for privatization to have a positive effect, then the effect may have appeared sooner in Hungary and Romania than in Russia and Ukraine.

FIGURE 4.9
Effects of Foreign and Domestic Privatization on Multifactor Productivity Growth (MFP)

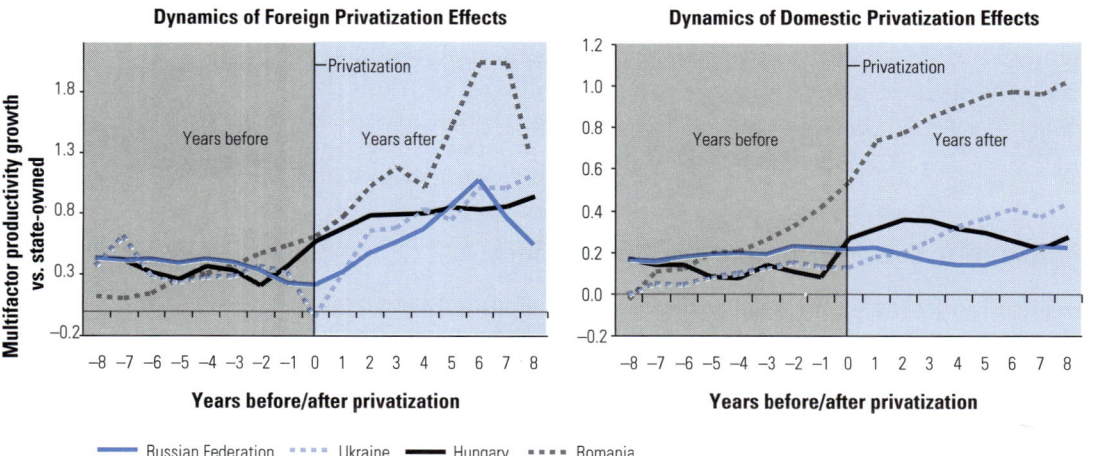

Source: Brown and Earle 2004.

Positive Effects on Job Creation Are Found among Foreign-Owned Privatized Firms

Privatization has also had significant effects on workers (see figure 4.10). Evidence from these four countries suggests that foreign privatization has increased employment and wages in all countries, though the effects are not always large. Domestic privatization has been less kind to workers, however, because wages suffered in all four countries and employment rose only in a few instances.

But there are also significant differences across types of workers. Thus, employment composition and relative wage changes have been significantly biased toward white-collar employees. This is consistent with the idea that foreign privatization, by promoting the upgrading of production processes with new technologies, tends to be skill-biased. It also suggests that although foreign privatization has improved the welfare of workers overall, it has also increased inequality.

How Many Firms Enter and Exit the Market in Transition Countries?

Much Creation and Some Destruction of Firms

As emphasized earlier, firm dynamics—especially firm entry—have been an essential driver of job creation and an engine for productiv-

FIGURE 4.10

Effects of Foreign and Domestic Privatization on Productivity, Employment, and Wages

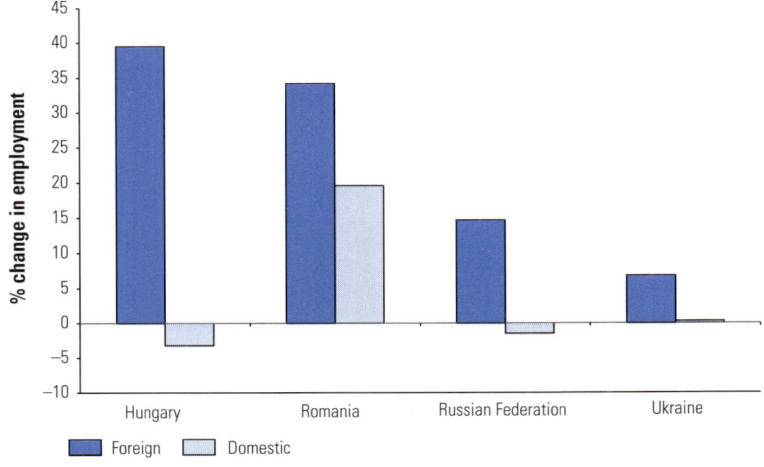

Source: Brown and Earle 2004.

ity growth. How many firms enter and exit the market in transition economies? What are their characteristics, compared with those of the incumbents?

A common fact in all market economies is that many firms enter and exit most markets every year. This is particularly true in transition economies where 20–25 percent of firms (with at least one employee) have entered or exited the market (on average) annually in the past decade (figure 4.11). Moreover, in transition economies, firm entry largely outpaced firm exit. Obviously, this is related to the process of transition and is not sustainable over the longer run. Still, it points to the fact that new firms not only displaced obsolete incumbents in the transition phase but also filled in new markets that were either nonexistent or poorly populated in the past. This is also reflected in the discrepancies between firm entry and exit across firm size. Indeed, the entry of firms is particularly large among microunits (20 or fewer employees). During the centrally planned system, there were relatively few of these microfirms; however, they exploded during the transition in most business service activities.

Even Successful Entrants Do Not Expand Significantly

A high entry rate is in itself a signal of market dynamism, and especially in transition economies, it is essential to develop new private activities. However, in most market economies, high entry sectors are also characterized by high exit rates, involving many young businesses that are censored by the market. So, how much do new firms displace old, obsolete units, and how high are failure rates among newcomers in the first years of their life?

FIGURE 4.11

How Many Firms Enter and Exit the Market?

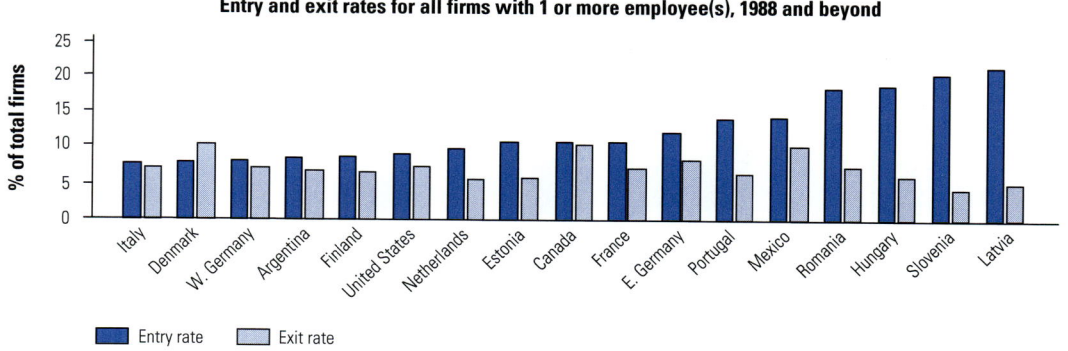

Source: Bartelsman, Haltiwanger, and Scarpetta 2004.

Compared with the OECD economies, new firms in transition countries seem to have higher survival rates (Scarpetta and Vodopivec 2005). Except for Romania, more than 70 percent of entrant firms are still in the market after four years, while the proportion is often around 60 percent in the OECD countries.

However, the expansion of successful new firms is limited, and new firms remain of relatively small size. This is common to many European countries and largely differs from other markets, including the United States, where successful entrants double in size in the early years of life.[10] These results point to the fact that the performance of new firms may be affected not only by entry conditions but also by factors that affect the decision to expand and hire more workers. These include access to finance, labor adjustment costs, and stability of the economic and regulatory environment (see chapter 5).

Summing Up: Entry Conditions and Incentives to Create Jobs Are Essential for Improving Job Creation in the Region

At the onset of transition, the presence of many inefficient state-owned firms offered a unique challenge for countries in the Region, but also a major opportunity for vast productivity improvements and sustained ameliorations of living standards. Because of large misallocation of resources, reallocation of labor and other resources—across firms, sectors, and locations—was perceived as one of the foremost tasks of transition. New control mechanisms of firm efficiency were put in place, dictating the pace and depth of restructuring. The process of creative destruction (that is, the exit of unprofitable firms, paving the way for the creation of new, more-productive ones), invigorated by privatization and competition, was expected to be exceptionally important in raising productivity in transition countries.

To a large extent, these expectations were borne out. Transition brought a remarkable surge of job flows. Firms destroyed low-productivity jobs and created high-productivity ones. The entry of new private firms in the market has been exceptionally large by international standards, contributing to the creation of many new jobs. But the exit of obsolete firms also accounted for a large share of job destruction. Because of restructuring and ensuing resource reallocation, the sectoral structure of employment strongly changed, with the increase of market services, deindustrialization, and reduction of employment in agriculture being the main outcomes. However, this general picture hides large differences across transition economies. For example, reflecting harsher adjustment conditions and slower progress in transforming the institutions to market standards, the share of agriculture in total employment increased in most CIS countries.

The reallocation of resources also proved to be efficiency-enhancing: although productivity increases have largely been driven by within-firm forces, resulting in defensive restructuring, firm entry has strongly increased productivity. In particular, not only have many new firms been relatively more productive than existing ones in transition—a fact that is uncommon in OECD countries—but their entry has also contributed to igniting competitive pressure on incumbents promoting their restructuring.

Investment climate conditions are also of great importance to stimulating the expansion of successful firms, often constrained by lack of access to finance or uncertainties about the institutional and market environment in which they operate. And by continuing to provide budgetary support to ailing firms (albeit often not as direct subsidies), many transition countries have not provided consistent and credible enforcement of firm exit (the share of job destruction resulting from exit of firms has been below that in nontransition countries, and increasing it would quite possibly be productivity- and welfare-increasing). These countries have therefore underutilized the potential exit of firms as a disciplinary device, as well as the actual exit of firms as a means of freeing resources to other, more-productive uses.

The main engine to enterprise restructuring has been the transfer of ownership to the private sector. Most pretransition firms have been privatized in Eastern Europe and the Former Soviet Union, although the method of privatization and the governance of the new private entities vary a great deal across countries of the Region. Most of these privatized firms have pursued defensive restructuring, with large layoffs. Their ability to move toward more strategic restructuring—with new investment and job creation—depends on the same investment climate conditions affecting newly created firms. The evidence that foreign-owned privatized firms have had better productivity and employment performance than domestically owned firms suggests possible difficulties in accessing new technologies, in exploring foreign markets, and in management.

The stance of the investment climate in transition economies and its impact on firm performance and job creation are reviewed in the next chapter of this report.

Notes

1. Previous studies have used two types of benchmark to assess how far away transition countries were from market economy structures and how much they had progressed over the transition periods toward these market structures. The first approach uses the GDP and employment structure of the neighboring Western European countries as a reference, using Northern and Southern European countries as two possible benchmarks (Aiginger and others 1999; Landesmann 2000). Alternatively, other studies have used regression analyses based on cross-country data for a large number of nontransition market economies (Raiser, Schaffer, and Schuchhardt 2003). The first approach is more relevant for accession countries, whose level of development is relatively close to their Western European counterparts; for these countries, both approaches yield similar conclusions. The second approach, however, is more adequate to assess CIS countries, whose market-structure benchmark is probably to be found in low- or low-to-middle–income developing countries and is used in this study.
2. The data refer to 1989–2002, although for a number of countries data coverage is more limited.
3. The distortion index is calculated as the sum of the observed distortion in each macrosector of the economy. The market benchmarks are obtained through regressions of sectoral employment shares on GDP per capita levels and its square. In this respect, the distortion index is a measure of the overall distance of an economy from a market economy with the same per capita income. See also Raiser, Schaffer, and Schuchhardt (2003) for more details.
4. Given data availability, the decomposition is limited to 14 manufacturing industries in 11 CEE countries. This limits the scope of the analysis because, as stressed above, most of the reallocation of labor has been driven by shifts away from manufacturing into business services, rather than within manufacturing. Still, it helps to assess whether market forces have promoted reallocation of labor toward those industries with greater growth potentials.
5. See Grosfeld and Roland (1996) for a discussion of defensive versus strategic restructuring.
6. The analysis focuses on Estonia, Hungary, Latvia, Romania, and Slovenia, and it is based on business register and enterprise survey data. For more details, see Bartelsman, Haltiwanger, and Scarpetta (2004).
7. It might be, however, that the correlation is resulting from the impact of technological advances for both continuing firms and for the creative destruction process. With technological advances, it can be observed that incumbents who survive increase productivity and that entering businesses (which presumably adopt the latest advances) are more productive than the exiting businesses. To focus on the contestability hypothesis more directly, Bartelsman, Haltiwanger, and Scarpetta (2004) also examine the relationship between the firm turnover rate and the productivity growth of incumbents. They again find a positive and statistically significant correlation. This latter finding provides even more direct evidence

of a connection between the competitiveness or contestability of markets and the productivity growth within incumbent firms.

8. Nearly all the studies covered by Djankov and Murrell (2002) are based on small surveys conducted soon after privatization. Since then, a few studies have used comprehensive manufacturing firm data with long time series to provide more rigorous tests of the effects of privatization. Orazem and Vodopivec (2003) find no effect of either domestic private or foreign ownership on total factor productivity in Slovenia during 1994–2001, but a strong effect of market competition. Lizal and Svejnar (2002) find a clear positive effect of foreign ownership on firm productivity and employment growth in the Czech Republic during 1992–98, but no effect of domestic ownership. The insignificant domestic ownership effect on productivity is surprising at first glance, given that the postprivatization ownership structure was concentrated in the hands of investment funds. These investment funds were poorly regulated, however, and many were at least temporarily owned by state banks.

9. Romania used management-employee buyouts early in the privatization process, but employees voted as a group, unlike in Russia and Ukraine.

10. Among the few CEE countries for which data are available, Romania is an exception: not only are failure rates higher than in the other countries but even successful entrants have very limited opportunities of expanding.

CHAPTER 5

The Investment Climate and Job Creation

This chapter analyzes the link between investment climate and job creation. It shows that differences in the investment climate account for a significant part of the variation of employment outcomes in the Region. It thus argues that improvements in the investment climate are critical for the creation of more and better jobs in the Region.

Although the investment climate varies considerably in the transition countries, it is generally worse than in both developing and developed countries with the most hospitable business environments. For example, it takes 11 days to start a business in Latvia and more than 100 days in Azerbaijan. In CEE, the average time to start a business is 50 days, compared with only 4 days in Denmark or the United States. The cost to register a business in low income CIS countries is significantly higher than in Thailand, for example.

In all of the transition countries, there is room for reducing the risks, costs, and barriers associated with business operation, although the nature and intensity of constraints vary across countries. In low income CIS countries, the dominant problem is underdeveloped institutions of a market economy (including security of property rights), economic and regulatory policy uncertainty, arbitrary and selective application of the regulations, corruption, and poor infrastructure. Middle income CIS countries, among them Russia, have a higher economic potential and perform better in some dimensions of the investment climate than do the poorer low income CIS countries. However, the challenges are still profound. Corruption is widespread. Burdensome regulations and bureaucratic harassment hamper business growth, as do underdeveloped financial markets.

In SEE, the playing field for firms is not level because of various—formal and informal—constraints on competition. The legal system does not function effectively, making contract enforcement difficult. Administrative barriers in some areas (for example, customs and trade) are still high, inhibiting firm growth and fuelling corruption. In CEE, institutions of a market economy are more developed and market-oriented reforms more advanced, easing some of the constraints. Yet, much can be done to lower the cost of doing business. High taxes, including taxes on labor, inhibit investment and hiring. Access to credit, although much easier than in other parts of the Region, is still seen as difficult by entrepreneurs. In some CEE countries, onerous regulations, including labor regulations, are a significant impediment to firm expansion. Finally, in some CEE countries, employers find it difficult to hire workers with necessary skills.

How to foster job creation in the Region? In low income CIS countries, the key issue is to develop institutions of a market economy and lower the risk associated with doing business. Property rights need to become more secure and infrastructure more reliable. In middle income CIS countries and SEE, focus should be placed on lowering the administrative barriers. Deregulation, less discretionary power in the hands of bureaucrats, product market competition, and a more effective legal system would address the most binding constraints. Finally, in CEE, priority should be given to addressing the demand for skilled workers, improving labor market flexibility, and lowering the monetary cost of doing business. One key measure is to reduce taxation, particularly taxes on labor, which are especially high in CEE. This requires carrying through difficult public expenditure reforms, particularly reforms of the pension and health care systems (see chapter 6).

But obviously, investment climate reforms need to consider country-specific obstacles to business growth. These can be identified by using investment climate surveys and focus groups of employers and—most important—by instituting authentic dialogue with the business community, including the newly established small private firms.

The rest of the chapter is organized as follows. Section 1 shows the link between the investment climate and employment. Section 2 presents major obstacles to firm operation and growth in the Region, as perceived by the employers. Section 3 provides empirical evidence of the investment climate's impact on job creation in the Region and shows that differences in employment outcomes are to a large extent accounted for by differences in the investment climate. Section 4 compares the investment climate in the transition countries to that in other regions and uses benchmarking to identify areas where there is room for improvement. Section 5 summarizes the main investment climate constraints in the Region and its subgroups of countries.

Importance of Investment Climate for Job Creation

As stressed in the previous chapter, the birth of new firms and the expansion of existing firms are prerequisites for employment growth and the reduction in unemployment. The importance of new firm creation as a source of new jobs is particularly large in a situation of massive reallocation of workers and jobs across sectors of the economy. New firms in the expanding sectors need to absorb workers released from firms in the declining sectors.[1] During the past decade, the Region's economies suffered a large displacement of workers (see chapter 4). Many SOEs went out of business once they were exposed to hard budget constraints and competition. Others have downsized. They reduced labor hoarding and shed redundant labor to reach the economically efficient size. As a result, the average firm size decreased and comes closer to that in market economies. For example, presently, the average size of a Polish firm is roughly 40 percent of that at the beginning of the transition. But if many firms downsize, as is the case in the Region, then the number of firms needs to grow for employment to increase.

A Sound Investment Climate Is Essential to Firm Creation and Expansion and Thus Employment Growth

Firm entry depends on the costs of starting a business and also on the expected benefits and costs of operating a business (Klapper, Laeven, and Rajan 2004). Similarly, firm growth depends on the rate of return to investment, which, in turn, is influenced by competitive pressures in the product market, internal governance, and access to new technologies. Institutions, policies, and regulations that affect firm entry, survival, and growth are referred to in this chapter as the "investment climate." The rest of this chapter examines the investment climate factors that hamper job creation in the Region through limiting firm entry and growth.

Employers' Views on the Major Obstacles to Firms' Operation and Growth in the Region

One way to assess the investment climate is to consider the entrepreneurs' opinions about their major constraints in running and expanding their businesses.[2] Additional valuable insights can be gained from focus group discussions (see box 5.1).

Entrepreneurs See Instability and Uncertainties as Major Obstacles to Business Expansion across the Region

Economic and regulatory policy uncertainty, along with macroeconomic instability, are top business concerns in the Region. One firm in three views these factors as major or severe obstacles to its operation and growth (figure 5.1). To a large extent, high business risk is an inherent feature of the transition, but bad governance often adds to this natural uncertainty. This includes frequent changes in regulations, lack of regulatory consistency and clarity, arbitrary interpretation of regulations and their selective enforcement, and (last, but not least) corruption. Although business is always associated with some

---

BOX 5.1

Small Entrepreneurs Complain about the Business Environment in Bulgaria

A few quotes from the survey of small entrepreneurs illustrate the problems they face in opening and running a business:

"If I had to start again, I would not even think of opening a business."

"I cannot even remember how many times I went for each permit. It just takes insanely long."

"During the inspections, they pick on every single thing. When they decide to pick up your money, there is no way out. They always find something to pick on."

"You must hold a law degree to be able to open a cafeteria."

"Instead of thinking how to be more efficient, we spend 60 percent of our time thinking how to cope with tax authorities and inspectors."

"There should be rules of the game, but clear ones and equally applicable to all."

Source: World Bank 2002a.

risk, reducing policy-induced uncertainty and improving governance are keys to improving the investment climate in the Region.

Uncertainty and macroeconomic instability, albeit important in all countries, are—as could be expected—deemed less severe not only in those CEE countries that are members of the EU but also (somewhat surprisingly) in the low income CIS countries. In contrast, uncertainty and instability are very frequently perceived as major constraints in SEE and middle income CIS countries.

Taxation, Access to Finance, and Corruption Also Severely Impede Business Activity

Firms in the Region frequently complain about taxation. This is natural, because taxes raise costs and lower returns on investment. At the same time, taxes are necessary to finance public goods and services. So setting tax rates is a difficult balancing act. However, in the transition countries, taxes are often unduly high because of inefficiencies in ser-

FIGURE 5.1
Most Frequently Reported Major Obstacles to Firm Operation in the Region

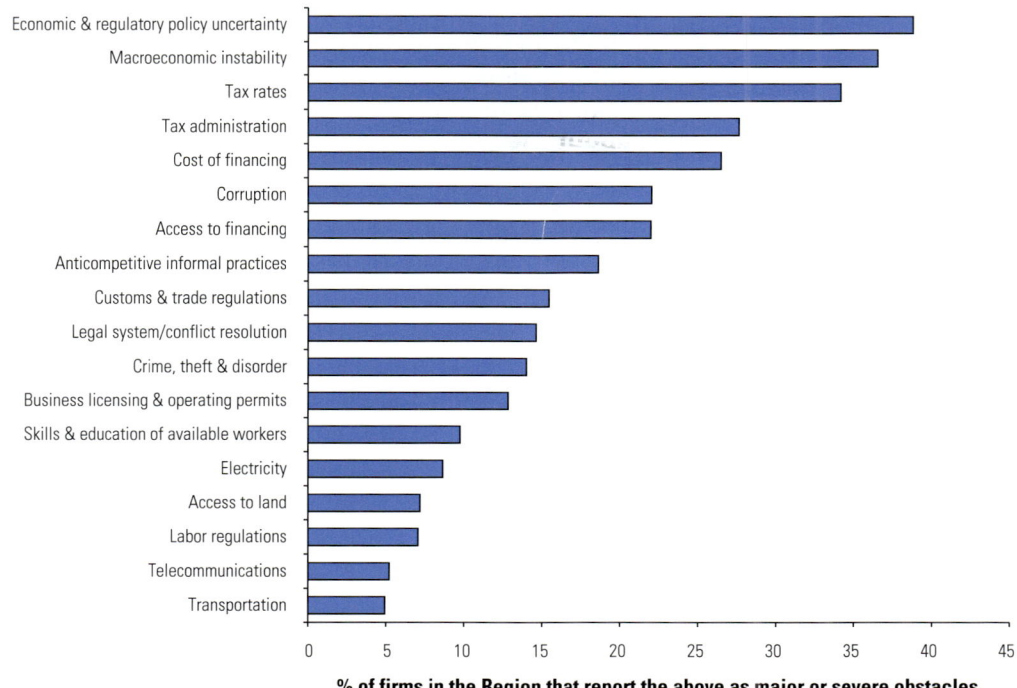

Source: EBRD–World Bank Business Environment and Enterprise Performance Surveys, 2002.

Note: Preliminary results from the new 2005 BEEPS are broadly consistent with those reported in this figure. However, some changes may have occurred for individual countries or subgroups of countries in the Region.

vice delivery, poor tax collection capacity, and a narrow tax base (resulting from a large informal sector), so there is room for reducing tax rates by improving efficiency without compromising important social objectives. One example is to reduce payroll taxes by reforming the pension and health care systems. This pertains especially to CEE and SEE countries, where payroll taxes are particularly high (see chapter 6).

An aspect of taxation that is more amenable to direct policy action is tax administration, which is seen as a major or severe obstacle by close to 30 percent of firms in the Region. Tax administration is a synonym for bureaucratic harassment (for example, disruptive and costly tax inspections), arbitrary interpretation of obscure tax regulations, selective enforcement, and associated extortion. As such, inefficient tax administration—an element of poor governance—contributes to both costs and risks faced by firms and so discourages investment. Tax administration is seen as a particularly severe issue in CIS countries, making it a policy priority.

Another top investment climate issue in the Region, as perceived by employers, is the high cost and difficult access to finance.[3] For more than one in four firms in the Region, the cost of credit is a major obstacle to firm growth. For more than one in five, difficult access (for example, high collateral requirements) is a major constraint. Evidence suggests that small firms are particularly hurt by poor access to credit, which limits their growth prospects (Beck, Demirguc-Kunt, and Laeven 2005). Improving access to finance, especially for small firms, is thus a priority in those cases where high real interest rates (or interest rate spreads) reflect an underdeveloped and noncompetitive banking system, which is particularly the case in low income CIS countries (De Nicoló, Geadah, and Rozhkov 2003).

Finally, firm growth in the Region is inhibited by widespread corruption and anticompetitive informal practices. Roughly, one firm in five sees these as major or severe obstacles to their operation and growth. Corruption and government interference are closely associated with numerous administrative barriers, red tape, and discretionary power in the hands of bureaucrats. These governance-related issues are particularly pronounced in SEE, while less so in the new EU-member countries.

Labor Regulations Are Seen as a Less Severe Obstacle in the Region

Labor regulations are not among top business concerns in the Region. According to the investment climate surveys, they are ranked 14 out of 18 obstacles.[4] They are seldom viewed as a major obstacle, but many firms see them as a moderate obstacle. Altogether, labor regulations pose a moderate, major, or severe obstacle to one firm in four in the Region, which is by no means a negligible fraction.

Labor Regulations Still Matter

Why are labor regulations perceived as less important in the Region? One reason is lax enforcement, especially in countries with poor administrative capacity. Another reason is that they are less important compared with other constraints. Labor regulations may constrain business operation, but other regulations and conditions may be much more constraining. In less-advanced economies, they are dwarfed by the overall uncertainty and instability, poor access to capital, corruption, and so forth.

Another potential reason may be cultural or historical: in many countries of the Region, employers take historically established labor regulations for granted. This is especially likely in countries where the interests of private businesses have not yet fully taken hold. The comparison between Croatia and Poland is illustrative. In Croatia, employment protection legislation is very strict, yet employers hardly complain about it. In contrast, in Poland, employment protection legislation is significantly more liberal; nonetheless, it ranks high among key business concerns. At the same time, the pace of enterprise restructuring has been much faster in Poland than in Croatia (Rutkowski 2003a). Therefore, the difference in perceptions is likely to reflect the fact that Polish employers are more aware of the role of labor regulations as an impediment to restructuring. This explanation is supported by the fact that restructuring firms (those that actually shed labor) more often report labor regulations as a significant obstacle than do firms that have not gone through downsizing (Pierre and Scarpetta 2004a).

Although labor regulations are not the top business concern, enhancing labor market adaptability is still essential for improving labor market outcomes in the Region. There are at least three reasons why the efficiency of the labor law needs to be improved:[5]

- The fraction of firms adversely affected by labor market regulations is significant in most the Region's subgroups of countries, and in some countries it is high. For example, in Poland, every second firm sees labor regulations as at least a moderate obstacle, and in Serbia and Montenegro and the Slovak Republic, labor regulations are seen as an obstacle by about one firm in three. In addition, as mentioned earlier, labor regulations tend to hurt firms that are most dynamic and are the source of growth and jobs.

- In many countries—mainly in the CIS—labor regulations are not seen as an obstacle only because they are not enforced (see chapter 6). But flexibility through nonenforcement is not an optimal solution; it undermines the rule of law and contributes to the uncertainty faced by both firms and workers.

- The need for greater efficiency of labor regulations is particularly pronounced in the Region, given the paramount challenge of restructuring and productivity catch-up (see chapters 4 and 6).

Worker Skills Can Constrain Firm Strategic Restructuring

Skill deficiencies are a significant obstacle to firm growth, especially in CEE, where restructuring has proceeded at a higher speed and is more advanced. For example, in the Czech Republic, Hungary, Latvia, and Poland, 35 to 40 percent of employers see the skills of the available workforce as a significant obstacle to the growth of their firms. In Estonia, this proportion reaches 65 percent. A special survey of labor demand in an intensively restructuring region of Azerbaijan found that the lack of workers with adequate skills is the third most important reason that prevents firms from hiring more workers (World Bank 2005a). One important source of the skills problem is a strong bias against workers with low educational attainment and skills, associated with enterprise restructuring and technological progress brought about by the transition (Commander and Köllő 2004).

Entrepreneurs' Perceptions of the Most Pressing Problems Vary by Region

Although many investment climate concerns are common across most transition economies, there is also substantial variation in their relative importance by country groups. In the transition economies that recently joined the EU (EU-8), labor-related issues, such as the skills of the available workers, labor regulations, and taxation, figure prominently in the surveys (figure 5.2, panel A). In other European transition economies, entrepreneurs highlight a combination of poorly functioning institutions (for example, ineffective legal system, industrial conflict resolution) and bad governance (for example, anticompetitive and informal practices, corruption) that limit firm growth and job creation (figure 5.2, panels B and C). In the middle income CIS countries, the predominant part is played by administrative barriers, such as numerous licenses and operating permits, burdensome tax administration (with associated bureaucratic harassment and extortion), and inefficient regulations (figure 5.2, panel D). Finally, in the low income CIS countries, the constraints are more basic and range from unreliable infrastructure to underdeveloped institutions of a market economy (figure 5.2, panel E).

It is striking that labor market issues—employment regulations and worker skills—affect firm growth prospects in CEE, while they apparently play a negligible role in the Region's other subgroups of countries.[6] One explanation is a faster pace of enterprise restructur-

FIGURE 5.2
Obstacles to Business Operation and Growth Vary by Subgroup
Panel A—CEE EU-Member Countries

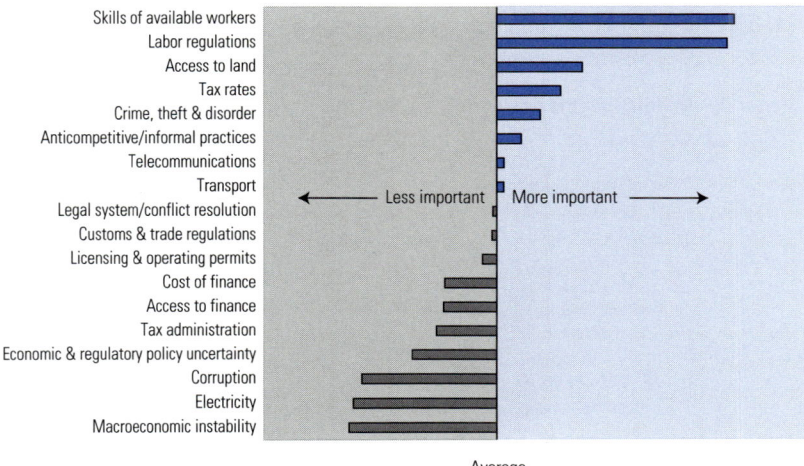

Panel B—CEE EU-Accession Countries: Bulgaria, Croatia, and Romania

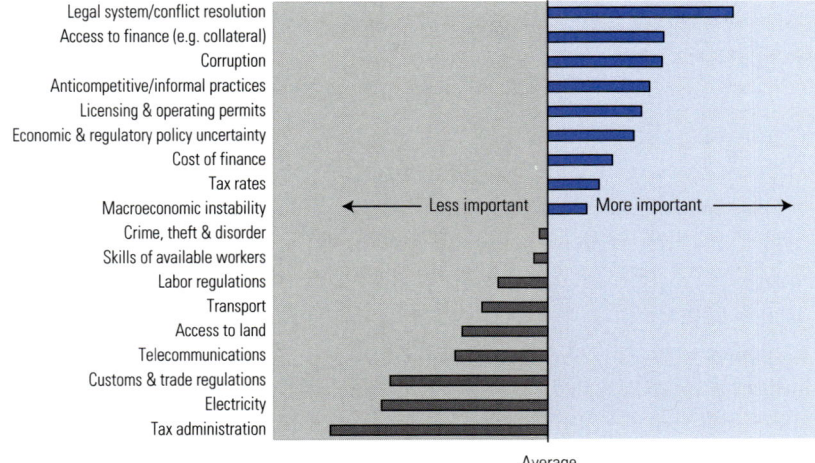

(*continues on the following page.*)

FIGURE 5.2 (continued)
Panel C—Southeastern European Countries

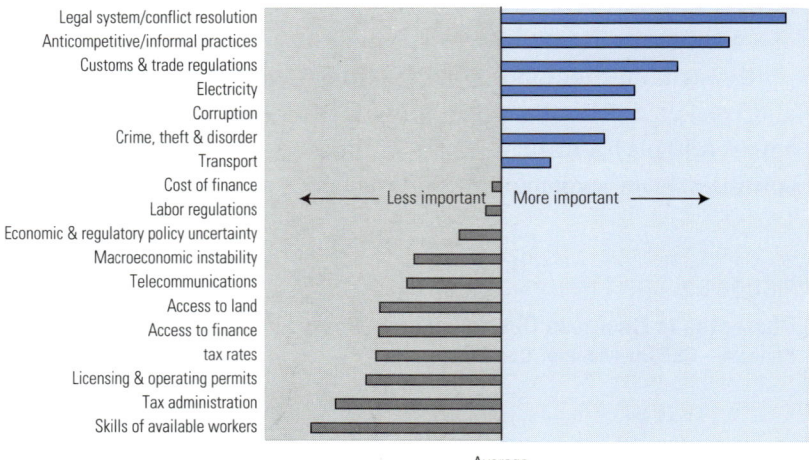

Panel D—Middle Income CIS Countries: Belarus, Kazakhstan, Russia, and Ukraine

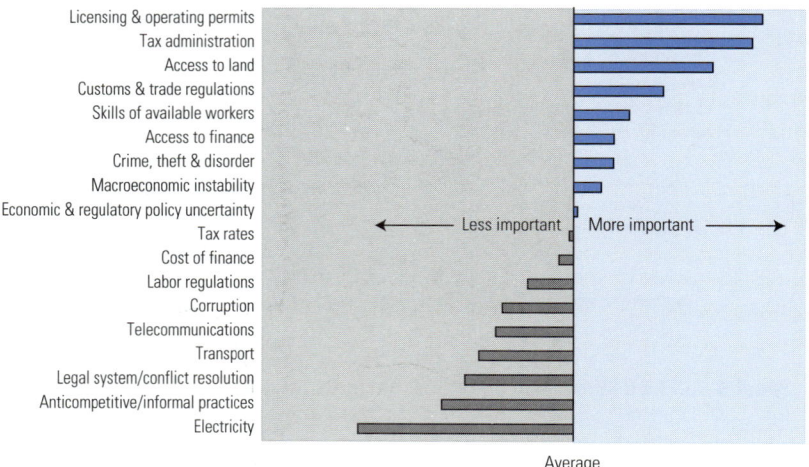

ing in CEE than in other parts of the Region, which affects the labor market in two ways. First, widespread job reallocation gives rise to skills mismatch because the newly created jobs differ in skill content from jobs that were destroyed. This explains why employers in CEE more often than in other regions view skills of available workers as a major constraint to firm growth. Second, labor regulations become an effective obstacle only if firms face competitive pressure and have to adjust the size and composition of their workforce to stay profitable. This in turn explains why employers in faster-restructuring CEE countries more often complain about labor regulations, although on the books they are less strict than in other subgroups.

FIGURE 5.2 (*continued*)

Panel E—Low Income CIS Countries: Armenia, Azerbaijan, Georgia, the Kyrgyz Republic, Moldova, Tajikistan, and Uzbekistan

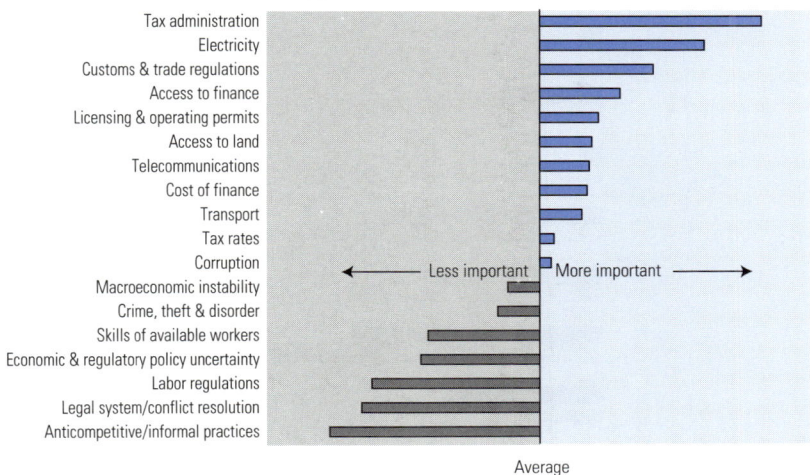

Source: EBRD–World Bank Business Environment and Enterprise Performance Surveys, 2002.

Note: Bars show the deviation from the regional and factor averages. Preliminary results from the new 2005 BEEPS are broadly consistent with those reported in this figure. However, some changes may have occurred for individual countries or subgroups of countries in the Region.

Smaller Firms Tend to Be Disproportionately Affected by Investment Climate Obstacles

Small firms are more sensitive to the investment climate than are larger firms. Results of multivariate regression analysis (figure 5.3) show that, controlling for other characteristics such as firms' age, smaller firms tend to be more affected by the main constraints identified above.[7] Smaller firms also tend to pay more bribes, and to pay bribes more often, than larger ones do (Gray, Hellman, and Ryterman 2004). Because smaller firms are the prime source of job creation, this implies that job growth is sensitive to investment climate changes (see chapter 4).

Policies to Foster Job Creation Need to Go beyond the Labor Market

Entrepreneurs' perceptions of the business climate suggest that the main constraints to job creation in the Region currently lie outside the labor market. It could also mean that labor market regulations are just a part of a broader institutional and policy framework that constrains firms' ability to grow and create new jobs. This has important implications for policies to foster employment and reduce unemployment. They cannot be limited to improving the workings of the labor

FIGURE 5.3
Smaller Firms Are More Constrained by the Investment Climate
Probability of reporting the following as major obstacle by size of firm

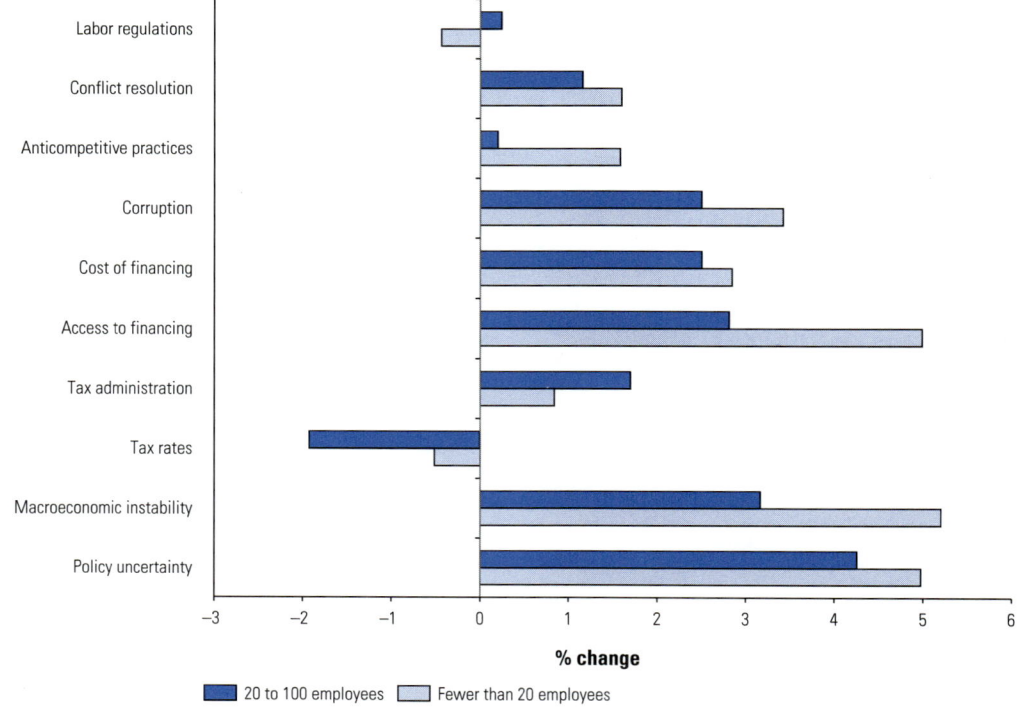

Source: EBRD–World Bank Business Environment and Enterprise Performance Surveys, 2002.

Note: Preliminary results from the new 2005 BEEPS are broadly consistent with those reported in this figure. However, some changes may have occurred for individual countries or subgroups of countries in the Region.

market; instead, they should aim at improving the overall investment climate and focus on the most severe obstacles to firm growth. Given the complexity of investment climate reforms, there is a need to set priorities and focus on the most binding constraints.

Macroeconomic instability and economic and regulatory policy uncertainty are seen as major obstacles for businesses across the Region. These two aspects catch various dimensions of the economic environment in which firms operate. In particular, they relate to the quality of institutions and governance. They are likely to encompass such elements as the unpredictability of policy changes, frequent regulatory changes, discretionary interpretation of laws and their selective enforcement, inconsistency in regulations, and discretionary power in the hands of bureaucrats (for example, the power to give permits) and bureaucratic harassment, associated with corruption and extortion.

Therefore, improving labor market outcomes entails a set of comprehensive and complex policy reforms to remove a wide range of constraints to business operation. This involves institutional reforms and changes in governance. Which particular issues should be given priority depends on country-specific circumstances (because key constraints differ by country) and on the extent to which various elements of the investment climate affect labor market outcomes.

The Impact of Investment Climate on Job Creation in the Region

This section attempts to shed light on two questions. Do countries with better investment climates have better labor market performance? Which institutions are most important for a good employment record? In the rest of this chapter, labor market performance is measured mainly through employment generated in the new private sector. The latter is proxied through service sector employment, as explained in box 5.2.

Differences in Investment Climate Explain a Substantial Part of Variation in Employment Outcomes in the Region

The results of a multivariate regression analysis show that differences in market services sector (used as a proxy for the new private sector) employment across the transition countries to a large degree reflect differences in the investment climate.[8] In other words, knowing various components of the investment climate, one can predict private sector employment reasonably well.[9] This supports the main claim of this section that a favorable investment climate is critical for job creation and employment growth in the Region. Table 5.1 shows how different components of the investment climate contribute to private sector employment (proxied by service sector employment controlled for GDP per capita[10]).[11]

The first row of table 5.1 reflects the actual change in service sector employment (corrected by GDP per capita). All countries have experienced an increase in service sector employment, above the one implied by economic development.[12]

The second row shows the change in service sector employment predicted by the model, given the impact of the time shock, country-specific effect, and investment climate in the country (see endnote 11). For the new EU member (first column), the model performs quite well, which means that the set of institutions constituting the

BOX 5.2

Service Sector Employment Rate as an Indicator of Job Creation Potential

The focus of this report is the employment generated by the new private sector. It might seem obvious to consider a country's total employment as an indicator of job creation potential, but there are difficulties.

Total employment is the sum of employment created by the public and private sectors. Countries with large public sectors have, in general, a large total employment rate, but can still have a bad business environment. In essence, public sector employment does not respond to the state of business environment institutions.

To overcome this difficulty, this report focuses on market service sector employment as a better indicator of an economy's job creation potential because in modern economies—and in transition economies, in particular—most job creation occurs in the market services sector. Therefore, employment opportunities are better in economies where the market services sector is large and expanding.

An index summarizing the government interference in the economy has been plotted against total and market service sector employment rates (figures A and B). As can be seen, the negative impact of the investment climate indicator on market service sector employment is much larger than the impact on the total employment rate.

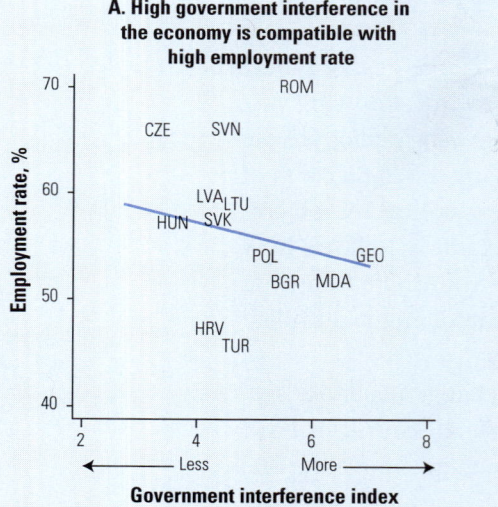
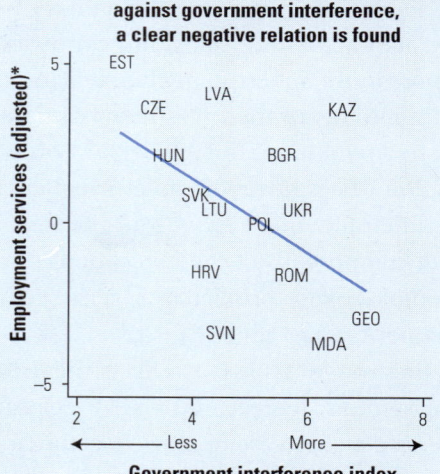

Source: Lopez-Garcia 2004.

Note: To control for the economic development, a regression of the service employment rate was run against the GDP per capita. The residuals from that regression represent the service employment rate not explained by the development of the economy. The residual is what is called the "service sector employment rate controlled for GDP per capita."

TABLE 5.1
Contribution of Investment Climate Components to Change in Service Sector Employment in the CEE EU Countries over the Past Decade

	Average: CEE, EU-member countries	of which:						Average: CEE, EU-accession countries a)	of which: Romania (94–02)	Average: Russia-Ukraine
		Lithuania (97–02)	Hungary (92–02)	Slovak Republic (94–02)	Poland (94–02)	Latvia (96–02)	Slovenia (93–02)			
Actual change in service sector employment	1.08	−1.83	1.11	0.66	1.33	1.89	0.61	1.06	−0.08	
Predicted change in service sector employment										
Of which:	1.09	0.13	1.92	0.42	1.51	1.26	0.98	0.76	0.30	0.39
Time shock	0.97	0.10	1.42	1.08	1.08	0.44	1.33	0.81	1.08	0.81
Start-up costs	−0.13	0.03	−0.57	−0.16	−0.26	0.17	0.02	0.23	0.53	−0.16
Access to finance	0.44	−0.02	0.70	0.02	0.52	0.39	1.03	−0.50	−1.75	−0.25
Market regulation	0.08	−0.01	1.00	−0.36	0.06	0.14	−0.53	0.15	0.06	−0.35
Tax burden	−0.26	0.04	−0.63	−0.16	0.11	0.12	−0.87	0.06	0.37	0.34

Source: Bank staff calculations.

Note: See annex 5.1 for the presentation of the regression model and definitions of explanatory variables.
Only statistically significant explanatory variables are shown in the table.
On average (considering all countries in the sample), corruption and the quality of the legal system were not significant; hence, they are not included in the table.
The averages for country groups are the unweighted average of the estimated contribution of each explanatory variable to the rise in market service employment within the group.
Low income CIS countries and Estonia were not covered by the regression analysis because of lack of data.
a) Bulgaria, Croatia, and Romania.

business environment is able to explain the employment performance in the private sector. The model is less powerful at predicting the actual service sector employment change in the next wave of accession countries. This results from the fact that corruption and the quality of the legal system play a far more important role in this group of countries than they did for the new EU members.

Poor Access to Finance, Excessive Market Regulations, Administrative Barriers, and High Taxes Are the Most Important Factors Impeding Job Creation in the Region

In CEE EU-member countries (EU-8), the most important driver of private sector employment growth has been by far the relatively good access to finance. To a lesser extent, employment growth has also been facilitated by relatively liberal market regulations.[13] However, a high tax burden and high administrative barriers (proxied by start-up costs) hindered job creation. For example, a better-than-average access to finance can explain the relatively good private sector employment performance of the Czech Republic, Hungary, and Latvia. Slovenia, another country where the access to finance is quite easy for entrepreneurs, would have performed much better if it had not been for the strict labor market regulations and high tax burden. The high tax burden has also hampered the employment outcomes in Hungary.

In CEE EU accession countries (EUA-3), the main contributors to the private sector employment growth have been relatively liberal market regulations and relatively low administrative barriers to new business formation. At the same time, private sector employment growth in these countries has been slowed by poor access to finance. For example, Romania saw a service sector employment change smaller than what would be expected, given its GDP per capita. This is mainly the result of poor access to finance. Indeed, Romania scores last in the ranking of the access-to-finance index because of its very high real interest rates, high collateral requirements, and, above all, lack of protection to creditors.

In Russia and Ukraine, growth in private sector employment has been achieved mainly thanks to a relatively low tax burden, but the poor investment climate has impeded job creation. Specifically, heavy market regulations, high administrative barriers to firm formation, and poor access to finance have all slowed the pace of private sector employment growth.

Access to finance stands out as the most important determinant of the growth in private sector employment in the Region. Access to finance alone can explain about 40 percent of the whole increase in service sector employment predicted by the regression model. Improving access to finance—along with other complementary measures to improve the investment climate—therefore carries the potential to foster job creation. Figure 5.4 illustrates this close relationship between access to finance and private sector employment.

However, other components of the investment climate matter too. Stringent market regulations discourage job creation (figure 5.5). Strict employment protection regulations may also discourage job creation, as has been the case in Croatia (box 5.3). Removing one particular constraint may therefore not be enough to engender employment growth. This is especially true, given the complementarities and synergies between various components of the investment climate. It is likely that countries will need to pursue a set of policies to improve the overall investment climate.

Overall, countries with favorable investment climate in the Region enjoy better labor market outcomes. Lower risk and costs of doing business and fewer administrative barriers lead to a faster pace of job creation and employment growth. Using a set of indicators of the investment climate, one can successfully explain much of the variation in private sector employment in the Region. The key determinants are access to finance, the tax burden, administrative barriers to firm creation, and market regulations. The importance of these components varies across subgroups. In European transition economies,

FIGURE 5.4
Market Service Employment Is Higher in Countries with Easier Access to, and Lower Cost of, Credit
Access to finance and service employment*

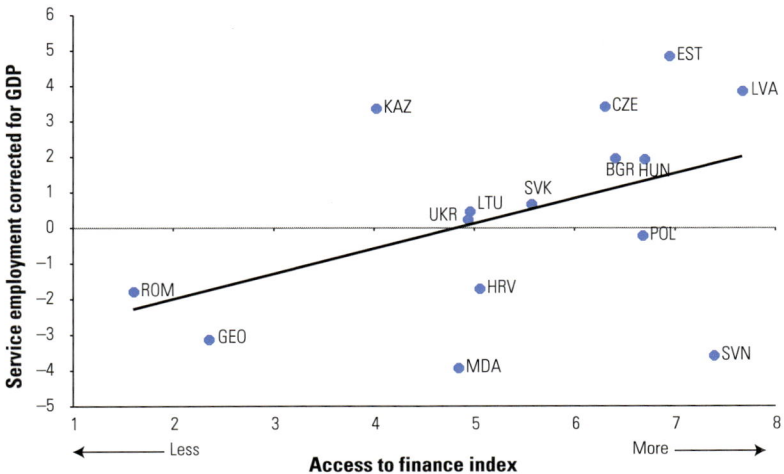

Source: Lopez-Garcia 2004.

Note: The access to finance index is a summary of data on the cost of credit, collateral required, credit to private sector, and protection to creditors (for details, please refer to annex 5.1).
* Controlled for GDP per capita.

FIGURE 5.5
Excessive Market Regulation Hurts Job Creation
Access to finance and service employment

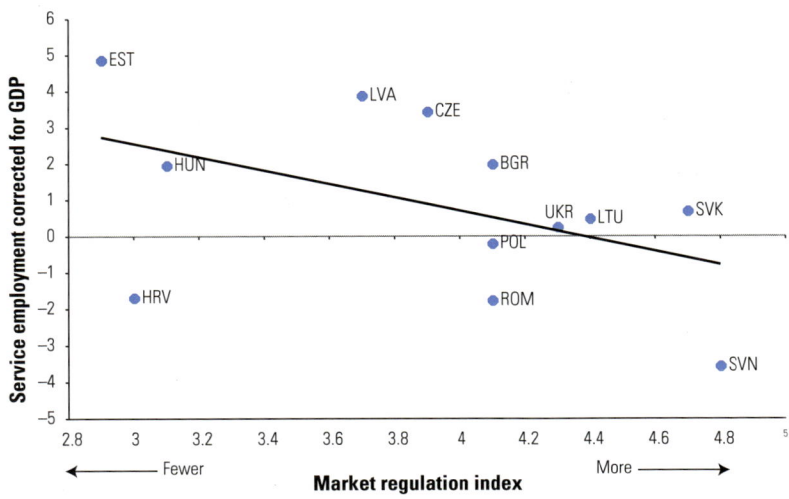

Source: Lopez-Garcia 2004.

Note: Market regulation includes credit and labor market regulations. The former refers to issues such as the percentage of deposits held in privately owned banks, the degree of competition from foreign banks and interest rate controls. Labor market regulation considers hiring and firing practices, impact of minimum wages, unemployment benefits, and union coverage.
* Controlled for GDP per capita

> **BOX 5.3**
>
> **Stringent Employment Protection Regulations May Forestall Job Destruction, but at the Same Time They Discourage Job Creation**
>
> A simple comparison between Croatia and Poland illustrates the point. Until recently, dismissal costs had been extremely high in Croatia, whereas they are relatively low in Poland. On a scale from 0 to 5, the OECD index of the cost of collective dismissal was 5.0 in Croatia and 3.9 in Poland (late-1990s data). Expectedly, the job destruction rate was much higher in Poland (about 12 percent in 1999) than in Croatia (5 percent in 2001). However, Poland enjoyed a much higher job creation rate than Croatia (10 percent against less than 4 percent, respectively). As a result, the job reallocation rate, which is a measure of industrial restructuring, was significantly lower in Croatia. In Poland, more jobs were reallocated away from declining firms and industries toward expanding ones.
>
> A similar pattern—low rates of both job creation and destruction, reflecting strict EPL—also prevailed in the Slovak Republic. In contrast, high rates of job creation and destruction occurred in countries with relatively flexible EPL, such as Latvia and Lithuania.
>
> As shown in chapter 4, the low job reallocation rate carries a significant cost in forgone productivity gains. Thus, policies to protect low-productivity, unsustainable jobs through high legislated dismissal costs are inefficient. An efficient approach is that of encouragement (that is, fostering job creation through enhancing labor market flexibility and improving the investment climate).
>
> *Sources:* World Bank 2001, 2002c, 2002d, 2003b, and 2003d.

job creation has been supported by better access to finance (especially in the new EU-member countries) and more efficient market regulations. At the same time, high business and labor taxation and some administrative barriers have impeded job creation. In contrast, in Russia and Ukraine (which are likely to be representative of other CIS countries), taxation is less of a problem, but inefficient market regulations, administrative barriers, and poor access to finance have hindered job creation. Table 5.2 summarizes these differences.

TABLE 5.2

The Importance of Determinants of Job Creation Varies by Subgroup in the Region

| | Impact of investment climate components on job creation ||
	Foster job creation	Impede job creation
CEE, EU-member countries	Access to finance	Taxation, start-up costs
CEE, EU-accession countries	Start-up cost, market regulations	Access to finance
Russian Fed. and Ukraine	Taxation	Market regulations, access to finance, start-up cost

Source: Bank staff calculations.

Investment Climate: International Comparisons and Variations within the Region

Perceptions from entrepreneurs, which were presented earlier in this chapter, are an important reality check of what matters to firms. However, they are difficult to compare across countries because they closely depend on the environment in which entrepreneurs operate and the standards they use as references (see box 5.4). This section uses selected objective measures of the investment climate to compare the experience of the transition countries relative to other countries.[14]

The focus is on those aspects of the investment climate that in the previous section were found to have a strong effect on job creation. Analysis starts by comparing selected elements of the investment climate in the Region to those in other regions. Then differences in the investment climate are examined across the Region's subgroups and across countries. All in all, the investment climate in the Region compares rather favorably to that in other regions, although in some key dimensions there is room for improvement. The study also shows that there are substantial differences in the investment climate among the Region's subgroups, as well as across countries. Generally, the cost of doing business is lowest in CEE and increases as one moves further east. The gap between the investment conditions in CEE and low income CIS countries is considerable.

Investment Climate in the Region Compares Favorably to That in Other Regions, but There Is Substantial Room for Improvement

On one hand, several elements of the investment climate in the Region compare well with those in other regions of the developing world. For example, the cost of market regulations (measured in management time spent dealing with them) is less than in other regions (figure 5.6). Unofficial payments to public officials to get things done (as a percentage of total sales) are smaller in the Region than in other regions (less than 2 percent of annual sales against more than 2 percent in all other regions).[15]

On the other hand, the comparison is less favorable in other dimensions of the investment climate. For example, property rights—an important element of the investment climate—are less protected in the Region than in some countries, and the costs of providing security are high (figure 5.7). The capital market is also less developed in the Region than in other areas of the world. This inhibits access to credit, which is likely, as shown earlier, to impede job creation (figure 5.8).

FIGURE 5.6
In Some of the Region's Subgroups, Time Spent Dealing with Government Regulations Is Still Substantial

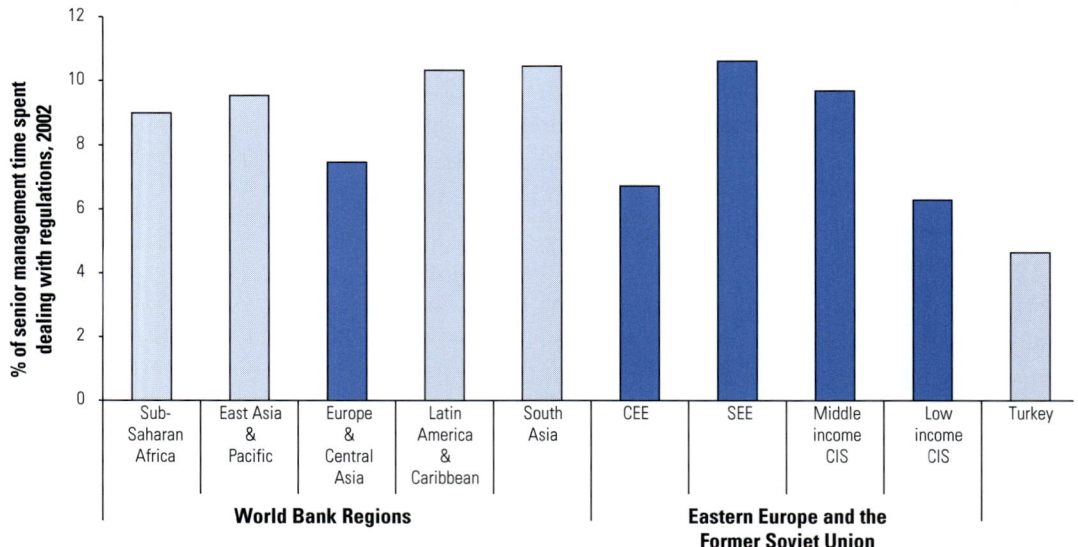

Source: EBRD–World Bank Business Environment and Enterprise Performance Surveys, 2002.

Note: Preliminary results from the new 2005 BEEPS are broadly consistent with those reported in this figure. However, some changes may have occurred for individual countries or subgroups of countries in the Region.

FIGURE 5.7
Protection of Property against Crime Can Be Costly

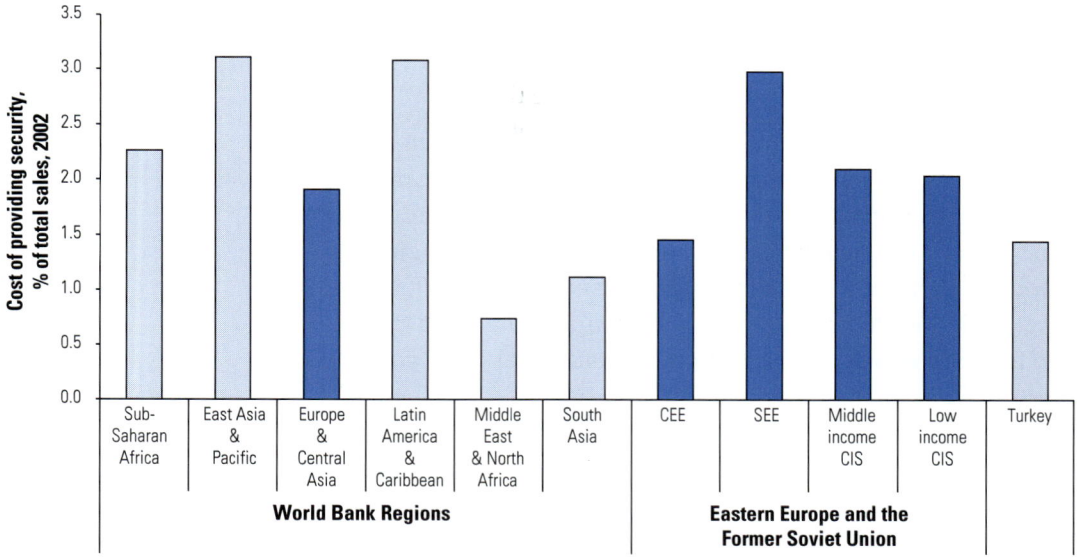

Source: EBRD–World Bank Business Environment and Enterprise Performance Surveys, 2002.

Note: Preliminary results from the new 2005 BEEPS are broadly consistent with those reported in this figure. However, some changes may have occurred for individual countries or subgroups of countries in the Region.

FIGURE 5.8
Firms in the Region Rely to a Lesser Degree on Capital Coming from Formal Institutions than Do Firms in Other Regions

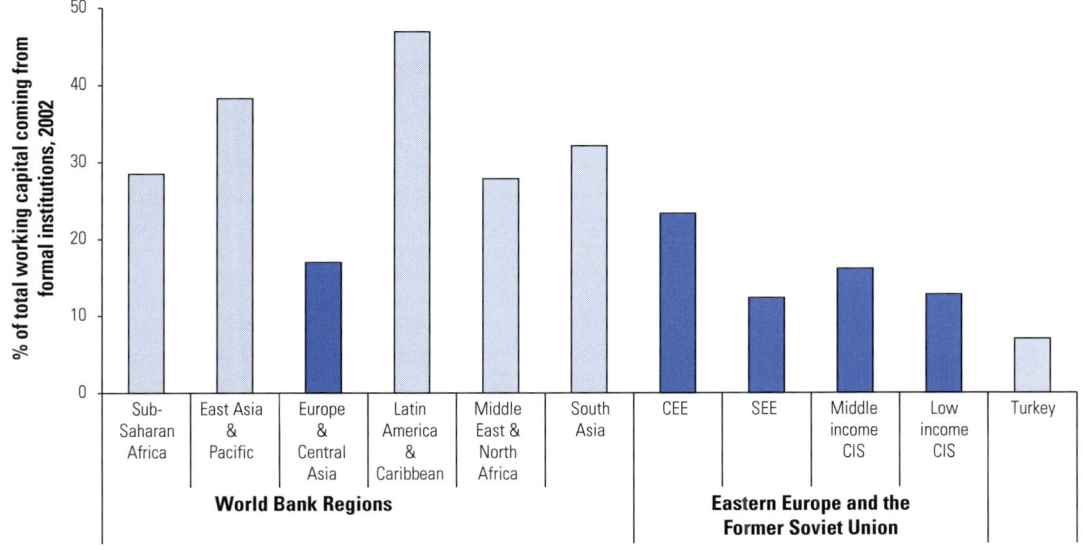

Source: EBRD–World Bank Business Environment and Enterprise Performance Surveys, 2002.

Note: Preliminary results from the new 2005 BEEPS are broadly consistent with those reported in this figure. However, some changes may have occurred for individual countries or subgroups of countries in the Region.

The Region's Subgroups Differ Substantially in Investment Climate

The comparison of the Region with other areas of the world is illustrative, but should not be taken too far. First, for more-developed countries of the Region, especially in CEE, the right comparators are developed market economies, rather than developing countries. For less-developed countries of the Region, especially the low income CIS countries, the appropriate comparators should be countries representing best practice among low and middle income countries. Second, the Region is heterogeneous, with substantial differences in the investment climate among subgroups and countries. Thus, even if the Region compares favorably to other regions (on average), this is not necessarily the case for some subgroups or countries of the Region. Below, the study looks more closely at variations in the investment climate within the Region and benchmark countries of the Region against investment climate "leaders."

In general, the investment climate is much better in CEE than in other parts of the Region. Consistent with earlier analysis, the cost of red tape in middle income CIS countries and SEE is much higher than in the rest of the Region and is also high by international standards (fig-

BOX 5.4

What the Official Data on Entry Barriers Do Not Show: Romania

Measurement matters. Different ways of measuring the same concept can yield different conclusions. The start-up costs in Romania are a good example.

According to *objective* data from the World Bank, opening a business is easy in Romania: no more than six procedures are required to start a business, one can go through the process in less than a month (against 37 days on average in Europe), and the cost of the process and minimum capital requirements are among the lowest in the transition countries.

However, when one looks at similar indicators of start-up costs based on *subjective* opinions, in this case those of managers of large corporations, the situation is quite different. According to the evaluation given to the sentence, "Starting a new business is generally easy," by the *Global Competitiveness Report*, Romania is one of the countries where starting a business is considered the most difficult (figure A).

Figure A: Subjective Perception of How Easy It Is to Start a Business

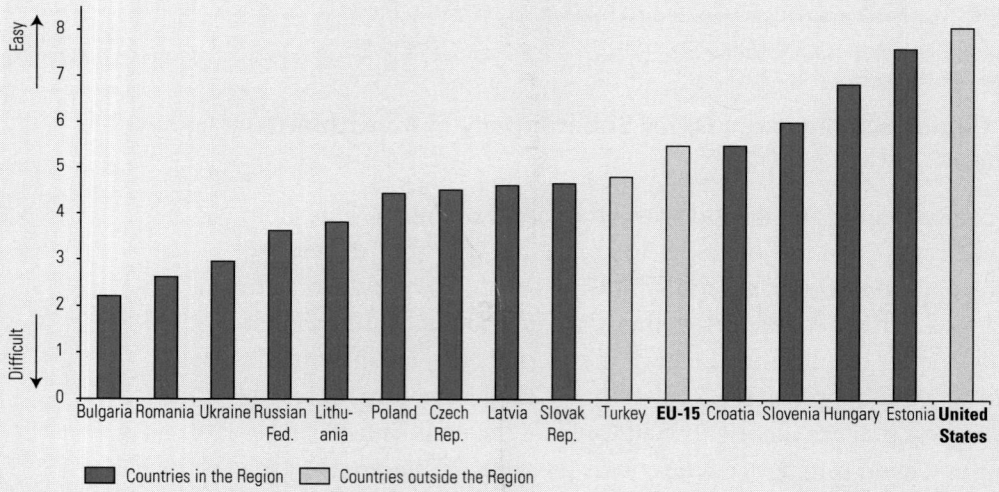

Source: World Economic Forum 2002.

Note: The index is based on managers' evaluation of the sentence, "Starting a new business is generally easy." The index varies from 0 to 10, with higher values indicating more favorable assessment.

This example shows that indicators based on perceptions in some cases can be preferable to objective indicators, since they reflect de facto rather than de jure conditions. But their inherent subjectivity limits their validity. On the other hand, objective indicators, although not distorted by subjectivity, often give only a partial picture and do not reflect all the dimensions of the problem. Given the limitations of both approaches, it is best to treat them as complementary.

ure 5.6). The cost of providing security (protecting firm property against crime) is especially high—also by international standards—in SEE and in the low income CIS countries (figure 5.7). Access to financing, as measured by proportion of working capital coming from formal institutions, is particularly poor in the low and middle income CIS countries and SEE (figure 5.8).[16] But, interestingly, it is still worse in Turkey—the only nontransition economy in the Region. Finally, corruption is a particular problem in the low income and middle income CIS countries. Countries of the Region that are poorer and less advanced in market reforms still have a long way to go to improve the investment climate to make it more conducive to firm growth and job creation.

On Most Key Dimensions of Investment Climate, the Transition Countries Lag behind World Leaders

The multivariate analysis presented earlier showed that low business start-up costs; easy access to, and low cost of, finance; and liberal market regulations are keys to the growth of the market services sector, and thus for employment. In all those dimensions of the investment climate, most of the transition countries lag behind world leaders. The gap is relatively small for the best-performing CEE countries, but is wide for most of the CIS and SEE countries. Below, the study benchmarks countries of the Region against selected developed and best-performing developing economies. The former are a natural benchmark for middle income countries of the Region, whereas the latter are a more adequate benchmark for low income countries of the Region.

Opening a Business Is Costly, Especially in SEE and Some CIS Countries

In most of the transition countries, the start-up costs are higher than in the United States (where it is least costly to start a business), the European Union (EU-15), or the dynamic developing countries, such as Korea, Malaysia, or Thailand (see annex table A5.2).[17] Among the transition countries, start-up costs are (on average) lowest in CEE, especially in the Baltic States. Costs of opening a business are also moderate in most CIS countries, although Belarus and Ukraine are clear outliers. Start-up costs are high in SEE by international standards (figure 5.9).[18]

The number of start-up procedures is limited to three in industrial countries with a liberal approach to entrepreneurship, such as Ireland or Sweden. In the Region, the most liberal country in this respect is Hungary, where one needs to go through five procedures. But in Belarus, where opening a business is most cumbersome, there are 19 necessary

FIGURE 5.9
Starting a Business Is Not Easy in Many of the Region's Countries

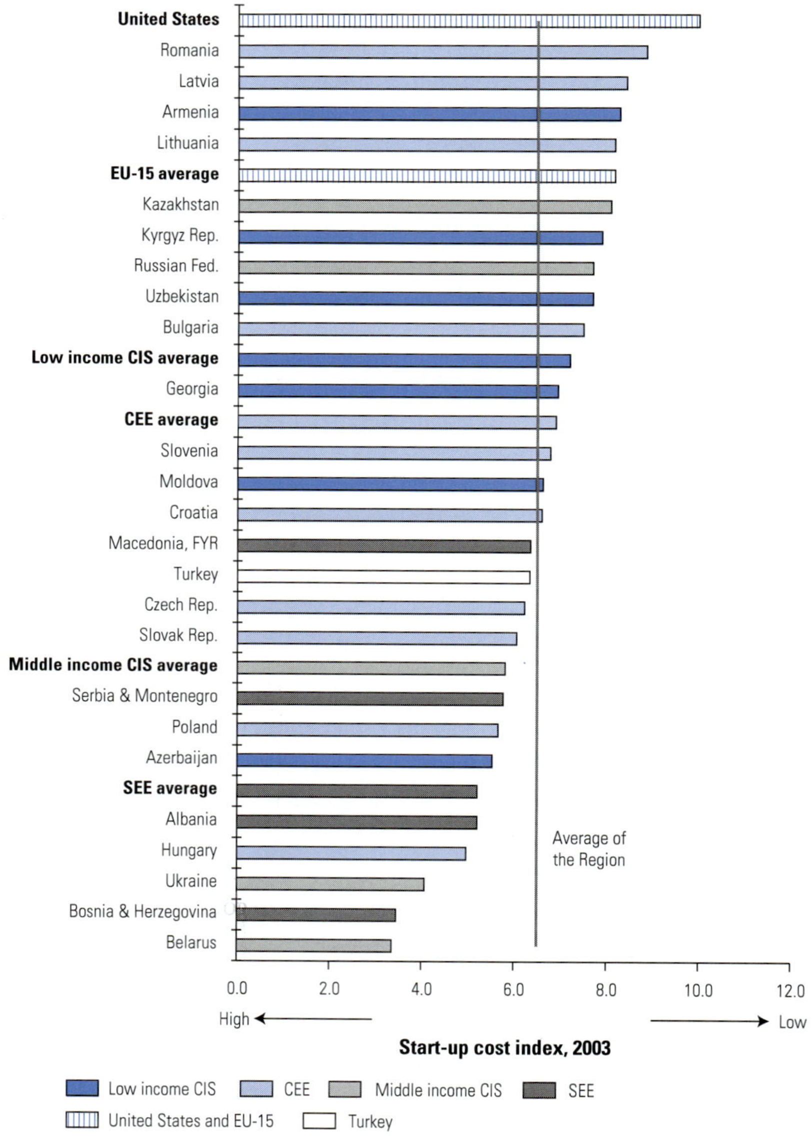

Source: World Bank, Cost of Doing Business Database.

Note: The index goes from 0 to 10, 0 being the most expensive. The start-up cost index was constructed by rescaling the four dimensions of start-up costs provided by the CODB database: number of procedures, total time, cost and minimum capital. Then a simple unweighted average of the four components was calculated.

procedures. Similarly, in many developed and developing countries, there is no minimum capital requirement to start a business. Within the Region, only in Azerbaijan is no start-up capital required. In Ukraine, the minimum required capital is almost five times the gross national income (GNI) per capita, which can effectively limit firm creation.[19]

Hungary exemplifies the point that even in countries with overall good investment climate, there is room for improvement. Procedural costs associated with opening a business are the lowest in Hungary, compared with those in other countries of the Region. At the same time, the monetary costs associated with registering a business are the highest. Thus, although (on average) start-up costs are moderate in Hungary, the country would benefit from improving the incentives for firm creation by lowering the registration costs.

To conclude, most of the transition countries can lower administrative barriers to firm entry and thus foster job creation. Opening a business can be made easier even in CEE countries, but the biggest room for improvement is in SEE and in some of the CIS countries.

Access to Finance Is Difficult, Especially in the CIS

Access to finance is substantially more difficult in the Region than in the EU-15 or in developing countries with developed credit markets, such as Korea or Malaysia, although better than in Turkey. Within the Region, access to finance is easier in European transition economies (especially in CEE) and more difficult in the CIS (especially in the low income CIS countries) (figure 5.10). But even in CEE, the credit market is notably less developed than in the EU-15. Domestic credit to the private sector (relative to GDP) is much less in CEE than in EU-15, and the interest rate spread is significantly larger.[20]

To illustrate, domestic credit to the private sector represents more than 100 percent of GDP in the European Union and some developing countries, such as Korea and Malaysia, but less than 30 percent in CEE. In middle income CIS countries, the ratio goes down to about 16 percent, and in low income CIS countries, it barely exceeds 10 percent.[21] This comparison shows that there is substantial room for developing the credit market and improving access to credit in all of the transition countries, but especially those in the CIS. Better access to credit, in turn, is going to support firm entry and growth and, ultimately, job creation. Moreover, better access to credit will provide incentives for firms to move from the informal to the formal sector, which in turn may lead to productivity gains.

Regulations Often Add Heavy Burden to Firms' Operation

There is still much room in the transition countries to make markets more liberal. In all of these countries, markets are more regulated than in the United States, and most of them are more regulated than in the EU-15. Again, European transition economies, especially new EU mem-

FIGURE 5.10
Job Creation in the Region Is Likely to Be Hampered by Difficult Access to Credit

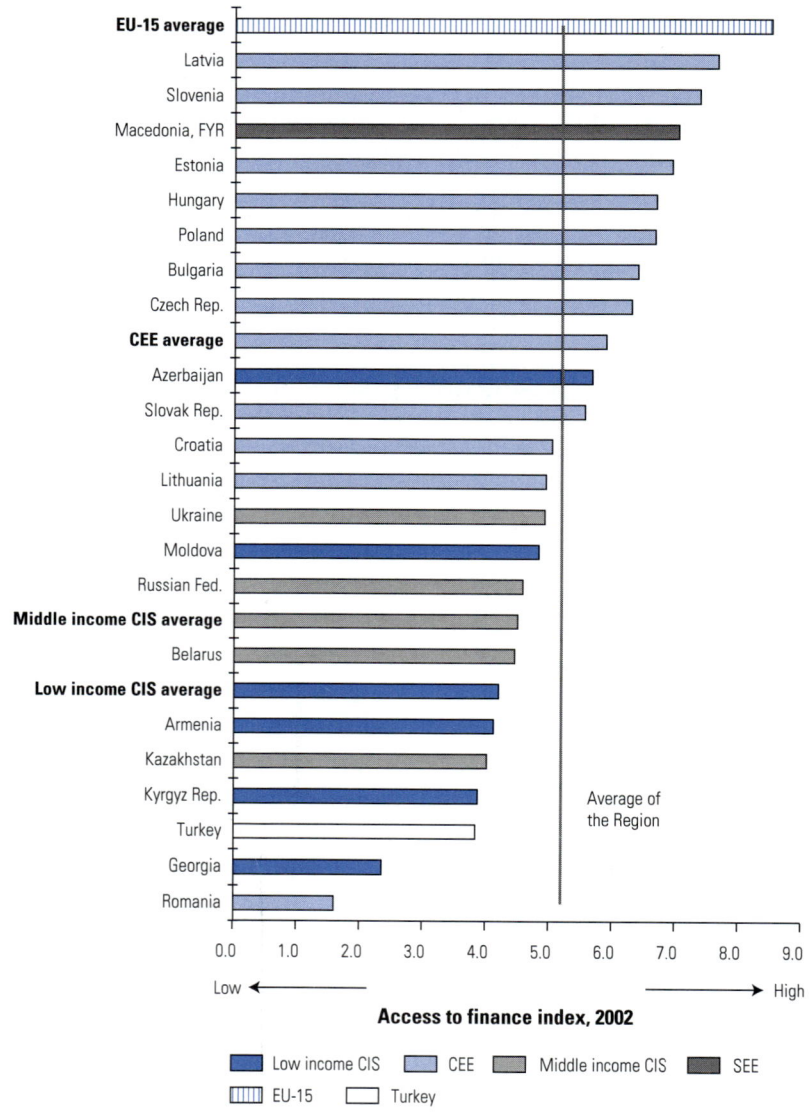

Source: World Development Indicators.

Note: The index goes from 0 to 10, 0 being the worst. The index is the combination of the following variables: ratio of domestic credit provided by deposit money to GDP, interest rate spread and real interest rate, ratio of deposit coverage to GDP and the index of creditors' protection (from the World Bank's Doing Business Database).

bers, tend to have less-regulated markets than the CIS and also Turkey do (figure 5.11). Thus, given that excessive market regulation has been shown to limit job creation, lessening the regulatory burden on business activity in the Region is yet another way to encourage job creation.

FIGURE 5.11
Markets in the Region Tend to Be Overregulated

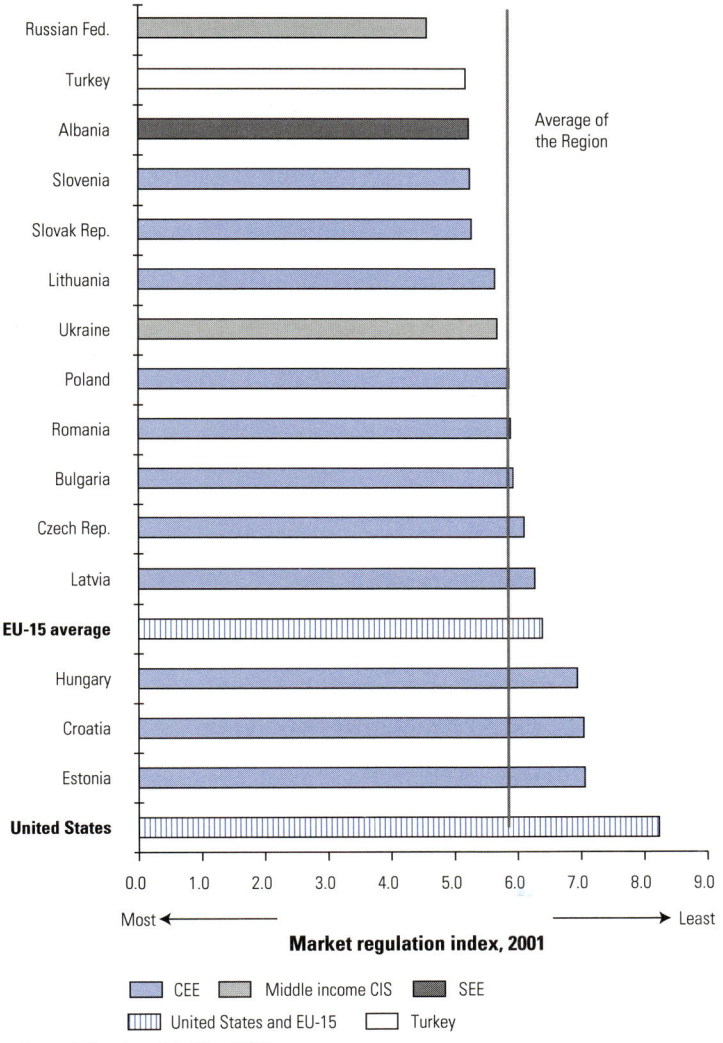

Source: Economic Freedom of the World 2003.

Note: The indexes go from 0 to 10, 0 being the most regulated. The market regulation index is an unweighted average of the credit market and labor market regulation indexes provided by the *Economic Freedom of the World's Annual Report* (Gwartney and Lawson 2003).

Corruption Adds Up to Heavy Regulations to Raise Costs of Doing Business

Corruption is closely related to excessive regulations, and it has been shown to be a severe obstacle to business formation and growth, as well as to job creation. Given that corruption looms large in the Region, its negative impact on employment is likely to be substantial.[22] Within the Region, the least corrupted are the CEE countries that are EU members. But even there, corruption is much more widespread than in the EU-15. In other European transition economies, corruption is a severe problem, and it is apparently rampant in the CIS countries (figure 5.12). But corruption is also a major issue in Turkey, which is a nontransition economy. Fighting corruption and its sources is thus critical to encouraging job creation.

FIGURE 5.12
Corruption Is High in the Region

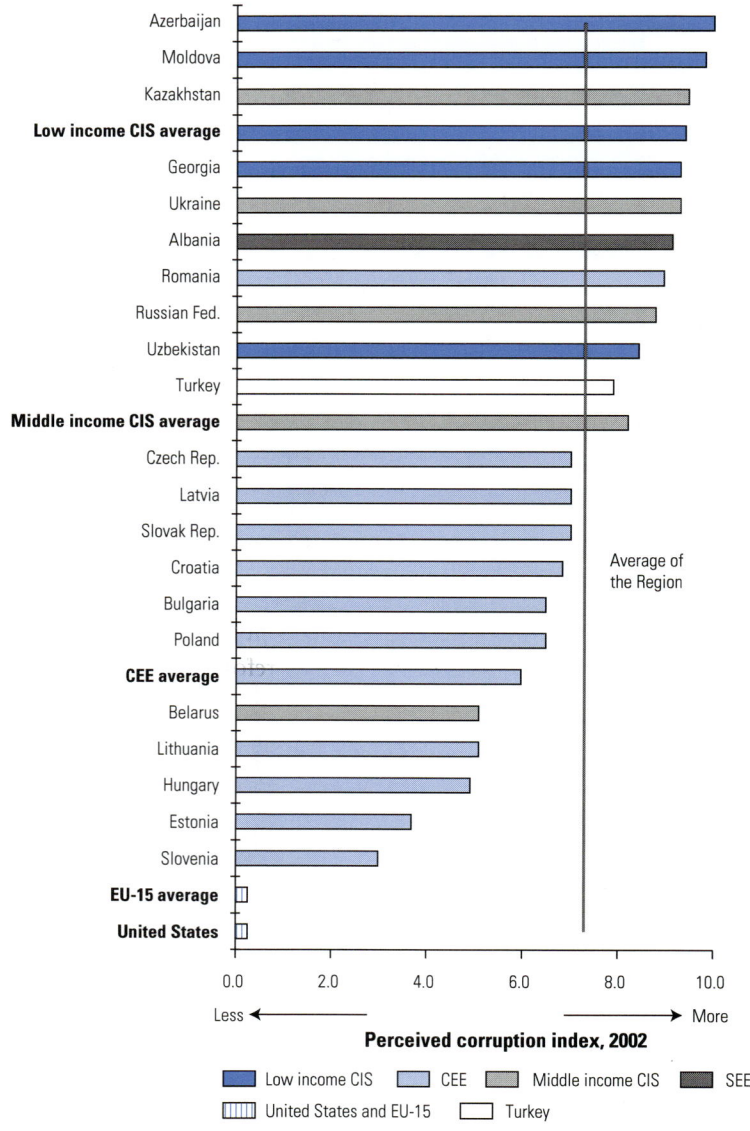

Sources: Transparency International 2002; Bank staff calculations.

Note: The index goes from 0 (best) to 10 (worst). The country ranking responds to the degree of corruption perceived to exist among public officials and politicians. It draws from 15 different polls and surveys from nine different institutions.

Summing Up: Promoting a Better Investment Climate to Foster Job Creation

Despite major structural reforms, the investment climates in many transition economies still suffer from significant shortcomings that negatively affect firms' incentives to invest and create more and better jobs. Therefore, better employment outcomes in the Region depend on further progress in structural reforms affecting the quality of the investment climate. Many investment climate challenges are common across the Region, although their importance varies by subgroup and country. The three challenges that stand out are the following:

- Strengthening macroeconomic stability and reducing economic and regulatory policy uncertainty.

- Lowering taxes, especially on labor, and simplifying tax administration. This is associated with public expenditure reforms, particularly with reforms to the pensions and health insurance systems. It also includes cutting programs that are not cost-effective and improving the efficiency in the delivery of public services. In addition, tax administration needs to be improved to reduce the burden on firms (for example, the costs associated with tax inspections) and to reduce the scope for corruption.

- Improving access to, and lowering the cost of, credit. This is associated with the reforms of the banking system, such as through enhancing competition.

Investment climate issues are also more pronounced in some regions than in others. The key elements of a reform agenda by subgroup are summarized here.

The Investment Climate Reform Agenda in CEE

Investment climate in the CEE EU-member countries is by far the most favorable among the transition countries. Nonetheless, even the most-advanced CEE countries lag behind world leaders in many dimensions of the investment climate, and there is significant scope for improvement. For example, starting a business in CEE is still considerably more difficult than in the United States or in the EU-15. Three issues are more of a constraint to firm growth in CEE EU-member countries than in other subgroups:

- High tax rates
- Labor regulations

- Skills of available workers

In the EU-accession countries, costs of doing business tend to be higher than in CEE EU-member countries. Additional investment climate issues that need to be addressed include the following:

- Corruption
- The efficiency of the legal system and conflict resolution
- Licenses and operating permits

The Investment Climate Reform Agenda in SEE

SEE countries are less advanced in investment climate reforms than are other European transition economies. There is considerable scope for reducing the risk and costs of doing business, as well as lowering administrative barriers and cutting the red tape. Reform priorities include addressing the following:

- Security of property rights
- High costs of starting a business
- Excessive regulation of business activities, including customs and trade regulations
- Anticompetitive or informal practices
- The quality of the legal system and conflict resolution
- Corruption

The Investment Climate Reform Agenda in the CIS

In most dimensions of the investment climate, the CIS countries, both middle income and low income, lag behind European transition economies. The institutions of a market economy are less developed and market-oriented reforms are less advanced than in European transition economies. Therefore, the risks associated with doing business are substantially higher, as are administrative barriers and associated bureaucratic harassment. Corruption is widespread, adding to the costs of doing business. To bridge this divide and to foster the creation of more-productive, formal sector jobs, the middle income CIS countries need to focus on addressing the following obstacles:

- Excessive market regulations, administrative barriers to business activity (for example, licensing and operating permits), bureaucratic harassment (for example, frequent and lengthy inspections), and associated corruption

- Business start-up costs (especially in Belarus and Ukraine)
- Underdeveloped credit market and access to finance

Investment climate constraints in the low income CIS countries are still more profound. In addition to the ones listed above, these countries need to overcome more-fundamental obstacles, such as the following:

- Security of property rights
- Underdeveloped infrastructure, including access to electricity
- Administrative barriers, including cumbersome customs and trade regulations

Reforms to Foster Job Creation Require Identifying Key Constraints to Firm Growth and the Active Involvement of the Business Community

Improving the investment climate is a complex task. Many of the reforms are interlinked and complementary and thus require appropriate sequencing. For example, fighting corruption requires deregulating business activities and lessening the discretionary power given to the bureaucracy. It also requires removing administrative barriers (for example, reducing the number of permits and licenses, simplifying customs procedures, and limiting the number of agencies that have the right to carry out inspections). Moreover, some reforms require substantial investments (for example, improvements in infrastructure, in the efficiency of the legal system, and in the institutions responsible for enforcement). Given the scarcity of resources, governments need to select priorities and focus on addressing the constraints that are the most binding. Improving the investment climate is a continuous process because the environment changes and new challenges emerge. Although investment climate reforms can be difficult and costly, the long-term social costs of abstaining from reforms are likely to be still higher. If firms' entry and growth is inhibited by high costs of doing business, job creation and employment will suffer.

The above-identified subgroup reform priorities define broad areas where the key constraints lie. Country-specific constraints and reform priorities need to be identified, using more-detailed information on the quality of business environment. Such information can be obtained from specially designed investment climate surveys or from focus groups of employers.[23]

The most important channel for identifying obstacles to job creation is ongoing government consultations and dialogue with the genuine representation of the business community, including the small private firms. Such dialogue has already been carried out in a number of the transition countries under different institutional forms. Bosnia and Herzegovina launched its so-called Bulldozer Initiative to involve the private sector in reforms. Latvia established a Steering Committee for Improvements of the Business Environment, which comprises representatives from key ministries and from associations of local firms, as well as foreign investors (World Bank 2003d). In Poland, a dynamic employers' confederation, representing the new private sector, is vocal in publicly articulating business concerns and actively takes part in a dialogue with the government on investment climate issues.

Thus in many of the transition countries, the institutional structure for voicing business concerns has already been created. The challenge is to overcome bureaucratic inertia and to mobilize political support for these necessary reforms that hurt the interests of those who benefit from the status quo.

Annex 5.1: Regression Analysis of the Impact of the Investment Climate on Employment in the Region

To capture the interaction between shocks and institutions, the following simple model (equation 5.1) was estimated:

$$u_{it} = c_i + d_t(1 + \sum_j \gamma_j X_i^j) + \epsilon_{it} \tag{5.1}$$

where u is the unemployment or employment rate in country i at time t, c are the country dummies, d are time dummies (that is, unidentified shocks assumed to be equal across countries[24]), and X is the time-invariant value over the period of the institution j in country i.

What the model is trying to capture is the way institutions shape the response of countries to a similar shock. All transition economies of the Region have been hit by a similar shock at a similar time, but their labor markets have responded differently. The objective is to determine whether this is the result of the institutional settings of the countries, and if so, which institutions had the strongest impact. To answer these questions, the model uses as explanatory variables the interactions of various institutions with some proxy to the shock. This is the most general specification, because no specific shocks are imposed; it is only assumed that a number of shocks over time, of equal dimension across countries, have hit the economies. Hence, the model allows one to isolate the impact of the (different) institutions from that of the shocks.

To estimate the coefficients corresponding to each of the institutions in the model, an unbalanced panel of 28 countries of the Region over 14 years (from 1989 to 2002) was used. Unfortunately, only one year of information for most of the institutional variables was available.

The list of institutions (explanatory variables) considered in the regression model is as follows:[25]

- *Start-up costs*. A composite index, constructed by using the World Bank's Doing Business Database, 2004.

- *Exit costs*. As above.

- *Access to finance*. A composite index, using the following variables: ratio of domestic credit to GDP from *World Development Indicators 2004* (World Bank 2004c), ratio of deposit coverage to GDP (IMF), and creditors protection index (Doing Business Database, 2004).

- *Quality of the legal system*. A composite index, combining indicators of contract enforcement (Doing Business Database 2004) and subjective evaluation of the quality of the legal system provided by the *Economic Freedom of the World 2003 Annual Report* (Gwartney and Lawson 2003).

- *Market regulations*. This is an unweighted average of the credit market and labor market regulation indexes, provided by the *Economic Freedom of the 2003 World's Annual Report* (Gwartney and Lawson 2003).

- *Corruption*. Transparency International Corruption Perception Index 2003 (www.transparency.org).

- *Tax burden*. Tax revenue as a percentage of GDP, from *World Development Indicators, 2004* (World Bank 2004c).

The results of the estimation of the regression are shown in table A5.1.

TABLE A5.1
Estimation Results

Type of regression: Common shocks across countries assumed

Variable	Service employment (corrected)		Unemployment	
	Coefficients	t-statistics	Coefficients	t-statistics
Shocks (given average institutions)	0.8%		0.85%	
Start-up cost index	−0.29*	(−1.45)	0.09	(0.26)
Exit cost index	−0.003	(−0.28)	−0.006	(−0.24)
Finance index	**0.41****	(2.95)	−0.18	(−0.42)
Legal system index	−0.04	(−1.13)	−0.05	(−0.86)
Mk. Regulation index	**−0.64****	(−2.45)	1.73*	(1.53)
Corruption index	0.06	(0.33)	1.57**	(2.37)
Tax burden	−0.08	(−1.11)	0.43**	(2.35)
Observations	106		104	
Adjusted R-Squared	0.95		0.77	

Source: Bank staff calculations.

Note: Nonlinear least square estimation
*significant at 15%
**significant at 1%

Annex 5.2: Investment Climate Indicators in Selected Transition and Developing Economies

TABLE A5.2
Investment Climate Indicators in Selected Transition and Developing Economies

	GDP per capita at PPP, 2002 (dollars)	Domestic credit/ GDP ratio (2002)	Starting a business			
			Number of procedures	Duration (days)	Cost (% GNI per capita)	Min. capital (% GNI per capita)
Armenia	3,230	6.9	10	25	7	4.5
Brazil	7,450	35.5	17	152	11.7	0
Hungary	13,070	35.3	6	52	22.9	86.4
Korea, Rep. of	16,960	115.6	12	22	17.7	332
Kyrgyz Republic	1,560	4.2	8	21	11.6	0.6
Malaysia	8,500	146.1	9	30	25.1	0
Moldova	1,600	17.6	10	30	18.6	24.6
Poland	10,450	28.8	10	31	20.6	237.9
Romania	6,490	8.3	5	28	7.4	0
Russian Federation	8,080	17.6	9	36	6.7	5.6
Serbia and Montenegro	—	—	11	51	9.5	120.3
Thailand	6,890	102.5	8	33	6.7	0
Ukraine	4,800	18	15	34	17.6	113.9
Vietnam	2,300	43.1	11	56	28.6	0

Sources: World Development Indicators (2004); Cost of Doing Business Database (2005).

Note: — = data not available.

	Hiring and firing workers				
	Difficulty of hiring index	Rigidity of hours index	Difficulty of firing index	Rigidity of employment Index	Firing costs (weeks)
Armenia	17	40	50	36	17
Brazil	67	80	70	72	165
Hungary	11	80	30	40	34
Korea, Rep. of	11	60	30	34	90
Kyrgyz Republic	33	40	40	38	21
Malaysia	0	0	10	3	74
Moldova	33	60	70	54	21
Poland	11	60	30	34	25
Romania	78	60	50	63	98
Russian Federation	0	60	20	27	17
Serbia and Montenegro	28	0	40	23	21
Thailand	67	40	20	42	47
Ukraine	33	80	80	64	94
Vietnam	44	40	70	51	98

Notes

1. Lopez-Garcia (2002) shows that the contribution to unemployment of barriers to entrepreneurship doubled in a sample of OECD countries, when worker reallocation was taken into account.
2. Such information is gathered in the investment climate surveys. These are the result of a partnership between the World Bank and country counterparts for the collection of data from large random samples of firms in more than 50 countries. The surveys collect objective quantitative data on measures of the investment climate, plus information on firm performance. This allows linking the investment climate indicators with performance to understand their impacts on productivity, investment decisions, and employment decisions. The surveys were launched in 2001, with about 20 new surveys conducted each year. So far, more than 26,000 formal firms have been interviewed, half of them with fewer than 50 employees.
3. This is consistent with the results in Pissarides, Singer, and Svejnar (2003), which provides evidence that constraints on obtaining external financing and the high cost of this financing are two of the top five constraints cited by managers of small and medium enterprises in Bulgaria and Russia.
4. Ranking is calculated according to the average score of each constraint.
5. Labor regulations are efficient if they support an efficient allocation of labor resources (see Estreicher and Schwab [2000], especially chapter 5).
6. This is also surprising, because on the books labor regulations are significantly more strict in the CIS and SEE than in CEE; however, the discrepancy between de jure and de facto strictness of employment regulations can be accounted for by differences in enforcement (see chapter 6).
7. Regressions are carried out using generalized ordered logit models. Perceptions for each type of constraint are estimated as a function of firms' characteristics (size, age, sector, innovating history, ownership, exports, imports, and foreign ownership) and country's income level.
8. Multivariate regression analysis was used to estimate the independent contribution of different components of the investment climate to employment. See annex 5.1 for the details, including the regression model, data used, and results.
9. The coefficient of determination (adjusted R^2) is 95 percent, meaning that the investment climate variables used in the model explain a large portion of variation in the market service employment rate across the sample of the transition countries.
10. To control for the economic development, a regression of the service employment rate was run against the GDP per capita. The residuals from that regression represent the service employment rate *not* explained by the development of the economy. The residual is what is called the "service sector employment rate controlled for GDP per capita."
11. This analysis is based on the argument that the institutional setting of a country shapes the impact that otherwise-similar shocks have on its labor market performance. The first economists to propose this idea were Michael Bruno and Jeffrey Sachs (1985). But it was only after the publication of the Blanchard and Wolfers (2000) model of equilibrium unem-

ployment that the interaction of shocks with institutions became a popular explanation among labor economists for the unemployment evolution of developed countries.
12. Lithuania is an exception, but this result needs to be treated with caution: comparisons of employment before and during the transition are inaccurate because of changes in methodology and data sources.
13. The indicator of market regulations is based on indexes of credit and labor market regulations.
14. One set of indicators corresponds to employers' answers to "objective" questions as part of the Investment Climate questionnaire (sample question: In a typical week, what percentage of senior management's time is spent dealing with requirements imposed by government regulations, including dealing with officials, completing forms, and so forth?). A second set of indicators reflects de jure conditions.
15. Based on the World Bank investment climate survey data.
16. Research on financial developments in the Region points to the poorly developed financial system in low income CIS countries as a major impediment to their sustained growth and emphasizes the "great divide" between the low income CIS countries and other subgroups, especially CEE countries (Nicoló, Geadah, and Rozhkov 2003).
17. Korea, Malaysia, and Thailand were chosen as comparators for the transition countries because their level of GDP per capita is similar to that in the middle income countries of the Region. For example, Korea has GDP per capita similar to that in Hungary and Poland, Malaysia to that in Bulgaria or Russia, and Thailand to that in Romania or Ukraine (see annex table A5.2 for data on GDP and selected investment climate conditions).
18. Because of the space constraint, the figures do not show countries outside the Region (except for the EU-15, which is a benchmark). Data for countries referred to in the text come from the same source as those used to construct the charts.
19. The data come from the World Bank Doing Business Database, 2003.
20. Interest rate spreads affect the cost of credit and thus investment. The level of spreads is determined by funding, operating and regulatory costs, rents accruing from banks' market power, and credit risk (Nicoló, Geadah, and Rozhkov 2003).
21. The data come from the World Bank (2004c).
22. The level of corruption is significantly negatively correlated with employment in the market services sector. However, the level of corruption tends to decrease with the level of economic development, and for this reason, the corruption variable turned insignificant in the employment regression reported in table 5.2. In other words, corruption matters for employment, but its impact is difficult to separate from that of economic development.
23. World Bank (2005a) provides an example of using focus groups and employer-based surveys for identifying constraints to job creation.
24. The first period is left out, so it becomes the constant. Therefore, the country dummies can be interpreted as the unemployment rate in the first period.
25. Detailed information on the construction of composite indices used in the regression is provided in Lopez-Garcia (2004).

CHAPTER 6

Labor Market Policy and Institutions: Combining Protection with Incentives for Job Creation

Enhancing job opportunities requires an adaptable labor market in which firms have the right incentives to create more jobs and workers receive support when coping with labor mobility. Improving the adaptability of the labor market requires interventions in several areas: wage determination and labor taxation, employment protection legislation, and social safety nets for the unemployed.

Although most transition economies of the Region have carried out significant labor market reforms over the past decade to improve labor market adaptability, there is substantial room for improvement. In most countries in the Region, employment relations are still overregulated, discouraging hiring. Much of the labor market flexibility comes from nonenforcement. In many countries, especially in SEE and the CIS, wage bargaining is not conducive to swift wage adjustments to changing demand-and-supply conditions. High taxes on labor, especially in CEE, discourage labor demand. Income support to the unemployed can be provided in a more efficient way, to provide protection to displaced workers and to encourage job reallocation, which is of particular importance in the CIS. Further labor market reforms are thus necessary to enhance the ability of the transition economies to cope with various shocks. Also, the reforms of the pension and health insurance systems need to be continued to make possible the reduction in labor taxation.

The chapter is organized as follows. Section 1 provides a brief discussion of the roles of labor market policies and institutions. Section 2 focuses on wage determination. Section 3 examines employment protection legislation in the Region. Section 4 deals with labor taxation. Section 5 analyzes active and passive labor market policies. Section 6 suggests direction for labor market reforms for the Region's subgroups.

The Role of Labor Market Policies and Institutions

Labor market policy and institutions are important, both in their potential impacts on labor market adjustment and in the incentives that they give firms (see box 6.1). They have direct and indirect impacts on wages, which in turn can be expected to influence both the structural level of (un)employment and the speed of labor market adjustment to shocks. Policies and institutions can impact wage and employment adjustment in a variety of ways, including truncating the lower end of the wage distribution (with impacts on the level and structure of employment), affecting firm incentives for hiring and firing, promoting (re)entry to employment for laid-off workers and new entrants, and affecting labor supply incentives. The interaction of different labor market institutions in specific country settings further complicates the analysis of the impact on labor market outcomes.[1]

In a context of major economic restructuring such as in the transition economies of the Region, the government has a role to play in balancing policies that facilitate the allocation of workers to more-productive jobs with policies that are designed to help workers cope with necessary adjustments. Most of the Region's countries have undertaken major reforms of labor market institutions during the transition, although the extent of reform has varied by subgroup and by specific element of the institutional framework. Despite reforms, excessive institutional rigidities appear to have contributed to unemployment among the low-skilled and in depressed regions and to have affected patterns of labor adjustment. However, they cannot be considered the primary cause of low labor market performance in the Region, which appears to be driven more by low labor demand, an unfavorable business environment, skills mismatch, and other factors.

The Divergent Paths of Wage Determination during the Transition

In market economies, a higher unemployment rate will have a dampening effect on wages: as outside options become less favorable,

BOX 6.1

The Role of Labor Market Policies and Institutions: Some International Evidence

Social Dialogue and Wage Bargaining

As illustrated by the experience of Western Europe and countries like Poland and South Africa, unions have a crucial role to play in promoting macro and structural reforms, as well as political openness and democracy. However, depending on the economic and social environment in which unions operate, collective bargaining has been found to affect the flexibility of wages and the performance of firms.

Union wage markup (a premium over the wage of similar workers in nonunionized firms) is an important indicator of union bargaining power and ability to influence labor market outcomes. The evidence suggests that union wage markups are small in industrial countries, but high in countries that have weak competition in output markets and large rents. For example, wage premiums are high in Bulgaria and Malaysia (5–20 percent) and South Africa (10–24 percent), but low in Korea (2–4 percent). High union wage premiums obviously benefit union members at the expense of the unemployed; however, wages set at above the competitive level lower labor demand and lead to less employment.

Unions also have other impacts. For example, in Mexico, unions have attempted to protect low-skilled jobs at the expense of higher productivity. In Guatemala, unionization is associated with lower productivity of coffee farmers. In Brazil, the improvement in productivity and profitability resulting from the greater participation of workers in certain aspects of company management was enhanced in unionized companies because unions facilitated communication between management and workers.

The level at which negotiations take place (firm, sector, or country) is also important. Experiences of developing and industrial countries have shown that sectors (industries) do not coordinate their wage demands, decreasing aggregate and relative wage flexibility.[a] To alleviate these effects, some industrial countries have reinforced the coordination between the different levels of bargaining. For example, in Denmark, Ireland, and the Netherlands, the basic wage increase is fixed through nationwide agreements, while further increases consistent with a firm's performance are left to firm-level negotiations. Following the systems in countries like Australia, New Zealand, and the United Kingdom, others have chosen to reinforce firm-level bargaining, which is more likely to reflect firms' and workers' performance.

Minimum Wages

Minimum wages have been found to have disemployment effects, small in aggregate, but significant among low-productivity workers. For example, in industrial countries, where minimum

(continues on the following page)

> **BOX 6.1** (*continued*)
>
> wages tend to be relatively low, they had a modest impact on low-technology firms and the employment of low-productivity workers. In Colombia, for every percentage point rise in the minimum wage, employment has been estimated to fall by 0.15 percentage points. In Indonesia, the significant increases in provincial minimum wages led to a fall in employment in small firms, but not in larger firms, although it was also associated with an increase in the number of workers below the minimum wage. At levels close to the average wage (as in several low-income countries), many private firms, especially those in low-technology activities, cannot afford to comply. In middle-income countries, the minimum wage is generally about half the average in the formal sector. Its coverage and enforcement tend to be low, but its impact on low-productivity firms and jobs can be large. In Latin America, for example, the largest proportions of workers who earn less than the minimum wage are found in countries where it is comparatively high: in Paraguay (where most workers earn less than two-thirds of the minimum wage), Nicaragua (40 percent of workers below the minimum), and Colombia (25 percent).
>
> **Employment Protection Legislation**
>
> The protection offered to permanent workers and the conditions for temporary employment vary considerably across and within regions. Countries in Latin America, Eastern Europe, and Central Asia tend to offer the most employment protection for permanent workers. By contrast, English-speaking industrial countries and East Asian economies have the lowest statutory protection. Evidence from several countries that recently reformed their stringent labor regulations suggests beneficial effects. By moving their employment protection legislation closer to the standards of the European industrial countries in the 1990s, Colombia and Peru experienced a higher response of employment-to-output growth, with speedier employment adjustment but also positive employment effects. The reform in Colombia also contributed to increased compliance with labor legislation by lowering the costs of formal production. During the past decade, Italy and Spain have eased their restrictive firing regulations, which has led to sizable positive effects on employment.
>
> *Source:* Pierre and Scarpetta 2004b.
>
> a. Each bargaining unit is strong enough to push wages above productivity, but at the same time, it is vulnerable to other units' wage strategies without being able to influence them.

workers' bargaining power is decreased. Under Communism, except for the former Yugoslavia, unemployment was essentially nonexistent, and wages did not respond to firms' performance.

The negative relationship between unemployment and wages, commonly called the "wage curve," appeared during the 1990s in several CEE countries (for example, Bulgaria, Hungary, Poland, and Slovenia), indicating that wages have become responsive to local labor market conditions.[2] But no such relationship exists in countries that have been less advanced in their market reforms (for example, Romania). A wage curve also exists in Turkey, except for women and young workers, pointing to the specificity of their labor force participation and working conditions.[3] In the central-planning period, because of the passive roles of unions and managers, there was no wage bargaining as such, but rather centralized wage setting, which mirrored price setting throughout the economy.[4] Although the countries of the Region began the transition with very high union membership, the monolithic official unions exerted no independent influence on wages, being integrated into management structures and considered "transmission belts" for the authorities. Enterprise managers were also part of the planning apparatus, focusing on production and full employment objectives, rather than profits.

The evolution from a common starting point of government wage setting and passive unions and management has been mixed across the Region's countries during the transition. What are the patterns and explanations for this? What is the evidence of the unions' impact on labor market outcomes?

Falling Union Bargaining Power in Most Transition Countries

Union density and bargaining coverage[5] have significantly declined in nearly all of the countries of the Region during transition, leading to diminishing impact of unions on wages. Under Communism, virtually all employees were members of the unions, and this was the case in most countries of the Region at the onset of the transition. As a new private sector developed, union presence and impact on wages declined in all transition countries, although there are clear subgroup variations in the extent of the decline. Figure 6.1 provides available information on density and coverage rates for a range of countries of the Region in the early 2000s.

The trends by subgroups are as follows:

- Official density rates in the waged sector in Belarus, Russia, and Ukraine and other CIS countries remain high by OECD standards (estimated between 55 and 90 percent), although effective coverage rates are likely to be lower, given large informal sectors and inflated membership numbers in most countries.[6]

- By contrast, average density and bargaining coverage rates fell more steeply in CEE, from more than 85 percent density and more than 90 percent coverage in most cases in 1989 to an average of around 30 percent density and less than 40 percent bargaining coverage by

FIGURE 6.1
Density and Bargaining Coverage, Early 2000s

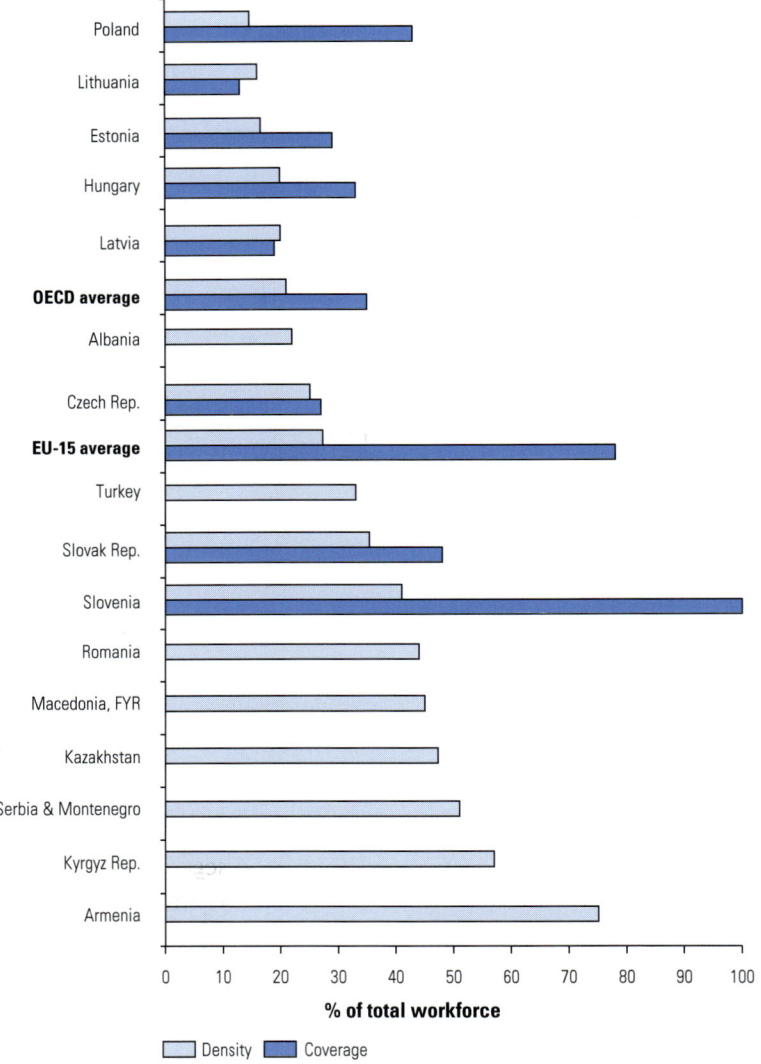

Sources: EIRO (2004); ILO (2002) for CIS; OECD (2004a); Micevska (2004) for Albania, Serbia and Montenegro, and FYR Macedonia.

the early 2000s. There is also substantial variation within CEE, the Baltic States being down to around 20 percent coverage and Slovenia maintaining 100 percent by the early 2000s.[7]

- SEE countries also witnessed substantial declines in union density and bargaining coverage, though estimates from different sources vary. Reasonable estimates of average union density are 22 percent in Albania, 45 percent in FYR Macedonia, and 51 percent in Serbia and

Montenegro.[8] Estimates of coverage rates have proven challenging to obtain. In some countries, such as Bosnia and Herzegovina (BiH),[9] they remain very high in the formal sector, because of the strong role of general and sectoral collective agreements. Although more research is needed, this pattern may be typical of former Yugoslav countries, reflecting the residual influence of worker self-management and the role of trade unions prevalent under the former regime. In both BiH and Serbia and Montenegro (SAM), automatic extension of collective agreements to all workers was only eliminated with the reform of labor legislation over the past five years.

Despite declining membership, union bargaining strength in specific sectors has remained relatively strong. Examples include natural monopolies, transport, heavy industry, and mining, which have been more likely to stay in public ownership. In contrast, expanding sectors comprising largely private enterprises, such as trade, business, and personal services, have tended to have much lower union presence. Similarly, union presence in newly created small and medium enterprises is low.

The scale of the decline in union bargaining power in the transition countries reflects several influences:

- Structural change in the formal sector—specifically the emergence of large private sectors (with typically much lower density and coverage rates) and the growth of service sectors at the expense of traditional industrial sectors (where unions are more strongly represented)

- A pattern—stronger in CEE—of increased segmentation and fragmentation of unions and union confederations, often with conflicting political and economic agendas[10]

- The increased level of informal sector activity

The differential legal position of unions across the Region is an important factor in influencing their behavior. At one extreme, nonreformers, such as Turkmenistan, retain mandatory membership in the successor unions, with automatic union fee deduction from salaries. Others, such as Uzbekistan, inhibit the formation of independent unions through high membership thresholds for union registration. Azerbaijan controls union activism through legal prohibition of political activity.[11] Other countries, such as Estonia, have no such limitations on union formation or activity, but have eliminated the privileges for unions in bargaining that continue to exist in many other countries of the Region (see box 6.2).

> **BOX 6.2**
>
> **Wage Bargaining in Estonia: A Radical Reformer**
>
> Because of explicit policy choices and a more general rejection of the Soviet inheritance, Estonia has seen the most fundamental changes in wage bargaining of any country of the Region. Together with Latvia and Lithuania, Estonia has witnessed the most dramatic decline in union density and bargaining coverage in the Region. By 2003, union density had fallen to around 16 percent, with 22 percent coverage. The private sector had only 8 percent density and around 19 percent coverage, in contrast to density and coverage rates of 28 and 31 percent, respectively, in the public sector. Although some sectors such as banking, construction, and services have very low unionization, others such as light industry, energy, education, and transport have strong unions, with much higher density. The small enterprise sector, which accounts for around 90 percent of private sector employment, has very limited unionization.
>
> The low density and coverage, especially in the private sector, are partly the result of a lack of legal privileges for trade unions. This is reflected in the Collective Agreements Act of 1993, which abandoned the former union monopoly to conclude agreements and to represent workers at the enterprise level. There are no restrictions as to who may be elected or in which proportion to workers. This principle has been upheld not only for collective agreements, but also in later legislation on worker representation, such as the Trade Union Law of 2000. Estonian laws do not restrict union activity, but they do not stipulate any special bodies for codetermination or representation that are reserved for unions, the right to demand the conclusion of collective agreements, or any obligation on employers to enter collective bargaining.

Divergent Patterns of Change in the Wage-Bargaining Process across Subgroups

Changes in unionization and in the role of unions in the economy have often radically affected the process of wage setting in transition countries. As seen in chapter 2, all of the transition countries have experienced widening wage differentials resulting from transition, suggesting that, in aggregate, wage determination has become more flexible. However, the aggregate patterns mask substantial cross-country variation in the evolution of wage-bargaining arrangements:

- At one end of the spectrum, countries such as Belarus and Turkmenistan retain the inherited system, with wage setting in the formal sector being highly centralized and entirely controlled by the

> Tripartite national bargaining began in 1992, with a Socio-Economic Council formed in 1999. Although the Council has a wide mandate to discuss economic issues, its only effective influence is on the minimum wage, the tax-free income threshold, and the level of unemployment benefit. For the public sector, negotiations focus only on the aggregate wage fund allocation, with substantial flexibility for employers to determine relative wages of workers beyond the minimum. The exception to date has been the education sector, where a more traditional wage coefficient structure has been retained in the face of a strong union. However, unions and employers accept the government view that budget and macroeconomic criteria are the primary determinants of wage outcomes. This can be seen in the large fluctuations in the real minimum wage during the second half of the 1990s and in the wage and pension freezes in the wake of the financial crisis in Russia. However, in 2001, there was a tripartite agreement on an increase in the ratio of minimum wage to average wage (MW/AW) from 32 percent in 2003 to 41 percent by 2008. Recent efforts of the government have focused on introducing performance-related pay, a move that has generally been resisted by the unions.
>
> Beyond the national-level negotiations, private sector bargaining in Estonia happens almost entirely at the firm level. Given low union density and limited rights of representation, individual employment contracts have a major role in determining the wages of workers. As a result, there are often high wage differentials within firms, and unions include many workers with limited individual bargaining leverage (such as low-skilled or Russians whose language skills limit their work opportunities).
>
> *Source:* Patzwaldt 2004.

government. A highly centralized model is also used in Slovenia, although the institutional mechanism is very different, leaving an important role for social partners in wage determination.

- At the other end of the spectrum, wage bargaining in most CEE countries has become highly decentralized in the growing private sector, and there are efforts to introduce more flexibility into public sector pay determination.

- Most of the other countries of the Region fall somewhere between these two extremes. Overall, Belarus, Russia, Ukraine, and other CIS countries still exhibit a strong legacy of socialist era wage determination in the formal sector. SEE countries represent an intermediate stage, with wage determination that is neither decentralized nor as dominated by government as in the CIS.

Compression of the Wage Schedule in the Public Sector

Key factors that distinguish the divergent evolution of wage bargaining in the transition countries include the size of public sector employment and the overall importance of government in economic decision making. The extent to which countries have reduced the role of the state in wage bargaining is thus the distinguishing feature of different subgroups of countries in the Region.

To assess the divergent subgroup developments, it is necessary to look first at public sector wage setting, because this has been the baseline wage determination mechanism from which countries have diverged at different speeds. Most of the transition countries have retained a coefficient-based system of wage determination in the public sector, under which wage adjustments cascade from adjustments in the base. This remains the model in Belarus, Russia, Ukraine, and other CIS countries and in SEE, with the public sector wage schedules exerting strong influence on formal private sector wage determination.[12] The coefficient system also applies in CEE public sector wage determination, although Estonia has eliminated the tariff schedule above the minimum in the public sector (except in education).

A key feature of such coefficient systems in most of the transition countries has been a compression of the wage schedule. Whereas the wage multiple from top to bottom of the public sector wage schedule in OECD countries has been around six to nine times, coefficient scales in the transition countries have typically been more compressed (for example, 2.3 in Romania, 2.8 in Moldova, 3.6 in Hungary, and so forth).[13] This is an issue that many of the Region's governments have examined as part of civil service reforms, but as of the end of the 1990s, a significant share of countries still had high public sector wage compression.[14]

Spillover Effects in the Private Sector

The primary significance of the coefficient system in economic terms in the transition countries is not its direct impact via public sector employment. The share of public sector employment in most of the transition countries is not very large—albeit higher than the market-benchmark for countries at the same level of income per capita (see chapter 4)—and public sector wages have remained fairly low, despite some recent increases, especially in the CEE countries.[15] However, the rigidities of the coefficient system assume wider significance in a labor market where there is a large state-owned sector that follows the same system, or where the formal private sector mimics the public sector wage-setting mechanism. A strict coefficient system with strong wage compression clearly limits the scope for adjusting wages to relative productivity levels and regional labor market characteristics. To the extent that this characterizes much of formal sector wage determination (public and private), the economic impacts could be expected to be negative.

In practice, the coefficient system brings varying degrees of rigidity in wage determination across subgroups. The trends in wage determination in different subgroups of the Region are strongly associated with the residual share of public sector and SOE employment in total wage employment and the overall degree of government intervention in the economy.[16]

- In CEE, greater wage flexibility has been mainly the result of a substantial decentralization in formal private sector wage setting, coupled with product market liberalization and associated competitive pressure. The most notable exception is Slovenia, which retains 100 percent bargaining coverage and highly centralized wage setting, even in the private sector.[17] In CEE countries, where wage-bargaining changes have progressed the most (for example, the Baltic States, the Czech Republic, Hungary, and Poland), enterprise-level wage bargaining developed spontaneously, largely in line with growth in the private sector and in the face of rather weak trade union influence at the firm level. For most CEE countries, wage bargaining takes place primarily at the enterprise level. The individual work contract is also a very important factor in the most-advanced reformers such as Estonia and Latvia.[18] By contrast, the role of sectoral bargaining is generally limited in CEE countries, with the exception of the Slovak Republic and Bulgaria—with around 40 percent of the workforce covered by sectoral collective agreements—and Slovenia.[19]

- By contrast, in Belarus, Russia, Ukraine, and other CIS countries, the government remains a much more pervasive force in formal sector wage determination. The formal private sector has more closely followed the public sector's lead in wage determination. Unions have not (for the most part) evolved into independent forces in bargaining; they have retained a dominant role, but are almost entirely subject to the determination of wages by the government. Employers often continue to place employment retention above productivity gains, commonly mimicking public sector wage setting in the formal private sector. Although the situation varies across countries (for example, Kazakhstan has active independent unions), the weakness of unions and employers is a shared feature of Belarus, Russia, Ukraine, and other CIS countries. As a result, they remain price takers from government in relation to formal sector wages and focus their efforts on negotiating soft budget constraints. At the same time, a large informal sector (accounting for more than 40 percent of employment) has provided very flexible wage determination for a large share of the workforce and is an important source of large wage disparities in the CIS. In Russia, flexible wage setting coexists with the use of the coefficient system in the private sector. Although most firms use firm-level wage scales, a significant fraction of private firms has adopted the public sector coefficient system.[20]

- There is less information on wage-bargaining developments in SEE countries. Generally, in countries of the former Yugoslavia, unions have been relatively influential, in part because of the inheritance of self-management. At the same time, the role of the government in formal sector wage setting remains strong, either directly (as in BiH and SAM), or less directly through the wage pull of the SOE sector. This in part reflects a weak role of employers in central or sectoral wage bargaining in some SEE countries. In Bosnia and Herzegovina, the trade union confederations also have a strong influence on wage setting, in the face of still underdeveloped employer organizations and the strong influence of governments. Overall, the importance of general collective agreements in SEE continues to be strong, which both limits the impact of EPL reforms and prolongs wage-setting practices such as automatic seniority increases and large location bonuses. There is also a strong role for sectoral unions and bargaining, the presence of employers as an independent voice again being negligible. Serbia and Montenegro and FYR Macedonia provide examples of more-fragmented union movements, although a general collective agreement and sectoral collective agreements have a strong role in both countries. There is also a strong wage pull from the SOE sector to other sectors, so that one has yet to see the desired level of decentralization in wage setting to develop.

Bargaining Structures in Transition Economies Are Still Evolving, and Their Labor Market Impact Is Underresearched

Overall, the link between wage-bargaining systems and labor market outcomes in the Region remains underresearched, in particular in CIS and SEE countries. With this caveat in mind, several patterns appear regarding bargaining arrangements and labor market outcomes in the Region:

- Changes in union density per se do not have a major impact on employment and unemployment rates, which is consistent with evidence from OECD countries. This is confirmed in multivariate regressions for CEE, Russia, and Ukraine, which control for country characteristics, including the depth of transitional reforms (using the EBRD transition index). The results for (un)employment outcomes also hold for job flow outcomes.[21] The finding is also confirmed in regression analysis on pooled data for OECD, CEE, and SEE countries for the second half of the nineties.[22]

- The typical negative correlation between bargaining coverage and earnings dispersion seen in OECD countries does not appear to hold at the cross-country level in transition economies. The most striking examples of this come from Russia and other CIS countries, which combine high union density rates with very large earning disparities (see chapter 2). However, the conclusion must be interpreted with caution in light of the perhaps misleadingly high density rates from Russia, Ukraine, and other CIS countries. Further research is needed to consider country and subgroup fixed effects.

- State-owned firms (which have higher union density) consistently have a greater share of firm surplus devoted to wages, reflecting insider bargaining power relative to both the privatized and de novo private firms. In the medium term, these firms may lack reinvestment capital; this may lead in time to slower growth and eventually lower employment. This pattern has been found in analyses of Bulgaria, Poland, and Russia.[23]

- Evidence from multivariate analysis for CEE, Russia, and Ukraine suggests that both highly centralized or coordinated systems and more decentralized systems are associated with higher employment and lower unemployment.[24] In other words, sectoral bargaining tends to deliver the worst employment outcomes, a pattern also observed in the OECD countries.[25] Slovenia provides an example of a flexible system whereby firms are allowed to deviate from the minimum wages associated with skills categories to reflect the performance of the firm or individual workers or both. The resulting within-firm wage flexibility appears to reduce excess turnover of workers (that is, improve the stability of employment) and to improve the match quality of workers (that is, improve the degree of adequacy between workers' characteristics and the requirements of their jobs).[26] These findings suggest a microlevel trade-off between wage differentials and employment.

Minimum Wages Vary a Great Deal across the Transition Countries

The minimum wage (MW) is an important element of wage determination. Particularly at the low end of the wage distribution, it may price out low-skilled, often young, workers. Minimum wages in the transition countries exhibit a clear divide between CEE and SEE on the one hand, where they average close to 40 percent of the average wage (AW) in 2002, and the CIS (except Ukraine) on the other hand, where they are only around 20 percent (and for several countries less than 10 percent) of the average wage (see figure 6.2). These ratios place CEE at the high end of the range of minimum wages by international standards and CIS at the low-to-modest end. In Ukraine, where the minimum wage is comparatively high, there is evidence that it is not enforced (see figure 6.3 and World Bank [2005c]). In SEE, both BiH and FYR Macedonia have high minimum-wage-to-average-wage ratios.

FIGURE 6.2
Minimum-Wage-to-Average-Wage Ratio, 2002 (percentage)

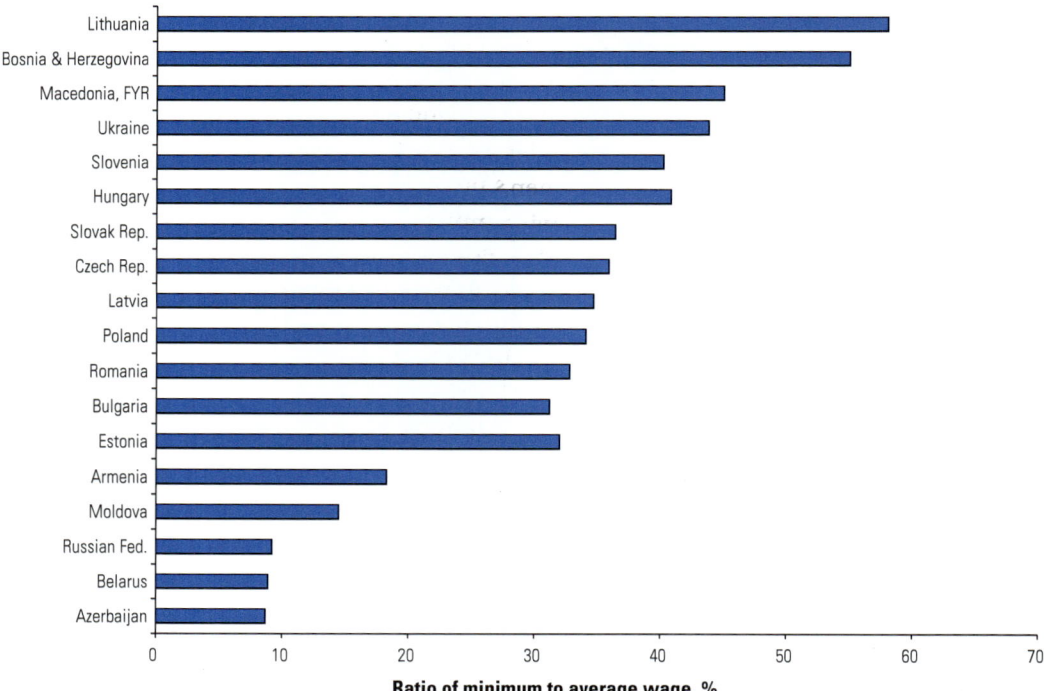

Sources: TransMonee and Bank staff calculations.

Note: BiH = FBiH only.

FIGURE 6.3
Minimum Wage in Ukraine Accounts for a High Percentage of the Market Wage of Low-Skilled Workers, but It Is Not Enforced

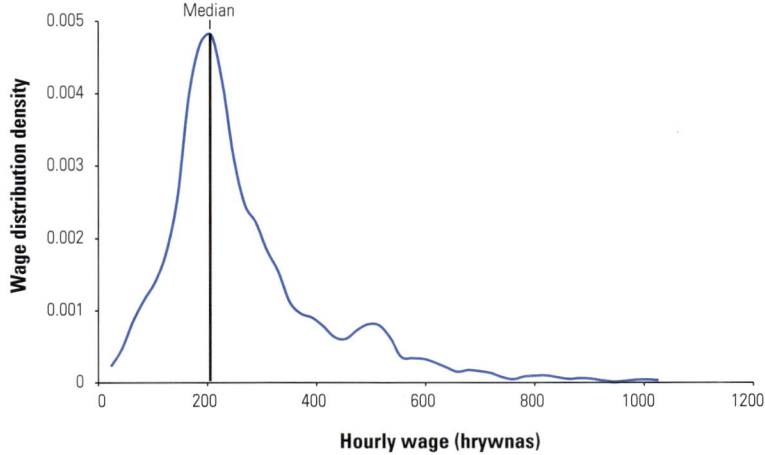

Sources: Ukrainian Longitudinal Monitoring Survey, 2004; World Bank 2005c.

Note: The vertical line indicates the minimum wage (205 hrywnas in June 2004). Low-skilled workers are workers classified as "unskilled" according to the ULMS.

Negotiated Minimum Wages Are Often Much Higher Than the Nationwide Minimum Wage

Minimum wages for some sectors are higher—often considerably so—than the national minimum wage. This is typically a product of bargaining at the sectoral level. Examples indicate that the increment of sectoral MWs over general wage floors can be substantial: in Bulgaria, 52 percent of sectoral collective agreements provide for minimum wages higher than the economywide minimum, with negotiated minimums 10–80 percent higher than the national minimum; in the Federation of Bosnia and Herzegovina (FBiH), the minimum wage in the 2004 telecommunications sector collective agreement was double the economywide minimum wage (itself a high 55 percent of the average wage) and equivalent to 110 percent of the economywide average wage.[27] Although the principle of varied minimum wages is desirable, the potentially negative employment effects of ratcheting MWs above already high national MWs need to be considered.

Minimum Wages Sometimes Set Social Benefit Minimums

In a number of the transition countries—most notably in Belarus, Russia, Ukraine, and other CIS countries—the role of the official minimum wage was perhaps more significant as the base around which certain social benefits were set. Many of these countries have abolished such linkages. Kazakhstan provides a case where this explicit welfare function of the minimum wage has been delinked, with a "base numerator" set instead as the base for determination of certain social transfers.

The Czech Republic, however, provides a good example where such delinkage was done without sufficient consideration for the value of the minimum wage relative to base social welfare benefits, with negative implications for work incentives.[28] From 1992 to 1998, various social benefits were linked to the minimum wage. Because of fiscal concerns, the government kept the minimum wage at a low level to avoid increased transfers obligations. However, this was changed in the late 1990s, with the introduction of a "subsistence wage" distinct from the minimum wage, which assumed the function of the benchmark for setting the level of the transfers.[29] If low-income workers earn less than this amount, the state tops up their income to the subsistence wage level. With the link to the transfers system, people receive the subsistence wage whether they work or not. Such an example raises the issue of using uniform national minimums in social benefit determination when regional labor markets may have very different market wages on offer. What appears as a reasonable benefits numeraire in the capital city may well have significant work disincentive effects in depressed regions.

Another notable feature of the minimum wage in some countries is its linkage to the revenue system. Croatia and FYR Macedonia constitute an interesting case. These countries do not have any economywide minimum wage as such, but they require that social benefit contributions be paid on the basis of a set minimum amount. Although such an explicit link may be sensible from a public finance perspective, it is questionable whether it is prudent from a labor market perspective.[30] In other countries, the relationship to public finances is not explicit, but disproportionately high shares of workers cluster on declared wages at or just above the minimum wage (with evidence of additional undeclared incomes above the minimum), creating incentives to sustain a high minimum wage to sustain tax revenue. For example, in Latvia, almost one-third of private employees earn declared income within 20 percent of the official minimum wage, although the average wage is around three times the minimum and public sector wages exhibit a more regular distribution.[31] This aspect of minimum wage policy in the Region requires further research.

Minimum Wages Have Stronger Disemployment Effects in Backward Areas and among the Low-Skilled

International evidence shows that high national minimum wages negatively affect employment chances of low-productivity workers, including workers with little labor market experience (for example, the youth), with low skills, and in backward regions (O'Keefe 2004). Large increases in minimum wage levels in the Czech and Slovak Republics (of 70 and 50 percent, respectively—but from very low levels) have led to limited job losses and to large increases in firm wages during 1999–2002.[32] However, for specific subgroups of workers, such as the low-skilled or the youth, minimum wages represent a much higher proportion of the reservation wage.[33] For example, in Poland, the minimum wage accounts for more than 80 percent of the wage received by low-skilled workers in high unemployment regions. Because the wage of low-paid workers is close to the minimum, they are the first to be affected by any increase in the minimum wage. Evidence shows that there is a negative relationship between MW/AW ratios and low-paid employment. This suggests that high minimum wages contribute to pricing marginal workers out of the workforce. Some evidence on the negative effects of minimum wage increases on employment rates among unskilled workers is found in regression analyses from Estonia and Hungary.[34] It is also consistent with high youth unemployment in the transition countries, particularly given the general absence of separate youth minimum wages (except in Poland).

Employment Protection Legislation Remains Strict despite Reforms, Although Enforcement Is Variable

Employment protection legislation (EPL) is a key labor market institution in ensuring secure and decent work. At the same time, it is important to balance its positive impacts on workers with jobs with the needs of the unemployed and those entering the labor market, whose prospects of being hired may be negatively affected by overly strict job-security provisions. There are also trade-offs from an economic viewpoint between the positive features of strict EPL (such as incentives to provide productivity-enhancing training to workers) and the need for sufficient ease of job turnover to promote efficient allocation of labor and contribute to macrolevel productivity improvements.[35] Given the complex balance to be struck in the design and enforcement of EPL, it is perhaps not surprising that research on its contribution to labor market outcomes, even in OECD countries, has reached contrasting findings.[36] Analysis of EPL in the transition countries is further complicated by several factors, including the relatively fast pace of change in EPL during the transition, the unusually high need for labor reallocation, and often weak compliance.

Nearly All Transition Countries Have Liberalized Employment Protection Legislation, Especially Those Moving into the EU

At the beginning of the transition, workers in the Region were among the most protected in the world. This was reflected in the socialist-era EPL, under which dismissals were very difficult, full-time permanent employment was the norm, and workers were entitled to a wide range of workplace benefits and protection. At the same time, protections such as severance pay and notice periods upon dismissal were largely unnecessary (because dismissals were prohibited, except for severe misconduct). Former Yugoslavia, which had very generous provisions on both, was a notable exception.

Nearly all transition countries subsequently carried out significant reforms of EPL, though at varying points during the transition. The direction of initial reforms has been toward greater flexibility in labor relations, including in hiring and firing (for example, lower direct dismissal costs or removal of trade union veto on dismissals), promoting temporary and part-time employment, allowing for opting out of collective agreements, and so forth. Most CEE countries achieved their first wave of EPL reforms early in the transition, while other regions such as SEE and the CIS often delayed reforms until the late 1990s. Many countries have continued to adjust reformed legislation, although in some cases reducing flexibility in later revisions (for example, Romania's second wave of EPL reforms after 1998 and Hungarian reforms effective from 1997).

EU Transition Countries Have Focused More on Liberalizing Temporary Contracts

Although the overall trend in EPL reforms is therefore clearly toward greater flexibility, the progression has not been linear. For 10 transition economies, information has been gathered on the evolution of employment protection legislation since the beginning of the 1990s (figure 6.4). These data suggest that transition economies that were approaching entry into the European Union (for example, Hungary, Poland, and the Slovak Republic) have been more aggressive in liberalizing EPL than others whose accession was further in the future (for example, Bulgaria and Romania) or not foreseen in the short term (for example, Ukraine). This suggests that EU accession could have played a disciplining role in promoting reforms.[37]

It should be stressed, however, that most of the reforms have been concentrated on liberalizing temporary contracts by extending maximum duration of fixed-term contracts or by legalizing temporary work agencies. In other words, following the experience of many continental European countries, EU transition economies have liberalized at the margin, lowering the costs of temporary employment, with more modest reductions in the protection of permanent workers. This may have contributed to the observed duality in the labor market whereby vulnerable groups, including youth, women, and the unskilled, churn from one job to another without being able to build a proper career, while those who maintain a regular contract still enjoy a significant degree of job protection.[38]

Despite Reforms, Regulations Remain Fairly Restrictive in Most Countries

Despite the importance of the many reforms, EPL in the Region remains (on average) stricter than in other regions in the world (figure 6.5). In particular, the stringency of EPL for permanent workers in the Region is (on average) higher than that in any other region except South Asia. However, there is also considerable variation in the Region in the stringency of employment protection, particularly regarding temporary employment (figure 6.6A).

There is no clear subgroup pattern to the relative levels of regular and temporary EPL (figure 6.6B). However, in some cases, the differentials are very pronounced, in both directions. For example, Bosnia and Herzegovina, Bulgaria, and Latvia mainly limit temporary employment and regulate permanent employment less, while Albania, Estonia, Kazakhstan, Poland, and Slovenia provide significantly more protection to permanent employment.

EPL Is Not Fully Enforced in Many of the Transition Countries

There is evidence of weak enforcement of EPL in most of the transition countries, except for CEE.[39] This appears to be particularly the case in the CIS and a significant factor in much of SEE. This suggests that the effective rigidity imposed by EPL varies from that indicated by simple comparison of legislation (see also box 5.4). The point is supported by the available evidence on settlement of labor disputes

FIGURE 6.4
Employment Protection Legislation in EU-8 and Other Selected Countries during the Transition

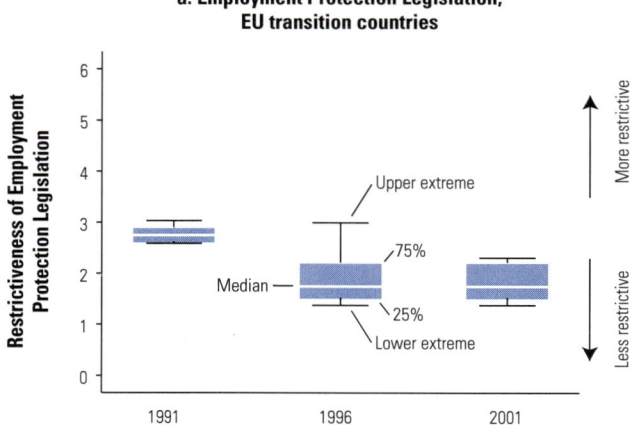

Source: Haltiwanger, Scarpetta, and Vodopivec 2003.

Note: The line in the middle of the shaded box represents the median. The shaded box extends from the 25th percentile to the 75th percentile, the so-called interquartile range (IQR). The lines emerging from the box extend to the upper and lower adjacent values. The former is equal to the 75th percentile plus 1.5 times IQR, while the latter is the 25th percentile minus 1.5 times IQR. Points more extreme than the adjacent values, if any, are outside values and are individually plotted. The employment protection legislation (EPL) index ranges from 0 (the least regulated) to 6 (the most regulated). The index measures regulations for both temporary and permanent employment contracts.

(for example, in Russia) and, for some countries, in the differences between the legislative difficulty of hiring and firing and the ease of both reported by employers (for example, in Romania and Ukraine).[40] In Belarus, Russia, Ukraine, and other CIS countries, there is widespread evidence of weak enforcement of EPL. It is seen

FIGURE 6.5

Transition Countries Have More-Stringent Regulations on Hiring and Firing than Do OECD Countries

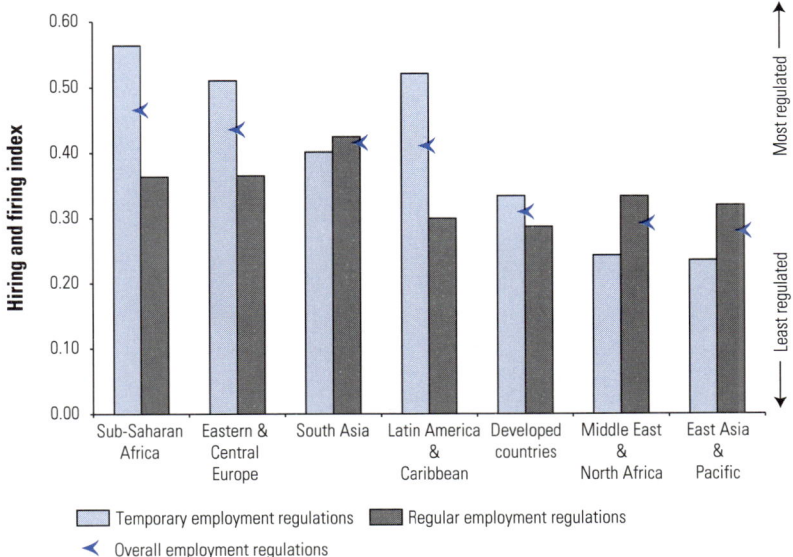

Source: Bank staff calculations based on Doing Business Database (2005). A higher index indicates more-stringent regulations; see annex 6.1 for the construction of the indexes.

most starkly in the massive scale of wage arrears in the subgroups during the 1990s and is supported by employer surveys. For example, in Moldova, despite strict EPL, employers identify labor regulations as their least important problem, which is consistent with the country's high job destruction rate. By contrast, CEE countries have less strict EPL (on average), but are considered more likely to enforce it (for example, evidence from Bulgaria, Lithuania, and Poland indicates that the costs of court challenges to dismissals act as additional disincentives to firing workers). Finally, there is evidence (for example, from Lithuania and Poland) that EPL is more strongly enforced in large firms, which typically have a stronger union presence.

Table 6.1 shows a tentative characterization of the transition countries according to the strictness of EPL and its enforcement. It is indicative only, but illustrates that the effective impact of strict EPL in the Region may be less than comparisons of labor legislation would suggest, with only Slovenia having both strict EPL and strict enforcement. Although the characterization is crude, it indicates that countries in the top right of the table need to focus more on credibly enforceable laws as opposed to "paper protections," which at best protect a limited share of formal sector workers.

FIGURE 6.6
There Are Significant Differences within the Region's Countries on EPL

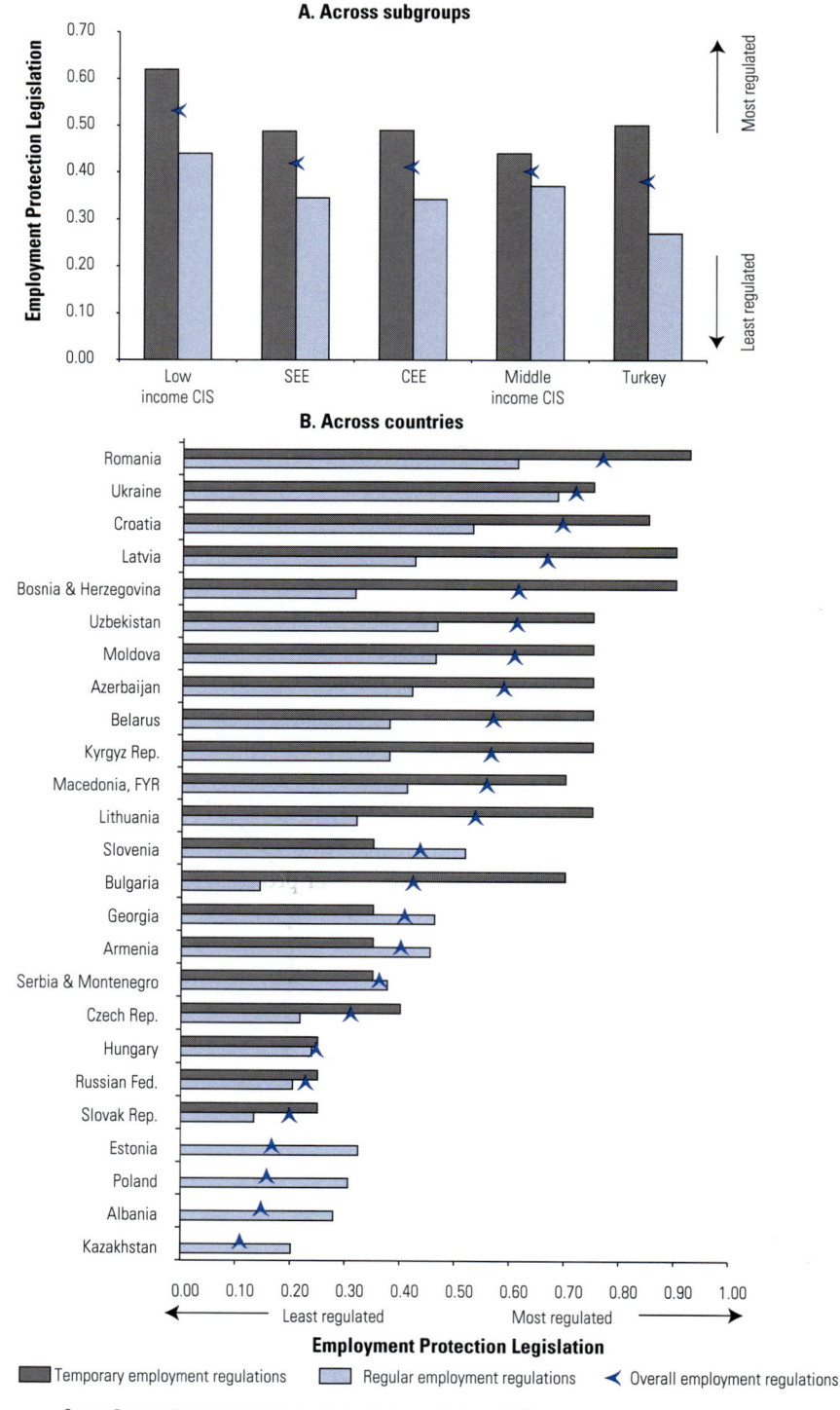

Source: Bank staff calculations based on Doing Business Database (2005).

TABLE 6.1
EPL and Enforcement Typology

	Flexible EPL	More restrictive EPL	Very rigid EPL
Weaker enforcement	Albania, Kazakhstan	Armenia, Georgia, Russian Federation, Serbia and Montenegro, Turkey	Azerbaijan, Belarus, Bosnia and Herzegovina, Kyrgyz Republic, Moldova, Ukraine, Uzbekistan
Intermediate enforcement		Bulgaria	Croatia; Macedonia, FYR; Romania
Stronger enforcement	Czech Republic, Estonia, Hungary, Poland, Slovak Republic	Latvia, Lithuania, Slovenia	

Source: Bank staff calculations.

Note: (i) Strictness defined as whether country EPL index below world average EPL index in Doing Business 2005, up to 20% higher and more than 20% higher; (ii) strength of enforcement based on share of informal sector employment. The degree of enforcement is proxied by the size of the informal economy; the higher the informal economy the weaker the estimated degree of enforcement (Schneider and Klinglmair 2004, and country studies where available). For Russia the EPL index was corrected toward stricter EPL following comments from Russian experts.

Even with Varying Enforcement, Strict EPL Has Had Some Negative Impacts on the Labor Market

Despite varying enforcement, available analysis indicates that there remain costs from strict EPL in the Region. First, strict EPL may promote informality, self-employment, and small firms (which often fall outside EPL). The positive correlation between strict EPL and the share of informal sector employment can be seen in figure 6.7. A similar positive association holds between the strictness of EPL and the share of self-employment.[41] Given that informal employment is frequently low-productivity, strict EPL can hamper productivity growth.

Second, strict EPL gives rise to less favorable employment outcomes in transition economies. The relationship between EPL and employment outcomes is difficult to identify statistically. One reason is that the system is still moving toward equilibrium, and thus the steady state (un)employment rate is not known. For example, cross-country regressions for the late 1990s suggest insignificant correlation between EPL and aggregate unemployment in countries from OECD, CEE, and SEE (Cazes and Nesporova 2003; Micevska 2004), although they find that stricter EPL increases the risk of long-term unemployment. However, these static studies do not capture the effects of the significant institutional changes that transition countries carried out over the 1990s, nor do they use a steady state unemployment rate as a dependent variable.

In contrast, more complex, cross-country, pooled regression analysis (which adds the time dimension to the relationship) finds negative

FIGURE 6.7
Informality Tends to Be Higher in Countries with Strict EPL

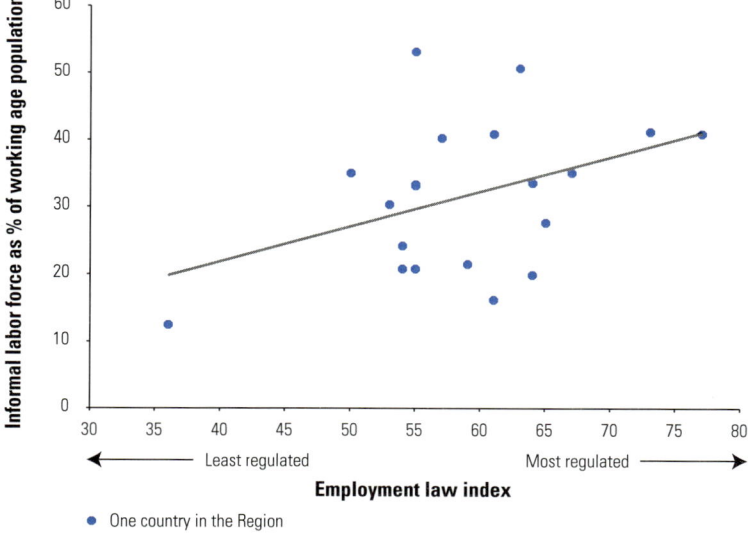

- One country in the Region

Sources: Doing Business in 2004 for EPL; Schneider (2002) for the size of the informal sector.

effects of strict EPL for CEE, Russia, and Ukraine.[42] In countries with low coordination among partners in wage bargaining,[43] strict EPL is found to weaken labor market outcomes, but in countries with a high degree of coordination, the effect is less marked. Significantly, the effects of EPL on employment rates are weaker in the Region than in OECD economies, while they are stronger for unemployment rates. This is consistent with strict EPL being unable to prevent job destruction, but still contributing to less formal sector job creation. It is also consistent with employer surveys, in which firms that are expanding are more likely to report EPL as a major obstacle in their operations, while nonexpanding firms are less likely to do so.

In addition, greater job security for those with jobs appears to come at a cost for the unemployed and new entrants in the labor market, so that (re)entry into formal sector employment is negatively affected. This "insider-outsider" impact on formal sector employment rates would appear to undermine the claim that strict EPL is "always good for workers" in the aggregate. Moreover, evidence from the Region indicates that reforms of EPL have not been associated with higher income inequality and that there are, if anything, higher income disparities in countries with stricter—but weakly enforced—EPL.[44]

A further important finding of regression analysis is that EPL has a significant association with the pace of labor reallocation. For CEE,

Russia, and Ukraine, regression analysis reveals that a more-stringent EPL is associated with lower job creation, lower job destruction, and thus lower job reallocation.[45] This in turn is likely to feed through to impacts on productivity. These findings are consistent with more-detailed country case studies (for example, in Croatia, Bosnia and Herzegovina, and the Slovak Republic). This supports the intuition that strict EPL dampens job flows, even with weak enforcement. Empirical findings on employers' perceptions of the impact of EPL also suggest that firms that are in the process of upgrading or developing new product lines and potentially need additional skilled workers are more affected by strict EPL than others (see chapter 5).

Finally, regression analysis on pooled data from OECD, CEE, and SEE countries for the second half of the 1990s finds that strict EPL influences the composition of unemployment: the strictness of temporary EPL provisions is positively correlated with higher youth and female unemployment, stricter EPL increases the risks of long-term unemployment, and stricter temporary EPL discourages labor supply.[46]

Taxes on Labor

Taxes on labor may impact equilibrium wages; this in turn may affect equilibrium employment. The extent of the employment impact is affected by the level of competition in the labor market. In particular, the impact of high taxes on labor use depends on the extent to which there is "tax shifting" of labor taxation onto the cost of labor (and hence labor demand), as opposed to shifting it onto take-home pay (and hence labor supply).

High Taxes on Labor Use, Especially in CEE Countries

The tax wedge on labor in the transition countries is high—in many cases, very high. At the same time, like most labor market institutions, it exhibits considerable variation across countries, both in aggregate level and composition (figure 6.8). Overall, the tax wedge on labor in CEE and Turkey is very high by any standard, while labor taxation in CIS countries is lower (on average). The tax burden on labor is at an intermediate level in SEE countries, but remains high by international standards.[47] On average, the tax wedge on labor in Belarus, Russia, Ukraine, and other CIS countries is more than 14 percentage points lower than that in CEE and Turkey, while for SEE, it averages around 11 percentage points lower than that in CEE and

Turkey (figure 6.9). The differences in payroll and effective personal income tax rates are likely to be amplified in practice by variable tax enforcement capacity across the Region.

For CEE, the comparison with OECD countries is of interest (figure 6.9).[48] The regional average tax wedge is around 8 percent lower than the OECD average (excluding CEE OECD countries). However, the averages mask considerable variety in both groupings. The tax wedge on labor in CEE countries is noticeably higher than the OECD average.[49] Once OECD countries are disaggregated into high, medium, and low labor tax wedge groups, CEE averages are 10 per-

FIGURE 6.8
The Region's Tax Wedge on Labor, 2003

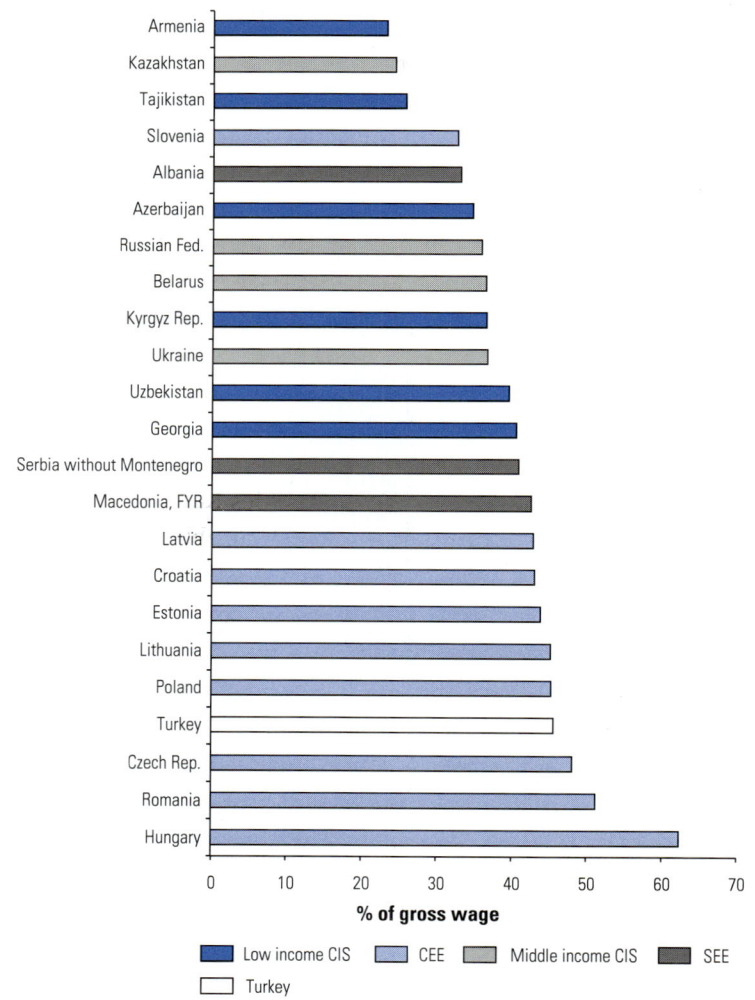

Sources: OECD (2004b) for Czech Republic, Hungary, Poland, and Turkey; Bank staff estimates for other countries.

Note: Tax wedge for nonagricultural worker on average wage without dependents.

FIGURE 6.9
Tax Wedge on Labor, the Region, and OECD, Early 2000s

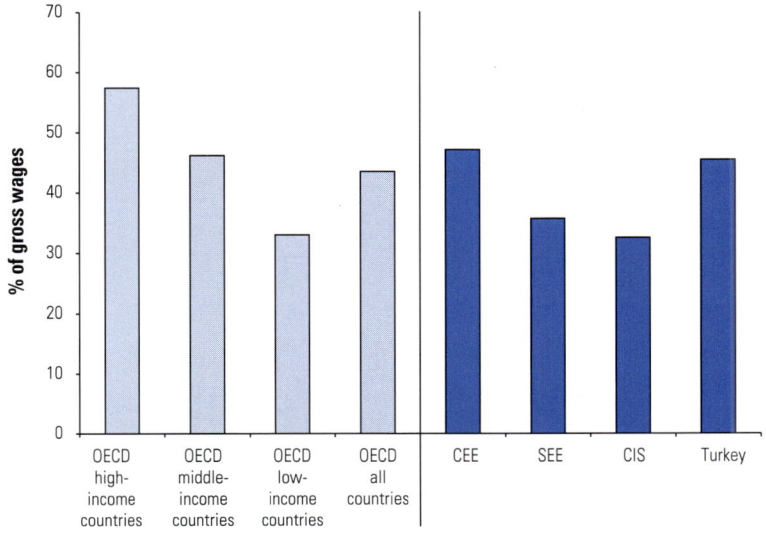

Sources: OECD (2004b) for OECD and CEE OECD, except Slovenia (based on 2001); Bank staff estimates for others (using 2003).

Note: Tax wedge calculated for nonagricultural AW worker without dependents in the Region and production AW worker without dependents in OECD. OECD groupings exclude CEE OECD: (i) low (less than 40% wedge) includes Australia, Iceland, Ireland, Japan, Korea, Mexico, New Zealand, Portugal, Switzerland, UK and USA; (ii) mid (40-50%) includes Canada, Denmark, Greece, Luxembourg, Norway, Spain and Sweden; (iii) high (51+ %) includes Austria, Belgium, Finland, France, Germany, Italy and Netherlands.

centage points lower than the average for the OECD group with the highest average tax wedge. Hungary is the only country of the Region that would fit firmly within the high labor tax OECD group. In contrast, CIS has an average tax wedge on labor equal to the average for the low-labor-tax OECD group, which includes Korea and Mexico, which are the only OECD members with comparable income levels. The SEE average is between the low- and medium-labor-tax OECD groups and somewhat below the overall OECD average.

For six CEE countries, there is also information on the evolution of the tax wedge during the 1990s (figure 6.10). Contrary to the patterns of employment protection and the decline in the generosity of unemployment benefits (see below), the tax wedge has increased (on average) in these countries, with a reduction in the cross-country dispersion of tax wedge rates. The surge in other social expenditures, predominantly pensions, has led to further increases in the fiscal burden on the use of labor. In this context, it is not surprising that many employers in the Region found the tax burden to be one of the most serious constraints to operating their firms (see chapter 5).

Although the high tax wedge in the Region is important, there is also considerable evidence—particularly in the earlier part of the

FIGURE 6.10
Surge in the Tax Wedge in EU Transition Countries during the 1990s

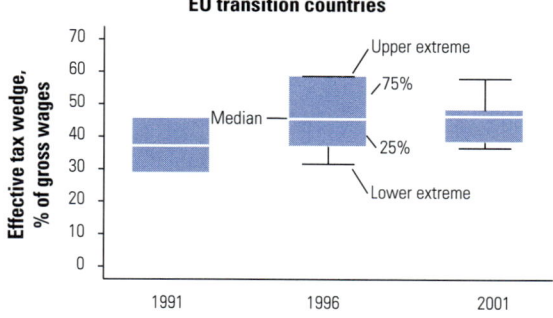

Source: Haltiwanger, Scarpetta, and Vodopivec 2003.

Note: See note to figure 6.4 for details on the construction of the graph. The tax wedge on labor use is the ratio of total taxes—income taxes and social security contributions—over wages plus employers' social security contributions. The *effective* tax wedge is based on tax, social security receipts and the wage bill, as opposed to the *notional* tax wedge which is based on average tax and social security rates for the average production worker.

transition, and before reforms of tax administration in a number of countries—of partial tax compliance, particularly in low-income countries and those affected by conflict. The combination of high taxes on labor and the low capacity of the public sector to enforce compliance points to ambiguous effects on aggregate (un)employment. However, the relatively stronger enforcement capacity of CEE countries, combined with their very high labor taxation, could raise labor costs and affect employment. This is true at least for countries with low-productivity potentials whose wages cannot fully compensate for the high taxes because of minimum-wage rules.

High Taxes on Labor Use Are Associated with Negative Labor Market Outcomes

Evidence from OECD countries suggests that the pass-through of taxes onto wages depends on wage-bargaining systems.[50] In countries with sectoral wage bargaining, where there is a lack of coordination between social partners, the pass-through onto wages is more limited because workers have fewer incentives to consider the effect of their bargaining on employment. In such countries, labor taxes are therefore found to have greater negative effects on labor market outcomes. Similar effects may be at work in the transition countries.

What are the findings on the impact of labor taxation on labor market outcomes in the Region? Available cross-section and panel regression analyses on the impact of taxes on labor in the Region, although limited, find impacts similar to those in OECD countries.[51]

This is reinforced by information on employer perceptions reported in chapter 5, identifying high taxes as a major constraint on firm operations. The high tax wedge on labor, especially in CEE, is associated with lower employment rates, higher unemployment rates, higher long-term unemployment rates, and higher youth unemployment rates.

It is clear that to foster job creation in the longer term, a number of countries in the Region need to consider significant reductions in their tax burden on labor. A challenge facing the transition countries is the need for a reduction in payroll taxes from a labor demand viewpoint amid social expectations of maintaining social insurance systems at current levels. This raises important reform issues in pensions and health insurance. Given demographic trends, further reforms of social insurance programs will be needed simply to avoid substantial increases in payroll taxes across the Region.

The Role of Passive and Active Labor Market Programs

High and persistent unemployment in many transition economies creates political demand for the use of passive and active labor policies. The case is reinforced by equity arguments, given the significantly higher-than-average poverty rates among households with unemployed heads in the transition countries (for European transition economies, mean expenditures of unemployed-head households is only 68 percent of the average, but in the CIS around 85 percent) and by political economy arguments at a time when significant reforms are necessary and public acceptance is crucial. However, because of poor incentive effects and moral hazard, passive labor market policies may create economic inefficiencies and entail large government expenditures. Active labor market programs (ALMPs) may also be very costly, and their success in helping the unemployed needs to be evaluated to justify such spending.

The developments in both passive and active programs for the unemployed have been rapid in the Region and have included major adjustments in many countries during transition. These interventions are a crucial part of the menu of policies that governments can use to help displaced workers and other disadvantaged groups find new jobs. This section draws from available empirical evidence to outline which types of policies and designs have been more successful. It argues that if there is adequate administrative capacity, ALMPs can be used to help disadvantaged worker groups and improve the matching function of the labor market. But they hardly increase aggregate employment. ALMPs are costly, and thus monitoring and evaluation are necessary to ensure that they have the net impact (for example, significantly improving the job-finding chances of program participants) that justifies the cost. The level of spending and the mix of programs will depend on what individual countries can afford in their financial and administrative capacity.

All Transition Economies Introduced OECD-Style Unemployment Insurance, and They Have Reduced Their Generosity to Contain Expenditures

The need for major reallocations of labor during transition led to the introduction of unemployment insurance systems in all transition countries by the early 1990s. They adopted OECD-type mandatory unemployment insurance (UI) schemes, financed in nearly all cases from payroll taxes, with some CEE countries introducing unemployment assistance following expiration of unemployment benefits (UB).

As in the OECD, unemployment benefits in the Region are typically earnings-related, though subject to floors and ceilings. In recent years, the range in replacement rates for UI has been 35–60 percent of the previous wage. This is equivalent to 60–100 percent of the national minimum wage and 10–45 percent of the national average wage in CEE. The effective replacement rate in some countries was also considerably below the legislated rate because of payment arrears (for example, in Russia, the low income CIS countries, and Serbia and Montenegro) and benefit ceilings (for example, Croatia).

The replacement rate has been adjusted downward in a number of CEE, SEE, and CIS countries during the 1990s in the face of fiscal constraints and significant flows into unemployment. It had reached an average of just more than 40 percent of the average wage by the end of the decade in EU transition countries (figure 6.11). The decline has, however, been accompanied by a widening of the replacement rates across these countries, with some (for example, Poland) moving to a flat level and others maintaining the earnings-related system.

Although replacement rates are broadly comparable to EU and OECD averages, it is important to note the significant variation in rates across countries and the implications of the typical practice in the Region of designing programs with benefit floors related to national benchmarks. This can result in replacement rates relative to average wages in depressed regions that can be very high, risking employment disincentives. This issue is a concern in CEE, in particular.

FIGURE 6.11

Unemployment Benefit Replacement Rates Have Declined in EU Transition Countries during the 1990s

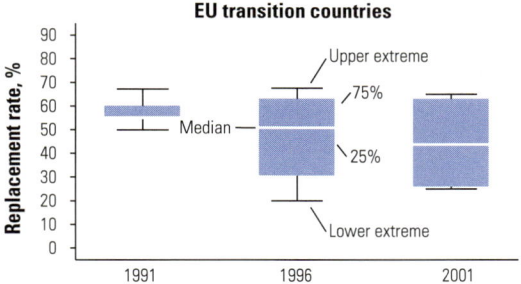

Source: Haltiwanger, Scarpetta, and Vodopivec 2003.

Note: See note to figure 6.4 for details on the construction of the graph. The replacement rate is the ratio of unemployment benefits over previous wage. It refers to a worker earning an average wage while at work and with sufficient work experience to claim benefits for the maximum duration.

Benefits duration in the transition countries falls within a range comparable to that in OECD countries—between six months and a year at the end of the 1990s. In some SEE countries, unemployment benefits duration reaches 24 months. Across the Region, there was a convergence in benefits duration during the 1990s, with a number of countries reducing high benefits duration in response to fiscal pressures and a growing pool of long-term unemployed.

Coverage Is Low, Especially in the CIS

Coverage rates of UI programs (that is, the share of the registered unemployed receiving unemployment benefits) vary between countries and over time. This is in part related to the varying treatment of noncontributing groups like school leavers and other special groups and to the extension of UI duration for older unemployed. It also reflects the growing pool of unemployed who have exhausted their benefits entitlement. On average, the share of registered unemployed receiving benefits is just under 30 percent in the Region, and it has been falling over time in most countries. In CEE, the average coverage rate was around 45 percent at the end of the 1990s, while for SEE the coverage was much lower, at around 12 percent, largely reflecting tighter qualification rules.

Overall, the combination of coverage and replacement rates and benefits duration means that UI systems in CEE and SEE are at the lower end of OECD generosity and well below such levels in the CIS. The very low generosity of the CIS systems has made UI systems increasingly irrelevant, contributing to low registered unemployment rates. The level of generosity is also reflected in spending shares on unemployment benefits, which in the late 1990s ran to an average of around 0.7 percent of GDP in CEE and SEE, but only 0.1–0.3 percent of GDP in the CIS. This compares with OECD and non-Region EU averages of around 1.4 and 1.7 percent, respectively.[52]

Two other considerations are important concerning UI in the transition countries:

- In a number of countries, a range of noncash benefits attached to registered unemployment status may have a strong impact on incentives to register. The most significant is free health insurance. There is evidence that in countries of former Yugoslavia, as well as in Poland, workers register as unemployed to ensure family health insurance coverage when no one in the household is paying social contributions. In Bosnia and Herzegovina, for example, only 25 percent of registered unemployed were actually unemployed, according to ILO definitions.[53] In Croatia, this proportion is still higher and was 40 percent in 2001. This contributes to substantially inflated official unemployment figures in some countries. Conversely, the effective absence of additional entitlements for registered unemployed in the CIS reinforces low incentives to register. Also in Russia and other CIS countries, the services provided by public employment agencies do not provide better alternatives than individual job search, so the payoff to registering is negligible.

- As suggested above, the stringency of work test enforcement varies substantially across the Region. Country studies, such as one for the Czech Republic, indicate that the stringency of work test enforcement has been a contributing factor to keeping registered unemployment rates low. In contrast, most countries in SEE and the CIS make minimal efforts to enforce work tests, in part because of low labor demand and in part because of low administrative capacity. However, in Russia, administrative restrictions often lead the long-term unemployed to be struck from the register.

More Generous UI Systems Have Been Associated with Poor Employment Outcomes

Multivariate analysis for CEE, Russia, and Ukraine suggests that, if too generous, unemployment benefits might have a negative impact on labor market outcomes, with the level of benefits negatively affecting employment rates, and duration of benefits being strongly associated with a higher unemployment rate, and especially a higher long-term unemployment rate.[54] This is consistent with OECD findings, but both the level and duration effects are stronger in transition than in OECD economies. In addition to these aggregate findings, studies of exits from unemployment in CEE confirm the negative effects of potential benefits duration on the probability of exit from unemployment to employment, with notable increases in exits to employment near benefits exhaustion.[55]

The findings support the point made above that the generosity of CEE unemployment insurance systems in the initial stages of transition acted as a floor on real wages, inducing lower exits from unemployment by raising the effective reservation wage. However, it is also important to note that subsequent tightening of UI through duration and level reductions had only a moderate impact on exits from unemployment to employment.[56] The explanations include weak labor demand, structural mismatches and informational failures associated with geographic and sectoral segmentation, and inherited attitudes of the unemployed toward the role of the state in providing employment.

Social Assistance Programs to Help the Long-Term Unemployed and the Poor

Social assistance systems may be important in terms not only of poverty alleviation but also of labor market adjustment. To the extent that they work effectively, they help to protect workers who have lost their jobs and exhausted other entitlements before finding new work. However, there is also a risk that, if not well-designed, they raise the reservation wage above market wages, thereby discouraging job search. In contrast, where social assistance systems provide negligible benefits, workers are more inclined to remain in poorly paid jobs, willing to tolerate extended wage arrears and periods of administrative leave. A well-designed and adequately financed social assistance system can therefore have a role to play in labor adjustment—both in ensuring adequate work incentives and in encouraging productivity-enhancing labor turnover.

The mix of social assistance–welfare programs within and between transition countries is complex. Apart from means-tested social assistance, there are typically child-family benefits; often benefits for utilities for poor households; in-kind benefits; and benefits for specific groups such as refugees, veterans, and survivor families. Although all countries in the Region introduced an OECD-style mix of social protection programs, the generosity and credibility of the systems have varied dramatically across the Region.[57]

Over the transition period, the evolution of basic social assistance programs has been varied. Some countries have remained with the initial mix of programs, while others have been more innovative in experimenting with minimum income guarantees (for example, Estonia and the Kyrgyz Republic) and benefits structured as negative income taxes (for example, Lithuania).[58] Others, such as Armenia and some oblasts of Russia (as well as Turkey), have introduced proxy means-tested programs for the poor. Others still, including Albania and Uzbekistan, have relied on community knowledge to target poor households. Moreover, following the experience of other developing countries, some economies of the Region have introduced programs that provide income support to poor families conditional on either basic needs triggers or behavioral changes (box 6.3).

The variations in the type and coverage of social assistance programs are in part a reflection of varying fiscal constraints and adminis-

---

BOX 6.3

Innovative Ways of Targeting the Poor

Two innovative ways of targeting the poor have gained momentum in developing countries and have been tested in some countries in the Region in recent years.

Conditional cash transfers are an innovative channel for the delivery of social services that is being implemented in an increasing number of countries.[a] They combine close targeting with capital accumulation by making income support conditional on either basic needs triggers or behavioral changes. Conditional cash transfers have virtually not been used in the Region so far, but they have been successfully implemented in Turkey, where there is evidence that they are resulting in higher attendance rates and higher continuation rates from primary to secondary education.

Social funds are investment funds that implement a bottom-up model in which communities and local institutions, rather than central governments, take the lead in identifying and carrying out community-level investments. The Armenia Social Investment Fund, created in 1996, was the first in the Region. A recent review of such funds in six developing countries, including Armenia, suggests that they are relatively successful. In Armenia, investments in education (school buildings, furniture, and basic equipment) are found to have increased primary enrollment rates, and investments in water and sanitation have decreased the frequency of illness in children.[b]

a. See Rawlings 2004.

b. See Rawlings, Sherburne-Benz, and Van Domelen 2004.

trative capacity, both between and within countries. Overall, there is a major gap between spending as a share of GDP on nonemployment programs in CEE, SEE, and the CIS. For example, during 1991–95, nonemployment benefits ranged from 1.6 percent of GDP in Bulgaria to 5 percent of GDP in Poland in CEE countries, while they represented only 0.3 percent in Ukraine and 0.6 percent in Russia.[59]

Social Assistance Benefits Are Linked to Minimum Wage or Other Social Minimums

An important factor in a number of countries is the connection between the minimum wages and social benefits. This may in some cases create work disincentives, as well as overburdening the minimum-wage-setting process. As shown above, the Czech Republic during the 1990s provides an example of both these effects.

A further factor about social welfare benefits and labor market outcomes relates to program incentives to (re)enter the workforce for those able to work. There has typically been limited effort to encourage this in transition economies, either through workfare or incentives in the benefits themselves. Bulgaria is an exception, with its "From Social Assistance Toward Employment" program, under which social assistance recipients (with a priority for long-term unemployed) must accept temporary work or risk a reduction or removal of benefits. The participants also receive pension and health insurance. Participation can be no more than three years. This has led to significant reductions in social assistance rolls (see box 6.4);[60] however, the longer-term impact of such programs is less clear. For example, no positive impact on employment was found in a follow-up study of a similar regime introduced in Hungary in 2000 (Galasi and Nagy 2003).

The Generosity of Social Assistance Is Associated with Wage and Labor Turnover Outcomes

Overall, the labor market impacts of social assistance programs are not well researched in the Region. However, some evidence from CEE indicates that social welfare benefits spending facilitated restructuring in the face of falling real wages.[61] By 1997, in CEE countries, there were more unemployed people on means-tested social assistance than on unemployment benefits.[62] By contrast, in the CIS and most of SEE, lower spending on social welfare benefits, combined with the less progressive incidence of most social transfer spending, meant that workers were willing to tolerate much greater falls in real

Although Not Increasing Aggregate Employment, ALMPs Have Had Positive Impacts When Supportive Preconditions Prevail

The available evaluations in the Region suggest that ALMPs can improve the labor market outcomes of target participants,[64] but only when some facilitating preconditions are met. It is important to stress that ALMPs achieve far less when labor demand is depressed and when the investment climate is poor. They are not a substitute for job creation by private firms. Even in conducive circumstances, they are only part of a menu of policies to support employment growth. Although ALMPs in the Region have in several cases improved the matching function of the labor market, they are only a supplemental tool for improving labor market outcomes, the effectiveness of which is largely dependent on employment-enhancing policies outside the labor market itself. Nonetheless, while ALMPs may not raise aggregate employment, redistributing job opportunities toward the disadvantaged worker groups may have more than typical value in the Region because of the larger stagnant pool of long-term unemployed.

Some ALMPs Have Proven More Effective Than Others

Evaluations of ALMPs in the Region are from CEE and some SEE countries only and are relatively few to date. In some cases, the employment impact of programs in the transition countries has been more positive than OECD comparators. This is most notable with training. Overall, however, they indicate that the net impact of ALMPs in the Region seldom exceeds 10 percent and is often lower.[65] Certain ALMPs work better and are more cost-effective than others, with the ranking of interventions varying according to specific labor market conditions and dependent on the effectiveness of local institutions. Questions remain on their relevance for the poorer and more informal economies in the Region, where informal networks may play a stronger role in finding employment. Although the effectiveness of specific programs in specific countries cannot be determined beforehand, some findings emerge from evaluations in the Region:[66]

- Multivariate regression analysis from CEE in the 1990s found significant positive effects of ALMPs on outflows to jobs among the unemployed in Bulgaria, the Czech Republic, Poland, and the Slovak Republic, while in Hungary the impact was never significant.[67]

- As in other regions, job search assistance in this Region—generally provided by public employment services—has proved the most cost-effective intervention to address the structural component of unemployment. The positive effects in reducing unemployment duration appear to be clearer in transition countries than in OECD countries.[68]

- The employment impact of training seems positive and notably better than that for the OECD, though the impact on earnings has been mixed. Training programs in the Region also appear to have been more cost-effective. Targeted small-scale programs focused on specific groups have tended to have a positive net impact, particularly for the low-skilled. For example, in Hungary and Poland, the net impact of training on workers with primary education was found to be 15–17 percent, while in Bulgaria it exceeded 20 percent. The available evaluations confirm a significant employment effect for the poorer and more informal economies in SEE. As noted above, net impact evaluations have not been carried out in the CIS.

- The evidence on the impact of wage subsidies is mixed. In some countries (for example, the Czech Republic and Hungary), they have proven effective in helping disadvantaged unemployed, with a net postprogram impact ranging from 10 to 15 percent. The effects have been particularly positive in high-unemployment regions in countries such as Bulgaria. The results are more positive than evaluations of similar programs in OECD countries. However, some evaluations also show negative employment effects of wage subsidies.

- Public works can act as effective safety net interventions, but the impact on the employment prospects of participants has been mixed. In general, the transition countries have relied on public works far less in their mix of ALMPs than both a number of OECD countries and other regions such as South Asia have. Outcomes range from significant negative impacts on future employment prospects and wages in Hungary and Poland, to no impact in Romania, to positive—though perhaps short-term—employment impacts in FYR Macedonia, the Slovak Republic, Slovenia, and Ukraine. However, it is important to view public works more as an income-support program than as a typical ALMP, so the temporary income impact on participants should probably be given higher weight than for other types of programs (see box 6.4).

- Programs that promote self-employment—typically credit or grant programs, often combined with business advisory services—have been less evaluated in the Region. The available evaluations indicate positive outcomes from such programs, but the results are limited because they target a small subgroup of the unemployed.

An important consideration in interpreting the above results is the institutional capacity of public employment agencies. There has traditionally been a tendency in the Region for employment agencies that operate both UI and ALMPs to run their own programs. In a number of cases, private employment agencies have been prohibited under the relevant legislation (although this is generally being remedied now). The public provision of ALMPs has in many countries resulted in programs that take limited account of local labor demand in their design. A further concern in some countries has been the governance of unemployment funds; for example, such funds may be used for political or other purposes, or there may be a lack of transparency, making it difficult to track the use of the funds. Finally, the design and evaluation of such programs are important factors in determining their efficiency.[69]

Further Reforms of Pension and Health Insurance Systems Will Also Be Required

In addition to the above, reforms of pension systems and (to a lesser extent) health insurance systems in the Region will continue to have significant effects on the labor market. These are direct (for example, with regard to the longer-term incentives for older workers to increase labor force participation) but also indirect (for example, in the large tax burden on labor imposed by social insurance programs in the Region).

Early in the transition period, countries of the Region have recognized the necessity of revising the ongoing pay-as-you-go monopillar pension systems that were under pressure because of a shrinking base of contributions and a growing number of beneficiaries. All countries revised the way benefits were adjusted toward rates that were feasible under available resources. Some also started to increase the retirement age, which was initially low and had even declined in some countries in the early 1990s. Others revised benefits formulae (for example, increasing the reference period). Beyond these initial changes, two groups of countries emerged.

One group of countries (including Albania, Armenia, Azerbaijan, Georgia, and Tajikistan) maintained minimally adequate income floors, which smoothed out any benefit differences resulting from years of contribution or previous earnings. The countries of the second group looked to introduce multipillar systems through shifting a portion of the mandatory contribution from the public pension to private institutions that established individual defined-contribution accounts for individual workers. As of 2004, nine countries[70] were already operating second pillars, while FYR Macedonia, Romania, the Slovak Republic, and Ukraine had some legislation about a second pillar. Despite problems, reversals, and some transitional costs, the systems are overall better than the old ones.

Outstanding issues remain, and reforms need to continue to bring full benefits (Holzmann and Hinz 2005). Specifically, three issues arise in the context of this report. First, the evolution of the labor market, combined with the desire to better link benefits with contributions, has left some individuals with inadequate pensions and relying on social safety nets. In a context of increasing real wages, there has been political pressure to increase the indexation of existing pensions, keeping contribution rates high. Although this has so far not threatened the competitiveness of the transition countries (because of their comparatively low wage rates), this trade-off may become binding as wages continue to increase.

Second, more fiscal pressures may arise because of rapidly aging populations and low fertility rates; most countries in the Region will need to continue reforms of the pension system to adjust the system dependency ratio to changing demographics.[71] Further increases in the retirement age may be necessary as life expectancy increases.

Third, countries of the Region also need to undertake other welfare reforms that will stimulate formal sector labor supply to improve the contributions base for a given working-age population. In addition, CEE and SEE countries will need to improve—and in many cases tighten—their eligibility rules and assessment mechanisms within their disability pension programs to avoid an unaffordable dependence on disability benefits by the working-age population. Furthermore, the need for health system reforms that will allow for gradual reduction in health insurance payroll taxes (particularly in SEE) is clear.

Summing Up: The Challenge of Labor Policy Reforms in Transition Economies

This chapter indicates that—like many other areas of the economy and society in transition countries—labor market institutions have been subject to major changes in what is a very short period in international comparative terms. It is likely that the full effects of these reforms have not yet been felt. Overall, CEE and, to a large extent, SEE countries have developed labor market institutions similar to those in mature market economies. Labor market reforms in Russia, Ukraine, and other CIS countries in contrast have been less thorough, with greater residual institutional rigidities diluted by weak enforcement and high informality. Across the Region, however, the remaining rigidities in labor market institutions continue to have negative impacts on employment outcomes, albeit probably not as acute as sometimes portrayed.

Although labor market institutions cannot be considered as the primary cause of unemployment in the Region, there remains a significant institutional reform agenda across the Region, more so as neighboring EU countries continue labor market liberalization. The specific elements of the agenda and the relative priority between them vary between subgroups, and often within subgroups. General conclusions that are appropriate for each country on all elements of reform are therefore overly ambitious. It is also very clear that labor market institutions and their impact on labor market outcomes constitute an area where substantially more research is needed.

With this major caveat in mind, broad patterns of an agenda for the reform of labor market institutions in the Region and priorities for each subgroup are apparent and will need to be assessed in the light of further research. The key elements of a reform agenda by subgroup are summarized below.

The Labor Market Institutional Reform Agenda in CEE Countries

There is a need for greater adaptability of real wages to productivity. This could be achieved by further decentralization of wage bargaining or by strengthening a social compact that links wage and productivity growth but retains the flexibility for firm bargaining within the aggregate wage adjustment parameter. This should avoid an increased role for sectoral bargaining, which appears to be associated with worse labor market outcomes. In public sector wage setting, there is probably a need for an increased flexibility in wage setting along the model developed (for example) in Estonia. Moreover, there is a need for reconsidering minimum-wage setting, which, albeit not binding on average, may be too high for the low-skilled and for workers in backward areas of many CEE economies. In this context, the possible impact of the rigid link between minimum wage and social benefits should be reassessed.

In the area of employment protection legislation, there is a need to review regulations for permanent employment contracts, which remain overly rigid also in light of the liberalization of temporary contracts. This should help avoid a significant segmentation of the labor market. There is also a need to further improve labor inspection methods to balance effective enforcement with avoidance of unnecessary impositions on firms, including an increased role for firm self-reporting.

There is also a need to reduce taxes on labor, which are currently very high in CEE, and appear to be a major impediment to increasing employment. However, this will need to be done gradually and in parallel with further reform of pensions and disability and health insurance to balance fiscal requirements, social protection of social insurance beneficiaries, and the need to improve labor market outcomes.

Unemployment benefits have now been reformed in many CEE countries, and their generosity is currently relatively low, limiting possible work disincentives. The main challenge is to strengthen the (re)activation of the long-term unemployed, both through incentives in the benefits and tax systems (for example, back-to-work allowances and tax credits for low-income working households) and through targeting active programs at those groups for whom their net impact is the highest. There is also a need to improve monitoring and evaluation of the effectiveness of different ALMPs to improve their design and targeting efficiency. Moreover, social assistance benefits in depressed regions need to be examined to ensure that eligibility thresholds and benefits levels do not contribute to localized work disincentives.

The Labor Market Institutional Reform Agenda in SEE Countries

Regarding wage determination in SEE countries, there is a need to (a) lessen the role of the government in collective bargaining and strengthen the voice of employers in an attempt to improve the wage and productivity linkage; (b) reduce the scope of general and sectoral collective agreements by promoting greater decentralization of bargaining to the firm level; (c) increase flexibility in minimum-wage setting by allowing for youth minimum wages; and (d) ensure that the minimum-wage-to-average-wage ratio is controlled and, in some countries (for example, BiH), reduced.

Further reform is also needed in the area of employment protection, where regulations on temporary employment contracts remain fairly strict. SEE countries should also ensure that more liberal EPL provisions are not undermined by continued rigidity of employment conditions in collective agreements. This should be accompanied by a significant improvement in labor inspection practices to balance effective enforcement with the avoidance of unnecessary impositions on firms, including an increased role for firm self-reporting of compliance.

SEE countries should aim for a gradual reduction in payroll taxes, with a particular focus on health insurance taxes. This should be accompanied by efforts to improve compliance on tax payments by firms, including SOEs. Moreover, many countries in this subgroup should improve on the (re)activation of the long-term unemployed, both through incentives in the benefit system (for example, back-to-work allowances) and through targeting ALMPs on those with low skills and in depressed regions. This could also imply some reallocation of funds across activities. This should be accompanied by encouraging private employment agencies to play a role in areas where local labor markets permit.

The Labor Market Institutional Reform Agenda in the Middle and Low Income CIS Countries

This group of countries is even more heterogeneous than the others, and it is thus more difficult to identify common policy objectives. Even so, some common elements could be identified. One concerns the wage-bargaining process, in which most countries in the subgroup should promote better representation of social partners and lower direct intervention from the government. This implies encouraging the emergence of independent unions and employers' associations that will assume a more active role in bargaining and moving away from wage schedules in which all wages are rigidly set as multiples of the minimum wage.

In the area of employment protection, most countries in this subgroup have had more limited reforms, with strict regulations being accompanied by pervasive nonenforcement. Focusing EPL on a core set of labor protections that can be credibly enforced and promoting a reform in labor inspection services could go some way in promoting labor reallocation within the formal sector.

Passive and active labor market programs are less developed in this subgroup than in most of the Region. Given the limited administrative capacity, large underreporting of activities, and limited financial resources, especially in the low income CIS countries, an appropriate choice could be to provide a minimum level of protection for some basic risks. Such protection could be financed through general revenues.[72] For example, the issue could be raised as to whether a move to flat-rate unemployment assistance is appropriate and whether this might be financed through general revenues, rather than the payroll tax.

More generally, moving toward universal social protection could be considered in some countries. Decoupling minimum pension schemes and health insurance from the labor market status of people (for example, through creating a universal minimum pension or expanding health insurance coverage to informal workers) are options currently under consideration in some emerging economies such as Mexico. Moreover, given widespread informality, the need to reinforce social protection for those without access to formal insurance mechanisms should be considered. This could include greater use of public works schemes that are open to all those willing to work at a program wage rate that is set at a level low enough to ensure self-targeting of the most-needy.

Countries that have not already done so should also consider using alternative approaches to targeting of social transfers, such as proxy means testing or community identification of beneficiaries within national guidelines. Improving targeting for programs aimed at vulnerable groups would enable more efficient redistribution of resources. Regarding social insurance, CIS countries should continue reforms of the pension system that will adjust the system dependency ratio to changing demographics, and encourage other reforms that will stimulate formal sector labor supply to improve the contributions base for a given working-age population.

Annex 6.1: Construction of Employment Protection Legislation Indexes

The indexes are calculated from the raw data provided in the World Bank's Doing Business Database (2005). All the variables range between 0 and 1. Either they are zero-one dummies (no-yes), or they are normalized over the sample. Variables for which higher values (x) represent looser regulations are normalized according to the simple formula (equation 6.1):

$$x_N = 1 - \left(\frac{x - \min(x_E)}{\max(x_E) - \min(x_E)}\right) \quad (6.1)$$

whereas variables for which higher values represent stricter regulations are normalized in the following way (equation 6.2):

$$x_N = 1 - \frac{(\max(x_E) - x)}{(\max(x_E) - \min(x_E))} \quad (6.2)$$

where x_N is the normalized value, $\max(x_E)$ is the maximum value that the variable takes over the sample of countries available from the database, and $\min(x_E)$ is the corresponding minimum value.

The *permanent employment weighted index* is constructed from the raw variables in the following way (weights in parentheses):

Procedures (1/2)	The employer must notify a third party before dismissing one redundant employee. (1/6)
	The employer needs the approval of a third party to dismiss one redundant worker. (1/6)
	The law mandates retraining or replacement before dismissal. (1/6)
	There are priority rules applying to dismissal or layoffs. (1/6)
	There are priority rules applying to reemployment. (1/6)
	Is redundancy considered a "fair" grounds for dismissal? (1/6)
Firing costs (1/2)	Legally mandated notice period for redundancy dismissal (in weeks) after 20 years of continuous employment. Normalized (1/2)
	Severance pay for redundancy dismissal as number of months for which full wages are payable after continuous employment of 20 years. Normalized (1/2)

The *temporary employment regulation index* is equal to the simple average of the following variables:

Fixed-term contracts are only allowed for fixed-term tasks.
What is the maximum duration of fixed-term contracts (in months)? Normalized

Finally, the *overall employment regulation index* is the simple average of the regular and temporary employment indexes.

Notes

1. Useful overviews of institutional issues in the Region's labor markets include Haltiwanger, Scarpetta, and Vodopivec (2003); Boeri and Terrell (2002); Riboud, Sanchez-Paramo, and Silva-Jauregui (2002); Garibaldi and Brixiova (1998); and Svejnar (1999 and 2002).
2. See Blanchflower and Oswald (1998); Köllő (1998); Basu, Estrin, and Svejnar (2004); and Iara and Traistaru (2004).
3. See Ilkkaracan and Selim (2003).
4. See Basu, Estrin and Svejnar (2004) and Flanagan (1998). Poland and (to a lesser extent) Hungary were partial exceptions to this general picture by the end of the communist period.
5. "Union density" refers to the proportion of workers who are members of a union. Union coverage refers to the proportion of workers who are covered by a collective bargaining agreement.
6. See ILO (2002, in Russian). Armenia provides an example of the difficulty of interpreting union density figures in the CIS, with 75 percent union density by official estimates, but 80 percent of workers claiming to "have nothing in common" with trade unions, and half of those claiming to be totally uninformed about unions. Often the inclusion of pensioners and segments of the registered unemployed in union membership numbers also inflates density data.

7. See, among others, EIRO (2004).
8. See Micevska (2004).
9. BiH includes two entities: Republika Srpska and the Federation of Bosnia and Herzegovina.
10. In many countries, this has been in part a political reaction against the "state unions" that monopolized the union movement during the socialist period.
11. See ILO (2002, in Russian) for case studies of CIS country social dialogue.
12. The Russian coefficient system tends to set lower bounds that are very low so that additional payments make up a significant amount of total earnings of public sector employees.
13. See Schiavo-Campo, de Tommaso, and Mukherjee (1997).
14. In many countries that have not reformed public sector pay determination, there has been a significant incidence of payments to employees that are not subject to the coefficient schedule. Such payments have been both formal, through allowances of various forms, and informal, through undisclosed payments to workers.
15. See Schiavo-Campo, de Tommaso, and Mukherjee (1997). By the mid-1990s, the Region's public-to-private-sector-wage ratio was the lowest of any region, though it was somewhat higher in CEE and SEE.
16. Although there are issues of recording and interpreting data on coverage and density, data generally refer to the formal economy (that is, they include both the state and private sectors).
17. Slovenia has general collective agreements for both the whole public sector and the whole private sector, with sectoral- and company-level agreements (EIRO 2004). The tripartite private sector agreement for 2004–5 includes provisions on principles for pay increases, aggregate increases, minimum increases for all workers, and the minimum wage, among others. These follow the general principle of restraining real-wage growth below productivity growth.
18. See EIRO (various years). Martin and Cristescu-Martin (2002 and 2003) also provide annual updates of developments in CEE industrial relations.
19. This is in contrast to the bulk of EU-15 countries, where wage bargaining takes place primarily at the sectoral level in most countries, though with a trend toward greater decentralization during the 1990s. CEE countries will be subject to social partnership arrangements as part of EU accession.
20. It is estimated that some 30 percent of blue-collar workers and 15 percent of white-collar workers in the private sector in Russia are paid according to public sector wage grids (Kapelyushnikov 2003).
21. See Haltiwanger, Scarpetta, and Vodopivec (2003).
22. See Micevska (2004).
23. See Luke and Schaffer (2000) for Russia, Dobbelaere (2004) for Bulgaria, and Grosfeld and Nivet (1999) and Mickiewicz and Bishop (2003) for Poland. Mickiewicz and Bishop also find that relative rent sharing by workers divides more strongly along old and new firm lines than state and private ones.
24. See Haltiwanger, Scarpetta, and Vodopivec (2003). This association does not necessarily imply causality. The result is at least in part driven by the

coincidence of centralized or coordinated bargaining in Russia and Ukraine with seemingly favorable labor market outcomes (see chapter 2). However, low open unemployment in Russia and Ukraine is mainly the effect of the nature of enterprise restructuring, rather than of the bargaining system. It is also worth noting that although Russia's wage-bargaining system appears centralized on paper, in practice managers have great flexibility at the level of the firm.

25. See OECD (2004a).
26. See Haltiwanger and Vodopivec (2003).
27. See EIRO (2004) for Bulgaria; ONASA (2004) for Bosnia.
28. See Eriksson and Pytlikova (2004).
29. Social benefits were set as a percentage of the "subsistence wage."
30. A minimum social security threshold that exceeds the actual wage implies a higher rate than the nominal tax rate on that wage. In consequence, this may discourage the demand for less-skilled labor.
31. See OECD (2003) for discussion of the Latvia case.
32. See Eriksson and Pytlikova (2004).
33. In some countries, the minimum wage is differentiated according to individuals' education and qualifications. For example, in Montenegro, while the "standard" minimum wage is around 17 percent of the average gross wage, the minimum wage for individuals with a university or higher education degree is at a high 54 percent of the average wage.
34. Kertesi and Köllõ (2003) provide evidence on the disemployment effects that the substantial hikes in minimum wage in Hungary had in backward areas in 2001; see Hinnosaar and Rõõm (2003) for Estonia.
35. Recent literature also points to other functions of EPL, including ensuring the income of workers (who are generally risk averse) against labor market uncertainty and providing incentives to employers to internalize the social costs of layoffs in the presence of a higher social than private value of employment. See OECD (2004a); Pissarides (2001).
36. See for example, Nickell (1997).
37. At the same time, the speed of market-oriented reforms, of which labor market reforms are a part, influenced the EU-accession process.
38. Evidence from Argentina, Colombia, France, Peru, and Spain suggests that asymmetric liberalization of contracts has led to significant shifts toward precarious jobs. In Argentina and Spain, these reforms were reversed after a few years, and in the latter, net job creation really picked up only after the government reformed regular contracts in the mid-1990s. In Spain, temporary employment reached almost one-third of the total workforce after the reform of temporary contracts in the mid-1980s (Dolado, García-Serrano, and Jimeno 2002). In Peru, the liberalization of temporary employment in the early 1990s led to an increase in temporary employment from 20 percent in 1990 to 55 percent in 2000. In Colombia, there was a similarly large increase (Saavedra 2003). See also Blanchard and Landier (2002) for France and Hopenhayn (2004) for Argentina.
39. Squire and Suthiwart-Narueput (1995) investigate the impact of labor market regulations in settings where compliance is incomplete.
40. See World Economic Forum (2002).
41. Although neither of these relationships is posited as causal, a link is supported by qualitative assessments.

42. The regressions are done on eight CEE countries: Bulgaria, the Czech Republic, Estonia, Hungary, Poland, Romania, the Slovak Republic, and Slovenia (Haltiwanger, Scarpetta, and Vodopivec 2003).
43. The coordination variable is the simple average of the degree of coordination among employers' associations and trade unions (Haltiwanger, Scarpetta, and Vodopivec 2003).
44. See World Bank (2004c).
45. See Haltiwanger, Scarpetta, and Vodopivec (2003).
46. See Micevska (2004).
47. The calculated tax wedge on labor in reduced form is defined as (labor cost − net pay)/labor cost*100. Labor cost comprises gross wage plus employer payroll contributions on wage. Net pay is calculated as gross wage less employee payroll contributions and personal income tax.
48. The comparison of the tax wedge should be treated with caution because of tax benefits and the treatment of social transfers to families with children, which vary across OECD countries.
49. See Riboud, Sanchez-Paramo, and Silva-Jauregui (2002).
50. See Daveri and Tabellini (1997); Elmeskov, Martin, and Scarpetta (1998).
51. See Haltiwanger, Scarpetta, and Vodopivec (2003); Cazes and Nesporova (2003).
52. Low registered unemployment may lead to artificially high spending per registered unemployed, such as in Russia.
53. See World Bank (2002b).
54. See Haltiwanger, Scarpetta, and Vodopivec (2003). One should bear in mind that reverse causality (endogeneity) may be at work here. Governments often are under pressure to respond to growing unemployment by lengthening the duration of unemployment benefits. This happened, for example, in Poland, where benefit duration is longer in regions of high unemployment. To the extent this is the case, the estimated regression coefficient is biased and overstates the impact of benefit duration on unemployment.
55. See Vodopivec (2004) for a comparative analysis of Estonia and Slovenia.
56. See, for example, Micklewright and Nagy (1996) for Hungary; Ham, Svejnar, and Terrell (1998 and 1999) for the Czech and Slovak Republics.
57. See Atkinson and Micklewright (1992) for pretransition safety net details.
58. See Staines and Isamiddinova (2004).
59. See table 5 in Boeri and Terrell (2002).
60. See Kuddo (2004).
61. See Boeri and Terrell (2002) and Garibaldi and Brixiova (1998).
62. See Boeri (1997).
63. See Commander and Lee (1998) on Russia, and Garner and Terrell (1998) on the Czech and Slovak Republics.
64. This applies to the employment rates of participants and (in some cases) to their postprogram wages.
65. The net impact is lower than the gross impact. The gross impact is the fraction of program beneficiaries who were placed in jobs. The net impact is the gross impact minus the estimated fraction of program beneficiaries

who would have found jobs anyway (the deadweight loss). The deadweight loss can be estimated using experimental or quasi-experimental techniques, as well as econometric methods.
66. See Betcherman, Olivas, and Dar (2004) for a summary of ALMP evaluations, including those for selected countries in the Region. See also Boeri (1997) and Bonin (1999).
67. See Boeri (1997).
68. See Fretwell, Benus, and O'Leary (1999) for cost-effectiveness analysis on ALMPs in CEE countries.
69. ALMPs often have several social and economic goals, which need to be both determined before a new program is designed and taken into account when carrying out impact evaluations.
70. Bulgaria, Croatia, Estonia, Hungary, Kazakhstan, Latvia, Lithuania, Poland, and Russia.
71. The system dependency ratio is the ratio of the number of pensioners to the number of contributors to the pension system.
72. There is scope for improving tax collection. For example, De Ferranti and others (2004) propose general principles to improve the efficiency and equitability of taxation in the context of Latin America.

Bibliography

Acquisti, Alessandro, and Hartmut Lehmann. 2000. "Job Creation and Job Destruction in the Russian Federation." Trinity Economic Paper 20001, Trinity College Dublin, Department of Economics, Dublin.

Aghion, Philippe, and Olivier J. Blanchard. 1994. "On the Speed of Transition in Central Europe." In *NBER Macroeconomics Annual 1994*: 283–320. Cambridge, MA: MIT Press.

Aiginger, K., M. Boeheim, K. Gugler, M. Pfaffermayr, and Y. Wolfmayr-Schnitzer. 1999. "Specialisation and (Geographic) Concentration of European Manufacturing." Working Paper 1, Enterprise DG 3, European Commission, Brussels.

Andrienko, Yuri, and Sergei Guriev. 2003. "Determinants of Interregional Mobility in Russia: Evidence from Panel Data." William Davidson Institute Working Paper 551, University of Michigan, Stephen M. Ross Business School, Ann Arbor.

Aslund, Anders, Peter Boone, and Simon Johnson. 1996. "How to Stabilize: Lessons from Post-Communist Countries." In *Brookings Papers on Economic Activity* 1: 217–313. Washington, DC: Brookings Institute.

Atkinson, Anthony B., and John Micklewright. 1992. *Economic Transformation in Eastern Europe and the Distribution of Income*. Cambridge, U.K.: Cambridge University Press.

Babetski, Jan, Alexandre Kolev, and Mathilde Maurel. 2003. "The Kyrgyz Labour Market in the Late 1990s: The Challenge of Formal Job Creation." *Comparative Economic Studies* 45 (4): 493–520.

Baily, Martin Neil, Eric J. Bartelsman, and John Haltiwanger. 2001. "Labor Productivity: Structural Change and Cyclical Dynamics." *Review of Economics and Statistics*, 83 (3): 420–33.

Baily, Martin Neil, Charles Hulten, and David Campbell. 1992. "Productivity Dynamics in Manufacturing Plants." *Brookings Papers on Economic Activity: Microeconomics*, 187–249. Washington, DC: Brookings Institute.

Baldwin, John, Timothy Dunne, and John Haltiwanger. 1998. "A Comparison of Job Creation and Job Destruction in Canada and the United States." *Review of Economics and Statistics*, 53 (3), 347–56.

Barlevy, Gadi. 2002. "The Sullying Effect of Recessions." *Review of Economic Studies* 69 (1): 65–96.

———. Forthcoming. "Credit Market Frictions and the Allocation of Resources over the Business Cycle." *Journal of Monetary Economics*.

Bartelsman, Eric, John Haltiwanger, and Stefano Scarpetta. 2004. "Microeconomic Evidence of Creative Destruction in Industrial and Developing Countries." Policy Research Working Paper 3464, World Bank, Washington, DC.

Bartelsman, Eric, Stefano Scarpetta, and Fabiano Schivardi. 2005. "Comparative Analysis of Firm Demographics and Survival: Evidence from Micro-Level Sources in OECD Countries." *Industrial and Corporate Change* 14 (3): 365–91.

Basu, Swati, Saul Estrin, and Jan Svejnar. 2004. "Wage Determination under Communism and in Transition: Evidence from Central Europe." William Davidson Institute Working Paper 717, University of Michigan, Stephen M. Ross Business School, Ann Arbor.

Beck, Thorsten, Asli Demirguc-Kunt, and Luc A. Laeven. 2005. "Finance, Firm Size, and Growth." Policy Research Working Paper 3485, World Bank, Washington, DC.

Betcherman, Gordon, Karina Olivas, and Amit Dar. 2004. "Impacts of Active Labor Market Programs: New Evidence from Evaluations with Particular Attention to Developing and Transition Countries." Social Protection Discussion Paper 0402, World Bank, Washington, DC.

Bilsen, Valentijn, and Jozef Konings. 1998. "Job Creation, Job Destruction, and Growth of Newly Established, Privatized, and State-Owned Enterprises in Transition Economies: Survey Evidence from Bulgaria, Hungary, and Romania." *Journal of Comparative Economics* 26 (3): 429–45.

Blanchard, Olivier, Rudiger Dornbusch, Paul Krugman, Richard Layard, and Lawrence Summers. 1991. *Reform in Eastern Europe*. Cambridge, MA: MIT Press.

Blanchard, Olivier, and Francesco Giavazzi. 2003. "Macroeconomic Effects of Regulation and Deregulation in Goods and Labor Markets." *Quarterly Journal of Economics* 118 (3, August): 879–907.

Blanchard, Olivier, and Michael Kremer. 1997. "Disorganization." *Quarterly Journal of Economics* 112 (4): 1091–1126.

Blanchard, Olivier, and Augustin Landier. 2002. "The Perverse Effects of Partial Labour Market Reform: Fixed-Term Contracts in France." *The Economic Journal* 112 (480): F214–44. London: Royal Economic Society.

Blanchard, Olivier, and Justin Wolfers. 2000. "The Role of Shocks and Institutions in the Rise of European Unemployment: The Aggregate Evidence." *The Economic Journal* 110 (462): C1–33. London: Royal Economic Society.

Blanchflower, David, and Andrew Oswald. 1998. "Unemployment, Well-Being and Wage Curves in Eastern Europe." Photocopy. http://www2.warwick.ac.uk/fac/soc/economics/staff/faculty/oswald/europeeast.pdf.

Boeri, Tito. 1995. "Unemployment Dynamics and Labour Market Policies." In *Unemployment, Restructuring, and the Labor Market in Eastern Europe and Russia*, ed. S. Commander and F. Coricelli, 361–83. Washington, DC: World Bank.

———. 1997. "Learning from Transition Economies: Assessing Labor Market Policies across Central and Eastern Europe." *Journal of Comparative Economics* 25 (3): 366–84.

Boeri, Tito, Michael C. Burda, and János Köllő. 1998. "Mediating the Transition: Labour Markets in Central and Eastern Europe." In *Mediating the Transition: Labour Markets in Central and Eastern Europe*, ed. L. Ambrus-Lakatos and M. Schaffer. Forum Report of the Economic Policy Initiative, No. 4. New York: CEPR.

Boeri, Tito, and Pietro Garibaldi. 2004. "Labor Market Performance in Transition Economies: A Macroeconomic Perspective." Background Paper for *Enhancing Job Opportunities: Eastern Europe and the Former Soviet Union*, World Bank, Washington, DC.

Boeri, Tito, and Stefano Scarpetta. 1996. "Regional Mismatch and the Transition to a Market Economy." *Labour Economics* 3 (3): 233–54.

Boeri, Tito, and Katherine Terrell. 2002. "Institutional Determinants of Labor Reallocation in Transition." *Journal of Economic Perspectives* 16 (1, Winter): 51–76.

Bonin, John, ed. 1999. "Special Issue on Unemployment and Labor Market Policies in Transition Countries." Journal of Comparative Economics 27 (1).

Bornhorst, Fabian, and Simon Commander. 2004. "Regional Unemployment and its Persistence in Transition Countries." Discussion Paper 1074, Institute for the Study of Labor (IZA), Bonn.

Brown, J. David, and John S. Earle. 2002a. "Gross Job Flows in Russian Industry Before and After Reforms: Has Destruction Become More Creative?" *Journal of Comparative Economics* 30 (1): 96–133.

———. 2002b. "Job Reallocation and Productivity Growth under Alternative Economic Systems and Policies: Evidence from the Soviet Transition." Discussion Paper 644, IZA, Bonn.

———. 2002c. "The Reallocation of Workers and Jobs in Russian Industry: New Evidence on Measures and Determinants." Staff Working Paper 02-83, W. E. Upjohn Institute for Employment Research, Kalamazoo, MI.

———. 2004. "The Microeconomics of Creating Productive Jobs: A Synthesis of Firm-Level Studies in Transition Economies." Background Paper for *Enhancing Job Opportunities: Eastern Europe and the Former Soviet Union*, World Bank, Washington, DC.

Bruno, M., and J. Sachs. 1985. *Economics of Worldwide Stagflation*. Cambridge, MA: Harvard University Press.

Caballero, Ricardo J., and Mohammad L. Hammour. 1994. "The Cleansing Effect of Recessions." *American Economic Review* 84 (5): 1350–68.

———. 1996. "On the Timing and Efficiency of Creative Destruction." *Quarterly Journal of Economics* 111 (3): 805–51.

———. 2000. "Institutions, Restructuring, and Macroeconomic Performance." Working Paper 7720, National Bureau for Economic Research (NBER), Cambridge, MA.

Campos, Nauro F., and Fabrizio Coricelli. 2002. "Growth in Transition: What We Know, What We Don't, and What We Should." *Journal of Economic Literature* 40 (3): 793–836.

Castanhiera, M., and G. Roland. 2000. "The Optimal Speed of Transition: A General Equilibrium Analysis." *International Economic Review* 41 (1): 219–39.

Cazes, Sandrine, and Alena Nesporova. 2003. *Labour Markets in Transition: Balancing Flexibility and Security in Central and Eastern Europe*. Geneva: ILO.

Chadda, B., and F. Corricelli. 1994. "Fiscal Constraints and the Speed of Transition." Discussion Paper 993, CEPR, London.

Chenery, H. B., and L. Taylor. 1968. "Development Patterns: Among Countries and Over Time." *Review of Economics and Statistics*, 50: 391–416.Claessens, Stijn, and Kyle Peters. 1997. "State Enterprise Performance and Soft Budget Constraints." *Economics of Transition* 5 (2): 305–22.

Commander, Simon, and János Köllő. 2004. "The Changing Demand for Skills: Evidence from the Transition." Discussion Paper 1073, Institute for the Study of Labor (IZA), Bonn.

Commander, Simon, and Une Lee. 1998. "How Does Public Policy Affect the Income Distribution? Evidence from Russia, 1992–1996." Photocopy, EBRD, London.

Coricelli, F., and V. Ercolani. 2003. "Deficits and Fiscal Rules on the Road to an Enlarged European Union." Working Paper 3672, CEPR, London.

Daveri, F., and G. Tabellini. 1997. "Unemployment, Growth and Taxation in Industrial Countries." Discussion Paper 9706, Brescia University, Brescia, Italy.

Davis, Steven J., and John C. Haltiwanger. 1990. "Gross Job Creation and Destruction: Microeconomic Evidence and Macroeconomic Implications." *NBER Macroeconomics Annual 1990*: 123–68. Cambridge, MA: MIT Press.

———. 1992. "Gross Job Creation, Gross Job Destruction and Employment Reallocation." *Quarterly Journal of Economics* 107 (3): 819–63.

———. 1999. "Gross Job Flows." In *Handbook of Labor Economics*, ed. Orley Ashenfelter and David Card, Vol. 3B: 2712–2803. Amsterdam: Elsevier.

Davis, Steven J., John C. Haltiwanger, and Scott Schuh. 1996. *Job Creation and Destruction*. Cambridge, MA: MIT Press.

De Ferranti, David, Guillermo Perry, Francisco Ferreira, and Michael Walton. 2004. *Inequality in Latin America and the Caribbean: Breaking with History?* Washington DC: World Bank.

De Nicoló, Gianni, Sami Geadah, and Dmitriy Rozhkov. 2003. "Financial Development in the CIS-7 Countries: Bridging the Great Divide." Working Paper 03/205, IMF, Washington, DC.

Decressin, Jörg W. 1994. "Internal Migration in West Germany and Implications for East-West Salary Convergence." *Weltwirtschaftliches Archiv* 130 (2): 231–57.

Djankov, Simeon, and Peter Murrell. 2002. "Enterprise Restructuring in Transition: A Quantitative Survey." *Journal of Economic Literature* 40 (3): 739–92.

Dobbelaere, Sabien. 2004. "Ownership, Firm Size and Rent Sharing in Bulgaria." *Labour Economics* 11 (2): 165–89.

Dobrogonov, Anton. 2002. "Social Protection in Low Income CIS Countries." Photocopy, World Bank, Washington, DC.

Dolado, Juan, Carlos Garcia-Serrano, and Juan Jimeno. 2002. "Drawing Lessons from the Boom of Temporary Jobs in Spain." *The Economic Journal* 112 (480): F270–95. London: Royal Economic Society.

Dorenbos, Ruud. 1999. *Labor Market Adjustments in Hungary and Poland*. Groningen: University of Groningen.

Duryea, S., G. Marquez, C. Pagés, S. Paternostro, and S. Scarpetta. 2005. "Assessing Informality in Transition and Emerging Economies." Photocopy, World Bank, Washington, DC.

Earle, John S., and Zuzana Sakova. 2000. "Business Start-Ups or Disguised Unemployment? Evidence on the Character of Self-Employment from Transition Economies." *Labour Economics* 7 (5): 575–601.

EBRD. 2003. *Transition Report 2003*. London: EBRD.

———. 2004. *Transition Report 2004*. London: EBRD.

Ederveen, Sjef, and Nick Bardsley. 2003. "The Influence of Wage and Unemployment Differentials on Labour Mobility in the EU." In European Union, AccessLab, *Workpackage 3: Analysing and Modelling Inter-regional Migration*. http://accesslab.wifo.ac.at/.

Elmeskov, J., J. Martin, and S. Scarpetta. 1998. "Key Lessons for Labour Market Reforms: Evidence from OECD Countries' Experiences." *Swedish Economic Policy Review* 5 (2): 205–52.

Eriksson, Tor, and Mariola Pytlikova. 2004. "Firm-Level Consequences of Large Minimum-Wage Increases in the Czech and Slovak Republics." *Labour* 18 (1): 75–103.

Eslava, Marcela, John Haltiwanger, Adriana Kugler, and Maurice Kugler. 2004. "The Effects of Structural Reforms on Productivity and Profitability Enhancing Reallocation: Evidence from Colombia." *Journal of Development Economics* 75 (2): 333–71.

Estreicher, Samuel, and Stewart J. Schwab. 2000. *Foundations of Labor and Employment Law*. New York: Foundation Press.

Estrin, Saul. 2002. "Competition and Corporate Governance in Transition." *Journal of Economic Perspective* 16 (1): 101–24.

European Commission. 2002. "Strengthening the Co-ordination of Budgetary Policies." Communication from the Commission to Council and the European Parliament, November 27, 2002. COM (2002) 668 final. Brussels: EC.

———. 2004. *Industrial Relations in Europe 2004*. Luxembourg: Office for Official Publications of the European Communities.

European Industrial Relations Observatory (EIRO). 2004. http://www.eiro.eurofound.eu.int/.

Faggio, Giulia, and Jozef Konings. 1999. "Gross Job Flows and Firm Growth in Transition Countries: Evidence Using Firm Level Data on Five Countries." Discussion Paper 2261, CEPR, London.

Faini, Riccardo, Giampaolo Galli, Pietro Gennari, and Fulvio Rossi. 1997. "An Empirical Puzzle: Falling Migrations and Growing Unemployment Differentials among Italian Regions." *European Economic Review* 41: 571–79.

Fatas, Antonio, Jürgen von Hagen, Andrew Hughes Hallett, Rolf R. Strauch, and Anne Sibert. 2003. *Stability and Growth in Europe: Towards a Better Pact*. Monitoring European Integration 13. London: CEPR.

Fidrmuc, Jan. 2004. "Migration and Regional Adjustment to Asymmetric Shocks in Transition Economies." *Journal of Comparative Economics* 32 (2): 230–47.

Flanagan, Robert. 1998. "Institutional Reformation in Eastern Europe." *Industrial Relations* 37 (3): 337–57.

Fleisher, Belton M., Klara Sabirianova Peter, and Xiaojun Wang. 2004. "Returns to Skills and the Speed of Reforms: Evidence from Central and Eastern Europe, China, and Russia." Discussion Paper 1182, Institute for the Study of Labor (IZA), Bonn.

Foster, Lucia, John C. Haltiwanger, and Cornell J. Krizan. 2001. "Aggregate Productivity Growth: Lessons from Microeconomic Evidence." In *New Developments in Productivity Analysis*, ed. Edward Dean, Michael Harper, and Charles Hulten, 303–72. Chicago: University of Chicago Press.

Foster, Lucia, John C. Haltiwanger, and Chad Syverson. 2005. "Reallocation, Firm Turnover, and Efficiency: Selection on Productivity or Profitability?" Working Paper 11555, NBER, Cambridge, MA.

Fretwell, David H., Jacob Benus, and Christopher J. O'Leary. 1999. "Evaluating the Impact of Active Labor Programs: Results of Cross-Country Studies in Europe and Central Asia." Social Protection Discussion Paper 9915, World Bank, Washington, DC.

Friebel, Guido, and Sergei Guriev. 2000. "Why Russian Workers Do Not Move: Attachment of Workers through In-Kind Payments." Discussion Paper 2368, Centre for Economic Policy Research (CEPR), London.

Gács, Vera, and Peter Huber. 2005. "Quantity Adjustments in the Regional Labour Markets of EU Candidate Countries." Working Paper 254/2005, Austrian Institute of Economic Research (WIFO), Wien. http://www.wifo.ac.at.

Galasi, Péter, and Gyula Nagy. 2003. "*A munkanélküli-ellátás változásainak hatása a munkanélküliek segélyezésére és elhelyezkedésére.*" (in Hungarian) ["The Effect of Changes in Unemployment Assistance on Benefit Receipt and Job Finding."] *Közgazdasági Szemle* 50 (7–8): 608–34.

Garibaldi, Pietro, and Zuzana Brixiova. 1998. "Labor Market Institutions and Unemployment Dynamics in Transition Economies." *IMF Staff Papers* 45 (2): 269–308. Washington, DC: IMF.

Garner, Thesia I., and Katherine Terrell. 1998. "A Gini Decomposition Analysis of Inequality in the Czech and Slovak Republics during the Transition." *Economics of Transition* 6, (1): 23–46.

Gimpelson, Vladimir, and Rostislav Kapelyushnikov. 2005. Background Note for *Enhancing Job Opportunities: Eastern Europe and the Former Soviet Union*. World Bank, Washington, DC.

Gorodnichenko, Yuriy, and Klara Sabirianova Peter. 2004. "Returns to Schooling in Russia and Ukraine: A Semiparametric Approach to Cross-Country Comparative Analysis." William Davidson Institute Working Paper 719, University of Michigan, Stephen M. Ross Business School, Ann Arbor.

Granberg, Alexander, and Ioulia Zaitseva. 2002. "Macroeconomy of the Russian Regions Neighboring with the European Union." Photocopy, Council for the Study of Productive Forces, Moscow.

Gray, Cheryl, Joel Hellman, and Randi Ryterman. 2004. *Anticorruption in Transition 2: Corruption in Enterprise-State Interactions in Europe and Central Asia, 1999–2002*. World Bank, Washington, DC.

Griliches, Zvi, and Haim Regev. 1995. "Firm Productivity in Israeli Industry, 1979–1988." *Journal of Econometrics* 65 (1): 175–203.

Grosfeld, Irena, and Jean-François Nivet. 1999. "Insider Power and Wage Setting in Transition: Evidence from a Panel of Large Polish Firms, 1988–1994." *European Economic Review* 34 (4–6): 1137–47.

Grosfeld, Irena, and Gerard Roland. 1996. "Defensive and Strategic Restructuring in Central European Enterprises." Discussion Paper 1135, Centre for Economic Policy Research (CEPR), London.

GUS (Central Statistical Office). 2003. *Demand for Labour in 2002*. Information and Statistical Papers series, Warsaw.

Gwartney, James, and Robert Lawson. 2003. *Economic Freedom of the World: 2003 Annual Report*. Vancouver, BC: Fraser Institute.

Haltiwanger, John C., Stefano Scarpetta, and Milan Vodopivec. 2003. "How Institutions Affect Labor Market Outcomes: Evidence from Transition Countries." Paper presented at the World Bank Economists' Forum, Washington, DC, April 10, 2003. Photocopy.

Haltiwanger, John C., and Milan Vodopivec. 2002. "Gross Worker and Job Flows in a Transition Economy: An Analysis of Estonia." *Labour Economics* 9 (5): 601–30.

———. 2003. "Worker Flows, Job Flows and Firm Wage Policies: An Analysis of Slovenia." *Economics of Transition* 11 (2): 253–90.

Ham, John, Jan Svejnar, and Katherine Terrell. 1998. "Unemployment and the Social Safety Net during Transitions to a Market Economy: Evidence from the Czech and Slovak Republics." *American Economic Review* 88 (5): 1117–42.

———. 1999. "Women's Unemployment during Transition: Evidence from Czech and Slovak Micro-Data." *Economics of Transition* 7 (1): 47–78.

Hazans, Mihails. 2004. "Determinants of Inter-regional Migration in the Baltic Countries." In European Union, AccessLab, *Workpackage 3: Analysing and Modelling Inter-regional Migration*. http://accesslab.wifo.ac.at/.

Hinnosaar, Marit, and Tairi Rõõm. 2003. "The Impact of the Minimum Wage on the Labor Market in Estonia: An Empirical Analysis." Research Paper 8, Eesti Pank (Bank of Estonia), Tallinn, Estonia.

Holzmann, Robert, and Richard Hinz. 2005. *Old-Age Income Support in the Twenty-first Century: An International Perspective on Pension Systems and Reform.* Washington, DC: World Bank.

Hopenhayn, Hugo A. 2004. "Labor Market Policies and Employment Duration: The Effects of Labor Market Reform in Argentina." In *Law and Employment: Lessons from Latin America and the Caribbean*, ed. James J. Heckman and Carmen Pagés, 497–516. Chicago: The University of Chicago Press.

Huber, Peter. 2003. "Intra-national Labour Market Adjustment in the Candidate Countries." Working Paper 218/2004, Austrian Institute for Economic Research (WIFO), Wien.

———. 2004. "Regional Labor Market Developments in Transition." Background Paper for *Enhancing Job Opportunities: Eastern Europe and the Former Soviet Union*, World Bank, Washington, DC.

Iara, Anna, and Iulia Traistaru. 2004. "How Flexible Are Wages in EU Accession Countries?" *Labour Economics* 11 (4): 431–50.

Ilkkaracan, Ipek, and Raziye Selim. 2003. "The Role of Unemployment in Wage Determination: Further Evidence on the Wage Curve in Turkey." *Applied Economics* 35: 1589–98.

ILO. 2002. *Social Dialogue in the CIS Countries: Ten Years of Independence*. National reports. Series Publications on Social and Labour Affairs in Eastern Europe and Central Asia, No. 13, in Russian. Moscow: ILO.

Jurajda, Stepan, and Katherine Terrell. 2000. "Optimal Speed of Transition: Micro Evidence from the Czech Republic." William Davidson Institute Working Paper 355, University of Michigan, Stephen M. Ross Business School, Ann Arbor.

Kallai, Ella. 2003. "Determinants of Regional Mobility in Romania." In European Union, AccessLab, *Workpackage 3: Analysing and Modelling Interregional Migration*. http://accesslab.wifo.ac.at/.

Kapelyushnikov, Rostislav. 2003. "The Mechanisms of Wage Formation in Russian Industry." (in Russian) Working Paper WP3/2003/07, State University Higher School of Economics, Moscow.

Kaufmann, Daniel, Art Kraay, and Pablo Zoido-Lobaton. 2004. "Governance Matters III: Updated Indicators for 1996–2002." Policy Research Working Paper 3106, World Bank, Washington DC.

Kertesi, Gábor, and János Köllő. 2001. "Economic Transformation and the Revaluation of Human Capital – Hungary, 1986–1999." Working Paper on the Labour Market 2001/4, Institute of Economics, Hungarian Academy of Sciences, Budapest.

———. 2003. "Fighting 'Low Equilibria' by Doubling the Minimum Wage? Hungary's Experiment." Discussion Paper 970, IZA, Bonn.

Keyfitz, Robert. 2004. *The Labor Market in Turkey.* Photocopy, World Bank, Washington, DC.

Klapper, Leora, Luc Laeven, and Raghuram Rajan. 2004. "Business Environment and Firm Entry." Policy Research Working Paper 3232, World Bank, Washington, DC.

Kolev, Alexandre, and Catherine Saget. 2003. "Towards a Better Understanding of the Nature, Causes and Consequences of Youth Labor Market Disadvantage: Evidence from South-East Europe." Social Protection Discussion Paper 0502, World Bank, Washington, DC.

Köllő, János. 1998. "Employment and Wage Setting in Three Stages of Hungary's Labor Market Transition." In *Enterprise Restructuring and Unemployment in Models of Transition*, ed. Simon Commander. Washington, DC: World Bank.

Konings, Jozef, Hartmut Lehmann, and Mark Schaffer. 1996. "Job Creation and Job Destruction in a Transition Economy: Ownership, Firm Size and Gross Job Flows in Polish Manufacturing, 1988–91." *Labour Economics*, Vol. 3 (3), pp. 299–317.

Kraft, Evan, and Milan Vodopivec. 1992. "How Soft Is the Budget Constraint for Yugoslav Firms?" *Journal of Comparative Economics* 16 (3): 432–55.

Kuddo, Arvo. 2004. "Public Works in Europe and Central Asia." *SPectrum* 2004 (Summer): 47–48. Washington, DC: World Bank.

Landesmann, Michael. 2000. "Structural Changes in the Transition Economies, 1989–1999." In *Economic Survey of Europe, 2000*. No. 2/3. Geneva: United Nations Economic Commission for Europe (UN/ECE).

Lizal, Lubomir, and Jan Svejnar. 2002. "Privatization Revisited: The Effects of Foreign and Domestic Owners on Corporate Performance." Photocopy.

Lopez-Garcia, Paloma. 2002. "Labour Market Performance and Start-up Costs: OECD Evidence." Discussion Paper 565, Centre for Economic Performance, London School of Economics and Political Science (LSE), London.

———. 2004. "Business Environment and Labor Market Outcomes in ECA Countries." Background Paper for *Enhancing Job Opportunities: Eastern Europe and the Former Soviet Union*, World Bank, Washington, DC.

Lucas, Robert E. B. 2005. *International Migration and Economic Development: Lessons from Low-Income Countries*. Cheltenham, U.K.: Edward Elgar Publishing.

Luke, Peter, and Mark Schaffer. 2000. "Wage Determination in Russia: An Econometric Investigation." Discussion Paper 143, IZA, Bonn.

Martin, Roderick, and Anamaria Cristescu-Martin. 2002. "Employment Relations in Central and Eastern Europe in 2001: An Emerging Capitalist Periphery." *Industrial Relations Journal* 33 (5): 523–35.

———. 2003. "Employment Relations in Central and Eastern Europe in 2002: Towards EU Accession." *Industrial Relations Journal* 34 (5): 498–509.

Micevska, Maja. 2004. "Unemployment and Labor Market Rigidities in Southeast Europe." Working Paper, Global Development Network Southeast Europe (GDN-SEE) and Vienna Institute for International Economic Studies (wiiw), Vienna.

Mickiewicz, Tomasz, and Kate Bishop. 2003. "Wage Determination: Privatized, New Private and State-Owned Companies: Empirical Evidence from

Panel Data." William Davidson Institute Working Paper 584, University of Michigan, Stephen M. Ross Business School, Ann Arbor.

Micklewright, John, and Gyula Nagy. 1996. "Labour Market Policy and the Unemployed in Hungary." *European Economic Review* 40 (3–5): 819–28.

Munich, Daniel, Jan Svejnar, and Katherine Terrell. 2005. "Returns to Human Capital under the Communist Wage Grid and During the Transition to a Market Economy." *Review of Economics and Statistics* 87 (1, February): 100–123.

Murrell, Peter. 1992. "Evolution in Economics and in the Economic Reform on the Centrally Planned Economies." In *The Emergence of Market Economies in Eastern Europe*, ed. Christopher C. Clague and Gordon Rausser, 35–53. Cambridge, MA: Blackwell.

Newell, Andrew. 2000. "Regional Unemployment and Industrial Restructuring in Poland." Discussion Paper 194, IZA, Bonn.

———. 2001. "The Distribution of Wages in Transition Countries." Discussion Paper 267, IZA, Bonn.

Newell, Andrew, and Barry Reilly. 1996. "The Gender Wage Gap in Russia: Some Empirical Evidence." *Labour Economics* 3 (3, October): 337–56.

———. 1999. "Rates of Return to Educational Qualifications in the Transitional Economies." *Education Economics* 7 (1, April): 67–84.

Nickell, Stephen. 1997. "Unemployment and Labor Market Rigidities: Europe versus North America." *Journal of Economic Perspectives* 11 (3): 55–74.

O'Keefe, Philip. 2004. "Labor Market Institutions and Policies in ECA." Background Paper for *Enhancing Job Opportunities: Eastern Europe and the Former Soviet Union*, World Bank, Washington, DC.

OECD. 1998. *Employment Outlook*. OECD: Paris.

———. 1999. *Employment Outlook*. OECD: Paris.

———. 2000. *Employment Outlook*. OECD: Paris.

———. 2003. *Employment Outlook*. OECD: Paris.

———. 2004a. *Employment Outlook*. OECD: Paris.

———. 2004b. *Taxing Wages: 2002–2003*. 2003 edition. OECD: Paris.

———. 2005. *Trends and Recent Developments in Foreign Direct Investment*. Photocopy, OECD, Paris. http://www.oecd.org/dataoecd/13/62/35032229.pdf.

ONASA. 2004. http://www.onasa.com.ba/NewsFlow/web/guest.nsf?OpenDatabase.

Orazem, Peter F., and Milan Vodopivec. 1995. "Winners and Losers in Transition: Returns to Education, Experience and Gender in Slovenia." *World Bank Economic Review* 9 (2): 201–30.

———. 2003. "Do Market Pressures Induce Economic Efficiency? The Case of Slovenian Manufacturing, 1994–2001." William Davidson Institute Working Paper 621, University of Michigan, Stephen M. Ross Business School, Ann Arbor.

Paci, Pierella. 2002. *Gender in Transition*. Washington, DC: World Bank.

Paci, Pierella, and Barry Reilly. 2004. "Does Economic Liberalization Reduce Gender Inequality in the Labor Market? The Experience of the Transition

Economies of Europe and Central Asia." Photocopy, World Bank, Washington, DC.

Patzwaldt, Katja. 2004. "Case Studies on Labor Market Institutions in Estonia, Russia, and Poland." Background Note for *Enhancing Job Opportunities: Eastern Europe and the Former Soviet Union*, World Bank, Washington, DC.

Peter, Klara Sabirianova. 2003. "Skill-Biased Transition: The Role of Markets, Institutions, and Technological Change." Discussion Paper 893, IZA, Bonn.

Phelps, Edmond. S. 1992. "Consumer Demand and Equilibrium Unemployment in a Working Model of the Customer-Market Incentive-Wage Economy." *Quarterly Journal of Economics* 107 (3, August):1003–32.

———. 1994. *Structural Slumps: A Modern Equilibrium Theory of Unemployment, Interest and Assets*. Cambridge, MA: Harvard University Press.

Pierre, Gaëlle. 2004. "The Investment Climate in ECA: Views from Employers." Background Note for *Enhancing Job Opportunities: Eastern Europe and the Former Soviet Union*, World Bank, Washington, DC.

Pierre, Gaëlle, and Stefano Scarpetta. 2004a. "Employment Regulations through the Eyes of Employers: Do They Matter and How Do Firms Respond to Them?" Policy Research Working Paper 3463, World Bank, Washington, DC.

———. 2004b. "How Labor Market Policies Can Combine Workers' Protection with Job Creation: A Partial Review of Some Key Issues and Policy Options." Background Paper for *World Development Report 2005*.

Pissarides, Christopher. 2001. "Employment Protection." *Labour Economics* 8 (2): 131–59.

Pissarides, Francesca, Miroslav Singer, and Jan Svejnar. 2003. "Objectives and Constraints of Entrepreneurs: Evidence from Small and Medium Size Enterprises in Russia and Bulgaria." *Journal of Comparative Economics* 31 (3): 503–31.

PKPP (Polish Confederation of Private Employers). 2003. "Monitoring Malych i Srednich Przedsiebiorstw Raport z badan (Monitoring of Small and Medium-Size Enterprises Research Report)." Warsaw.

Profit, Stefan. 1999. "Twin Peaks in Regional Unemployment and Returns to Scale in Job-Matching in the Czech Republic." Discussion Paper 2135, Centre for Economic Policy Research (CEPR), London.

Raiser, Martin, Mark E. Schaffer, and Johannes Schuchhardt. 2003. "Benchmarking Structural Change in Transition." Working Paper 79, EBRD, London.

Rashid, Mansoora, and Jan Rutkowski. 2001. "Labor Markets in Transition Economies: Recent Developments and Future Challenges." Social Protection Discussion Paper 0111, World Bank, Washington, DC.

Rawlings, Laura. 2004. "A New Approach to Social Assistance: Latin America's Experience with Conditional Cash Transfer Programs." Social Protection Discussion Paper 0416, World Bank, Washington, DC.

Rawlings, Laura, Lynne Sherburne-Benz, and Julie Van Domelen. 2004. "Evaluating Social Funds: A Cross-Country Analysis of Community Investments." Regional and Sectoral Studies, World Bank, Washington, DC.

Riboud, Michelle, Carolina Sanchez-Paramo, and Carlos Silva-Jauregui. 2002. "Does Eurosclerosis Matter? Institutional Reform and Labor Market

Performance in Central and Eastern European Countries in the 1990s." Social Protection Discussion Paper 0202, World Bank, Washington, DC.

Römisch, G. 2001. "Regional Disparities within Accession Countries." Paper presented at the East-West Conference of the Oesterreichische Nationalbank, November 5–6, 2001.

Rowthorn, R., and R. Ramaswamy. 1997. "Deindustrialization: Causes and Implications." Working Paper 42, IMF, Washington, DC.

Rutkowski, Jan. 1996. "High Skills Pay-Off: The Changing Wage Structure during Economic Transition in Poland." *Economics of Transition* 4 (1): 89–112.

———. 1999. "Labor Markets and Poverty in Bulgaria." Social Protection Discussion Paper 9918, World Bank, Washington, DC.

———. 2001. "Earnings Inequality in Transition Economies of Central Europe: Trends and Patterns during the 1990s." Social Protection Discussion Paper 0117, World Bank, Washington, DC.

———. 2003a. "Does Strict Employment Protection Discourage Job Creation? Evidence from Croatia." Policy Research Working Paper 3104, World Bank, Washington, DC.

———. 2003b. "Rapid Labor Reallocation with a Stagnant Unemployment Pool: The Puzzle of the Labor Market in Lithuania." Policy Research Working Paper 2946, World Bank, Washington, DC.

———. 2003c. "Why Is Unemployment So High in Bulgaria?" Policy Research Working Paper 3017, World Bank, Washington, DC.

———. 2004a. "Firms, Jobs and Employment in Moldova." Policy Research Working Paper 3253, World Bank, Washington, DC.

———. 2004b. "Labor Market Developments during Economic Transition." Background Paper for *Enhancing Job Opportunities: Eastern Europe and the Former Soviet Union*, World Bank, Washington, DC.

Rutkowski, Jan, and Marcin Przybyla. 2002. "Poland: Regional Dimensions of Unemployment." In *Labor, Employment, and Social Policies in the EU Enlargement Process*, ed. B. Funck and L. Pizzati, 157–75. Washington, DC: World Bank.

Saavedra, Jaime. 2003. "Labor Markets during the 1990s." In *After the Washington Consensus: Restarting Growth and Reform in Latin America*, ed. Pedro-Pablo Kucynski and John Williamson, 213–63. Washington, DC: Institute for International Economics.

Sapir, Andre, Philippe Aghion, Giuseppe Bertola, Martin Hellwig, Jean Pisani-Ferry, Dariusz K. Rosati, Jose Vinals, Helen Wallace, Marco Buti, and Mario Nava. 2004. *An Agenda for a Growing Europe: The Sapir Report*. Oxford: Oxford University Press.

Scarpetta, Stefano. 1995. "Spatial Variations in Unemployment in Central and Eastern Europe: Underlying Reasons and Labour Market Policy Options." In *The Regional Dimension of Unemployment in Transition Economies*, ed. Stefano Scarpetta and Andreas Wörgötter, 27–54. Paris: OECD.

Scarpetta, Stefano, Philip Hemmings, Thierry Tressel, and Jaejoon Woo. 2002. "The Role of Policy and Institutions for Productivity and Firm Dynamics:

Evidence from Micro and Industry Data." Economics Department Working Paper 329, OECD, Paris.

Scarpetta, Stefano, and Peter Huber. 1995. "Regional Economic Structures and Unemployment in Central and Eastern Europe: An Attempt to Identify Common Patterns." In *The Regional Dimension of Unemployment in Transition Economies*, ed. Stefano Scarpetta and Andreas Wörgötter, 206–33. Paris: OECD.

Scarpetta, Stefano, and Milan Vodopivec. 2005. "Restructuring, Productivity, and Job Creation in Eastern Europe and the Former Soviet Union." Background Paper for *Enhancing Job Opportunities: Eastern Europe and the Former Soviet Union*, World Bank, Washington, DC.

Schiavo-Campo, Salvatore, Giulio de Tommaso, and Amitabha Mukherjee. 1997. "Government Employment and Pay: A Global and Regional Perspective." Policy Research Working Paper 1771, World Bank, Washington, DC.

Schneider, Friedrich. 2002. "The Size and Development of the Shadow Economies of 22 Transition and 21 OECD Countries." Discussion Paper 514, IZA, Bonn.

Schneider, Friedrich, and Robert Klinglmair. 2004. "Shadow Economies around the World: What Do We Know?" Discussion Paper 1043, IZA, Bonn.

Singer, Slavica, Sanja Pfeifer, Djula Borozan, Natasa Sarlija, and Suncica Oberman. 2003. "What Makes Croatia a(n) (Non) Entrepreneurial Country?" Global Entrepreneurship Monitor (GEM) 2002 Results for Croatia. Zagreb: CEPOR.

Solanko, Laura. 2003. "An Empirical Note on Growth and Convergence across Russian Regions." BOFIT Discussion Paper 9, Institute for Economies in Transition, Bank of Finland, Helsinki.

Squire, Lyn, and Sethaput Suthiwart-Narueput. 1995. "The Impact of Labor Market Regulations." Policy Research Working Paper 1418, World Bank, Washington, DC.

Staines, Verdon, and Dilnara Isamiddinova. 2004. "Social Assistance in Transition Countries of Europe and Central Asia." *SPectrum* 2004 (Summer): 21–26. Washington, DC: World Bank.

Steves, Franklin, Samuel Fankhauser, and Alan Rousso. 2004. "The Business Environment in the CIS-7 Countries." Photocopy, EBRD, London.

Svejnar, Jan. 1999. "Labour Market in the Transitional Central and East European Economies." In *Handbook of Labor Economics*, ed. Orley Ashenfelter, and David Card, 2810–57. Vol. 3 of *Handbooks in Economics*, Elsevier Science Series. Amsterdam: North-Holland.

———. 2002. "Transition Economies: Performance and Challenges." *Journal of Economic Perspectives* 16 (1, Winter): 3–28.

UNDP. 2004. *W Trosce o Pracê: Raport o Rozwoju Spolecznym Polska 2004 (Working Out Employment: Human Development Report Poland 2004)*. Warsaw.

UNICEF. 1999. "Women in Transition." Regional Monitoring Report 6, UNICEF, Florence.

———. 2000. "Young People in Changing Societies." UNICEF, Innocenti Research Centre, Florence.

Vecernik, Jiri. 1995. "Changing Earnings Distribution in the Czech Republic: Survey Evidence from 1988–1994." *Economics of Transition* 3 (3): 355–71.

Verme, Paolo. 2004. "Constraints to Growth and Job Creation in Low Income CIS countries." Background Paper for *Enhancing Job Opportunities: Eastern Europe and the Former Soviet Union*, World Bank, Washington, DC.

Vodopivec, Milan. 1991. "The Labor Market and the Transition of Socialist Economies." *Comparative Economic Studies* 33 (2): 123–58.

———. 2004. *Income Support for the Unemployed: Issues and Options*. Regional and Sectoral Studies. Washington, DC: World Bank.

World Bank. 1993. *The East Asian Miracle: Economic Growth and Public Policy*. New York: Oxford University Press.

———. 1998. "FYR Macedonia: Country Economic Memorandum: Enhancing Growth." Report 18537-MK, World Bank, Washington, DC.

———. 1999. *FYR Macedonia: Focusing on the Poor*. 2 vols. Washington, DC: World Bank.

———. 2000. *Making Transition Work for Everyone: Poverty and Inequality in Europe and Central Asia*. Washington, DC: World Bank.

———. 2001. *Poland Labor Market Study: The Challenge of Job Creation*. Washington, DC: World Bank.

———. 2002a. *Bulgaria: Poverty Assessment*. Washington, DC: World Bank.

———. 2002b. "Labor Market in the Postwar Bosnia and Herzegovina: How to Encourage Businesses to Create Jobs and Increase Worker Mobility." Report 24889-BIH, World Bank, Washington, DC.

———. 2002c. *Lithuania: Country Economic Memorandum. Converging to Europe: Policies to Support Employment and Productivity Growth*. Washington, DC: World Bank.

———. 2002d. *Slovak Republic: Living Standards, Employment, and Labor Market Study*. Washington, DC: World Bank.

———. 2002e. *Transition: The First Ten Years: Analysis and Lessons for Eastern Europe and Former Soviet Union*. Washington, DC: World Bank.

———. 2003a. "A Study of Informal Labor Market Activity in the CIS-7." World Bank, Washington, DC.

———. 2003b. *Croatia: Country Economic Memorandum. A Strategy for Growth through European Integration*. Washington, DC: World Bank.

———. 2003c. *FYR Macedonia: Country Economic Memorandum: Tackling Unemployment*. Washington, DC: World Bank.

———. 2003d. *Latvia: Country Economic Memorandum: The Quest for Jobs and Growth*. Washington, DC: World Bank.

———. 2003e. *Moldova: Public Economic Management Review*. Washington, DC: World Bank.

———. 2003f. *Russian Labor Market: Moving from Crisis to Recovery*. Europe and Central Asia Region, Human Development Sector Unit. Washington, DC: World Bank.

———. 2004a. *Moldova Poverty Assessment: Recession, Recovery, and Poverty in Moldova.* Washington, DC: World Bank.

———. 2004b. *Poland: Convergence to Europe: The Challenge of Productivity Growth.* Investment Climate Assessment. Warsaw: World Bank.

———. 2004c. *World Development Indicators 2004.* Washington, DC: World Bank.

———. 2004d. *World Development Report 2005: A Better Investment Climate for Everyone.* Washington, DC: World Bank.

———. 2005a. "Azerbaijan: Enterprise Restructuring and Labor Redeployment." Photocopy, World Bank, Washington, DC.

———. 2005b. *Growth, Poverty, and Inequality: Eastern Europe and the Former Soviet Union.* Washington, DC: World Bank.

———. 2005c. "Ukraine Jobs Study. Fostering Productivity and Job Creation." Photocopy, World Bank, Washington, DC.

———. Forthcoming. *Enhancing Gains through International Labor Migration in Europe and Central Asia.* Washington, DC: World Bank.

World Economic Forum. 2002. *Global Competitiveness Report 2002–2003.*

Wyplosz, Charles. 2002. "Fiscal Discipline in EMU: Rules or Institutions?" *National Institute Economic Review* 191 (1): 64–78.

Yoon, Yang-Ro, Barry Reilly, Gorana Krstic, and Sabine Bernabè. 2003. "A Study of Informal Labour Market Activity in the CIS-7." Paper prepared for the Lucerne Conference of the CIS-7 Initiative, January 20–22, 2003.

Index

administrative barriers, 42,
    53–54, 169–172
    middle income CIS, 50–52
administrative costs, 32–33
agriculture and agricultural
    regions, 129–131
    jobs, 13
    low income CIS, 79
    unemployment, 83
Albania, start-up costs, 60*n*.37
ALMP. *See* labor market programs, active
Armenia
    obstacles to business operation and growth, 33, 165
    union density, 238*n*.6
Azerbaijan, 3
    business start-up costs, 33
    obstacles to business operation and growth, 33, 165
    wage differentials, 92

backward areas, 81–82
bargaining. *See* wage bargaining
bargaining power, trade unions,
    197–200
bargaining structures, 204–206
Belarus
    business start-up costs, 33
    obstacles to business operation and growth, 32, 164
blue-collar jobs, 13
Bulgaria
    business environment, 158
    obstacles to business operation and growth, 31, 163
    unemployment, 12
    wages, 122
    workfare program, 229
business environment, 4
    business operation
    cost of, 25, 27–35
    obstacles, 30, 31, 58*n*.20

business environment, (continued)
   start-up costs, 32–33, 45, 60n.37

capital
   formal institutions, 175
   formation, gross fixed (GFCF), 115, 116, 117
   investment, new, 115
Central and Eastern Europe (CEE), 55, 64
   employment structure, 127
   high-technology industries, 141
   inflation, 112
   investment climate reform, 183–184
   labor costs and labor supply, 44–48
   labor market institutional reforms, 234–235
   manufacturing and productivity growth, 137
   obstacles to business operations, 163–164
   policies to improve labor market outcomes, 45
   taxes on labor use, 217–220
   unemployment, 66, 67
   wage curve, 196–197
   wage distribution, 92
   wage inequality, 91
   wage flexibility, 203
   see also Bulgaria; Croatia; Czech Republic; Estonia; Hungary; Latvia; Lithuania; Poland; Romania; Slovak Republic
Central Asia, EU vs, 62
circular migration, 73
coefficient system, 202, 203, 239n.12
Commonwealth of Independent States (CIS)
   employment, 113
   employment structure, 127
   investment climate reform, 184–185
   labor market institutional reforms, 236–237
   minimum wage, 92
   wage determination, 203–204
   wage inequality, 91
   wages, 114
commuting, 85
competition, 34, 35, 49, 62
   SEE, 48–50
competitiveness, 56n.5
conditional cash transfers, 226
contestability, 153–154n.7
contracts
   liberalization, 47
   temporary, 210–211, 240nn.37,38
coping strategies, 100
corruption, 49, 159–160, 181–182, 187, 191n.22
costs
   of doing business, 25, 27–35
   of labor, 44–48
   of living, 39
credit and access to credit, 29–30, 43, 171, 173, 175, 180, 183
Croatia
   credit market, 29
   jobs, 13
   minimum wage, 207
   obstacles to business operation, 31, 163
   unemployment, 60n.38
Czech Republic
   investment rate, 40
   jobs, 13, 15

Czech Republic, (continued)
  labor productivity growth, 140
  labor reallocation, 129
  minimum wage, 207
  taxes, 28
  unemployment, 66, 67
  wage differentials, 92
  wages, 122

decomposition, 153n.4
deregulation, 156
disemployment, 240n.34
distortion index, 153n.3
dual labor markets, 98

earnings dispersion. *See* wage dispersion
education, employment and, 84
educational wage premiums, 90
employers, 42
  obstacles to firms' operation and growth, 158–167
employment, 54
  female, 14, 77, 80–81, 103n.8
  gender gap, 77
  investment climate and, 167–169
  macroeconomic policy and output, 119–120
  measurement, 103n.11
  Moldova, 69
  output and, 108–118
  prospects, 118, 120–123
  sector distribution, 126
employment protection legislation (EPL), 4, 26, 36–38, 42, 49–50, 51, 53, 59n.30, 60n.36, 196, 209–221, 234–236, 240n.35
  construction of indexes, 237–238

employment protection legislation, (continued)
  enforcement, 59n.31, 211–213, 215–217
  EU transition countries, 210–211
  job creation and destruction, 172
  relations, 47, 153n.1
  revision, 42
  structure, 215–217
  subgroup variation, 214
  typology, 37
employment rates, 71–75, 75–76, 100, 241n.64
  investment climate and, 169
  male, 76–77
  service sector, 168
employment structure, 126–127
  economic development and, 128
employment-to-working-age ratio, 2, 11, 76
enterprise restructuring. *See* restructuring
entrepreneurs
  Bulgaria, 158
  obstacles to firms' operation, 158–167
  regional variation, 162–165
entry rate, 133
Estonia
  job creation, 23
  job flows, 8, 9
  jobs, 14
  wage bargaining, 200
European Union
  accession countries, 55
  Central Asia vs, 62
  employment rate, 99
  member countries, 55
  taxes on labor use, 220
exit costs, 187

exit rate, 133

finance, access to, 28–29, 42, 43, 159–160, 169–172, 179, 187, 190n.3
financial system, 191n.16
firm-level database, international, 132–133
firms
    creation and expansion, 157
    creation, destruction, and productivity, 143–145
    data, 133
    demographics, and labor reallocation, 23–24
    entering and exiting, number of, 149–151
    entry, conditions and job creation, 151–152
    foreign-owned privatized, 149
    job creation and, 131–137, 149
    obstacles to activity, 28
    productivity and output and, 137–147
    restructuring, 19–23, 131–147
    small, investment climate, 165, 166
    turnover, 23, 24
fiscal deficits, 58n.18
fiscal policy, 116–118
foreign direct investment, 60n.35
foreign privatization, 23
foreign-owned privatized firms, job creation and, 149
formal sector, 239n.16
    institutions to support, CIS, 52–54
    structural change, 199

GDP, 27, 118, 119–121, 153n.1

gender
    labor force, 57n.8, 77
    pay differential, 16
    see also women
geopolitical regions, 64–65
    differences, 6–7
    government effectiveness, 65
    labor market disparities, 17–19
    unemployment rates, 81–82
Georgia
    competition, 34
    obstacles to business operation and growth, 33, 165

health insurance systems, 232–233
high-technology industries, 141, 146
housing
    benefits, 88
    market inefficiencies, 19, 87–88
human capital, investments, 48
Hungary
    employment, 103n.7
    investment climate, 179
    job creation, 23
    job flow rates, 136
    labor productivity growth, 140
    taxes, 28
    unemployment, 2, 66, 67
    unemployment benefits, 59–60n.33
    wages, 122

industry, 129–130
    downsizing, 128, 130
    high-technology, 141, 146
    low income CIS, 79
    productivity and staffing, 139, 141, 142

inequality, 56*n*.3
inflation, 110, 112
   employment, 113
informal sector employment,
   12–13, 81, 87, 93, 94–95,
   102*n*.2, 103*n*.11, 105*n*.29
   patterns, 95
informality, strict EPL and, 216
infrastructure, 53, 59*n*.25, 85
instability, 158–159
institutions, 24–35, 52–53, 156
   challenges, 42–43
   geopolitical location and, 6
   job creation and, 193–242
   role, 194, 195–196
interest rates, 114–116,
   123*nn*.4,7, 191*n*.20
   fiscal policy and, 26–27
investment climate, 24, 27, 30,
   45, 60*n*.34
   CEE, 48–49, 183–184
   CIS, 184–185
   employment and, regression
     analysis, 186–188,
     190–191*n*.7–11
   indicators, 188–189
   information, 190*n*.1,
     191*n*.14
   international comparisons
     and within-region varia-
     tion, 173–181
   job creation and, 155–191
   job creation, regional,
     167–172
   new firms, 152
   reform, 183–186
   SEE, 184
   small firms, 165, 166
   subgroup variation, 175–177
investments, 4
   economic growth and job cre-
     ation and, 40
   rate, by country, 41

job creation, 3, 4, 45–46, 115,
   133
   determinants, 172
   EPL and, 36
   firm productivity and, 22
   firm restructuring and,
     131–137
   fiscal policy and, 58*n*.19
   foreign-owned privatized
     firms, 149
   geopolitical location, 8
   high costs and, 27
   investment climate and,
     155–191
   job destruction and, 7, 8, 9,
     135
   labor market policy and insti-
     tutions, 193–242
   low-income CIS, 78–79
   market regulation and, 171
   new firms, 23, 25, 134–137
   policies, 39–56, 165–167
   productivity and restructuring
     and, 125–154
   reforms, 185–186
   Turkey, 68–69
   urban areas, 82–85
job destruction, 23–24, 131–134
   job creation and, 135
job flow, 134, 230
   rates, 136
jobless growth, 5, 26, 110
jobs
   changing nature of, 7, 12–14,
     15, 93–97
   newly created, 30–31
   opportunities, 100
   productive, 8–12
   protection, 36
   reallocation, 4, 6, 13, 133
   search assistance, 230–231
   security, 93, 216
   stability, 34

jobs, (continued)
    turnover, 134
    see also employment protection legislation

Kazakhstan
    minimum wage, 207
    obstacles to business operation and growth, 32, 164
knowledge-driven economy, 56n.5
Kyrgyz Republic
    credit market, 29
    jobs, 13, 15
    labor reallocation, 129
    obstacles to business operation and growth, 33, 165

labor costs, 117
labor demand, 58n.17, 70, 123n.5
    drivers of, 19–24
labor force
    female, 14, 57n.8, 80–81, 103n.8
    hiring and firing, 36, 37, 51, 213
    less-skilled, 12–14, 77–81, 102, 209
    male, 76–77
    mobilizing, CEE, 44–48
    participation, 70
    productivity, 56n.3
    rates, 9
    reallocation, 4–5
    skills, 48
    underutilization, 99–100
    withdrawal, 70–71
    young workers, 77–81
labor markets, 5–19, 54, 56, 61–105
    adaptable, 4–5
    CEE, 234–235
    changing nature of jobs, 12–14, 15
    CIS, 236–237
    disparities, 8, 17–19, 97–98
    dual, 98
    dynamic, 71–74
    flexibility, 156
    geographical disparities, 17–19
    imbalances/disparities, 85, 83
    institutional reforms, 234–237
    macroeconomic variables, 111
    outcomes, 97–99
    persistent unemployment, 8–12
    policy, job creation and, 193–242
    programs, 222–233, 236, 241–242nn.65,69
    programs, active, 50, 231–233
    regional disparities, 101–102, 103–104nn.13,14,16
    role, 194, 195–196
    SEE, 235–236
    segmentation, 101
    wage growth, inequity, and low-paid jobs, 14, 16–17
labor mobility, 85–88
labor productivity growth, 133, 140
labor reallocation, 21, 52, 129–130
    firm demographics and, 23–24
    productivity growth and, 138
labor regulations, 160–162, 163, 190nn.5,6
Latvia
    credit market, 30
    job creation, 23
    job flow rates, 136

Latvia, (continued)
  labor productivity growth, 140
  wages, 122
law enforcement, SEE, 48–50
legal systems, 42, 187, 199
legislation, 51
  labor, 30, 38
  see also employment protection legislation; regulations
liquidity, 88
  constraints, 19, 104n.19
Lisbon agenda, 56n.5
Lithuania
  investment climate, 191n.12
  labor productivity growth, 140
  wages, 122
low income CIS, 55, 64
  inflation, 112
  institutions to support the formal sector, 52–54
  job creation and growth, 78–79
  labor markets, 56, 66
  obstacles to business operations, 165
  policies to improve labor market outcomes, 45
  see also Armenia; Azerbaijan; Georgia; Kyrgyz Republic; Moldova; Tajikistan; Uzbekistan
low-skilled workers, 12–14, 77–81, 102, 209

Macedonia
  minimum wage, 207
  unemployment, 66, 67
macroeconomic policy, 25, 26–27
  employment and output and, 119–120

manufacturing
  jobs, 13
  productivity growth, 137–139
  service sector jobs vs, 96–97
market discipline, firms and, 20
market economy
  economic structure and, 126–127
  institutions, 156
markets
  credit and, 171
  disparities, regional, 81–82
  regulations, 187, 191n.13
  services, 129–130, 171
  see also urban areas
middle income CIS, 55
  administrative barriers, 50–52
  inflation, 112
  obstacles to business operations and growth, 164
  policies to improve labor market outcomes, 45
  restructuring, 50–52
  safety nets, 50–52
  see also Belarus; Kazakhstan; Russia; Ukraine
migration
  circular migration, 73
  internal, 18–19, 86–87, 104n.16
  international, 71, 72–73
  receiving country, 73
  return migration, 73
  sending country, 73
minimum wage, 17, 35, 49, 92, 195–196, 206–207, 240n.33
  employment and, 209
  negotiated, 207
  social assistance benefits and, 227
  social benefits and, 207–208
  subminimum wage, 46–47

minimum wage, (continued)
    Ukraine, 207
    wages and, 206
Moldova, 3
    employment, 69
    job creation and, 22
    obstacles to business operation and growth, 33, 165

new firms, 154nn.9,10
    entry barriers, Romania, 176
    job creation and, 134–137
    productivity and, 146–147
    start-up cost, 177–179

OECD countries
    taxes on labor use, 218–219
    unemployment benefits, 222–223
output, employment and, 108–118
    macroeconomic policy and, 119–120

pensions and pension systems, 38, 232–233, 242n.71
Poland
    competition, 34
    investment rate, 40
    jobless growth, 5
    jobs, 14
    labor demand, 58n.17
    labor productivity growth, 140
    unemployment, 2, 12
    unemployment benefits, 59–60n.33
    wage distribution, 16
    wages, 46, 122
policy, 24–39, 42–43
    challenges, 43–44
    constraints, 46
    employment-output link, 114–118

policy, (continued)
    fiscal, 116–118
    job creation, 39–56, 165–167
    labor market outcomes, 45
    macroeconomic, 107–123
    priorities, 44, 45
poverty, unemployment and, 3
priorities
    constraints, 46
    policy, 44, 45
private sector
    employment, 169–170
    spillover effects, 202–204, 239n.17
privatization, 23, 34–35, 152, 154n.8, 9
    domestic, 59n.27, 148
    existing firms and, 147–148
    foreign, 148
productivity, 57n.9, 104–105n.22, 23
    firm turnover and, 24, 25
    output per capita growth, 109
    restructuring and job creation and, 125–154
productivity growth, 88, 153–154n.7
    between component, 143
    decomposition of, 143
    firm creation and destruction, 143–145
    labor reallocation and, 138
    privatization and, 148
    sources, 145
    wages and, 139, 141, 142
    within component, 143
profitability, 62
property rights, 156
public sector
    pay determination, 239n.14
    wage schedule compression, 202
public works, 228–229, 231

reallocation, labor-productivity
 growth and, 144
reforms, 44
 payoffs, 2
 within-enterprise, 20–22
regulations, 169–172, 179–181,
 191n.13, 211
 labor, 160–162, 163,
 190nn.5,6
 time spent, 173, 174
 see also employment protection legislation; legislation
rent, 59n.29
resource reallocation, 19, 20
 new firms, 152
restructuring, 30–31, 121–123
 defensive, 20–21, 57n.14, 139
 existing firms and, 147–149
 middle income CIS, 50–52
 output-jobs link, 112–113
 productivity and job creation
 and, 125–154
 strategic, 22–23, 57n.14, 162
 within-industry, 137–139
retirement, 38
return migration, 73
risk reduction, 33–34
Romania
 credit market, 30
 job creation, 23
 job flow, 9, 136
 labor productivity growth,
 140
 labor reallocation, 130
 new firm entry barriers, 176,
 154nn.9,10
 obstacles to business operation and growth, 31, 163
 taxes, 28
 unemployment, 66, 67
 wages, 122
Russia
 coefficient system, 239n.12

Russia, (continued)
 job flow, 8, 9, 136
 jobs, 14
 labor market, 103n.10
 labor reallocation, 21
 obstacles to business operation and growth, 32, 164
 reallocation, labor-productivity growth and, 144
 wages, 92, 104–105n.23,
 239n.20

safety nets
 informal, 19
 middle income CIS, 50–52
sectoral bargaining, 205–206
security costs, 173, 174
self-employment, 12–13, 93, 96,
 102n.2, 103n.11, 231–232
Serbia & Montenegro
 start-up costs, 60n.37
 wage differentials, 92
service sector, 13
 employment rate, 168
 investment climate and, 169
 manufacturing jobs vs,
 96–97
services
 nonmarket, 129–130
 see also market services
severance pay, 51, 60n.39
size threshold, 133
skills
 deficient, 162, 163
 jobs and, 13–14
 mismatch, 19, 57n.6, 86–87,
 105n.30
Slovak Republic
 investment rate, 40
 labor productivity growth,
 140
 unemployment, 2, 12
 wages, 122

Slovenia
   job creation, 23
   job flow, 8, 9, 136
   labor productivity growth, 140
   private sector spillover effects, 239*n*.17
   unemployment, 66, 67
   wage differentials, 92
   wages, 122
social assistance programs, 225–227
   wage and labor turnover outcomes and, 227–228
social benefits, 19, 26, 38–39, 57–58*n*.16
   minimum wages and, 207–208
social dialogue, 195
social funds, 226
social partnerships, 42
social protection, 54, 237
   mechanisms, 87
social safety nets, 4–5, 51–52
social security threshold, 240*n*.30
social transfers
   alternatives, 236
   targeting, 52
Southeastern Europe (SEE), 55, 64
   competitive markets, 48–50
   inflation, 112
   investment climate reform, 184
   labor market institutional reforms, 235–236
   law enforcement, 48–50
   obstacles to business operations, 164
   policies to improve labor market outcomes, 45
   stability, 48–50

Southeastern Europe (SEE), (continued)
   unemployment, 66, 67
   wage bargaining, 204
   see also Albania; Bosnia & Herzegovina; Macedonia, FYR; Serbia & Montenegro
stability, 183
   SEE, 48–50
staffing, 139
start-up costs, 32–33, 45, 60*n*.37, 177–179, 187
state-owned firms, 205

Tajikistan, obstacles to business operation and growth, 33, 165
targeting the poor, 226
taxes, 27–28, 29, 45, 49, 51, 58–59*nn*.21,22, 156, 159–160, 169–172, 183, 187
   CEE, 217–220
   collection, 242*n*.72
   labor use, 217–221, 235, 241*nn*.47,48
   payroll, 28, 236
technological advances, 153–154*n*.7
telephone service, unemployment and, 85
temporary employment, 13
trade unions, 35, 42, 59*n*.32, 195
   bargaining power, 197–200
   density, 205, 238*nn*.5,6
   state, 239*n*.10
training, 231, 57*n*.6
transition economies, 1
   taxonomy, 56*n*.1
transition shock, 24
Turkey, 56*n*.1
   job creation, 68–69
   unemployment, 11–12
Turkmenistan, 56*n*.1

Ukraine, 3
    job flow rates, 136
    minimum wage, 207
    obstacles to business operation, 32, 164
uncertainties, 158–159
underemployment, 63–75
    job creation and destruction and, 135
unemployment, 9–12, 60n.38, 63–75, 105n.32
    flows into and out of, 74
    inflated figures, 224
    job creation and destruction and, 135
    long-term, 47, 48, 68, 70
    open, 100
    outflows, 103n.9
    persistent, 3, 8–12, 71–75, 97–99, 100
    registered, 241n.52
unemployment benefits, 38, 47, 50, 51, 59–60n.33, 222–223, 235, 241n.54
    coverage, 223–224
    employment and, 224–225
    noncash benefits, 224
    replacement rate, 222
unemployment rate, 103n.12
    regional disparities, 81–82
"unemployment trap," 47
unions. See trade unions
urban areas, job creation, 82–85
Uzbekistan
    business start-up costs, 33
    obstacles to business operation and growth, 33, 165

wage bargaining, 195, 205, 239–240n.24
    bargaining structures, 204–206
    change within subgroups, 200–201

wage bargaining, (continued)
    Estonia, 200
    EU countries, 239n.19
    SEE, 204
    trade unions, 197–200
wage determination, 51, 53, 194, 235
    CIS, 203–204
    public sector, 239n.14
wage disparities, 3–4, 57n.12, 92–93, 105n.27
    bargaining and, 205
wages, 49, 57n.12, 59n.28, 100–101, 104n.20, 21, 117
    adaptability, 46
    adjustments, 113–114
    CEE, 203
    differentials, 89–93, 105n.31
    distribution, 14, 16, 89
    flexibility, 25, 35–36, 92–93, 203
    gender gap, 81
    growth, 7–8, 14
    inequality, 16, 18, 90–91, 98, 101, 105n.26
    output-jobs link, 112–113
    productivity and, 57n.9, 141, 142
    public sector, 122
    rebounding, 88–93
    Russia, 239n.20
    schedules, compression, 202
    subsidies, 231
    "wage curve," 196, 105n.28
wage-setting mechanism, 14
white-collar jobs, 13
women, employment, 14, 77, 80–81, 103n.8
workers; workforce. See labor force
workfare, 228–229

young workers, 77–81